Moses and Pharaoh

Perspectives on Exodus

Philip Quenby

ONWARDS AND UPWARDS PUBLISHERS
Berkeley House, 11 Nightingale Crescent, West Horsley, Surrey, KT24 6PD, UK.
www.onwardsandupwards.org

Copyright 2014 © Philip Quenby

ISBN: 978-1-910197-03-5

First edition published in 2014 by Onwards and Upwards Publishers.

The right of Philip Quenby to be identified as the author of this work has been asserted by him in accordance with the Copyright, Designs and Patents Act 1988.

All rights reserved.

No part of this publication may be reproduced or transmitted in any form or by any means, electronic or mechanical, including photocopy, recording or any information storage and retrieval system, without permission in writing from the author or publisher.

Unless otherwise indicated, scripture quotations are taken from the HOLY BIBLE, NEW INTERNATIONAL VERSION. Copyright © 1973, 1978, 1984 by International Bible Society. Used by permission.

Scripture quotations marked (RSV) are from the Revised Standard Version of the Bible, copyright © 1946, 1952, and 1971 the Division of Christian Education of the National Council of the Churches of Christ in the United States of America. Used by permission. All rights reserved.

Scripture quotations marked (NRSV) are from the New Revised Standard Version Bible, copyright © 1989 the Division of Christian Education of the National Council of the Churches of Christ in the United States of America. Used by permission. All rights reserved.

Scripture quotations marked (TLB) are taken from The Living Bible copyright © 1971. Used by permission of Tyndale House Publishers, Inc., Carol Stream, Illinois 60188. All rights reserved.

Scripture quotations marked (GNT) are from the Good News Translation in Today's English Version- Second Edition Copyright © 1992 by American Bible Society. Used by Permission.

Scripture quotations marked (KJV) are from The Authorized (King James) Version. Rights in the Authorized Version in the United Kingdom are vested in the Crown. Reproduced by permission of the Crown's patentee, Cambridge University Press.

Scripture quotations marked (NKJV) are taken from the New King James Version®. Copyright © 1982 by Thomas Nelson, Inc. Used by permission. All rights reserved.

Every effort has been made to obtain the necessary permissions with reference to copyright material. We apologise for any omissions in this respect and will be pleased to make the appropriate amendments in future editions.

Cover design: LM Graphic Design

Printed in the UK

Dedication

'Tis only the splendour of light hideth Thee.

Acknowledgements

God said of Adam, "It is not good for the man to be alone. I will make a helper suitable for him." (Genesis 2:18). For blessings new every morning, and above all for the gifts of wife, children, family and friends, I praise my Maker. For their unfailing consideration, kindness, generosity, forbearance and love, I give heartfelt thanks and acknowledge my debt to each.

Contents

Maps and Plans 6
List of Illustrations 7
Preface 9
1. Encountering God 12
2. Belonging to God 28
3. Worshipping God 44
4. Knowing God 60
5. Reflecting God 76
6. Relying on God 92
7. Recognising God 106
8. Obeying God 122
9. Serving God 136
10. Remembering God 152
11. Living for God 168
12. The Presence of God 184
Epilogue 198
Appendix I 203
Appendix II 229
Appendix III 237
Appendix IV 239
Appendix V 243
Appendix VI 247
Glossary 251
Bibliography 261
Notes 263
Index of Scripture References 337
Subject Index 347

Maps and Plans

The Egyptian Empire in the XVth Century BC.

Upper and Lower Egypt.

Administrative divisions (nomes) of Lower Egypt.

Administrative divisions (nomes) of Upper Egypt.

Plan of Akhet-aten.

Areas of settlement by the Twelve Tribes of Israel after the conquest of Canaan.

List of Illustrations

Plate I: Peristyle hall of Thutmoses IV at Thebes.

Plate II: Temple of Isis, first pylon, Philae.

Plate III: Papyrus growing by the Nile.

Plate IV: Colossal statue of Amenhotep III.

Plate V: Bust of Amenhotep III.

Plate VI: Akhenaten and Nefertiti worshipping Aten in the form of the sun-disc.

Plate VII: Locusts on the move.

Plate VIII: Portrait study from the workshop of royal sculptor Thutmoses at Amarna, believed to represent Amenhotep III.

Plate XIX: Ammit, Devourer of the Dead, Eater of Hearts and Great of Death.

Plate X: Soufrière Hills Volcano, Montserrat 1995.

Plate XI: Mount Galanggung, West Java, Indonesia, 1982.

Plate XII: Mount Rinjani, Lombok Island, Indonesia, 2010.

Plate XIII: Mummified head of Amenhotep III.

Plate XIV: The colossi of Memnon, fronting a now vanished temple built by Amenhotep III.

Plate XV: A desert oasis.

Plate XVI: Commemorative scarab of Amenhotep III.

Plate XVII: Mount Sinai.

Plate XVIII: Statue of Akhenaten in early Amarna style.

Plate XIX: Bust of Akhenaten.

Plate XX: Bas relief portrait of Akhenaten.

Plate XXI: Akhenaten in the guise of the Sphinx worships Aten.

Plate XXII: One of the Amarna letters.

Plate XXIII: Treasures from the tomb of Tutankhamun.

Plate XXIV: Statue of the Apis bull.

Moses and Pharaoh

Preface

"I will hear, for I am compassionate." (Exodus 22:27).

Few, if any, lands have a lineage longer or more splendid than ancient Egypt.[1] The monumental remains of the Nile valley and the tantalising glimpses they offer of a vanished civilisation have evoked wonder and fascination throughout the ages. Though much is now reduced to dust and fragments, enough remains to spark awe, admiration and delight. The domain of the pharaohs[2] has influenced nations near and far, antique and modern. Once her reach extended over large parts of the ancient Near East and East Africa, until at length her strength ebbed and she was supplanted by others. Yet to this day she has kept her capacity to beguile. This former greatness whose trace we perceive but dimly was no mere happenstance, for the Lord "raised [her] up for this very purpose, that I might show [her] my power and that my name might be proclaimed in all the earth." (Exodus 9:16). The collision between the overweening pride of a venerable culture and the settled purposes of the Almighty that is described in the second book of the Bible forms one of the climactic moments of all history. It is fundamental to understanding God's plan for his world and for each human being. The story is as fresh and relevant today as at the moment it was written, revealing much about the human heart and the excuses we are all apt to make for not following God's template for our lives, about the nature of our society, about where we need to go and about how to get there.

Ascribing dates to the events described in Exodus is not straightforward. So far, no Egyptian record has been found that allows us to identify the era of the Israelites' oppression and escape beyond any shadow of doubt. Of their wandering in the wilderness there is as yet no trace.[3] Coupled with the miraculous nature of their deliverance, this has led some to assert that the Bible account is wholly fanciful, or at best an embellishment. We would do well to reflect long and hard before reaching any such conclusion. There was a time when some denied the very existence of a man called Pontius Pilate, till a stone bearing his name was unearthed in Israel in 1961.[4] The kings of Egypt were no strangers to propaganda and news management. As this book will relate, in dealing with one particular period of trauma, they and their subjects were capable of an act of collective amnesia that equals any modern airbrushing of inconvenient photographs. The simple fact is that the Bible has never been proven wrong. It remains as solid and reliable a guide on matters of fact as on those of faith and morals. There is no reason to disbelieve or discount what it says about Moses and his mission to free God's people.

This work aims to highlight how Exodus applies to us today, exploring twelve broad themes against the backdrop of a turbulent period in Egyptian history. The message is timeless. It holds regardless of when the Israelites' captivity, departure from Egypt and time of testing in the desert took place. Nevertheless, we have to fix these happenings somewhere. The supposition made here, if true, may perchance illumine a particularly murky episode in the annals of those who lived along the banks of the Nile. To avoid cluttering the narrative, dating methodology is described in an appendix. A word of caution is in order, however: if the theory is shown not to fit what Scripture says, then the theory is wrong, not the Bible. Above all, beyond any issue of timing lies the fact that the living Word of God remains true for every age and will speak to us if only we will listen.

Our nation is presently in slavery, suffering hard bondage no less real than was Israel's under the rulers of The Two Lands.[5] We desperately need to heed the call of our Saviour, who longs to lead us back to a life of freedom with Him. Our choice is stark: to stand before Him or kneel before the enemy.

London 2013.

Gad

Whose meaning is, *good fortune*

Of whom Jacob prophesied,
*"Gad will be attacked by a band of raiders,
but he will attack them at their heels."*
(Genesis 49:19).

1. Encountering God

Breaking with the past.

"Say to the Israelites, 'The LORD, the God of your fathers — the God of Abraham, the God of Isaac and the God of Jacob — has sent me to you. This is my name for ever, the name by which I am to be remembered from generation to generation.'" (Exodus 3:15).

Even as ruins, the palaces and temples that sit astride the Nile at cities such as Thebes, Memphis and Heliopolis can still amaze. Their stones and hieroglyphs are testament to the ambition, sophistication and continuity of the civilisation that built them. In the Valley of the Kings lie more wonders, the burial places of royalty from time immemorial. The first dynasty of ancient Egypt was established more than three thousand years before the birth of Christ. Its thirty-one successors held sway until the coming of the Romans and the dawn of the Christian era.[6] At its high point, the Egyptian Empire stretched from Sudan in the south to the borders of Turkey in the north. Tribute from conquered peoples and allies made Egypt rich and self-confident. The attainments of her building projects are astounding for any epoch. The Great Pyramid of Cheops (Khufu), standing just over 480 feet high and for over four thousand years the tallest structure on earth, was crafted by a people who had neither iron, nor wheel, nor capstan, nor pulley. It reputedly holds enough stone to build a wall ten feet high and five feet wide from Calais to Baghdad. For this to have been constructed by a society without modern technologies is almost beyond comprehension.[7] Not surprisingly, Egyptians were proud of their heritage and valued the old ways. Well might they have considered themselves and the land they inhabited to have been blessed with good fortune.

Yet in the fourteenth century BC, towards the end of Egypt's Eighteenth Dynasty, something quite remarkable happened. Centuries of tradition were overturned. A new ruler compelled the court to quit the ancient capital for a metropolis built from scratch on the edge of the desert.[8] Leaving behind the treasured places of his forefathers and moving to virgin land was deeply symbolic, but greater upheavals were to come. This same pharaoh signalled a change of spiritual allegiance by altering his name, turning his back on the old pantheon of gods and instituting novel forms of worship. He promoted radical and innovative art forms so shocking in their representation of the human body that some believe they indicate hereditary disease in the royal family. There appears to have been a period of national self-absorption or introspection that left the country largely paralysed in the face of military and political threats from beyond its north-eastern borders. Most revolutionary, divisive and cataclysmic of all for a people steeped in polytheism, the monarch insisted on worship of one god above all others. By the time the seventeen years or so of his reign had passed, Egypt was in turmoil, her old ascendancy abroad vanished. She was never to recover her former hegemony fully.

The pharaoh who did these things was so reviled by later generations that he was called "criminal," "rebel" or "enemy".[9] His erstwhile subjects quickly did their best to put the dislocations of his reign behind them, his name being deliberately omitted from the king lists which were routinely recited to ensure nourishment to the departed in the afterlife. The aim was no less than to bring about the personal obliteration of a man whose very memory was anathema, for Egyptians believed that only through such commemoration was rebirth possible.[10] Within a short space of the heretic's passing, Thebes was again the capital and temples to the old gods had been re-opened. There followed a self-conscious national act of forgetting that attempted to erase all trace of this unique experiment.

The pharaoh's name was Akhenaten.[11] To this day he remains an enigma, a character apparently so divorced from the society that spawned him that later generations have constantly been tempted to project onto him their own fantasies and to ascribe to him their own motives. So little is known for sure about this occupant of the throne and the true nature of the changes he wrought that his reign has been the subject of avid speculation and vivid re-imagining. Yet whilst keeping the wilder flights of fancy in check, any serious attempt to grapple with the many curiosities and contradictions of his rule must grasp the nettle of how the monarch came to upend so many of the customs of his people in a land that greatly revered and venerated the example of its forefathers.

The finger of God.

We inhabit a world where change is the norm. From cradle to grave we imbibe an atmosphere in which it is promoted, expected, even glorified. Whether couched in the language of innovation, re-engineering, or personal growth, the message is the same: to stand still in business or personal life is to be a dullard, a loser, consigned to the margins. From the Industrial Revolution onwards, we have seen the pace of development quicken: transforming hierarchies and institutions, refashioning social conventions and economic life, undermining traditional morality and spirituality, altering the ethnic make-up of our land. It is thus difficult in the extreme for us to put ourselves in the shoes of a people for whom change was rare, unwelcome and almost always to be regarded with suspicion. A great effort of imagination is required if we are to comprehend fully the aversion to change of traditional societies and the radical contusions of thought or environment that were needed to bring it about.

Akhenaten's overturning of the past was no modern lifestyle choice. Neither was it the mere whim of a tyrant. Something of great moment must have happened to trigger it. His reforms were not lightly undertaken, nor without impact on others. They went to the root of the life of the nation. It is hardly likely that they were anything other than long considered, turned this way and that in the mind, agonised over and much reflected upon. They bear the hallmark of experiences sufficient to shake the perceptions, attitudes and education of someone in a position of privilege, trained from childhood to esteem and uphold the accepted way of doing things, a man who was no mere figurehead, but was indeed guardian, pivot and pinnacle of the life of the nation. It would scarce be going too far to say that, whatever happened to turn this potentate from the path trodden by his ancestors, it must have been deep felt, perhaps shattering.

The book of Exodus tells of heavenly interventions so powerful that they left no-one untouched. Even the pagan magicians of Egypt were moved to acknowledge "the finger of God" (Exodus 8:19)[12] when they saw the plagues that the Lord brought upon their land. So mighty were these works and so incontrovertible the evidence that, when the Israelites left Egypt, "Many other people went up with them" (Exodus 12:38). We cannot know for sure whether these were simply the slaves and downtrodden of subject races or classes, or whether they perhaps included "officials of Pharaoh who feared the word of the LORD" (Exodus 9:20), but at all events it is clear that it was not Hebrews alone who recognised the presence and activity of the one true God. This should be no surprise; when the High King of heaven moves, we can anticipate that every human being will be aware of a force that is above and beyond them. Some may choose to avert their eyes, but none who reflect honestly can fail to acknowledge the Almighty for who he is and recognise his deeds as the work of his hands. Others may delve deeper, to a personal encounter with the one who made them.

Heartbreak.

Moses was one such. His story should greatly encourage, for he was not someone to whom his later role as leader, deliverer, prophet, judge, lawgiver and "friend" (Exodus 33:11) of God came early or easy. His life is a reminder that, before the Lord asks us to undertake something, he will equip and train us. Almost by definition, this is a process which is likely to take time. It will not always be free of care or trouble, and neither can we expect it to be painless. Ground has to be prepared and we have to be brought to the right place physically, mentally, morally and spiritually. Amongst other things, this means that we must be ready to accept that we cannot achieve anything truly lasting or worthwhile on our own, but only through the power of God working in us. At first, Moses did as we are all far too apt to do, thinking that his own plans and initiatives would suffice. This led him to take the law into his own hands: "He saw an Egyptian beating a Hebrew, one of his own people. Glancing this way and that and seeing no-one, he killed the Egyptian and hid him in the sand." (Exodus 2:11-12). Fired by hatred of injustice, conscious of his own position of privilege and responsibility, earnestly desiring to right a dreadful wrong, Moses thought that the ends justified the means. It is a perennial fallacy of many who seek to create a better world. The result on this occasion was precisely what has been seen all too often throughout the ages when godly insight and perspective take a back seat and morality is cast to the wind. Moses became a murderer.[13]

Such drastic action did not endear him to those he sought to help, for the soil was not yet ready for planting: "Moses thought that his own people would realise that God was using him to rescue them, but they did not." (Acts 7:25). This hints that the prince might already have had some inkling of the Lord's wish to make of him the means by which Israel would be delivered, but if so his outlook at this point was sorely limited. Perhaps being raised as a prince of Egypt had made him proud, reliant on his own abilities, conscious of being "no ordinary child" (Acts 7:20 and Hebrews 11:23) and of having been "instructed in all the wisdom of the Egyptians" (Acts 7:22).[14] Whatever the case may have been, the future prophet appears at this stage to have been aware neither of God's methods nor of his timing and to have had only the faintest grasp of any coherent plan of action. He responded in the heat of the moment without divine authority, and as a result neither his words nor his actions carried weight with men: "The next day he went out and saw two Hebrews fighting. He asked the one in the wrong, 'Why are you hitting your fellow Hebrew?' The man said, 'Who made you ruler and judge over us?'" (Exodus 2:13-14). The irony is that, in the fullness of time, the Lord would indeed raise Moses up as both ruler and judge over all Israel.

Moses' experience has lessons for us as we contemplate the dire state of this nation and our people's desperate need for deliverance from the things that bind them. No amount of human striving will avail if we are not doing things in God's way, according to his timing, for "If the LORD does not build the house, the work of the builders is useless" (Psalm 127:1, GNT). It is not our earthly achievements and human qualities that will be the deciding factor, but the extent of our inspiration, anointing and commissioning by God. Fine phrases and well-intentioned deeds will be of no account unless they are rooted in prayer. Above all, the attitude of our hearts must be right: the methods that we use are of fundamental importance. If these are wrong, then others will be justified in expecting that the same flawed approach will carry over into other walks of life. The likelihood then is that they will reject both messenger and message. So it was that the Israelite who questioned Moses' right to intervene in a fight asked, "Are you thinking of killing me as you killed the Egyptian?" (Exodus 2:14).

It is often said that, before God can use us, he must break our hearts. Moses' heart was broken on seeing the oppression and pain of his people. It was broken again as his first attempts to help them ended in failure, and broken countless times more over the years of desert wandering as he saw their seemingly endless self-pity, backsliding, ingratitude and sinfulness, as he became the butt of their continual murmurings of discontent and the rebelliousness even of his own brother and sister. There is no doubt that Moses suffered grievously, but it was not without purpose. Someone with a broken heart seldom has room for pride. God took a man of uncommon ability, marked from birth by signs of special favour, who heard the call of destiny and spoke to his Creator "face to face, as a man speaks with his friend"(Exodus 33:11),[15] and made him "more humble than anyone else on the face of the earth." (Numbers 12:3). Only in that frame of mind was he a suitable instrument for his Lord to wield.

Groundwork.

Preparation of Moses began from before the moment of his birth, but more than this: all those other individuals who were to play a part in the Lord's plan for Moses' life and ministry were also being positioned or raised up and the circumstances necessary for the fulfilment of his mission put in train so that they were brought to fruition at just the right time and in exactly the right place.[16] Nothing takes God by surprise, nor catches him unawares. The first two chapters of Exodus are a study in the way the Almighty works out his purposes, regardless of and despite the plans of men. Sometimes his interventions are obvious and dramatic. On occasion only miracles can account for them, but most usually he achieves his ends through human agency and his hand is veiled. The Almighty especially delights in operating through the despised and downtrodden, the unprepossessing, unexpected and weak. In response to St Paul's pleas for removal of a "thorn in the flesh" (2 Corinthians 12:7, NKJV) he told the apostle that "My grace is sufficient for you, for my power is made perfect in weakness." (2 Corinthians 12:9). Time and again Pharaoh's efforts to suppress Israel were thwarted by women, whose position in the societies of the ancient Near East was almost always subservient, servile or subordinate. Yet in flagrant disobedience to the commands of the civil power and completely disregarding all threats that might be levelled at their wellbeing or livelihood, a succession of brave, resourceful and caring women – first the Hebrew midwives Shiphrah and Puah[17] (Exodus 1:15-21), then Moses' mother (Exodus 2:1-3 and 8-9) and sister Miriam (Exodus 2:4 and 7-8), and finally even Pharaoh's own daughter (Exodus 2:5-6 and 10) – were used by God to be the means of saving and protecting the babe, nurturing him and bringing him to a position of prominence. Though from earliest boyhood the youngster was raised in an Egyptian palace, his mother was nevertheless able to give him such a firm grounding in the faith of his forebears that this stayed with him even when he was surrounded by unbelievers.[18] It was doubtless this faith that sustained him, first in the face of all allurements of power and luxury and then during long years of hardship and apparent failure.

Again, we should take heart. With the possible exception of Pharaoh's daughter, it is likely that none of these women regarded themselves as in any way exceptional. It could be that they went to their graves without having a personal experience of God. Yet they were faithful, compassionate and careless of reputation or safety. Their contributions mattered. Without them, none of what came later would have been possible. We should never imagine that what we have to offer is of no account, neither to suppose that we need direct personal revelation from the Lord in order to do his will. If we are true to what he has said in his Word contained in the Bible, we are guaranteed a great harvest, albeit one that we may not see fully or at all until we go to join him in heaven. Nor should we overlook the blessings that the Almighty bestows in reward for faithfulness: "God blessed the midwives because they were God-fearing women. So the people of Israel continued to multiply and to become a mighty nation. And because the midwives revered God, he gave them children of their own." (Exodus 1:20-21, TLB).

An upbringing as an Egyptian prince doubtless assured the foundling of material comfort, status, literacy, worldly knowledge, administrative experience and the habit of command. Often we are tempted to conceive that blessing lies in these things and these alone, yet much more was needful for the task that God had in mind. The Most High did not intend his prophet to be corrupted by a life of ease and indolence, but to carry on growing morally and spiritually until he was fit for what lay ahead.[19] A radical change of direction was required, for which the catalyst was necessarily dramatic. Only an event such as slaying a fellow creature and learning that "When Pharaoh heard of this, he tried to kill Moses" (Exodus 2:15) could have spurred flight and eventual refuge amongst nomads in the desert and scrub of regions beyond full Egyptian control. With the benefit of hindsight, we can see that God was intent not just on preserving the life and integrity of his chosen instrument, but on giving him valuable contacts, adding to his knowledge, bringing him new skills and above all building his character. None of this would have been evident to the fugitive at the time, however. From Moses' point of view, when he "fled from Pharaoh and went to live in Midian" (Exodus 2:15), that must have seemed an unmitigated disaster, the wreck of all his hopes. The cherished dream of freeing his people would have been in tatters. This bears reflection when things do not appear to be going well in our own lives. We too readily expect everything to be plain sailing, to have things drop into our laps without effort or pain, but life is not like that. Hardship is often the best means by which God can shape and craft us.

So it was with Moses. Through a series of events that some might call coincidence but which were in fact ordained by God, in Midian he met Reuel, "priest of Midian" (Exodus 2:16, NRSV), who in due course became his father-in-law.[20] The Israelites were thereby assured of a friendly reception when passing through Midianite lands in years to come, whilst Moses gained the benefit of advice and support from an experienced leader when grappling with issues of administration that threatened to wear him down (Exodus 18:13-27).[21] Since the territory of Midian spanned both sides of the Gulf of Aqaba and down into Sinai, most probably Moses came to know much of the country through which the Israelites were later to trek during their escape from Egypt and subsequent forty years of wandering in the wilderness. He would have learnt survival in hostile terrain, handling of flocks and herds, the routines of a nomadic life, the habits and nature of surrounding tribes, the positions of wells, oases and Egyptian garrisons, with much else besides.

Most important of all was the moulding of character. During his time in Midian, Moses learnt to be husband (Exodus 2:21), father (Exodus 2:22 and 18:3-4) and shepherd (Exodus 3:1). It is no accident that the Bible uses each of these roles as metaphors for the activity of God and the presence of his kingdom. Jesus likens the kingdom of heaven to a bridegroom (Matthew 25:1 and 5), teaches us to pray to God as "Our Father in heaven" (Matthew 6:9 and Luke 11:2) and describes himself as "the good shepherd" (John 10:14, NKJV). If we wish to maximise our effectiveness as servants of his kingdom, it follows that we must learn the qualities that belong to the highest conception of these functions. In a society where our sense of what it means to be husband and father is sadly diminished and where our understanding of matters pastoral is slight, this demands extra effort and application. For a nation that sets such store by material things and worldly achievement, it is especially important to recognise that in domesticity and the lowly can be more of God than anything we might encounter in the courts of kings and princes. If the Lord is by our side, the everyday need not be humdrum.

Fire.

Eighty years was Moses in the making before he was ready for summoning to his life's work.[22] He had acquired earthly knowledge, but learnt its limitations; had dallied on the heights of human experience yet also plumbed its depths; had once been sure of his ability and prowess, only to have his weakness made plain. Through decades of waiting he had perforce to learn patience and self-control. These are characteristics we all need, and indeed they are amongst the many fruits of the Holy Spirit (Galatians 5:22), but there is a danger of allowing them to become confused with fatalism, blind acceptance or connivance in wrongdoing. Moses went through times of bitter disappointment. He came late to marriage, fatherhood and being a shepherd. It would therefore have been entirely understandable had he failed to realise that God did not intend him to see out his days solely within the surrounds of family and clan. Bonds of love and mutual obligation were instead to be precursors to something of global and timeless significance, a balm to the suffering and the means by which in due course the shackles of man's slavery would be broken once and for all. Yet, discouraged as he must have been by years of apparently fruitless yearning and seemingly unanswered prayer, in all likelihood Moses would have seen what God intended as springboards to greater achievement as the confines of his world. When he had lived in Egypt, Moses' ambition was too large for what he was capable of achieving. Now the opposite was true: he needed the Lord to expand his vision. By definition the same applies to each of us, since God "is able to do immeasurably more than all we ask or imagine, according to his power that is at work within us" (Ephesians 3:20).[23]

The Bible does not specifically address Moses' state of mind at the time he "was tending the flock of Jethro his father-in-law, the priest of Midian, and he led the flock to the far side of the desert and came to Horeb, the mountain of God." (Exodus 3:1). It would be reasonable to suppose that he might from time to time have learnt at least the broad outline of events in Egypt from passing caravans.[24] Presumably he was aware that "The Israelites groaned in their slavery and cried out" (Exodus 2:23), and no doubt he groaned and cried out with them. We cannot know what depths of despair he might have plumbed, what regrets and missed opportunities may have played upon his mind, what anguished thoughts have lain heavy on his heart. All we can be sure of is that God's promise to later generations would have held good for him, as for us: "You will seek me and find me when you seek me with all your heart." (Jeremiah 29:13). Despite all appearance to the contrary, the Lord had good fortune in store – for Moses, for Israel and for the world.

Against this background came the decisive call: "There [on Mount Horeb][25] the angel of the LORD appeared to him in flames of fire from within a bush." (Exodus 3:2). This fire was unique, for it blazed but did not consume: "Moses saw that although the bush was on fire it did not burn up. So Moses thought, 'I will go over and see this strange sight – why the bush does not burn up.'" (Exodus 3:2-3). The occurrence was so remarkable, so life-changing and so central to Moses' mission that it would be astounding if he did not relate it widely and often. It may be that he told Pharaoh of it, either in an effort to make his demand for the Israelites' freedom more persuasive or when asked his reasons for returning to Egypt. At all events, it is not unreasonable to think that the story became known in Egyptian court circles, whether from Moses' own lips or from another source. If that were so, it gives an intriguing glimpse into the theology of Akhenaten. For just like the bush, the sun burns but is not consumed. The sun-disc was the outward sign of Akhenaten's invisible god Aten, held up as supreme deity by this most enigmatic of pharaohs.[26]

Fire is a symbol of God's presence and power throughout Scripture – not God himself, but a sign and agent of his activity, a fitting counterpoint to the fire and sun worship of those pagan religions which repeatedly, misguidedly and ultimately fatally persisted (and still do to this day) in mistaking created things for the Creator. When the three Israelites Shadrach, Meshach and Abednego were cast into the flames of a furnace by the Babylonian despot King Nebuchadnezzar, they too experienced fire that did not burn: "…the satraps, prefects, governors and royal advisors crowded around them. They saw that the fire had not harmed their bodies, nor was a hair of their head singed; their robes were not scorched, and there was no smell of fire on them." (Daniel 3:27). Fire is a metaphor of salvation and judgment. It was appropriate indeed as the means by which God first gained Moses' attention on Mount Horeb, for there was to be salvation for Israel and judgment on Egypt.

Revelation.

The way in which Moses' encounter with God occurred is an object lesson for any who complain that the Almighty is absent or non-existent. We are told that "When the LORD saw that [Moses] had gone over to look, God called to him from within the bush, 'Moses! Moses!' And Moses said, 'Here I am.'" (Exodus 3:4). It is not merely that God must speak and move, but that man must look, explore and respond.[27] Before God revealed his plans to Moses, there were a number of things that Moses had to do. He had to take notice of a phenomenon that was unusual and not immediately explicable. He then needed to investigate what was going on. Only once he had done this did God call his name. As the final piece in the jigsaw, Moses was required to reply. Often we do precisely the opposite of these things. We fail to apply our minds properly to what is around us, either being completely blind to what is happening or dismissing any possibility of God's involvement out of hand. We never see the bush burning in the first place, or neglect to examine dispassionately what might be the cause of this "strange sight" (Exodus 3:3). On other occasions we may go over to take a look, but ignore the Lord's voice.[28] If we do not pay heed and do not reply, we can hardly be surprised when God ends the conversation.

Yet once we respond, the High King of heaven speaks. He does not leave us groping in the dark, unsure of his character or of what we need to do. His appearance to Moses on Mount Horeb was significant not only in terms of the particular task that one man was told to undertake. It was part of the Lord's continuing disclosure to mankind of who he is and how he works, building towards the ultimate revelation of himself in the coming of Christ.[29] The Almighty confirmed to Moses that:

He is the same yesterday, today and forever: "I am the God of your father, the God of Abraham, the God of Isaac and the God of Jacob." (Exodus 3:6).

He has not turned his back on the world, but is intimately concerned with every detail of what goes on in it: "I have seen the deep sorrows of my people in Egypt ... I have seen the heavy tasks the Egyptians have oppressed them with." (Exodus 3:7 and 3:9, TLB).

He is not indifferent to our plight, but suffers with and alongside us: "I have heard them crying out because of their slave drivers, and I am concerned about their suffering." (Exodus 3:7).

He does not stand aloof, but takes an active part in righting injustice and oppression: "So I have come down to rescue them from the hand of the Egyptians and to bring them up out of that land into a good and spacious land, a land flowing with milk and honey" (Exodus 3:8).

He delegates much of this work to us, using humans as his representatives: "So now, go. I am sending you to Pharaoh to bring my people the Israelites out of Egypt." (Exodus 3:10).

He does not send us into the unknown, alone and ill-equipped. Rather, he gives firm proof and assurance of his activity, and goes with us every step of the way: "I will be with you. And this will be the sign to you that it is I who have sent you: When you have brought the people out of Egypt, you will worship God on this mountain." (Exodus 3:12).

He provides the authority that underpins what we need to speak: "I AM WHO I AM. This is what you are to say to the Israelites: 'I AM has sent me to you.'" (Exodus 3:14).

He has a name and thus is fully personal: "Say to the Israelites, 'The LORD, the God of your fathers – the God of Abraham, the God of Isaac and the God of Jacob – has sent me to you.' This is my name for ever, the name by which I am to be remembered from generation to generation." (Exodus 3:15).

He knows things all things and nothing is beyond his power: "But I know that the king of Egypt will not let you go unless a mighty hand compels him. So I will stretch out my hand and strike the Egyptians with all the wonders that I will perform among them. After that, he will let you go." (Exodus 3:20).

He can change the hearts and dispositions of men, providing for us in the most unlikely of circumstances: "And I will make the Egyptians favourably disposed towards this people, so that when you leave you will not go empty-handed." (Exodus 3:21).

Throughout the Bible, disclosure of a new name or title for God marks the giving of a new or more complete revelation of himself, and so it was on Horeb: "God ... said to [Moses]: 'I am the LORD. I appeared to Abraham, Isaac, and Jacob as God Almighty, but by my name "The LORD" I did not make myself known to them.'" (Exodus 6:2-3, NRSV).[30] To Moses, however, was revealed not just the name but its meaning: "I AM WHO I AM" (Exodus 3:14), which could equally be rendered "I will be who I will be".[31] This conveys a sense of God's being outside and independent of time, whose experiences are felt in a continually existing present, whom Scripture deservedly describes as "the Alpha and the Omega" (Revelation 1:8, GNT; 21:6, GNT; and 22:13, GNT), "the First and the Last, the Beginning and the End" (Revelation 22:13). This is the Creator, the First Cause and the Prime Mover, uncreated and everlasting, all-knowing and all-powerful. Over the course of the next forty years, he was to reveal to Moses more of himself and of the means by which he would take the family of

Abraham and make of it "a great and powerful nation" (Genesis 18:18), just as he had sworn to do many centuries before.[32]

Commissioning.

The start of this journey was not exactly promising. Moses' responses showed the extent to which fear and doubt had replaced self-assurance in his mind. He was diffident and reluctant to take risks. Though later generations described him as being "powerful in speech and action" (Acts 7:22), he complained of being "a poor speaker, slow and hesitant" (Exodus 4:10, GNT). In the face of such weakness the Lord was sympathetic, patient and forbearing, as he is with us in similar circumstances, "for he knows how we are formed. He remembers that we are dust." (Psalm 103:14). We might judge that in asking, "What if they do not believe me or listen to me and say, 'The LORD did not appear to you'?" (Exodus 4:1) the future prophet did no more than quite reasonably seek guidance as to a perfectly foreseeable eventuality.[33] This seems to be precisely how God treated the question. Indeed, such was the Lord's graciousness that by way of reply he thrice gave Moses signs so miraculous that only a supernatural force could have been behind them:

His staff became a snake: "When Moses threw it [his staff] down, it turned into a snake, and he ran away from it. Then the LORD said to Moses, 'Reach down and pick it up by the tail.' So Moses reached down and caught it, and it became a [staff] again." (Exodus 4:3-4, GNT).

His hand was made leprous and then healed: "The LORD spoke to Moses again, 'Put your hand inside your robe.' Moses obeyed; and when he took his hand out, it was diseased, covered with white spots, like snow. Then the LORD said, 'Put your hand inside your robe again.' He did so, and when he took it out this time, it was healthy, just like the rest of his body." (Exodus 4:6-7, GNT).

He was given power to turn the Nile to blood: "The LORD said, 'If they will not believe you or be convinced by the first miracle, then this one will convince them. If in spite of these two miracles they still will not believe you, and if they refuse to listen to what you say, take some water from the Nile and pour it on the ground. The water will turn into blood.'" (Exodus 4:8-9, GNT).

These portents were given "to prove to the Israelites that the LORD, the God of their ancestors, the God of Abraham, Isaac, and Jacob, has appeared to you" (Exodus 4:5, GNT), but they were also for Moses' benefit. Nevertheless, he still raised objections: "I have never been a good speaker, and I haven't become one since you began to speak to me. I am a poor speaker, slow and hesitant." (Exodus 4:10, GNT). This may have been an exaggeration, perhaps an outright falsehood, but even so God still answered kindly: "I will help you to speak, and I will tell you what to say." (Exodus 4:12, GNT).[34] Not until Moses pleaded, "No, Lord, please send someone else." (Exodus 4:13, GNT) are we told that "the LORD became angry with Moses" (Exodus 4:14, GNT). The scene is one with which we can each have sympathy. It is in our fallen nature to build obstacles to God and to the work that he wishes to do in us, through us and with us. Few would not have trembled at the size of the task that this man was asked to undertake.[35]

Moses was commissioned by God for great things when he was told, "I am sending you" (Exodus 3:10). We tend to forget or conveniently overlook that we have each been commissioned, too, for works both large and small. It was not a select few but all believers whom Jesus addressed when he said, "As the Father has sent me, I am sending you." (John 20:21). Every follower of Christ is included in the command to "Go ... and make disciples of all the nations, baptizing them in the name of the Father and of the Son and of the Holy Spirit, teaching them to observe all things that I have commanded you" (Matthew 28:19-20, NKJV). The finger of God has pointed at us, whether we are conscious of it or not: "For we are God's workmanship, created in Christ Jesus to do good works, which God prepared in advance for us to do." (Ephesians 2:10). Instead of bemoaning the suffering in the world, we would do well to reflect that it is our failure to undertake the tasks allotted to us which enables free rein to evil and vice. It is childish to expect that there will always be quick and bloodless victories in the fight to see God's kingdom come – seven times Moses exhorted Pharaoh on behalf of the Almighty to "Let my people go" (Exodus 5:1, 7:16, 8:1, 8:20, 9:1, 9:13 and 10:3) before at last the promised release came. Of one thing we can be sure, however: the extent to which we experience the fullness of that kingdom in this life depends in no small measure on us.

Conclusion.

A decisive break with the past requires that we set our eyes and heart on what lies ahead and leave former things behind. In the desert the Israelites repeatedly struggled with this, as in truth do most of us at some point or another. Faced with the challenges of the journey on which God was leading them, they yearned for the security and comfort they mistakenly convinced themselves had once been theirs: "If only we had died by the LORD's hand in Egypt! There we sat round pots of meat and ate all the food we wanted, but you have brought us out into this desert to starve this entire assembly to death." (Exodus 16:3). Confronted with the hard reality of the life of faith and the need for personal responsibility, they preferred instead the seductive yoke of slavery: "If only we had meat to eat! We remember the fish we ate in Egypt at no cost – also the cucumbers, melons, leeks, onions and garlic. But now we have lost our appetite; we never see anything but this manna!" (Numbers 11:5). Either overlooking God's miraculous provision entirely or treating it as if it were a thing of no account, they persistently viewed Egypt through rose-tinted spectacles, forgetful of the fact that there they had been "[oppressed] ... with forced labour" (Exodus 1:11), that taskmasters had "[imposed] tasks on the Israelites, and made their lives bitter with hard service in mortar and brick and in every kind of field [labour and] were ruthless in all the tasks that they imposed on them." (Exodus 1:13-14, NRSV).

God does not wish us to be slaves, but free. Through Jesus Christ he offers "freedom for the captives and release from darkness for the prisoners" (Isaiah 61:1, quoted in Luke 4:18). He yearns to usher us into "the glorious freedom of the children of God." (Romans 8:21). This liberty, however, does not come free of charge. It cost Jesus an agony of suffering on the cross to buy us back from bondage and living the life of freedom bought at such a price makes demands of us, too. Yet those who stay the course testify repeatedly that it is worth it. The Israelites' time of testing in the desert was not an end in itself but a mere way-station on the road to the Promised Land. Had they kept in mind their ultimate objective, they would have reached it swiftly and in good order. Instead, failure to root out tendencies towards romanticising the past, mischaracterising evil and cheapening the things of God led them to pay dearly. In this they were like Lot's wife, who "looked back, and she became a pillar of salt." (Genesis 19:26). The reality is that once we are embarked on the Christian life there ought to be no looking back and no turning aside. We should press on remorselessly towards our goal – an encounter with God that will end with our presentation before him "as one approved by him, a worker who has no need to be ashamed" (2 Timothy 2:15, NRSV) with the commendation "Well done, good and faithful servant!" (Matthew 25:21). Then all that we have had to endure in this life will be revealed as "light and momentary troubles [which] are achieving for us an eternal glory that far outweighs them all." (2 Corinthians 4:17).

Encounters with God take many forms. They are seldom as dramatic as those experienced by Moses, but then few are those called to endeavours of such magnitude. Meetings with our Maker lurk in the everyday as much as in the unusual, in the quotidian just as in the extraordinary. Too often we pass them by without a second glance, never pausing to look or listen. Yet if we wish to come face to face with the source of all that is beautiful, good and true, to experience in our lives his power, healing and restoration, to see him overturn the things in our past that hold us back and bring deliverance to our nation, the lessons of Exodus must apply to us as to previous generations. They involve:

Keeping alert to the Lord's activity and for his call;

Being ready to have our hearts broken;

Yielding to his shaping and guiding;

Staying responsive to his vision for our lives, church and country;

Allowing ourselves to be touched by the fire of his Spirit; and

Remaining unflinching in our willingness to go wherever he might send.

Coming before God is not reserved only for exceptional people. It is not for those who have never made a single mistake. If it were, the murderer Moses could not have been received and neither could we. Instead, it is our undeserved good fortune that the Lord lays himself open to everyone. On Mount Horeb, "Moses, Aaron, Nadab, Abihu, and seventy of the elders of Israel went up into the mountain. And they saw the God of Israel" (Exodus 24:9-10, TLB). Today our access to the Almighty is even greater because Jesus' death on the cross decisively broke the barrier which human sin placed between man and his Creator, an event symbolised as Christ "gave up his spirit" (Matthew 27:50) by the fact that "The curtain of the temple was torn in two" (Matthew 27:51 and Mark 15:38). The veil which used to keep separate the Holy of Holies, which only the High Priest was permitted to enter, and that just once a year, has been taken away. We can all encounter God.

Simeon

Whose meaning is, *one who hears*

Of whom Jacob prophesied,
"Simeon and Levi are brothers – their swords are weapons of violence. Let me not enter their council, let me not join their assembly, for they have killed men in their anger and have hamstrung oxen as they pleased."
(Genesis 49:5-6).

2. Belonging to God

Allegiance and character.

"I will take you as my own people, and I will be your God." (Exodus 6:7).

In the sixth year of his reign Akhenaten publicly, decisively and irrevocably chose to identify himself with Aten by changing his name. This was a statement of future orientation and direction that for many of his subjects, perhaps even most, must have been deeply shocking.[36] Their monarch had originally been called Amenhotep, in honour of the god Amun. This deity had hitherto been regarded as chief of the Egyptian gods. He was the divinity of reproduction and the life-giving force, into which other gods had progressively been assimilated so that he became Amun-Ra, the supreme creator. From the start of the New Kingdom[37] he was venerated as a victorious national god, with a cult temple at Weset (Thebes). For the king to turn his back on him was a denial tantamount to outright betrayal. Such apostasy in a sense involved turning the world upside down. It meant that in one fell swoop the very person who should have been ultimate guardian of the nation went against some of its most important norms and in doing so undermined key pillars of church and state. In the process he must have alienated many who in normal circumstances ought to have been natural supporters. It was by any stretch of the imagination an astonishing departure, and this by a man come relatively new to the throne, who we can reasonably suppose might still have needed to consolidate his power after succeeding a long-lived predecessor. The animosity of the influential priestly caste must have been enormous. We get some measure of it from the opprobrium heaped on Akhenaten after his death.

The name that Akhenaten selected for himself went beyond a simple badge of allegiance. It was no passing fancy, no issue of style or fashion but of the gravest import. In the ancient Near East names were of tremendous significance. They were indicators of respect, devotion, belonging, authority, vassalage, reputation and character.[38] To adopt a name incorporating that of a deity was to pledge lifelong fealty to the god concerned. In the clearest terms, Akhenaten announced that he was the liege-man and subject of Aten, but at the same time he made bold claims for himself in terms of personality and function. Instead of continuing to bear the title *Amun is Satisfied* he desired to be known as *Effective Spirit of Aten*.[39] The choice of epithet was designed not just to signify loyalty to his god but also to project Akhenaten's view of his own relation to the deity, proclaiming that the very spirit of the divine was at work in the king and made manifest through him. Whilst it was hardly entirely unprecedented for monarchs to make grandiose assertions about being above the ordinary run of mortals, the ambition of the claim was enormous and could scarcely have been lost on contemporaries as more and more reforms were put in place: people were to be left in no doubt that the pharaoh and his immediate family were to act as the primary (and, as far as Akhenaten was concerned, perhaps even the sole) mediators between god and man. In the process, a large part of the existing priestly caste was effectively rendered redundant.[40]

That this momentous step was not the act of a natural revolutionary is attested by Akhenaten's deep conservatism in other areas. Notwithstanding the radical changes which were made in years to come in matters of worship, texts used to teach scribes remained the traditional ones, often dating from the Middle Kingdom. It is true that references which were politically or religiously unacceptable to the new regime were removed, such as the manner of rendering the names of gods and goddesses. Nevertheless, despite the new ideology time-honoured manuals were not replaced in their entirety, as might have been expected and indeed has tended to happen throughout the ages wherever and whenever radical departures in thought occur. The results were in some instances surprising: among those materials whose use Akhenaten continued to allow was *The Teaching of King Amenemhat I,* which had first been produced in the Twelfth Dynasty, some five hundred years earlier. Given that the name of the king in its title translates as *Amun is Foremost* and bearing in mind that the name of Amun was in the process of being carefully erased from inscriptions across the country, permitting such a document to remain in circulation is, to say the least, curious. Yet in view of the thoroughness of the expurgations carried out elsewhere, it seems logical to conclude that this reflected deliberate policy rather than oversight. For such a commonly used text to have been left untouched reinforces the extraordinary nature of those alterations which were in fact made.

The snake king.

Allegiance inevitably impacts belief, for it involves choices about what we think worthy of respect, devotion and attention. In turn, beliefs influence character since we cannot long remain unaffected by the things we hold dear. Character drives action because the inward seeks outward expression: we naturally yearn to give effect to our heartfelt desires and imaginings, just as we long to see our ideals become reality. So it was with Akhenaten, whose allegiance required of him deeds that ran counter to much that his forebears held sacrosanct. Such things have been true throughout the ages, not least with the protagonists of Exodus. The confrontation between Pharaoh and Moses described in Scripture shows not merely the interplay of human emotions and ambitions. It is above all about decisions of personality, mind and will – as to where we place our allegiance and what character we develop in consequence.[41] On a spiritual level it is a classic battle of good against evil, in which the participants are representatives and instruments of those divine or demonic forces that motivate and stand behind them. Moses, Aaron and the Israelites were aligned with the one true God whilst Pharaoh and his people were in thrall to dark forces. The conflict is one that goes back to the earliest days of humanity, in which identical actors in the spiritual realms played out their eternal enmity on the same battleground of the human soul.[42] In such tales, albeit of faraway lands and long ago, are elements which resonate deeply with our current circumstances. They remind us that appearances can be deceptive, that earthly wisdom is not the same as the heavenly kind, that we have the ability to choose whose side we take and that the battles we fight are part of a wider picture.

APPEARANCES CAN BE DECEPTIVE.

Pharaoh presided over a magnificent civilisation, whose power and wealth were at that time without compare. All that was noblest in the arts and crafts, in architecture and science would have been at his behest.[43] He was to all outward appearance at the pinnacle of earthly achievement, surrounded by luxury, housed in a palace, arrayed in the finest raiment, clean-shaven and pomaded, attended by servants. This was the very embodiment of a god-king, who held the lives of his subjects in his hands and whose words were law. By contrast, Moses had spent forty years eking out a living in a harsh desert landscape, tending animals and living in a tent. From a human point of view, he had come down in the world. Indeed, he could scarcely have fallen further, a prince turned horny-handed son of toil,[44] clad most like in the homespun of a shepherd, bearded and ragged, a fitting agent for a race of slaves. With him came no fine retinue. There were no big battalions at his command, neither waiting chariots nor fleet archers, nor weaponry of any kind.

During the first clashes between these two adversaries, who on the face of it were so ill-matched, Pharaoh would have had every reason to feel confidence, and not just because of the disparity in temporal resources. For there was power, too, in the false gods and occult practices of Egypt.[45] When "Aaron threw his staff down in front of Pharaoh and his officials, and it became a snake" (Exodus 7:10), the Egyptian ruler does not seem to have been unduly discomforted. Instead, "Pharaoh then summoned the wise men and sorcerers, and the Egyptian magicians also did the same things by their secret arts." (Exodus 7:11).[46] Twice more the same thing happened. When the Hebrew leader "raised his staff in the presence of Pharaoh and his officials and struck the waters of the Nile, and all the water was changed into blood" (Exodus 7:20) and when "Aaron stretched out his hand over the waters of Egypt, and the frogs came up and covered the land" (Exodus 8:6), on each occasion "the Egyptian magicians did the same things by their secret arts" (Exodus 7:22 and 8:7). This is worthy of careful reflection, for the situation that men face in each age is no different. St Paul reminded his readers in one of the embattled early Christian communities that "our struggle is not against flesh and blood, but against the rulers, against the authorities, against the powers of this dark world and against the spiritual forces of evil in the heavenly realms." (Ephesians 6:12).

Applying this spiritual perspective to the contest between Moses and Pharaoh leads to a number of conclusions about the forces of good and evil:

Outward similarities: There might be superficial similarity between the outward effects of some works of God and those of the powers of darkness. We need wisdom, discernment and insight to disentangle the two.

A misleading surface: The signs which were wrought before Pharaoh through the agency of Moses, Aaron and the magicians of Egypt were things which brought affliction. Yet we might equally be faced with circumstances where we need to weigh things which appear on their face to be benevolent or enjoyable, for "Satan himself masquerades as an angel of light. It is not surprising, then, if his servants masquerade as servants of righteousness." (2 Corinthians 11:14).

Alluring counterfeits: It follows that just because something seems beautiful or desirable on the outside does not automatically mean that it is good. The evil one is perfectly capable of producing things that look pleasing at first sight or touch. He cannot create as God does, but he can imitate. He is the great counterfeiter, dressing himself up in borrowed clothes, camouflaging his real intent and beguiling us with sufficient truth for us to be misled. Jesus calls him "a liar and the father of lies" (John 8:44).

Deceptive signs: To a degree the forces of darkness can copy and hence we should expect "the work of Satan [to be] displayed in all kinds of counterfeit miracles, signs and wonders, and in every sort of evil that deceives those who are perishing" (2 Thessalonians 2:9-10).

Tell-tale indications: Counterfeits might look impressive at first sight, but closer investigation will reveal the truth. Although "Each one [of the Egyptian magicians] threw down his staff and it became a snake, [nevertheless] Aaron's staff swallowed up their staffs." (Exodus 7:12). The superiority of the God of Israel was thus clearly shown from the start.

Powerlessness revealed: Similarly, the Egyptian wise men and magicians were able to repeat the effects of the first three plagues, but could but reverse them, which was what Pharaoh and his people really needed. The plague of blood and the plague of gnats seem to have run their natural course, but the plague of frogs was lifted specifically because Moses asked God to remove it (Exodus 8:12-13), not because of anything the Egyptians did or said.

Limits exposed: There are limits to what evil forces can do.[47] The Egyptian wise men and sorcerers could not repeat the effects of the fourth plague: "When the magicians tried to produce gnats by their secret arts, they could not." (Exodus 8:18). After this, they recognised "the finger of God" (Exodus 9:19) and made no further attempts to intervene. By the time of the sixth plague their helplessness had been completely exposed: "The magicians could not stand before Moses because of the boils that were on them and on all the Egyptians." (Exodus 9:11).

We are surrounded by counterfeits both religious and secular. Many are those who masquerade as servants of righteousness whilst pursuing an agenda that has nothing to do with seeking and doing the will of God. The language of justice, fairness and truth is manipulated and misused, as it is ever wont to be. The devil's tactics have not changed. Just as he has done throughout the ages, Satan seeks to undermine belief in God or to channel our spiritual impulses in ways that lead away from Christ and consequently cut us off from the salvation that only Jesus can bring, since he alone is "the atoning sacrifice for our sins." (1 John 4:10, NRSV). As much as at any time in the past, we therefore need to know how to tell the difference between the real and the counterfeit, the true and false, the genuinely good and what is attractively packaged but rotten underneath. We need to know how to keep to the right path day by day and not be led astray. The way in which to do this is no secret. It is writ clear as day in God's Word. By obeying what this says we can access true wisdom and godly insight instead of having to rely solely on the knowledge and cleverness that we often mistake for such things.

EARTHLY AND HEAVENLY WISDOM.

The ancient Egyptians possessed scientific, mathematical and engineering skill of the highest order. Year upon year they were able to mobilise and organise manpower sufficient to build pyramids, palaces, colossal statues, columned halls and towering temples.[48] They had "secret arts" (Exodus 7:11, 7:22 and 8:7) which enabled them to mimic some of the handiwork of God. The achievements of modern science and technology are similarly spectacular. Such is their reach, so great the ability they give mankind to order and control daily life that they, too, might seem to take us into realms that have until now always been acknowledged as belonging to the Creator alone. This tempts some to imagine that we can relegate God to the sidelines, redefine him in a way more to our liking or even do away with him entirely. The foolishness of such an approach should be obvious. The reasoning ability and intellect that God has given us so that we can "work [his Creation] and take care of it" (Genesis 2:15) are a mechanism, neither more nor less. They need to be kept in proper perspective. The questions that God put to Moses are equally apposite in the modern world: "Who gave man his mouth? Who makes him deaf or mute? Who gives him sight or makes him blind? Is it not I, the LORD?" (Exodus 4:11). The proof of the pudding is this: all the finest of human minds cannot create a single genuinely new thing. No man is able to bring something out of nothing. All we can do is to work with what God has given, be it our physical strength, our mental capacity or the stuff of the world around.[49]

Not only do we puff ourselves up with pride in our dealings with God. We also elevate ourselves in relation to those who have gone before us or who live in less technologically advanced societies, imagining that we have avoided the traps into which the ancients fell.[50] We believe that science has removed us from the realms of superstition and that our pursuit of the rational means that we could never be misled by the fancies of heathen religions. When we read that "You must not worship the LORD your God in their way, because in worshipping their gods, they do all kinds of detestable things the LORD hates. They even burn their sons and daughters in the fire as sacrifices to their gods" (Deuteronomy 12:31), we tend to smile inwardly. Our reaction often is to regard the injunction as intolerant, old-fashioned and unsuited to current circumstances. Accounts of human sacrifice we consider exaggerated or fanciful[51] or at least so far removed from the present day as no longer to be relevant. To the extent that we engage at all with heathenism in modern form, we are apt to think of it as characterised at home by a harmless dabbling in horoscopes or crystals, and abroad as a quaint show for tourists, part of the background to provide local colour for our diversion. It rarely occurs to us that such things might have an impact in the real world. It seldom troubles our sleep that our widespread practice of abortion amounts to child sacrifice on a horrific scale. Neither do we scent danger when debates over issues such as euthanasia are couched in terms of the utilitarian rather than recognising the fundamental dignity of all human life.

In truth, we have not advanced as far beyond our ancestors as we would like to think. The issues that confronted them are the same as those that confront us, for what we believe or fail to believe affects every aspect of our lives and of the society in which we live. Both the Bible and human experience through the ages tell us that if we rely solely on the things of this world and the products of our own imaginations, at some point we will come unstuck. If we place ourselves in the hands of false gods, both we and those around us will ultimately suffer for it. Sooner or later our behaviour will reflect the creed we espouse, for in the same way that the presence of the Holy Spirit brings forth good fruit in our lives and characters, the presence of spiritually harmful influences will bring forth bad fruit.[52] So it was with Pharaoh, whose dealings with Moses showed what his gods really represented:

Pride and wilful ignorance: "Who is the LORD, that I should obey him and let Israel go?" (Exodus 5:2).

Mercilessness: "That same day Pharaoh gave this order to the slave drivers and foremen in charge of the people: 'You are no longer to supply the people with straw for making bricks; let them go and gather their own straw. But require them to make the same number of bricks as before; don't reduce the quota.

They are lazy; that is why they are crying out … Make the work harder for the men so that they keep working and pay no attention to lies.'" (Exodus 5:6-9).

Ingratitude: "Pharaoh summoned Moses and Aaron and said, 'Pray to the LORD to take the frogs away from me and my people, and I will let your people go and offer sacrifices to the LORD.' … But when Pharaoh saw that there was relief, he hardened his heart and would not listen to Moses and Aaron, just as the LORD had said." (Exodus 8:8 and 15).

Disavowal and wilful disobedience: Pharaoh exclaimed, "I do not know the LORD and I will not let Israel go." (Exodus 5:2). Later "he would not listen to Moses and Aaron … Instead, he turned and went into his palace, and did not take even this to heart." (Exodus 7:23).

Deceit: "Pharaoh said, 'I will let you go to offer sacrifices to the LORD your God in the desert, but you must not go very far. Now pray for me.' … But this time also Pharaoh hardened his heart and would not let the people go." (Exodus 8:28 and 32).

Sinfulness: "Then Pharaoh summoned Moses and Aaron. 'This time I have sinned,' he said to them. 'The LORD is in the right and I and my people are in the wrong. Pray to the LORD, for we have had enough thunder and hail. I will let you go; you don't have to stay any longer.' … When Pharaoh saw that the rain and hail and thunder had stopped, he sinned again: he and his officials hardened their hearts." (Exodus 9:27-28 and 34).

By contrast, Moses displayed the qualities that God seeks in those who would truly follow him:

Humility: "Moses was a very humble man, more humble than anyone else on the face of the earth." (Numbers 12:3).

Compassion expressed in godly action: "Some shepherds came along and drove them [the daughters of Reuel, priest of Midian] away, but Moses got up and came to their rescue and watered their flock." (Exodus 2:17).

Thankfulness: "I will sing to the LORD, for he is highly exalted. The horse and the rider he has hurled into the sea. The LORD is my strength and my song; he has become my salvation. He is my God, and I will praise him, my father's God, and I will exalt him." (Exodus 15:1-2, the great song of praise and thanksgiving sung by Moses after Pharaoh's horses, chariots and horsemen were lost in the Red Sea.)

Submission to the will of God: "Moses said to the LORD … 'If you are pleased with me, teach me your ways so I may know you and continue to find favour with you…'" (Exodus 33:12-13).

Truthfulness: "...let Pharaoh not deal deceitfully anymore in not letting the people go to sacrifice to the LORD." (Exodus 8:29, NKJV).

Righteousness: "When Moses approached the camp and saw the calf and the dancing, his anger burned and he threw the tablets out of his hands, breaking them to pieces at the foot of the mountain. And he took the calf they had made and burned it in the fire; then he ground it to powder, scattered it on the water and made the Israelites drink it." (Exodus 32:19-20).

As we reflect upon these contrasting qualities, we should consider what kind of character and what manner of society we wish to build: one based on pride or humility; mercilessness or compassion; ingratitude or thankfulness; disobedience of God or submission to his will; deceit or truthfulness; sinfulness or righteousness? To choose the path of virtue requires that we acknowledge and give pride of place to God rather than to idols.[53] Only by doing so can we expect to reflect his character to any meaningful degree in our own lives and in the life of our nation. To whom we give our allegiance is neither ephemeral nor of only passing importance: it is a matter of life and death.

A SECOND CHANCE.

Although Pharaoh and his people were initially aligned with dark forces, it was not inevitable that they should remain so. There was nothing that meant they were forever condemned to play this role without hope of reform or redemption. In the course of this conflict, as throughout history, human beings were given real choices: to side with God or to reject him. Time and again Pharaoh had the option of doing the right thing. He was shown the might of the one true God. The limitations of what could be done by his magicians were clearly displayed. The false gods of Egypt were shown up for what they were. The consequences of his choices were clearly spelt out to him beforehand, with warnings being given before each set of plagues.[54] There was nothing unfair or disproportionate in his treatment that could have provided the least excuse for further rebellion against the High King of heaven. His failure to do the right thing was neither through lack of evidence, nor because Egyptians were incapable of seeing things as they really were; even their pagan magicians were brought at length to acknowledge "the finger of God" (Exodus 9:19) and there were "officials of Pharaoh who feared the word of the LORD" (Exodus 9:20).

At the height of the seventh plague a moment of recognition seemed to dawn on the Egyptian ruler for the first time: "Then Pharaoh summoned Moses and Aaron. 'This time I have sinned,' he said to them. 'The LORD is in the right and I and my people are in the wrong.'" (Exodus 9:27). Recognising our sinfulness and taking responsibility for it are the first steps on the road to salvation. We need to lay aside all excuses and accept that we alone bear the blame for what we have done wrong. Once we sincerely say sorry, the way is open to turn decisively from the path of evil and to embrace the forgiveness that God has made possible through the death of Jesus on the cross. Doing so will not automatically mean that everything suddenly becomes perfect and that all troubles will be removed, but it will effect a change in the orientation of our lives that will bear great fruit over time. Pharaoh's confession of sin lifted the threat of judgment and thus brought immediate relief from affliction: "Moses replied, 'When I have gone out of the city, I will spread out my hands in prayer to the LORD. The thunder will stop and there will be no more hail, so you may know that the earth is the LORD's.'" (Exodus 9:29). This was a watershed moment, a chance to translate words of repentance into the genuine article by acting accordingly. There was still time to turn judgment to blessing, for despite all that had taken place Egypt was not yet beyond the point of no return: "All the flax and barley were knocked down and destroyed (for the barley was ripe, and the flax was in bloom), but the wheat and the emmer were not destroyed, for they were not yet out of the ground." (Exodus 9:31-32, TLB).[55]

Yet it soon became obvious that Pharaoh's words did not reflect a true change of heart, as Moses had recognised from the start, admonishing the king, "But I know that you and your officials still do not fear the LORD God." (Exodus 9:30). Nevertheless, the monarch was given yet another chance. It is an extraordinary example of the mercy of God and his willingness to forgive over and over again, but the opportunity was wasted. The ruler did as human beings do all too often, saying whatever was convenient for the passing moment but swiftly retracting when danger seemed to have been averted. The result was a further plague, swiftly followed by another about turn: "Pharaoh quickly summoned Moses and Aaron and said, 'I have sinned against the LORD your God and against you. Now forgive my sin once more and pray to the LORD your God to take this deadly plague away from me.'" (Exodus 10:16-17). Against all the odds, Pharaoh was again given the benefit of the doubt: "Moses went out from Pharaoh and entreated the Lord, and he sent a very strong west wind that blew the locusts out into the Red Sea, so that there remained not one locust in all the land of Egypt!" (Exodus 10:18-19, TLB). There was relief from the plague, but the ruler's persistence in wrongdoing had brought Egypt to the brink of disaster, for the locusts had "[devoured] everything growing in the fields, everything left by the hail." (Exodus 10:12). With fields stripped bare and famine beckoning, the desperate situation was obvious to all except the man in charge: "Pharaoh's officials said to him, 'How long will this man [Moses] be a snare to us? Let the people go, so that they may worship the LORD their God. Do you not yet realise that Egypt is ruined?'" (Exodus 10:7).

Even at such a late hour, choice remained, but Pharaoh spurned all thought of turning. His reaction when the ninth plague (that of darkness) struck sounded the death knell for thousands of Egyptians. Still stubbornly refusing to free the Israelites and hot with anger, "Pharaoh said to Moses, 'Get out of my sight!

Make sure you do not appear before me again! The day you see my face you will die.'" (Exodus 10:28). There was death, all right, but not as the god-king envisaged. At the very outset of his mission, the Lord had instructed Moses that once he had "perform[ed] before Pharaoh all the wonders I have given you power to do" (Exodus 4:21), the prophet should "Then say to Pharaoh, 'This is what the LORD says: Israel is my firstborn son, and I told you, "Let my son go, so that he may worship me." But you refused to let him go; so I will kill your firstborn son.'" (Exodus 4:22-23).[56] So it transpired, just as the monarch had been forewarned: "At midnight the LORD struck down all the firstborn in Egypt, from the firstborn of Pharaoh, who sat on the throne, to the firstborn of the prisoner, who was in the dungeon, and the firstborn of all the livestock as well. Pharaoh and all of his officials and all the Egyptians got up during the night, and there was loud wailing in Egypt, for there was not a house without someone dead." (Exodus 12:29-30).

These events show the interaction of free will and predestination. To know beforehand what is going to happen is not the same as making it come about. God knew in advance how Pharaoh would react and where this would lead, but this did not absolve the occupant of the throne from responsibility for what came to pass. The ruler showed repeatedly that he could not be trusted. There was never genuine repentance on his part, for he would say anything to get himself off the hook and then renege on promises the very next moment. The blame for all that happened thus squarely lay at his door, for "Pharaoh hardened his heart" (Exodus 8:15 and 32). It is true that God told Moses, "I will harden his [Pharaoh's] heart" (Exodus 7:3) and there are six occasions when the Bible says that "the LORD hardened Pharaoh's heart" (Exodus 9:12, 10:1, 10:20, 10:27, 11:10 and 14:4). Nevertheless, it is clear that there were times where the choice was Pharaoh's alone and the hardening was his.[57]

The entire Egyptian nation suffered for Pharaoh's decisions, but this was not unjust. The Egyptian ruling class were fully complicit in what was said and done since "his officials [also] hardened their hearts." (Exodus 9:34). Though "Those officials of Pharaoh who feared the word of the LORD hurried to bring their slaves and livestock inside" (Exodus 9:20) so as to avoid the effects of the seventh plague, the hardening of their hearts as soon as this plague was lifted shows their response was a pragmatic one aimed at avoiding Moses' prediction that "every man and animal that has not been brought in and is still out in the field ... will die" (Exodus 9:19). It was not evidence of real spiritual change, for the moment their feet were no longer being held to the fire they instantly reverted to their previous attitudes and actions. Even these officials' willingness during the eighth plague to counsel Pharaoh to "let the people go" (Exodus 10:7) seems to have been based on expediency more than on morality or faith. They still referred to "the LORD their God" (Exodus 10:7) as though this were someone who belonged to Israel but with whom they did not identify personally. In fact, so wedded to sin was the whole polity that "When the king of Egypt was told that the people had fled, Pharaoh *and his officials* changed their minds about them and said, 'What have we done? We have let the Israelites go and have lost their services!' So he had his chariot made ready and took his army with him" (Exodus 14:5-6, emphasis added), with disastrous consequences.[58]

Pharaoh and his people doomed themselves. They were neither victims of a malign fate, nor helpless puppets in the hands of a cynical deity. Like us, they were free and independent actors with the self-same ability to make unfettered choices that we all have. That every single one of them retained to the last a genuine opportunity to choose is shown by the fact that others made precisely that determination, for when Israel left Egypt "Many other people went up with them" (Exodus 12:38).

THE WIDER PICTURE.

The circumstances surrounding the contest recounted in Exodus demonstrate that this was no chance occurrence. It was not an accidental or meaningless tussle that could just as well have happened in another time or place, or not at all. Instead it is shown to be unfinished business from the past, a continuation of a conflict that goes back to before the beginning of human history and continues today.[59] The first letter of the Hebrew text of Exodus is *waw* (*vav*), meaning, *and*, connecting Exodus explicitly with the narrative which immediately precedes it in a self-conscious continuation of what is related in Genesis. The thematic connections between the two books are many, with echoes of God's creation of the world and of Man's fall from the Garden of Eden:

Heritage: The genealogy which announces the arrival of Israel in Egypt in Genesis 46:8-14 also (in condensed form) announces her departure in Exodus 1:1-5.

Fruitfulness: The fruitfulness and multiplication of God's people that was envisaged when God said, "Be fruitful and multiply, and fill the earth" (Genesis 1:28 and 9:1, NKJV) is reflected in the fact that in Egypt the Israelites "multiplied and spread" (Exodus 1:12) and "continued to multiply and to become a mighty nation" (Exodus 1:20, TLB).

A new people: The birth of Moses was not merely the coming into the world of one man, but represented the creation of a new people, who were to be "a kingdom of priests and a holy nation." (Exodus 19:6). The prophet was the vehicle through which God brought this fresh entity into being, and creation language is used to describe him: "Moses' mother saw that he was a goodly child" (Exodus 2:2, KJV) in the same way that "God saw that it was good" or "very good" (Genesis 1:4, 10, 12, 18, 21, 25 and 31, KJV) at the end of each stage of creation.[60]

Places of refuge: To save him from Pharaoh's order that Israelite baby boys should be killed, Moses' mother put him into what is rendered in English as "a papyrus basket" (Exodus 2:3) and set him upon the waters of the river Nile. In the original Hebrew the word for this vessel is used only twice in the entire Bible: in this verse and to describe the "ark" (Genesis 6:14, KJV) built by Noah to save himself and his family from the Flood.

Evil incarnate: Pharaoh is an historical character, but also symbol and archetype, a front man for malign forces. He was the snake king; as a mark of divinity or kingship Egyptian gods and royalty were frequently shown wearing the uræus, a diadem in the form of a spitting cobra's head. Snakes were conjured up by Pharaoh's magicians. A serpent was the creature through which the devil tempted Adam and Eve: "The serpent was the craftiest of all the creatures the Lord God had made. So the serpent came to the woman. 'Really?' he asked. 'None of the fruit in the garden? God says you mustn't eat any of it?'" (Genesis 3:1, TLB).[61]

Dividing: The language used of the parting of the Red Sea is the same as that employed to describe the separation of water and land on the second day of Creation. Of the later event it is said that "The waters were divided, and the Israelites went through the sea on dry ground, with a wall of water on their right and on their left" (Exodus 14:21-22) whilst of the earlier, "God said, 'Let there be an expanse between the waters to separate water from water.'" (Genesis 1:6).[62]

Separation and distinction: Similarly, Israel was set apart and treated differently from the nations around her: "The LORD makes a distinction between Egypt and Israel" (Exodus 11:7). This separating out applied not only to humans but even to animals: "…the LORD will make a distinction between the livestock of Israel and that of Egypt, so that no animal belonging to the Israelites will die." (Exodus 9:4). Exactly as promised, "not one animal belonging to the Israelites died." (Exodus 9:6).

Creating and re-creating: giving of the Law on Mount Sinai was an act of re-creation, part of the means by which God fashioned Israel for himself: "Now if you obey me fully and keep my covenant, then out of all nations you will be my treasured possession. Although the whole earth is mine, you will be for me a kingdom of priests and a holy nation." (Exodus 19:5-6). The phrase "The LORD said to Moses" is repeated seven times in the course of describing Israel's stay at Sinai (Exodus 25:1, 30:11, 30:17, 30:22, 30:34, 31:1 and 31:12),[63] underlining the correspondence between this and the original Creation, each day of which starts with the phrase, "And God said" (Genesis 1:3, 1:6, 1:9, 1:11, 1:14, 1:20 and 1:24).[64]

Exodus emphasises that Israel belongs to God in a special and unique way: "I am the LORD, and I will bring you out from under the yoke of the Egyptians. I will free you from being slaves to them, and I will redeem you with an outstretched arm and with mighty acts of judgment. I will take you as my own people, and I will be your God. Then you will know that I am the LORD your God, who brought you out from under the yoke of the Egyptians." (Exodus 6:6-7). On leaving Egypt, the Israelites are portrayed as God's army on the march: "It was this same Aaron and Moses to whom the LORD said, 'Bring the Israelites out of Egypt by their divisions'" (Exodus 6:26). Similar military terminology is repeated later: "Now the length of time the Israelite people lived in Egypt was 430 years. At the end of the 430 years, to the very day, all the LORD's divisions left Egypt." (Exodus 12:40-41).

Specialness and collective belonging encompassed the whole community, for God had clearly said that "Israel is my firstborn son" (Exodus 4:22). This was expressed symbolically through the need to "Redeem with a lamb every firstborn donkey, but if you do not redeem it, break its neck. Redeem every firstborn among your sons." (Exodus 13:13).[65] The same principle was to apply "When you take a census of the Israelites to count them, [for] each one must pay the LORD a ransom for his life at the time he is counted." (Exodus 30:12). As a result of God's widening of his covenant promises to embrace all believers, Israel was not confined to genetic descendants of Abraham. To be part of God's family is a matter of faith rather than blood line: "…know that only those who are of faith are sons of Abraham." (Galatians 3:7, NKJV). The result is that all – man, woman and child – have the chance to belong to God. As with Moses and as with Pharaoh, so with us: the issue is one of choice.

Conclusion.

To make right choices we have to see through false appearances, and for this we need the help of God's wisdom, insight and discernment. In exercising our free will we should strain every nerve and sinew to examine facts dispassionately, to make reasoned judgments based on the fullest evidence and to do so with minds unclouded by prejudice or preconception. It is of the utmost importance that we should open ourselves to the widest possible enquiry, not denying possibilities merely if they discomfort or challenge us. The options before us may appear legion, but in truth they come down to the same ones that people had to weigh in the days of Moses. In assessing the alternatives, our determinations will involve how we respond to and act upon what we hear – an allegiance which ultimately will determine both our character and our destiny. There is no middle course and no way in which decision can be avoided, for as Jesus observed, "He who is not with me is against me." (Matthew 12:30). From one side beckons Pharaoh, representing the powers of anti-Creation, who beneath the blandishments of power and luxury in fact offers only imprisonment and enslavement for humanity and the destruction of life: "…if it [an Israelite baby] is a boy, kill him" (Exodus 1:16, NRSV). In this he does no more than follow his real master, for Satan's aim and delight is to "steal and kill and destroy." (John 10:10). On the other side stands the great lawgiver of Israel and behind him the one true God, whose Son Jesus has "come that [we] may have life, and have it to the full." (John 10:10). To any rational mind there should be no doubt as to which choice is the better. Belonging to God is what we were made for and the means by which we find our greatest fulfilment. Rejecting him means that life is ultimately empty and meaningless. The events recounted in Exodus brought salvation for Israel and judgment for Egypt. We, too, must make our choice.

Akhenaten turned his back on the traditional deities of Egypt to embrace new ideas about the divine and novel ways of worship. Moses chose to be obedient to the Lord. Each claimed to belong to the one true God, but with very different results. The monarch comprehensively failed to turn round the ship of state and carry his people with him. The religious reforms he put in place were a chimera, for after his death Egyptians continued to venerate their traditional gods until converted to Christianity a millennium and a half later. The heretic pharaoh's teaching is nowhere expounded in those texts which his rule has bequeathed to posterity. The worship of Aten is long forgotten, the sovereign's inheritance little more than dust. Not so with Moses. He penned the first five books of the holy Bible (together accounting for a substantial proportion of the entire Old Testament), led a nation out of slavery in the teeth of opposition from the most sophisticated and powerful country on earth, kept them together and succoured them though forty years of desert wandering, saw off rebellions and countered backsliding, and in the midst of it all organised a moral framework and system of law that has been the underpinning of much of the world's civilisation ever since. Allegiance, character and belief kept him going notwithstanding repeated ingratitude and in spite of attacks from within and without. They sustained him throughout forty years of trial and moments of deepest disillusion, frustration and despair. This was the fruit of a man who truly belonged to God.

Moses and Pharaoh

Levi

Whose meaning is, *attached*

Of whom Jacob prophesied,
"Cursed be their anger, so fierce, and their fury, so cruel! I will scatter them in Jacob and disperse them in Israel."
(Genesis 49:7).

3. Worshipping God

Sacred and profane.

*"Then the cloud covered the Tent of Meeting,
and the glory of the LORD filled the tabernacle." (Exodus 40:34).*

Temple-building programmes in favour of Aten began almost as soon as his princely partisan came to the throne, but constructing an entirely new city at Akhet-aten was of an altogether different order of magnitude. It was a mammoth undertaking, some six years and more in the building.[66] Even the resources of a kingdom that was skilled in erecting monuments on an extravagant scale would have been tested by it in good years and strained almost beyond endurance in less happy times. Pharaohs throughout the ages had felt the need to make grandiose statements in brick and stone, but to modern eyes at least the call for this particular means of expressing a break with the past is not immediately self-evident. To our way of thinking, the splendour of the king, the delights of his new theology and the superiority of his god could have been proclaimed equally well in traditional centres of Egyptian power. In some respects it might be thought that to have usurped the bastions of other deities in this manner would have been an even clearer signal of the precedence of the new over the old. It would certainly seem to have made more sense in terms of spreading the word amongst ordinary people and enabling the ruler to monitor and exercise control over dissidents.

For the occupant of the throne, however, only the untouched ground of what became Akhet-aten would do. This was not out of dislike for other places, since he seems to have continued to use royal residences in other parts of the country throughout his reign. No doubt he was enthused by having a clean slate on which to build and enamoured of the chance for a pristine environment untainted by association with other gods. Perhaps he was influenced by wishing to avoid intrigue or even forestall sabotage by a disgruntled priesthood. In his mind's eye he may have pictured the perfect site for his new undertaking being positioned (as Akhet-aten fortuitously was) more or less equidistant between the historically competing centres of Thebes and Memphis and astride the no-man's-land between their corresponding regions of Upper and Lower Egypt. The fundamental underlying impetus, though, went beyond the practical and beyond all considerations of cementing national unity or sidestepping regional rivalries. Indeed it flew in the face of practicality, for as the rapid later abandonment of the new city by officialdom confirmed, its location was unsuitable as a large population centre, or at any rate as the seat of government. As for burying past enmities and bringing the nation together, the divisive nature of Akhenaten's novel experiment was clearly exposed after his death.

The primary motive for the creation of Akhet-aten was in fact unashamedly theological. Akhenaten himself asserted that divine inspiration was behind the move, leaving around the boundaries of his selected location a series of monumental inscriptions in which he outlined his reasons for alighting there and a list of buildings which made clear his architectural intentions. Whether we take such proclaimed intent with a pinch of salt or not, the physical setting which he chose for his new capital would certainly have been striking to ancient Egyptian eyes, accustomed as they were to reading contours and landscape in a way that we are not. The city was constructed on a plain laid between two sharply rising escarpments, making the perfect surroundings for viewing the ascent of the sun. When its disc was seen first thing in the day with cliffs to either side the result was a natural environment which formed a circle enclosed by lines left, right and beneath – the hieroglyph for Akhet-aten (meaning, *Horizon of Aten*). Thus to adherents of the king's favoured cult the very landscape announced and enfolded the supreme divine name, putting the unmistakable stamp of the highest god upon the curve and fall of its terrain, and in doing so proclaiming the title which the city to be built there in his honour was to bear.[67] Framed as were its dwellings, temples, palaces, workshops, warehouses, government buildings and tombs by rock formations sculpted at divine behest rather than hewn by any tool of man,[68] they occupied a place that Akhenaten was at pains to make clear had hitherto belonged to no mortal and to no other deity. To all intents and purposes it was entirely virgin land, unblemished, set apart from the beginning of time to be dedicated to the one who had made it, made ready from the first for the very day and hour of its eventual discovery by the king. Doubtless such compelling geographical evidence was seized upon as confirmation that the choice of location was apt and wielded as proof not only that Aten was indeed above all other gods but also that his royal servant was touched by heaven in a unique and very special way.[69]

The remoteness of the recently built metropolis, described by the pharaoh as "this distant place," brought other advantages, too; for the labourers, courtiers and functionaries whom he dragooned to populate his new creation would have found it difficult to return regularly to Thebes to attend family religious ceremonies there. They were to extent virtual prisoners of the regime and kept away from what their overlord might have regarded as the temptations of the outside world. To cap it all, the layout of Akhet-aten had another happy resonance. In contrast to the former capital Thebes (whose necropolis lay to the west of the Nile), the new city was constructed so as to rest entirely on the east bank of the river. To the Egyptians of this time the east, whence the sun was reborn each morning, was the place of life. The west was the region of the setting sun, and therefore the domain of death. Akhet-aten and its god thus stood for integrating life and afterlife, sacred and profane, commonplace and transcendental in a way that the old order did not, just as there were brought together and unified in Aten those characteristics that previously had been parcelled out between other gods. By way of emphasising both the spatial unity and cohesion of sacred landscape and the novel thinking which now obtained, the pharaoh pointedly commanded "a tomb [to] be made for me in the eastern mountain [of Akhet-aten] and let my burial be made in it" – a reference to the valley east of the city which leads to the desert, and in which the king almost straightaway began having tombs for his family excavated, abruptly abandoning the tomb which was then in the process of being made for him in the Valley of the Kings outside Thebes.

To some degree Akhenaten seems to have treated the natural amphitheatre of desert, plain, cliffs and river as a vast performance space. Inside his freshly minted capital, the pharaoh processed regularly by chariot along the 100-yard-wide boulevard known as 'the king's road' which joined the Great North Gate and the South Gate and continued past the royal palace beside the Nile to Gem-pa-Aten,[70] the enormous temple complex which he caused to be raised in honour of his god. This journey enacted the sun's progress as it traversed the heavens from sunrise to sunset, symbolically moving as it did so between earthly and spiritual, light and dark, life and death. To mimic the ceremonial carrying abroad of divine images during the religious festivals of previous reigns,[71] the king paraded frequently amongst the citizenry. These displays emphasised the close relationship between crown and deity, in the process underlining the fact that obeisance to the pharaoh was part and parcel of the worship of Aten. The same point was driven home through the architecture and orientation of the main royal palace, aligned on an east-west axis as traditionally were the temples of Egypt and furnished like them with open courts flanked by colossal statues of royalty in the guise of gods.[72] Upon its balconies Akhenaten, his chief queen Nefertiti and their children could bask in the radiance of Aten.[73] There, too, they could be observed and venerated by adoring subjects. Tomb carvings show the royal family reaching down from on high to lavish gifts upon grateful courtiers, in emulation of how their god might stoop from heaven to bestow blessing. Thus were phenomena both natural and artificial enlisted to portray the new orthodoxy and to underscore the pivotal role played by the king.[74]

The city as sacred microcosm was by no means an entirely novel concept. Akhenaten's father, for one, had redesigned and integrated the monuments of east and west Thebes to make a ceremonial stage for religious pageantry. The symbolism of various styles of building was well understood and used accordingly. Yet appropriating entirely virgin land on such a scale and with such overt religious intent was nonetheless an unusual departure, for ancient Egyptians generally liked sacred sites to be hallowed by long use. Furthermore, the notions of the past were adapted in a unique way in Akhet-aten by dividing the site symmetrically so as to give equal prominence to the magnificent temple of Gem-pa-Aten on the one hand and to the king's own tomb on the other.

Thereby was religious and ceremonial architecture employed in the exaltation of the king and his closest family, elevating them to be if not equal to the great sun god then at least within the ranks of those who stood closest to him in love, loyalty, esteem and trust, making them worthy deputies for him on earth and assured of being his beloved companions in the life to come.

Making space for God.

The events of roughly the first half of the book of Exodus, covering Israel's slavery in Egypt through to the call of Moses and on to the plagues of Egypt, the crossing of the Red Sea, the giving of the Law on Sinai, God's miraculous provision for Israel in the desert and her prostration before the Golden Calf tend to be familiar, in outline if not in detail. Yet important as they are, these happenings do not comprise the dominating concern of the text as a whole. They form the backdrop and the necessary outworking of God's activity in saving his people and drawing them to himself, but it is the question of worship that looms large above all else – the creating of sacred space and its use, the means by which man might draw near to an all-powerful, just and holy God, the rightful context in which and method by which to display reverence, the proper aids to adoration of the High King of heaven and the appropriate rituals for their consecration, dedication and hallowing. These issues were manifest from the moment that God told Moses on Horeb, "Do not come any closer ... Take off your sandals, for the place where you are standing is holy ground" (Exodus 3:5). Little wonder that the man who heard those words should record with such care the Lord's instructions for making the tabernacle and its accoutrements, the Almighty's commands as to the role and function of the priesthood and the laws which were ordained in order to enable Israel to walk with her God in holiness. These things together take up fifteen out of forty sections in Exodus: chapters 25 to 31 explain exactly how and from what materials the tabernacle and its fittings and furnishings are to be built, whilst almost the entire remainder of the book (chapters 35 to 40) details their actual construction.[75]

In view of the importance of worship to all that happens in Exodus, it is hardly surprising that Moses should have been of the tribe of Levi,[76] from whose descendants the Lord also selected "Aaron and his sons, so that they may serve me as priests." (Exodus 28:4).[77] Yet the focus in Exodus is far from being solely on one man, one family or even one nation. The contrast with the theology, temples and forms of worship instituted by Akhenaten is instructive, for nothing that Exodus describes was designed with a view to elevating Moses or celebrating his relationship with God merely for its own sake; the signs of God's presence were not only upon the Creator's chosen prophet, but with all the children of Israel (and even foreigners, too, if they chose to join God's people) regardless of age, sex or status. Indeed, the radical inclusiveness of the vision which God outlined for the entire Israelite community was shown from the very first by Moses' insistence that women and children were to be active participants in the worship that Israel was to offer God. This straightaway aroused Pharaoh's suspicions, since his assumption apparently was that adoration of the Hebrew deity was properly the concern of Jewish men alone: "Pharaoh said, 'The LORD be with you – if I let you go, along with your women and children! Clearly you are bent on evil. No! Let only the men go; and worship the LORD, since that's what you have been asking for.' Then Moses and Aaron were driven out of Pharaoh's presence." (Exodus 10:10-11).[78]

In the event, Moses had his way and all Israel was freed to serve and worship God. In this they were the first fruits and prototype of future generations, both Jew and Gentile. The eternal importance and worldwide significance of their escape from Egypt and their subsequent worship and service of the Almighty is underscored not just by the value, quantity and quality of the work and materials required in building the tabernacle and all that went with it, but also by the intricate and extremely specific elaboration of how to fashion and put together the various parts that go to make up the whole. Of prime concern, too, was the setting within which these were to be placed and the Sabbath observance that was part and parcel of God's plan for a community entirely dedicated to holiness. Such minute attention to what might appear mere incidentals should alert us to the fact that what is being described is not simply concerned with outward appearance. If we look beyond the surface we are brought face to face with God's template for enabling man to enjoy again some measure of the closeness to his Maker which Adam had experienced when the Lord came "walking in the garden [of Eden] in the cool of the day" (Genesis 3:8, NKJV). The careful exposition in Exodus is there not so that we may become bogged down in a morass of particulars but so that we may comprehend the fine and overarching plan of which they are fruit.

The experience of Moses helps understand the broader picture, for the prophet's groundbreaking meeting with God on Horeb was amongst other things an act of worship. After first explaining who was speaking (Exodus 3:6), why he was doing so (Exodus 3:7-9) and the role that the chosen leader was to play (Exodus 3:10), the Lord assured Moses that he would be with him in the trials to come (Exodus 3:12) before declaring, "And this will be the sign to you that it is I who have sent you: When you have brought the people out of Egypt, you will worship God on this mountain." (Exodus 3:12). In other words, there was to be something about the worship that was to take place after Israel had been set free which would show uncontrovertibly that their deliverance had been at the hand of the one true God. This eventual goal of the nation worshipping on "the mountain of God" (Exodus 3:1), which was itself but a staging-post on the journey to the Promised Land and an equipping for the life of faith that Israel was to lead thenceforth, was to some degree presaged by the response when "Moses and Aaron brought together all the elders of the Israelites, and Aaron told them everything the LORD had said to Moses ... And when they heard that the LORD was concerned about them and had seen their misery, they bowed down and worshipped." (Exodus 4:29-31). These two incidents demonstrate that, when seen through the prisms of God's activity and man's proper reaction to it, worship is not blind subservience demanded by a megalomaniac deity; it is above all for our benefit, being a sign, a privilege, a blessing and a pleasure, an expression of thanksgiving for all that has been done for us, comprising the ultimate aim and fulfilment of our eternal destiny.[79]

Worship can be defined as paying divine honour to God, being a feeling or act of adoration, of loving or admiring devotion and submissive respect. It is linguistically related to the word 'worth' and thus encompasses qualities such as value, merit, excellence, honour, deference and respect.[80] The Lord deserves worship (the ascribing to him of worth) precisely because he is worthy, being the archetype of all that is good, true and beautiful and the yardstick by which such qualities are to be measured. To adore such a one involves receiving as well as giving, because worshipping brings us into the very presence of the Most High and allows some of his holiness to rub off on us. We cannot worship with every fibre of our being if we are enslaved. That is not to say that we cannot worship at all, merely that we will be constrained in the degree to which we are able to offer our Maker all that we are and all that we can be. Breaking free of the things that bind us is seldom easy or instantaneous, but we need to persevere. Seven times Pharaoh was enjoined to let the Israelites go "so that they may hold a festival to [the LORD] in the desert" (Exodus 5:1) or "so that they may worship [the LORD]" (Exodus 7:16, 8:1, 8:20, 9:1, 9:13 and 10:3) before the king, faced with ruin on every side, for the first time reluctantly conceded, "Go, worship the LORD your God." (Exodus 10:8). Even then, as Exodus 10:10-11 and 10:24-27 describe, he twice had second thoughts before at last his hand was irrevocably forced and he exclaimed, "Up! Leave my people, you and the Israelites! Go, worship the LORD as you have requested. Take your flocks and herds, as you have said, and go." (Exodus 12:31-32).

God's freeing of the Israelites from their worldly bondage fulfilled the first precondition for their being able to worship him fully, richly and unreservedly. They had to take advantage of the freedom that was offered, for they could after all have chosen to remain in Egypt, but the activity which led to their being released was wholly God's.[81] The second precondition, however, required that they take positive steps of their own. If we are to worship God we need to make space for him. This involves preparing "holy ground" (Exodus 3:5) to serve as a link between heaven and earth, a place in time and space where the Lord may be encountered. Since the coming of Jesus this holy ground is no longer identified with a particular patch of land or with a given building, and neither is it in any way restricted temporally, for now God's people have the Holy Spirit dwelling permanently within. Consequently we "are the temple of God" (1 Corinthians 3:16, NKJV), "[our] bodies are a temple" (1 Corinthians 6:19) and "we are the temple of the living God" (2 Corinthians 6:16). Nonetheless, there remain valuable lessons to be had from considering the plan which God framed for the Temple in Jerusalem and, before that, for the tabernacle; human circumstances may have changed, but the Lord "is the same yesterday and today and for ever." (Hebrews 13:8). Hence the requirements of the holy place that Moses was told to craft apply equally (albeit metaphorically rather than physically) to us.[82] In effect, we need to make a tabernacle in our hearts. Doing so to the fullest extent requires that we break free of the things that bind us and move beyond desert regions where growth is hampered or haphazard into territory where "rivers of living water ... flow" (John 7:38, TLB).

Crossing the desert.

Sinai is mountainous, arid and forbidding. The land is unsuitable for farming and rain seldom falls. Though sudden cloudbursts are capable of turning ravines for a short while to raging torrents, it is hardly terrain one would ordinarily associate with streams of water, living or otherwise. Blistering heat by day and bitter cold by night enhance the outward appearance of desolation. It is of course true that the peninsula is not one uniform tract of monotonous desert, the northernmost expanses from El Arish to the Suez Canal consisting of broad sand valleys, the central region of El The being a wide plateau of limestone, and the triangular tip of the peninsula further south forming a moonscape of granite peaks, amongst them Mount Moses, Mount Catherine, Mount Serbal and Umm Shumar. Neither is the area entirely devoid of life, for to this day it is home to wolves and foxes, hyenas and wild goats, eagles and gazelles. Yet still it is a forbidding prospect for any stranger to cross, the more so if the needs of large bodies of men must be met. This was the wilderness navigated by Israel on the way to Horeb, and in this apparently hostile environment God provided for his people's needs through repeated miracles: manna (Exodus 16:1-35), quail (Exodus 16:13) and water from the rock (Exodus 17:1-7).[83]

Like the Israelites of old, we need to find a way through barren places so that we might come into the presence of God. The wilderness that we face may lie within or be circumstances that oppress us from without. The Hebrew for wilderness is *midbar*, which literally means, *from a thing* or *from a word*. The sense this conveys is an out-of-the-way place, a physical or mental landscape of solitude without distractions, free of material things and idle chatter. It depicts a clearing away of clutter that is needful to prepare our hearts and minds to receive God, as well as that necessary void which must be crossed in order to ascend beyond the mundane in search of the only true and lasting freedom, the liberation of our spirits and souls. Exodus depicts the sea as the threshold or opening of this void.[84] In Hebrew the stretch of water which the Israelites crossed to escape the pursuing Egyptian chariots is called *Yam Suf* which literally means, *sea of reeds* (though habitually rendered into English as the *Red Sea*). Since biblical Hebrew was written without vowels, *suf* might also be read as *sof* (meaning, *end*) or *saf* (meaning, *threshold*) – the expanse which the tribes had to traverse being the boundary or end of one world and the entrance to a new one.

Before the sea parted, "the angel of God, who had been travelling in front of Israel's army, withdrew and went behind them." (Exodus 14:19). The change in position was an act of protection, ensuring that Pharaoh's forces could not approach until the moment was right. Yet like so much else in the Exodus story, it is also redolent with symbolism, the Israelites' journey being a physical acting out of our own spiritual quest. It emphasises that, whilst the Lord may lead us to the threshold, we will not be wafted over it without effort on our part; we need both a decision to make the crossing and the necessary action to bring a crossing about, in each case undertaken of our own volition and free will. Both the requisite thoughts and the resultant action require faith. For Joshua to begin the conquest of Canaan it was needful that the "priests [carrying the Ark of the Covenant] stepped into the river [before] the water stopped flowing" (Joshua 3:15-16, GNT) and it became possible for the Israelites to cross the Jordan. Jewish tradition has it that in the same way the people had to step into the water before the Red Sea parted. It is no different for us; we must first take a step of faith if we wish God's power and glory to be revealed in our lives.

To cross the threshold is only the first step. It is not the end in itself, merely the start of our journey. There will inevitably be inhospitable regions to be traversed and challenges to be faced on the way, since life is bound to throw up difficulties for every traveller. The important point to keep in mind is that we are not left alone and friendless in our wanderings. They need not be aimless. Nor do they have to be made in pursuit of a mirage. They can instead be the agency by which we progress, albeit often hesitatingly and unsure, to our ultimate goal: an eternity of joyful fellowship and meaningful activity with God in heaven. Attaining this end requires application and concentration. As in the days of Moses, finding a way in the desert involves a combination of our activity and God's.[85] There is no magic formula which will form an unalterable script for our passage since free will and human choice are at play. The way ahead is signposted nevertheless: by God's Word in the Bible, by the example of those who have trod the path before us and by the prompting of the Holy Spirit.

The Bible is sparing in its descriptions of exactly how we should worship. We are told to "Give to the LORD the glory due His name; Bring an offering, and come before Him [and to] worship the LORD in the beauty of holiness" (1 Chronicles 16:29, NKJV, substantially repeated in Psalm 29:2 and Psalm 96:8-9). We know that "since we are receiving a kingdom that cannot be shaken, [we should] be thankful, and so worship God acceptably with reverence and awe, for our God is a consuming fire." (Hebrews 12:28-29). We are encouraged to worship "with gladness" (Psalm 100:2), "in spirit and truth" (John 4:24, NKJV), "offer[ing our] bodies as living sacrifices, holy and pleasing to God [as a] spiritual act of worship." (Romans 12:1). Yet the New Testament prescribes no unvarying formula of words and accompanying gestures of the kind found in Islam. The result is that we must walk by faith, as others have done beforehand, sustained by knowing that God is far more interested in the substance of what is in our hearts than the forms we adopt to show him reverence.

These things should neither perplex nor confound us. Such has been the experience of all who have sought the face of the God of Abraham, Isaac and Jacob. When the Israelites first set out from Egypt they had only the vaguest idea of where they were headed and of what God would demand of them on arrival. As regards some of the particulars, even Moses was in the dark: "Our livestock too must go with us; not a hoof is to be left behind. We have to use some of them in worshipping the LORD our God, and *until we get there we will not know* what we are to use to worship the LORD." (Exodus 10:26, emphasis added). At the outset not even their leader was aware of precisely what would take place at Horeb and what would be expected of the people there, but that was no good reason to put off the journey. We have even less excuse for delay or malingering, since we enjoy advantages that our spiritual forebears did not. For not only do we have the template of their walk, but we also have the Holy Spirit – our very own "pillar of cloud to guide [us] on [our] way and … pillar of fire to give [us] light, so that [we can] travel by day or night." (Exodus 13:21). The prize for those who persevere on the journey is that we have the chance to dwell with God, and he with us.

Dwelling with God.

Worshipping our Maker involves carving out sacred space and sacred time so that we might come into his presence. This in turn requires hallowing or making holy – a self-conscious setting apart and dedicating to the Almighty. For precisely this reason the Lord told Moses: "Go to the people and consecrate them today and tomorrow. Make them wash their clothes and be ready for the third day, because on that day the LORD will come down on Mount Sinai in the sight of all the people." (Exodus 19:10-11). Consecration was so important and the consequences of coming into the presence of the Almighty without it so dire[86] that God emphasised that "even the priests, who approach the LORD, must consecrate themselves, or the LORD will break out against them." (Exodus 19:22, the latter part repeated in Exodus 19:24). The process of consecration which the Israelites were commanded to undertake was twofold: both positive by turning deliberately to God and negative by painstakingly curtailing, restricting and excluding the profane, separating it from the sacred. Thus it was that Moses was enjoined to "Put limits for the people around the mountain and tell them, 'Be careful that you do not go up the mountain or touch the foot of it.'" (Exodus 19:12; see also Exodus 19:23).

It is by means of similar positive and negative steps that we are brought spiritually (as the Israelites were brought physically) to a place where the

Almighty may be encountered in the greatest fullness. It is in our abiding with him in that place that we are enabled to worship in ways that most please him and most benefit us. Exodus describes the putting in place of precisely what is needed to bring this about: the crafting of the tabernacle to form sacred space and the observance of Sabbath to create sacred time, in each case meticulously marking off sacred from profane. Through building of the tabernacle, setting apart one day in seven and giving the Law, God effectively recreated heaven on earth. By entering the tabernacle, Israel entered God's heavenly house. By keeping the Sabbath, she entered God's heavenly rest. By obeying the Law, she engaged in heavenly conduct. The Lord's aim through all this was that Israel should be holy, as God himself is holy, and moreover that in time she should be the vessel through which salvation was brought to all mankind. It follows that our own consideration of what tabernacle and Sabbath involve is important not so much for the sake of their outward forms but so as to lay hold of the inner truths which these reveal, mindful that the presence of the Holy Spirit has superseded both tabernacle and Temple and that in heaven all believers will enjoy not just periodic visitation by the Almighty but his continual presence (see Revelation 21:22-23).

GLORY.

For the Israelites to have a place where God came to meet them was in every degree extraordinary, all the more so given what they would have experienced in Egypt. As slaves in that land they would not have been allowed to enter the temple courts of the gods, being considered ritually impure. By contrast, in their new-found freedom those who once had been despised and downtrodden, mere chattels to satisfy the whim of a taskmaster, were given a place where the Lord committed himself to come and dwell with them as his people. Indeed, what the Almighty had in store for Israel went beyond even this. He told Moses: "This is what you are to say to the house of Jacob and what you are to tell the people of Israel: 'You yourselves have seen what I did to Egypt, and how I carried you on eagles' wings and brought you to myself. Now if you obey me fully and keep my covenant, then out of all nations you will be my treasured possession. Although the whole earth is mine, you will be for me a kingdom of priests and a holy nation.'" (Exodus 19:3-6). Linguistic resonances and echoes in the original Hebrew reinforce God's underlying message and purpose, for the word rendered into English as tabernacle (*mishkan*) derives from a root meaning, *to dwell*. From the self-same root (*sh-k-n*) comes the word *shekinah*, used to describe both the visible glory and indwelling presence of God. The scheme that the Lord put in place thus envisaged that worship should first and foremost be about coming into his presence. In keeping with the role of the tabernacle as the dwelling-place of the Most High and the place where his glory would be powerfully manifest and visible on earth, its dedication was not complete until he came to dwell in it. Indeed, only through the presence of the Almighty was the space properly sanctified: "There I will meet you and speak to you; there also I will meet with the Israelites, and the place will be consecrated by my glory." (Exodus 29:43).[87]

ILLUMINATION.

Symbolism abounds in all aspects of the tabernacle and its furnishings. As later with the Temple, the plan of the tabernacle self-consciously mirrored the threefold division of the world, its courtyard corresponding to the sea, the Holy Place to the land and the Holy of Holies to the heavens, each of these distinct areas marking varying degrees of closeness to God. The curtain which separated the Holy Place from the inner sanctum comprising the Holy of Holies consisted of four kinds of thread, "blue, purple and scarlet yarn and finely twisted linen" (Exodus 26:31), possibly to represent the supposed four elements of earth, wind, air and fire, though the colours are also those of royalty.[88] The lamp-stand (*menorah*) was viewed as a picture of the "lights in the firmament of the heaven" (Genesis 1:14, KJV), its seven branches alluding to the seven days of creation but also to the light of God's presence as men draw near their Creator in worship. Patterned on an almond tree reaching upwards (Exodus 25:31-40), alone of all the main tabernacle furnishings this was "hammered out of pure gold." (Exodus 25:36, though the plates, dishes, wick trimmers and trays mentioned in Exodus 25:29 and 25:38 were also of pure gold). As such, in Jewish thought it has been taken to depict the human soul, untarnished by base material, striving upwards to blossom fully in encounter with God, each part of its ornamentation in this schema representing stages of our spiritual journey. The first of these embellishments, appearing a sixth of the way up and consisting of a flower petal alone, is taken to stand for the completion or flowering of childhood.[89] A third of the way up follows the first fully complete bloom, depicting a more complete adult development and hence comprising not only flower petals (corolla, Hebrew *perach*), but also flower-cup (calyx, Hebrew *gevi'a*) and flower-bowl (reproductive capsule, Hebrew *caftor*). The shafts which branch off halfway up the menorah show the various spiritual paths which we might choose in life, each topped by petals and flower-bowl athwart three flower-cups and hence picturing the yet greater fullness of what is to come if we are serious, sincere and persevering in our seeking after God.[90]

INSTRUCTION.

The tablets of stone inside the Ark of the Covenant on which were "inscribed by the finger of God" (Exodus 31:18 and Deuteronomy 9:10) the Ten Commandments embody divine revelation and the instruction of God's laws. The whole tabernacle was a transportable structure for, as in the present, those who belong to the Lord were to be a pilgrim people, travelling light, forever on the move and ready to decamp at a moment's notice upon receiving God's command to do so. As a result, several of the tabernacle furnishings had rings for carrying poles. Yet in the case of the Ark the poles did not simply perform a practical function but were central to its symbolism. Unlike those for the altars and the table, "The poles [were] to remain in the rings of this ark; they [were] not to be removed." (Exodus 25:15). Some Jewish thinkers have consequently seen the poles as representing the nerves connecting the brain to the two senses necessary for receiving the Law: sight, so as both to see and to perceive; and hearing, so as understand as well as merely to hear. By remaining in place, the poles emphasised that we should always be connected to the Word of God, which is not static but changes those to and through whom it speaks, for it does "not return to [God] empty but … [achieves] the purpose for which [he] sent it." (Isaiah 55:11). The poles kept in the Ark thus serve to remind us that it is by remaining close to God in prayer and worship, remembering his saving acts and studying his Word that we are enabled to access the thoughts and do the will of the one who made us.

SUSTENANCE.

Bread was placed on a table in the tabernacle to invite blessing from God and ensure his day-to-day provision, but the Hebrew for showbread (*panim*) discloses deeper purpose and meaning. The word encompasses both 'facing' (hence, showing) and 'inward', emphasising that the source of what truly sustains is spiritual. The bread on the table and the "manna … [which was kept] for the generations to come" (Exodus 16:32) in the Ark (see Hebrews 9:4) were a reminder that "the LORD your God led you all the way these forty years in the wilderness, to humble you and test you, to know what was in your heart, whether you would keep His commandments or not. So He humbled you, allowed you to hunger, and fed you with manna which you did not know nor did your fathers know, that He might make you know that man shall not live by bread alone; but man lives by every word that proceeds from the mouth of the LORD." (Deuteronomy 8:2-3, NKJV). As such, showbread and manna were further goads to worship at the deepest level, by sparking thankful recollection of all that God had done.

FORESHADOWING.

The tabernacle and its furnishings were ultimately pointers to the coming of Christ. In the same way that this structure provided a focal point for God's glory to be revealed in the world, so Jesus was the greater manifestation of that glory (see for example the transfiguration described in Matthew 17:1-8, Mark 9:1-8 and Luke 9:28-36). The menorah provided illumination, but Jesus is "the light of the world" (John 8:12, NKJV). The tablets of the Law gave instruction, yet Christ is "the Word [who] became flesh and made his dwelling among us." (John 1:14). Showbread and manna were only reminders and pictures of divine sustenance, whereas the Son of Man is "the bread of life" (John 6:35 and 6:48), "the bread that came down from heaven" (John 6:41) and "the living bread that came down from heaven." (John 6:51). Everything about the tabernacle and its contents thus directed the people to those ultimate purposes of God which would in due course be revealed in Christ.

SABBATH AND SACRIFICE.

Scripture makes explicit the connection between tabernacle and Sabbath: "Observe my Sabbaths and have reverence for my sanctuary. I am the LORD." (Leviticus 19:30 and 26:2). Sabbath marks the crowning moment of creation, providing a spiritual focus in time as counterpoint to the tabernacle's focus in space and a chance for man to reflect as did his Maker after he "finished all the work he had been doing ... [and] rested" (Genesis 2:2). Sabbath symbolises and demands interaction, relationship and partnership between Creator and creature, putting reciprocity at the heart of tabernacle and Temple service, with their accompanying animal sacrifice; for whilst there be varied and sometimes culturally conditioned means for expressing worship,[91] its essentials lie in the condition of our hearts, spring from an exercise of our wills and are an outward expression of yearning for togetherness with God.[92] The Lord proclaimed that the Sabbath "will be a sign between me and you for the generations to come, so that you may know that I am the LORD, who makes you holy." (Exodus 31:13).[93] Since Christ "is Lord of the Sabbath" (Matthew 12:8) now our aim should be to rest in him. As Jesus often observed in confronting the Pharisees, it is not absence of work that is the crucial feature of Sabbath observance, but the presence of holiness, from which truest worship flows.

False worship.

In chapter 32 of Exodus, almost exactly in the middle of those sections which most directly address worship, is the incident of the Golden Calf. Israel's idolatry on this occasion was not simply about an object of misplaced veneration, nor even the fact that there was an attempt to set up an alternative system of worship to rival that described in chapters 35 to 40 of Exodus. It was much more, being nothing less than wholesale and wilful rebellion against God involving a negation and rejection of his entire saving activity in bringing Israel out of slavery in Egypt. The choice of the calf as symbol was far from accidental; bull worship was prevalent in Egypt, there being three major bull cults and a number of minor ones.[94] Setting up the Golden Calf meant deliberately turning the clock back so as once more to embrace spiritual bondage, for even though the people had left the lands bordering the Nile behind physically, the lure of all that Egypt represented remained. The events which Exodus 32 recounts were thus akin to spitting in the face of God; despite miracles aplenty before, during and after the flight from Pharaoh and notwithstanding the Lord's making good on his promise through Moses that "The Egyptians you see today you will never see again" (Exodus 14:13), those who "were out of control and so [had] become a laughing-stock to their enemies" (Exodus 32:25) effectively treated God as though he were untrustworthy, his blessings worthless and his promises unsure.

Israel's prostration before the Golden Calf points up the same issues that face us, as individuals and as a society. Now, as then, there are two competing systems of worship, belonging to two mutually exclusive world views and two completely different visions of mankind and its destiny. Now, as then, the issue is whether we take God at his word or dispute his truthfulness, reliability and power. Like rebellious Israelites, we say, "Come, make us gods who will go before us" (Exodus 32:1) as though we had never had the pillar of fire and cloud to guide and protect throughout our long history. Like them, we devote to idols that treasure which should be employed in working to the glory of God (see Exodus 32:2-4). Just as they did, we ascribe to others or to inanimate forces the things that God alone has done, saying: "These are your gods, O Israel, who brought you up out of Egypt." (Exodus 32:4). In similar fashion we claim to be honouring God, announcing that "Tomorrow there will be a festival to the LORD" (Exodus 32:5) when in reality we merely seek an excuse to "indulge in revelry" (Exodus 32:6). Whatever else all this may be, "it is not the sound of victory" (Exodus 32:18). We, too, "have committed a great sin" (Exodus 32:30).

Conclusion.

Worship involves attachment. We either revere the only true God or bow down to one of the myriad alternatives, behind which (whether we are conscious of it or not) lurk malign spiritual forces. We can follow the Law of the Lord or go our own way, where only ruin and destruction await. That same choice which confronted Israel in the days of Moses and has faced mankind in each and every age stands before our nation now; since by volition or by default we will be attached to something, will it be freedom and righteousness or slavery and sin? Akhenaten devoted staggering sums to worship, yet his object of veneration was misplaced and all was wasted. God cursed and scattered the tribe of Levi for its cruelty and unrighteous anger, though his wish is always to bless and hence this outcome was not his desire. It is the devil who aims "to steal and kill and destroy" (John 10:10), whereas Jesus has come so that we "may have life, and have it to the full." (John 10:10). Satan delights to scatter, but the Lord wishes to gather us for fellowship with him in the place where he dwells, where we may worship fully and unreservedly, and in doing so find both our true destiny and greatest joy.

Reuben

**Whose meaning is, *see, a son*,
sounding like, *he has seen my misery***

Of whom Jacob prophesied,
*"Reuben, you are my firstborn, my might, the first sign of my strength,
excelling in honour, excelling in power."*
(Genesis 49:3).

4. Knowing God

Relationships and influences.

"If you are pleased with me, teach me your ways so that I may know you and continue to find favour with you. Remember that this nation is your people." (Exodus 33:13).

Neither the time nor the whereabouts of Akhenaten's birth is certain. Nothing is known about his upbringing, beyond what can be conjectured in general terms from the manner in which Egyptian princes were habitually raised and educated. Little is understood of the reality that lay beneath the surface of his family relationships. We cannot tell how he behaved in private with parents, siblings, children, wives or concubines.[95] Even the nature and tenor of more public interactions such as those with nobility and priesthood is at best speculative. We may only guess at the ties which bound and those which burdened. Of all rulers of ancient Egypt, he is amongst the most enigmatic. His claim to uniqueness rests on the religious reforms he put in place and on the actions which seemingly flowed inexorably from them, yet even here much is seen through a glass darkly. Whether he really believed in one god to the exclusion of all others (rather than merely elevating Aten above other deities in the pantheon) is open to doubt. The extent to which he genuinely made a decisive break with the past or simply took existing trends to a new level is debatable. Opinions differ as to the degree to which those distortions in artistic representation that his reign witnessed reflected attempts to render a true likeness of the pharaoh and his family. What really lay behind Egypt's apparent lack of vigour in responding to developments beyond her north-eastern frontier is now almost impossible to discern with absolute certainty. As with all matters where archaeology is uncorroborated by a reliable and at least moderately complete written record, there is the distinct possibility that suppositions about the Amarna period are fatally skewed by the accidents of what has and has not been unearthed.

Given this background, it is clearly unrealistic to expect that we should be able to reconstruct every detail of the king's beliefs. Nevertheless, though nowhere is a comprehensive theology set out, there are broad outlines at least for which there is either direct evidence or where reasonable deductions can be made. For example, depictions of Aten in tomb carvings, paintings and such like show both a progression throughout the reign and, with it, an increasing departure from what had gone before. As the years went by it is evident that this god was seen more and more as one who could not and should not be represented in human or animal form. In this, he was quite unlike any other deity of ancient Egypt, whether it be the jackal-headed Anubis (protector of the dead, who was thought to control weighing of the heart after death and preside over mummification),[96] the falcon-headed sun god Horus or even Amun himself, variously shown as a goose, a curly-horned ram or hawk-headed when appearing in his guise as Amun-Ra.[97] The treatment of Aten was in stark contrast not only to each of these but to all other gods of this most polytheistic of societies. By the end of the court's sojourn at Akhet-aten, the one whom the pharaoh asserted to be the Supreme Being and creator of all things was signified exclusively by a stylised sun-disc. From this orb projected rays which ended in hands that reached out to or caressed the occupant of the throne and his nearest family, although even this depiction seems to have been understood purely as outward sign and manifestation of an invisible god.[98] Gone were images from earlier in the reign where Akhenaten had been content to honour the composite sun god Ra-Harakhty-Aten, shown with a human body, the head of a falcon and the sun emblazoned above.[99]

Such changes in representation point up a fundamental issue in man's relationship with the divine. For by definition a god who has no human or animal form needs another medium by which to make himself known to and knowable by humankind, since without means to show himself or intervene in the mortal world he must perforce remain forever distant from earthly creatures, so different from himself in power, majesty, character and essence. Aten therefore needed a human interpreter, and Akhenaten presented himself (together, in lesser degree, with other members of his immediate family) as filling this role. One way in which this was done was through the so-called hymns to Aten, authorship of which is commonly ascribed to the pharaoh himself.[100] These replaced those formal speeches which traditionally were exchanged between kings and the deities into whose mouths they put suitable responses, dialogues of this kind often being recorded on temple walls in preceding and subsequent reigns. The hymns to Aten were of a different order and seem to have been connected both to developments in pictorial representation of Aten and to equivalent evolution in the manner of transcribing that god's name which occurred at more or less the same time.[101]

Given the steps that Akhenaten took to act out his beliefs, and bearing in mind how costly these were to both ruler and subjects not only in terms of time and treasure but also in their upheavals and consequent expenditure of political capital, there is little reason to doubt the sincerity of the praise and worship which the monarch's poetic declamations accord to Aten. Yet at the same time it has justly been said that their real thrust concerns kingship. For as well as eulogising the deity, these devotional works elevate the ruler and his chief wife Nefertiti to such an extent as to make them virtually on a par with Aten. They end with cascades of royal titles, emphasising at one and the same time both the pharaoh's importance and his intimacy with the godhead. By extension, the message they conveyed was that the sovereign's rule on earth was ultimately endorsed, upheld and sanctified by heavenly power. Taken together, these things were ambitious beyond mere assertion of divine right of kings; they averred that, whilst everyone might be able to see the sun and benefit from its life-giving power, only the monarch and his closest relatives had true and unrestricted access to the great god Aten himself. In effect, as well as making vaulting claims for himself in terms of temporal power and authority, the fount of worldly law and embodiment of the nation also arrogated to his own office the role of Chief Priest (First Prophet) of his chosen cult.[102] In this he seems to have aimed at nothing less than abolition of all intermediaries between heaven and earth apart from himself and his nearest blood relations. All in all, these were devastating blows to the accepted pieties of Egypt.

Between heaven and earth.

For man in any meaningful sense to know his Maker requires two things at the minimum: that God should reveal himself, for what we can discern of him through the created order is limited;[103] and that he should be active in the world (immanent), so that relationship with him may be possible. Set against that background, it is significant that later depictions of Aten show hands reaching from the sun disc to point towards or touch the pharaoh and his family, for thereby was the activity of the god in this world displayed. There was thus the hope that there might be epiphany (revealing or showing) and, as a result, connection. It was such an event which occurred when Moses stood on Horeb and the Lord "called to him from within the [burning] bush" (Exodus 3:4). From that moment onwards is pictured the deepening interchange between the Almighty and his chosen prophet, bringing a mere mortal to the point where in due course he was able to speak to his Creator "face to face, as a man speaks to his friend." (Exodus 33:11).

Moses acted as mediator[104] between God and man and advocate for his people, but in neither case as Akhenaten seems to have envisaged his own fulfilment of equivalent roles, nor out of any desire to exclude others. There is not one single part of Scripture which so much as hints that Israel's great deliverer and lawgiver was ever tempted to court the slightest element of exclusivity, still less any personal advantage. Though he was in many ways the interface between heaven and earth, at no point is he to be seen seeking advancement either for himself, for his immediate family or even for his wider clan. On the contrary, he exclaimed, "Oh, that all the LORD's people were prophets and that the LORD would put His Spirit upon them!" (Numbers 11:29, NKJV). Humility and self-sacrifice were his watchwords throughout, as shown in all sorts of ways and on every kind of occasion by his:

Putting the wellbeing of others before his own wishes and safety: "Then Moses went back to Jethro his father-in-law and said, 'Let me go back to my own people to see if any of them are still alive.'" (Exodus 4:18).[105]

Bearing repeated hardship and unfair criticism for the sake of the work to which God had called him: "So the people grumbled against Moses, saying, 'What are we to drink?'" (Exodus 15:24).[106]

Risking life and limb for the sake of obedience: "Then Moses cried out to the LORD, 'What am I to do with these people? They are almost ready to stone me.'" (Exodus 17:4).

Encouraging others to step into the fullness of what God held in store for them: "Moses said to the people, 'Do not be afraid. God has come to test you, so that the fear of God will be with you to keep you from sinning.'" (Exodus 20:20).

Venturing into regions where others feared to tread: "The people remained at a distance, while Moses approached the thick darkness where God was." (Exodus 20:21).

Turning his back on the opportunity to win glory and honour for himself by becoming the father of a new chosen nation: "'I know how stubborn these people are. Now, don't try to stop me. I am angry with them, and I am going to destroy them. Then I will make you and your descendants into a great nation.' But Moses pleaded … '…Remember your servants Abraham, Isaac, and Jacob. Remember the solemn promise you made to them to give them as many descendants as there are stars in the sky and to give their descendants all that land you promised would be their possession forever.'" (Exodus 32:9-11 and 13, GNT).

Interceding with God on behalf of all Israel: "But Moses sought the favour of the LORD his God. 'O LORD,' he said, 'why should your anger burn against your people, whom you brought out of Egypt with great power and a mighty hand? Why should the Egyptians say, 'It was with evil intent that he brought them out, to kill them in the mountains and to wipe them off the face of the earth?' Turn from your fierce anger; relent and do not bring disaster on your people.'" (Exodus 32:11-12).

Counting his own life as nothing: "The next day Moses said to the people, '… I will go up to the LORD; perhaps I can make atonement for your sin.' So Moses went back to the LORD and said, 'Oh, what a great sin these people have committed! They have made themselves gods of gold. But now, please forgive their sin – but if not, then blot me out of the book you have written.'" (Exodus 32:30-31).

Pleading for God's presence to be with all the people: "Moses bowed to the ground at once and worshipped. 'O LORD, if I have found favour in your eyes,' he said, 'then let the LORD go with us.'" (Exodus 34:8-9).

Not setting himself above others but acknowledging his own fault and seeking forgiveness along with everyone else: "Although this is a stiff-necked people, forgive our wickedness and our sin" (Exodus 34:9).

Eschewing personal advantage by entreating God to reward all the people equally: "O LORD, if I have found favour in your eyes ... take us as your inheritance." (Exodus 34:9).

Such things did not come out of thin air. They were the fruit not merely of encounter with God, but of the heartfelt and considered response to that meeting, seen firstly in the pledging of allegiance and obedience to God's commands, and thereafter in the continual and deepening changes which were wrought in terms of character, devotion to true worship, questing after holiness and relegation of things profane to their rightful place. The example of Moses shows that knowing God requires first and foremost that we should put our trust in one greater than ourselves and thereafter that we should strive to the utmost to do what the Lord wishes in the precise way and at the exact moment he asks. By these means we are enabled both to draw near to him and thus to learn from him, whilst in the same instant having our desires and impulses properly directed so that they flow into those channels in which they were always designed to run. The achievements of Moses were nothing more or less than the outgrowth of deep relationship – a natural consequence of putting words into deeds so consistently and over such a long time that right conduct in all aspects of daily life became second nature. It was through growing into the will of his Maker in this fashion that Moses more and more came to reflect the nature of the Creator himself.[107] The prophet's every word and act was the result of his becoming intimate with the Almighty in a manner that few before or since have been able to hope for, let alone achieve. This did not mean that he was in every respect perfect. The Bible makes no bones about the mistakes that Moses made[108] and the weaknesses from which he suffered, but for all that he was of uncommon spiritual stature, a worthy prophet for the dawn of a new age.

Drawing nearer.

Moses' spiritual progression as the story of Exodus unfolds can be seen in all kinds of ways, but the fullest extent of it is perhaps most amply illustrated by the fact that the man who once "hid his face, because he was afraid to look at God" (Exodus 3:6) not so very much later reached a point where he dared ask his Maker, "Now show me your glory." (Exodus 33:18). It was by any measure a bold and altogether astonishing request – so much so that we might even be tempted to think that by making it Moses stepped beyond proper bounds, demonstrating both a degree of disrespect and an element of effrontery. There was indeed a steadily increasing crescendo of issues that Israel's representative raised with the Lord on this occasion, building from "If you are pleased with me, teach me your ways so that I may know you and continue to find favour with you" (Exodus 33:13) through to the plea for the continual Presence of God that is contained in Exodus 33:15-16. Yet at no point is there a sense that the

Almighty was in any measure displeased with what Moses said, and still less did he censure him for his temerity. It is true that he replied that "you cannot see my face, for no-one may see me and live" (33:20), but all indications are that this was uttered by way of explaining why the prophet's desire was not granted in full rather than by way of rebuke.[109]

This has a valuable lesson for us since, in examining how and why Moses should have been able to speak with God in this way, we may come to grasp more of what it means to grow in knowledge of the Most High and his ways. This is a continual process, building on the firm foundations of his Word so as to increase in nearness to him.[110] It can only come about through:

Dialogue and understanding: "Moses said to the LORD, 'You have been telling me...'" (Exodus 33:12);

Instruction and resultant action: "Moses [was told by the LORD] ... 'Lead these people'" (Exodus 33:12);

Faith and trust throughout all uncertainty: "Moses [complained that God had] ... not let me know whom you will send with me" (Exodus 33:12) yet did not baulk at the task;

Intimacy and relationship: "You have said, 'I know you by name ...'" (Exodus 33:12);

...these things leading progressively to:

Blessing and reward: "You have said, '...you have found favour with me.'" (Exodus 33:12); and

Approval and delight: "And the LORD said to Moses, '... I am pleased with you...'" (Exodus 33:17).

This bears reflection. If we are to grow in knowledge of God we must not simply hem him in with our requests but must also allow him to speak to us, being prepared in the process to go beyond mere hearing to a place of listening attentively and grappling with the full implications of what is said. Only in such fashion can we come to any worthwhile degree of understanding and application, enabling thought, word and deed to come together and feed the one into the other, for the message needs to be lived if it is to realise its greatest potential in us and in the world around us. None of this will come about automatically. Hence we need to develop the discipline of regular prayer and reading of the Bible; since Scripture is the living Word of God it has power to speak to us day by day, but for it to do so we need to delve into it, asking questions of the text and of ourselves in order to discern its import for us in the present. Through doing so we may expect to be instructed, to learn and to grow, such things being not merely for their own sake but also in order that we might be changed, made more and more spiritually mature and spurred to action as a result; we ask the Lord to "teach [us] your ways" for a purpose – that of "know[ing] you and continu[ing] to find favour with you" (Exodus 33:13), which in turn means that there will be steps we need to take in order to keep alongside and in alignment with the teaching we receive. In thus setting our hand to the plough to be about the "good works, which God prepared in advance for us to do" (Ephesians 2:10), there will inevitably be things which are from time to time unclear. Our challenge then is to keep going in faith and trust, accepting that we cannot know every detail of what lies ahead but that in all things our heavenly Father "works for the good of those who love him, who have been called according to his purpose." (Romans 8:28). When we do our honest best to make all these things a reality of our daily living, then even more than at present we will cause the one who should have pride of place in our lives to "take great delight in [us] … [to] quiet [us] with his love … [and to] rejoice over [us] with singing" (Zephaniah 3:17).

With all this in mind, we would do well to take the experience of Moses and the lessons of his life to heart. He spent long years in the parched landscapes of Midian and a further forty years in those wilderness regions through which the Israelites later wandered. Though the heavy burdens he bore as leader and the pressing demands on him through times of change, challenge and strife were such as to put him at various points under almost intolerable strain, he did not entirely lack opportunity for quiet reflection. During such periods he was able amongst other things to commit to writing the five books which form the Pentateuch[111] and to carve out moments from the demands of everyday living to be with God.[112] These oases of intimacy and relationship were the bedrock on which were built each and every one of his achievements. They remind us of a hugely important truth: if we pray and do not act, our prayers will be in vain but by the same token if we act and do not pray, our actions will be in vain. What emerges strongly from Moses' story is that mankind comes to know the Almighty not mainly through philosophical or mystical speculation but by studying his Word, abiding in his presence in prayer and attaining the refinement of character which comes with putting his commands into practice. These are our routes to fuller knowledge of God. It is through knowing him as best we are able and by virtue of relationship with him forming the wellspring of all we do that we are able to build the truest and most lasting monuments.

The mountaintop.

Moses learnt the hard way that there was nothing he could do to save Israel in his own strength, but that God alone was able to bring salvation. When eventually he came to tread the path of humility, he found released in himself such depth of faithfulness, such sensitivity of heart and such ambition for the things of God that by stages the Lord graciously made himself known in greater and greater measure. Three times[113] Moses stood on Horeb in the presence of the Almighty: when first called to his life's work (Exodus 3:1 to 4:17 inclusive), when first receiving "the tablets of stone inscribed by the finger of God" (Exodus 31:18) with the Ten Commandments (Exodus 20:21) and once again when God told him to "come up to the LORD, you and Aaron, Nadab and Abihu, and seventy of the elders." (Exodus 24:1).[114] Yet the experience on these occasions was a mere foretaste of what was to come next. In loving answer to the prophet's request for the Alpha and Omega to "show me your glory" (Exodus 33:18), God provided a glimpse of perhaps the greatest measure of himself that mortal flesh and blood can stand.[115] Before doing so, he explained to Moses what was about to happen, saying:

"I will cause all my goodness to pass in front of you..." (Exodus 33:19).

"I will proclaim my name, the LORD, in your presence..." (Exodus 33:19).

"...I will have mercy on whom I will have mercy, and I will have compassion on whom I will have compassion." (Exodus 33:19).

"There is a place near me where you may stand on a rock." (Exodus 33:21).

"When my glory passes by, I will put you in a cleft in the rock and cover you with my hand until I have passed by." (Exodus 33:21-22).

"Then I will remove my hand and you will see my back, but my face must not be seen." (Exodus 33:21 and 23).

The face reflects our inmost being. It gives the lie to thoughts, emotions, personality and even experiences. To look something or someone in the face involves steady, unflinching confrontation. In asking to discern the face of the Almighty, Moses requested that the Lord reveal himself in all his fullness and in every particular so that his earthly servant would espy not "a poor reflection as in a mirror; [but see] ... face to face ... [and] know fully, even as I am known." (1 Corinthians 13:12). In all probability even the great prophet did not fully comprehend the extent of his request, just as Jesus had to tell his disciples James and John,[116] "You don't know what you are asking" (Matthew 20:22 and Mark 10:38) when they desired to be seated at either side of him in heaven. In the event, whilst God reiterated that "My face must not be seen" (Exodus 33:23), as he had previously warned, "Do not come any closer" (Exodus 3:5), all the same he did disclose essential elements of himself:

In terms of character: his "goodness ... mercy [and] ... compassion" (Exodus 33:19);

In terms of sovereignty: his unfettered ability to decide "on whom I will have mercy, and ... on whom I will have compassion." (Exodus 33:19);

In terms of power, beauty and holiness: his "glory" (Exodus 33:22); and

In terms of reputation and eternal, uncreated nature: his "name, the LORD" (Exodus 33:19).

It is worth pondering why God chose to show those aspects of his character that are encapsulated by our words 'goodness', 'mercy' and 'compassion', and not others from among his myriad attributes. It is perhaps not immediately apparent at first sight, for example, why these three things should on this occasion have taken precedence over "love, joy, peace, patience, kindness … faithfulness, gentleness and self-control" (Galatians 5:22), these along with goodness being "the fruit of the Spirit" (Galatians 5:22) and hence amongst the qualities that describe at least a part of God's essence.[117] It can only be conjecture, but it is possible that the traits which were disclosed were what Moses most needed to experience. He had thrilled at and trembled before the power of the Most High, but power is not always or necessarily benign. He had witnessed judgment come upon the Egyptians, but in the midst of judgment it is easy for us to lose sight of mercy.[118] He had been present at a great deliverance, but it is possible to deliver and remain disinterested and emotionally disengaged. So, alone on Horeb, to Moses was shown what King David later described, "The LORD … merciful and gracious, Slow to anger, and abounding in mercy [who] will not always strive with us, Nor will He keep His anger forever … [who] has not dealt with us according to our sins, Nor punished us according to our iniquities … As a father pities his children, So the LORD pities those who fear Him." (Psalm 103:8-10 and 13, NKJV).[119] Were he ever in doubt about it until then, from that point onwards Moses would have realised that the God he worshipped and served was both "Lion" (Revelation 5:5, NRSV) and "Lamb" (Revelation 5:6, NRSV), capable in a manner and to a degree that human beings can barely comprehend of tempering justice with mercy, of balancing righteous anger with deepest compassion, of exercising with exquisite gentleness and self-control a power beyond the capacity of anyone or anything to withstand, of being under no duress or compulsion save that of his own nature yet nevertheless choosing to suffer the pain, anguish and humiliation of allowing men to reject him. These are among the paradoxes of the divine nature, as shown later in yet fuller measure in the person of Jesus Christ, who urged that we "take my yoke upon you and learn from me, for I am gentle and humble in heart, and you will find rest for your souls. For my yoke is easy and my burden is light." (Matthew 11:29).

God's ultimate disclosure of himself in Christ Jesus is particularly intriguing in light of the reference to there being "a place near me where you may stand on a rock" (Exodus 33:21), for many times in Scripture the Lord is described as a rock. He is "the Shepherd, the Rock of Israel" (Genesis 49:24), "the Rock [whose] works are perfect" (Deuteronomy 32:4), a "rock [and] fortress"

(2 Samuel 22:2 and Psalm 18:2), "an everlasting rock" (Isaiah 26:4, NRSV), "Rock and ... Redeemer" (Psalm 19:14). King David says that "he set my feet on a rock" (Psalm 40:2), another psalmist that "he is my Rock, and there is no wickedness in him." (Psalm 92:15). For the Christian, of course, the Rock on which we stand in order that we might glimpse God without being destroyed in the process is Jesus, that self-same "spiritual rock that went with [the Israelites as they came out of Egypt]; and that rock was Christ himself." (1 Corinthians 10:4, GNT). It is therefore with justice that New Testament writers were so clear in seeing the activity and presence of Jesus throughout the events recounted in Exodus, in drawing parallels between the happenings of that time and their own and in applying the lessons of that distant past to the whole New Testament dispensation. Hence, for example, it is said by the writer of Hebrews that Moses "regarded disgrace for the sake of Christ as of greater value than the treasures of Egypt, because he was looking ahead to his reward." (Hebrews 11:26).[120]

Moses is also said to have "persevered because he saw him who is invisible" (Hebrews 11:27). Again, the wording of Exodus provides justification for this claim. Since God had affirmed that "When my glory passes by, I will put you in a cleft in the rock and cover you with my hand until I have passed by" (Exodus 33:21-22), the implication seems to be that right up to that point the prophet was allowed to remain standing on the rock which was positioned at a "place near me" (Exodus 33:21). It was from this vantage point that "the servant of God" (Revelation 15:3) would thus have been able to watch whilst his Maker "cause[d] all [his] goodness to pass in front of [him]..." (Exodus 33:19) and "proclaim[ed his] name, the LORD, in [the prophet's] presence..." (Exodus 33:19). These were lofty things to experience and surpassing in wondrousness, for there is not only beauty but also might in the Name and the Word of God: "When Jesus said, 'I am he,' they [the soldiers who came to arrest him on Gethsemane before his trial and crucifixion] drew back and fell to the ground." (John 18:6).[121] Indeed, such was the impact and splendour of that manifestation of the Almighty which is his full, unmediated glory that it was necessary for Moses to be shielded from it until the Lord had passed by. He could only be allowed to glimpse its retreating shadow once the first overwhelming, blinding,[122] glaring, stupefying beauty and brightness of it had somewhat abated. It was then that God would have "[removed his] hand [so that Moses would] see [his] back" (Exodus 33:23). As he did so, the erstwhile prince of Egypt would have come to perceive yet more of that excellence which is to be found in our Creator alone, an "excelling in honour, excelling in power" (Genesis 49:3) above and beyond anything that his forebear Jacob could have imagined. This was the God of whom Moses had spoken after the crossing of the Red Sea, one "majestic in holiness, awesome in glory, working wonders" (Exodus 15:11).

Back with a bump.

Much as we might like, we cannot remain on the mountaintop forever. The Lord has work for us to do in this world, which means that, just as Moses did, we need to come down from the mountain to confront the difficulties, compromises, challenges and ugliness of the present, gazing unflinchingly on all that men have made of a once perfect Creation. The question when we descend is to what use we should put such knowledge of God as we have been able to gain in the interim. It ought not to be an abstract thing, but rather to inspire, spur and enable all we are to be and all we are to do. The key to using it to the best possible effect is relationship – with God and with our fellow men, the love of these being the essence of all that was revealed through Moses. As Jesus replied to one who wanted to know which was the most important of God's laws, "'Love the Lord your God with all your heart, soul, and mind.' This is the first and greatest commandment. The second most important is similar: 'Love your neighbor as much as you love yourself.' All the other commandments and all the demands of the prophets stem from these two laws and are fulfilled if you obey them." (Matthew 22:37-40, TLB, substantially repeated in Mark 12:30).

Relationship necessarily involves vulnerability, since the more we open ourselves to others the more we create opportunity for disappointment and hurt. Moses' life had no lack of such things:

Abandonment: the orphan heart of a boy whose mother (albeit under the most appalling duress) consigned him to "a papyrus basket ... among the reeds along the bank of the Nile." (Exodus 2:3);

Separation: the estrangement from true family that resulted when his mother "took him to Pharaoh's daughter and he became her son." (Exodus 2:10);

Confused identity: the guilt, pain, accusations, threats and divided loyalties that would have been triggered as "By faith Moses, when he had grown up, refused to be known as the son of Pharaoh's daughter." (Hebrews 11:24);

Failure and remorse: the terrible realisation of having killed in vain resulting from the fact that "Moses thought that his own people would realise that God was using him to rescue them, but they did not." (Acts 7:25);

Exile: the need to flee the land of his birth and seek refuge in less congenial surroundings, so that when "Zipporah [Moses' wife] gave birth to a son ... Moses named him Gershom, saying, 'I have become an alien in a foreign land.'" (Exodus 2:22);

Disappointment: being let down badly not only by strangers but even by his elder brother as "Moses saw that the people were running wild and that Aaron had let them get out of control." (Exodus 32:25);

Ingratitude: being the butt of repeated unfair criticism from those for whose rescue he had sacrificed everything, as the people "grumbled against Moses" (Exodus 15:24, 16:2 and 17:3, Numbers 14:2) over and over again;

Untrustworthy companions: being unable to leave the camp even for as little as forty days without the Israelites forgetting all they had seen and heard and starting to doubt him, saying "As for this fellow Moses, we don't know what has happened to him." (Exodus 32:23);

Betrayal: finding that his very brother and sister were fomenting discontent as "Miriam and Aaron began to talk against Moses because of his Cushite wife, for he had married a Cushite." (Numbers 12:1); and

Thwarted hope: being denied entry to the Promised Land as "the LORD said to Moses and Aaron, 'Because you did not trust in me enough to honour me as holy in the sight of the Israelites, you will not bring this community into the land I give them.'" (Numbers 20:12).

Moses was the perennial outsider: a Jew amongst pagans, a slave amongst royalty, a foundling of uncertain parentage amongst those of proud ancestry, an intended victim amongst his would-be murderers, an educated man amongst untutored ruffians, a prince amongst nomads, a shepherd at the court of kings, a stranger amongst his family, a foreigner amongst his own people. Yet he did not allow these things to embitter, distract or cripple him. Instead he pursued knowledge of, relationship with and obedience to God. As a result, the power of the Almighty was released in him to transform, overcome and transcend what might otherwise have been grave handicaps. Hence in due course:

Reconciliation took the place of abandonment: "[Aaron] is already on his way to meet you and his heart will be glad when he sees you." (Exodus 4:14). In the months to come, the two brothers stood united in dealing with the Israelites and in confronting Pharaoh.

Togetherness and fellowship replaced separation: "[Aaron] went to meet [Moses] at the holy mountain; and when he met him, he kissed him. Then Moses told Aaron everything that the LORD had said when he told him to return to Egypt; he also told him about the miracles which the LORD had ordered him to perform." (Exodus 4:27-28, GNT).

Certainty of whom he served and to whom he belonged resolved all confusion of identity: Moses' second son "was named Eliezer, for he said, 'My father's God was my helper; he saved me from the sword of Pharaoh.'" (Exodus 18:4).

The power of God supplanted and made up for all human failure and guilt: "I am making a covenant with you. Before all your people I will do wonders never before done in any nation in all the world. The people you live among will see how awesome is the work that I, the LORD, will do for you." (Exodus 34:10).

The exile was to be brought into a new and better homeland: "And I have promised to bring you up ... into ... a land flowing with milk and honey." (Exodus 3:17).

Disappointment was redeemed through forgiveness and fresh anointing: "Bring Aaron and his sons to the entrance of the Tent, and have them take a ritual bath. Dress Aaron in the priestly garments, anoint him, and in this way consecrate him, so that he can serve me as priest. Bring his sons and put the shirts on them. Then anoint them, just as you anointed their father, so that they can serve me as priests. This anointing will make them priests for all time to come." (Exodus 40:12-15, GNT).

The love of God allayed the ingratitude of man: "I know you by name and you have found favour with me" (Exodus 33:12).

The trustworthiness of God proved more enduring than human venality: "I will drive out nations before you and enlarge your territory, and no-one will covet your land when you go up three times each year to appear before the LORD your God." (Exodus 34:24).

The loyalty, fellowship and provision of God salved betrayal at the hands of kith and kin: "Moses was there with the LORD forty days and forty nights without eating bread or drinking water." (Exodus 34:28).[123]

Consolation was provided in the face of thwarted hope: "There [on Mount Nebo] the LORD showed [Moses] the whole [of the Promised] land ... [and] said, '... I have let you see it with your eyes, but you will not cross over into it.'" (Deuteronomy 34:1 and 34:4).

Knowing God will not lead to past hurts being entirely forgotten or undone but, as Moses' life shows, it is the route by which bad experiences can be turned to good account and our destiny reclaimed.

Conclusion.

Moses' relationships and influences are writ clear in the Pentateuch, warts and all. His experience of the Lord was profound and oft repeated, his knowing of him greater and deeper than that of almost any mortal. Though schooled in all the subtle arts of the Egyptians, he yet held to the simple faith of his fathers. God was his focus; to him he directed his gaze and from him he sought guidance, so that the excellence of the Master found its reflection in the humility of the servant. By contrast, the truth about Akhenaten is shrouded. It is impossible to know the extent to which he might have glimpsed the one true God. Whilst he claimed divine command was the reason for his causing the new city of Akhet-aten to be built, in this he did no more than echo the claims of pharaohs before and since. On its face, his religion reflects a concept of the divine that was partial at best, consistent perhaps with someone who witnessed or had knowledge of at least some of the events of Exodus 1 to 14 but was ignorant of all that came before or happened afterwards.[124] He had no context of a covenant with Abraham in which to place his understanding, no conception that the Lord desires to be accessible to all men, no idea that God might be fundamentally different in character from an earthly king.

Family relationships are amongst our earliest and most profound influences. A welter of sadness and hurt lay behind the birth of Reuben, whose coming into the world caused his forlorn mother Leah to hope, "Surely my husband will love me now." (Genesis 29:32). Yet of this boy, whose start in life (like that of Moses) was so unpromising, Jacob prophesied in his old age, "Reuben, you are my firstborn, my might, the first sign of my strength, excelling in honour, excelling in power." (Genesis 49:3). God alone made him so. He will do the same for us if we but allow ourselves to know him.

Zebulun

Whose meaning is, *honour*

Of whom Jacob prophesied,
"Zebulun will live by the seashore and become a haven for ships; his border will extend towards Sidon."
(Genesis 49:13).

5. Reflecting God

Art, representation and association.

"When Aaron and all the Israelites saw Moses, his face was radiant, and they were afraid to come near him." (Exodus 34:30).

Before Akhenaten came to the throne the conventions of Egyptian painting, carving and statuary were well-defined and rigidly followed. Pharaohs were shown in heroic style, with what appear to be limited attempts at lifelike representation. Form and layout were strictly controlled, leaving little room for individual expression on the part of the artist. Canons of proportion dictated how much of a scene each human figure should occupy[125] so that only posture and facial features were capable of different interpretation. Given this background, the art of the Amarna period marks an extraordinary rupture with what went before. It amounted not merely to tinkering around the edges but to tearing up the whole rule book. Nowhere is this more apparent than in depictions of the ruler and his family. The king, his chief wife Nefertiti and their daughters are portrayed with distended skulls, elongated necks and other physical peculiarities which appear to modern eyes as deformities. The pharaoh's body is given what appear to be female as well as male characteristics, with wide hips, rounded belly and breasts. So great was the dislocation caused by these aberrations that the former certainties of Egyptian art were never fully recovered.[126]

In another way, too, Amarna art dispensed with the formalities of bygone years. Its scenes of royal family life are unique in giving a picture of domestic intimacy that is repeated nowhere else in what has survived from ancient Egypt. Akhenaten was shown dandling his daughters on his knee in a way that no other pharaoh before or since ever was. The sudden coming into being of such representations and their equally swift disappearance once one short reign was over demands explanation. Opinion is divided as to whether depictions of this ruler's body are intended to be naturalistic or not. Those who say they are believe the monarch suffered from ailments or genetic disorders which have been variously diagnosed, with leading candidates including the conditions known as Fröhlich's Syndrome and Marfan's Syndrome.[127] Those who prefer to read symbolically have produced an equal flurry of speculations to support their cause. Yet whichever it might be, the same question arises, namely why someone able to exercise complete control over artistic output should command or permit that he be displayed in a manner so apparently unflattering, so seemingly contrary to all contemporary ideas of royal dignity and so different from the rigid conventions of preceding ages.

As with so much else involving Akhenaten, definitive proof is hard to come by. Such evidence as is available suggests that threads both naturalistic and symbolic were interwoven.[128] Recent analysis of the skull of Tutankhamun indicates that he, sprung from the same stock as "the enemy of Akhet-aten", had the distinctive head shape which Amarna art ascribes to Akhenaten and his daughters.[129] The likelihood, therefore, is that this element of the royal family's representation, at least, had its basis in real life. Yet as for other aspects of how the pharaoh and his close kindred are shown, it is perfectly possible that the aim was not realism but propaganda: a portrayal of the king as confidant of and mediator for the supreme god, designed to make the occupant of the throne seem a creature so above and beyond the human that he was pictured inhabiting a different body, a fleshly tent into which were gathered all attributes, including those both male and female, in the same way that Aten had subsumed all other gods. This certainly would be consistent with the name by which Akhenaten chose to be known, for as well as meaning, *beneficent*, its *akh* component embraces notions such as transfiguration or transmutation, bright shining brilliance and personal union with the sun god, re-enacted each daybreak. It points moreover to the border between earthly and spiritual, human and other-worldly; for once mummification was complete, the dead were thought to become *akh* spirits, thereafter acting as intercessors for those who remained behind.[130]

Seen in this context, Amarna art looks like a further attempt to elevate Akhenaten beyond the level of a mere mortal and to regions surpassing the run of everyday things. In other areas, too, there was a continuing erosion of formerly distinct boundaries between god and royalty. From about the ninth year of the pharaoh's reign the names of Aten began to be written inside cartouches, a device which hitherto had been used purely to enclose the titles of pharaohs and their consorts. At more or less the same time, the sun-disc which was used to designate Aten started to be shown wearing one of the most prestigious items of royal and divine regalia: the uraeus, a diadem in the shape of a spitting cobra's head. Alongside these developments came alterations in building methods and in temple architecture. Though the early work of Akhenaten's reign was stylistically and structurally similar to that of his predecessors, within a year or two the pattern of temples to Aten that were being raised in Thebes began to look quite different. As well as plan and orientation being rethought, even basic materials and the manner of construction altered, with stone structures starting to be crafted from so-called *talatat* set in a strong mortar. Not only the content of but also the terminology in which monumental inscriptions were expressed was changed, with a move away from the old-fashioned language which had traditionally been used in favour of an idiom which better reflected the spoken vernacular of the day.[131] Whether this aimed at making the new cult more accessible it is impossible now to say with any degree of certainty. What is clear is that the relentless shifting of the ground beneath their feet must have been deeply unsettling to a great many of the king's subjects. It is not fanciful to think that a significant proportion of Egyptians, elite and commoners alike, would most probably have been at first nonplussed, then increasingly frustrated before finally waxing outraged, angry and embittered by the ever-growing crescendo of religious reforms. Yet momentous as these might have been, they were but straws in the wind presaging a wholesale shift in the wider regional balance of power and an undermining of Egypt's once unrivalled place in the world.

Signs and wonders.

The idea that form follows function is nowadays associated with twentieth century architecture and industrial design,[132] but the underlying concept is hardly new. Artists and craftsmen throughout the ages have followed it, whether consciously or not. In all fields of endeavour we tend to work from what we know to develop or understand what is new. Thus it is that even a radical departure such as Akhenaten made seldom springs altogether fully formed into the daylight, being more apt to ease itself into being through a stuttering series of progressions from what has gone before. Hence, too, our frequent difficulty in describing or even envisaging what is truly groundbreaking; whatever does not fit into the neat categories we love to build on the basis of previous experience often leaves us flummoxed. We have no reason to feel superior to the ancients in this respect; in the present there is much that we shy away from simply because it is unfamiliar, uncomfortable or so far beyond our capacity to understand that to reject it out of hand is easier than to grapple with its full implications. A Trinitarian God who works miracles causes us to feel particularly out of our depth, our discomfort increased by the need to hold in tension those aspects of the divine which to us often appear at one and the same time paradoxical, nonsensical or contradictory.

Nevertheless, Exodus clearly portrays just such a God. It was miraculous that Moses survived beyond infancy, let alone that he should subsequently have been enabled to be the agent of Israel's delivery from Egypt. It required daily miracles for the Hebrew multitudes to obtain adequate food and water during their desert wanderings. That "the cloud of the LORD was over the tabernacle by day, and fire was in the cloud by night, in the sight of all the house of Israel during all their travels" (Exodus 40:38) was a constant sign of supernatural agency, a continual reminder of "all the wonders [God had given Moses] … the power to do." (Exodus 4:21). Likewise, the handing down of the Ten Commandments was attended by powerful indicators of the power and presence of God (see Exodus 19:16-19). It thus follows that we cannot engage fully or properly with the Exodus story without in some way grappling with the idea of miracles. Much modern thinking on this topic can be traced back to the formulations of Scots philosopher David Hume (1711-1776); for him, any miracle was a logical impossibility since he defined such an event as "a transgression of a law of nature by a particular volition of the Deity, or by the interposition of some invisible agent".[133] The conclusion is unsurprising given the starting point, but utterly fails to take account of the possibility of God's working miracles without breaching those natural laws which he himself has put in place. In fact, Exodus (in common with the rest of Scripture) makes it abundantly clear that the Almighty has often used human agency to bring about much of what he purposed to achieve.[134] As for those events which were beyond either the capacity or the control of man, there are perfectly good explanations of how they might have come to pass without need to do violence to those rules which govern the workings of our universe.[135]

The fact that the Bible frequently recounts the miraculous should hardly catch us unawares; it is an inevitable result of God's being neither remote nor distant nor uncaring, but engaged with all that he has created and deeply concerned about each of his creatures. It is natural that such a person should intervene in human history and take a hand in helping those who serve him. Endued with attributes beyond the full comprehension of man, and strength past our ability to conceive or understand, he is "able to do immeasurably more than all we ask or imagine" (Ephesians 3:20). It is childish to believe that to bring about his purposes he might have need of circumventing boundaries which he himself established. It is simplistic to think that just because we do not see with the same clarity that Moses saw on Horeb this must mean that our Creator cannot still be at work, now as then; his activity is as evident all around in our age just as it was in epochs of long ago, when pharaohs bestrode the earth and fancied in their delusion that they could ignore the decrees of the Almighty, fly with impunity in the face of the moral order that he has commanded, and say "Who is the LORD, that I should obey him and let Israel go?" (Exodus 5:2). The issue is not and never has been whether the Lord works wonders and provides signs to warn or enlighten men. Instead it is a question of whether we care to gaze full upon such things, see them for what they are and recognise the hand at work behind them. Even at the time of the events that Exodus describes, there were opportunities aplenty for a sceptic to deny God's work in the saving of Israel. It was done by saying of the Golden Calf, "These are your gods, O Israel, who brought you up out of Egypt" (Exodus 32:4), and through questioning the wisdom and authority of the one whom God had ordained to lead Israel,[136] but could equally well have been effected by choosing (as is the fashion in our day) to ascribe events to natural causes rather than divine activity. It seldom takes long before voices begin to murmur that it was all just:

The action of the waves: when in fact, "The horse and its rider he has hurled into the sea." (Exodus 15:1);

The movement of tides: when in truth, "Pharaoh's chariots and his army he has hurled into the sea." (Exodus 15:4);

The vagaries of chance: when without doubt, "Your right hand, O LORD, was majestic in power. Your right hand, O LORD, shattered the enemy." (Exodus 15:6);

The blowing of the wind: when in reality, "You unleashed your burning anger; it consumed them like stubble. By the blast of your nostrils the waters piled up." (Exodus 15:7-8); and

The aftermath of a storm: when although "The enemy boasted ... you blew with your breath, and the sea covered them." (Exodus 15:9-10).

This should challenge us deeply: to consider whether we desire to pay heed merely to the shadow or to look for the reality behind it, to analyse the effect or seek to discern the cause which has triggered it, to enquire only after the movement or attempt to comprehend what has set it in motion. For any who wish to search diligently and in good faith, the truth is that all about lie circumstances that point to and reflect our Maker, in the natural world no less than in the characters and affairs of men – and in these latter perhaps most of all, whom "God created ... in his own image" (Genesis 1:27). There is no need to search for that which is undiscovered or trawl distant galaxies for hidden things, for these fundamentals are writ clear in words uncontested, conditions undisputed and findings solidly based; the very fact of our planet's being capable of incubating and sustaining life is a miracle, the odds of its happening by chance so dauntingly great[137] that those who wish to deny the hand of a Creator in designing, framing and setting in place the cosmos are driven to egregious convolutions. The human body is "fearfully and wonderfully made" (Psalm 139:14) beyond the reaches of mere happenstance,[138] the structure of the simplest cell almost as complex as the organisms which they combine to form. There is no lack of signs and wonders, though sadly many "have eyes, and fail to see ... [and] ears, and fail to hear" (Mark 8:18, NRSV).

Holding up a mirror.

The art of the Amarna period reflected the beliefs and character as well as the political and religious agenda of its ultimate architect, inspiration and presiding genius, Akhenaten. The universe as it was when first brought into being, when he who "set the sun and the moon in their places" (Psalm 74:16, GNT) "saw all that he had made, and it was very good" (Genesis 1:31), in the same way reflected its sole designer, artist and craftsman. Though what was once perfect has been scarred and misshapen by generations of sin, enough traces of the original divine work remain for there to be no difficulty in discerning that what God moulded was at its inception and in every aspect orderly, structured, fruitful, harmonious, benign, pleasant and beautiful.[139] Such qualities can be seen in the crafting of the tabernacle and its accoutrements, which Moses commissioned at the Lord's command and to a heavenly template, for God told his prophet to "Make this tabernacle and all its furnishings exactly like the pattern I will show you"(Exodus 25:9) so as to enable his glory to shine in the world.[140]

TEMPLATE.

God did not leave his people flailing about for ways to give effect to what he asked them to do, nor cause Moses to bear the entire burden unaided. Instead he provided what was needed, giving an initial vision and then enabling this to be translated into reality through the inspiration and direction of his Holy Spirit.[141] Thereby were things which initially were only described or pictured brought into being, as those who were to undertake the various tasks were equipped to do so, as those allocated to provide the requisite time, talents and materials had stirred up within them the necessary desire, anticipation and heart eager for service, and as those with skill and knowledge had bestowed upon them the means to pass these to others so that there would be help in the present and a continuing resource for the future.[142] Thus was a mirror held up to the world, showing God's plan for men and his deepest desire that they should be in close and lasting relationship to him, basking in his radiance and in his love. The result was:

Ordered, with absolute precision in measurement required, as is evident not just with regard to the tabernacle itself but also in the specifications of other objects such as the ark (see for example Exodus 25:10 and 25:17);[143]

Structured, in the precise positioning of decoration and careful interrelationship of objects the one to the other – this is seen with regard to the ark (Exodus 25:12-16 and 18-21) but also in many other aspects of the design;[144]

Fruitful, by intent and in result, the "flower-like cups, buds and blossoms" (Exodus 25:31), "almond flowers" (Exodus 25:34) and "buds and branches" (Exodus 25:36) of the lampstand signifying and encouraging the harvest which flows from heartfelt prayer, dedication to holiness and true worship, and obedience to God's commands;

Harmonious, representing "the work of a skilled craftsman" (Exodus 28:6), its overall unity of design, materials and execution evident in the fact that the "skilfully woven waistband [of the ephod was] … of one piece with the ephod [itself]" (Exodus 28:8 and 39:5),[145] whilst the components of the tabernacle were to form "a unit" (Exodus 26:6, 26:11, 36:13 and 36:18);

Benign, the engraving of the names of the twelve Israelite tribes on onyx stones worn by the high priest (Exodus 28:9-12) vouchsafing that "Whenever Aaron enters the Holy Place, he will bear the names of the sons of Israel over his heart on the breastpiece of decision as a continuing memorial before the LORD"

(Exodus 28:29) – God's remembrance of his people and loving-kindness towards them thereby being assured;

Pleasant, the tabernacle becoming the abode of the Most High, wherein he dwelt and which in due course was filled by "the glory of the LORD" (Exodus 40:35); and

Beautiful, with "gold, silver, and bronze; fine linen; blue, purple, and red wool; cloth made of goats' hair; rams' skin dyed red; fine leather; acacia wood; oil for the lamps; spices for the anointing oil and for the sweet-smelling incense; carnelians and other jewels" (Exodus 25:3-7, GNT).

In all of this, the tabernacle (and before that, the entire Creation which was its model) did no more than reflect something of the great and glorious God who brought it into being.

VISION.

With regard to all that was to be made, Moses was told, "They [the ones whom God had selected to carry out the work] are to follow exactly the directions I gave you."(Exodus 31:11, TLB). Yet it seems that the prophet was not merely given verbal instructions. In the case of the altar he was also told that "it is to be made just as you were shown [not told] on the mountain" (Exodus 27:8) and similarly he was to "set up the tabernacle according to the plan shown you on the mountain" (Exodus 26:30). These statements imply that, at the very least, images of altar and tabernacle were revealed so that Moses could more readily visualise how the completed item was to look, and it is reasonable to infer from this that he was probably shown the various other things as well. It is well that he should have been, for it is difficult to derive their precise appearance merely from the words recorded in Exodus, hence the differences (albeit usually slight) in modern attempts at reconstruction. Though to some degree those artists and craftsmen who translated vision into completed work may have been given rein for self-expression, faithful adherence to the divine plan was the uppermost consideration. So should it be in the case of that work to which we are called; fulfilment of the tasks we are allotted in the time, place and manner of God's choosing is the overriding concern, notwithstanding that in his grace the Lord allows us to give effect to our instructions in ways that are commensurate with our particular character, abilities and circumstances.

All of those conditions that went into construction of the tabernacle, its fixtures and fittings did not simply involve the making of a given set of things at a fixed place and time. There is a more general lesson to be drawn from these events and circumstances: if we are to be a faithful reflection we must start with clear vision. Otherwise, the image we project stands no chance of bearing anything approaching a true likeness, still less of doing proper justice to what it seeks to represent. Profound spiritual truths lie behind those things that Israel acted out and experienced in the physical realm, which it behoves us to ponder and take to heart. To do so is not a work of sheer imagination and neither does it require a shot in the dark. Our task is akin to that of the Israelites themselves, whom the Lord "humbled ... causing you to hunger and then feeding you with manna, which neither you nor your fathers had known, to teach you that man does not live on bread alone but on every word that comes from the mouth of God" (Deuteronomy 8:3), but to whom at the same time he provided visual symbols to help them see from whence they might derive that spiritual nourishment which all of us crave at the most profound level, whether we know it or not. In reflecting Creation and giving means by which to draw near the Creator, the tabernacle and its contents were also signposts to the source of all that is best and most truly satisfying. Just as in days of old, the sustenance that the Lord offers any who seek him today is no optional extra; it is a fundamental and basic requirement for worthwhile living, attaining true wholeness, health, wellbeing and peace,[146] and the means by which we may set our feet on the path to becoming what our Maker intended us to be. Without it, not only will we fail to flower, fail to bring forth the harvest of which we are capable and fail to reflect the Lord's glory in the world, but ultimately our souls will wither and die. This is true of individuals. The same applies at a corporate level, as family, church, or nation, for "Without vision the people perish" (Proverbs 29:18, KJV). It is thus of the gravest concern that we consider whither and to whom we should look to attain vision and how we might set about seeing more clearly.

INSPIRATION.

Exodus makes no bones about it: the most exalted genius in any field of endeavour derives from and is dependent on God. Correspondingly, its proper and most worthwhile use is in his service. Those of the Israelites who were touched by the Holy Spirit so as to be fitted for work on the tabernacle and its furnishings were endowed with creative capacity and practical expertise of the very highest order. Were Bezalel at work amongst us today, he might seem a giant, a new Leonardo or Michelangelo, for "The LORD said to Moses, 'I have chosen Bezalel, the son of Uri and grandson of Hur, from the tribe of Judah, and I have filled him with my power. I have given him understanding, skill, and ability for every kind of artistic work – for planning skillful designs and working them in gold, silver, and bronze; for cutting jewels to be set; for carving wood; and for every other kind of artistic work.'" (Exodus 31:1-5, GNT, substantially repeated by Moses in Exodus 35:31-33). He was not the only one, since the Lord "appointed Oholiab (son of Ahisamach of the tribe of Dan) to be his assistant" (Exodus 31:6, TLB) and alongside him "all who are known as experts, so that they can make all the things I have instructed you to make: the Tabernacle; the Ark with the place of mercy upon it; all the furnishings of the Tabernacle; the table and its instruments; the pure gold lampstand with its instruments; the altar of incense; the burnt offering altar with its instruments; the laver and its pedestal; the beautifully made, holy garments for Aaron the priest, and the garments for his sons, so that they can minister as priests; the anointing oil; and the sweet-spice incense for the Holy Place. They are to follow exactly the directions I gave you." (Exodus 31:6-11, TLB).

In principal (Bezalel), trusted lieutenant (Oholiab) and associated artisans we see clearly that the gifts and activity of the Holy Spirit are not limited to areas for which we reserve the epithet 'spiritual', but extend just as much to the practical. The Bible does not teach a distinction between mind and matter of the kind espoused by elements of ancient Greek philosophy.[147] Instead, it embraces the unity of Creation, counsels the pursuit of integrity[148] in all its aspects, and advises that in and through God we should seek wholeness in body, mind and spirit. Amongst the Israelites of Moses' day, gifts of artistry and craftsmanship were poured out liberally, both in terms of the numbers of people who were thereby inspired and in the sheer breadth of the capabilities given; those taught by Bezalel and Oholiab are described as having "skill to do all kinds of work as craftsmen, designers, embroiderers in blue, purple and scarlet yarn and fine linen, and weavers – all of them master craftsmen and designers." (Exodus 35:35). Such things were without precedent in the annals of God's people, for never before had the Holy Spirit been seen at work inspiring the activity of men on a scale so vast.[149]

These were momentous events, their fruit being constructions and artefacts which not only were of outstanding beauty but were of immense significance in the outworking of the Almighty's plan for Israel. We might sometimes be tempted to believe that such things belong only to a distant past and that anything remotely equivalent could never be in our own day. Yet that is not what Scripture says. At the first Pentecost the apostle Peter deliberately applied Old Testament prophecy to explain to an amazed crowd the extraordinary events which accompanied the coming of the Holy Spirit: "These people are not drunk, as you suppose; it is only nine o'clock in the morning. Instead, this is what the prophet Joel spoke about: 'This is what I will do in the last days, God says: I will pour out my Spirit on everyone. Your sons and daughters will proclaim my message; your young men will see visions, and your old men will have dreams. Yes, even on my servants, both men and women, I will pour out my Spirit in those days, and they will proclaim my message.'" (Acts 2:15-18, GNT; quoting Joel 2:28-29). The implication of the fact that the Holy Spirit no longer comes only to certain individuals for the fulfilment of specific tasks (as in Old Testament times) but is now poured out on all flesh is that we can expect manifestations just as great, indeed even greater, than those which Moses witnessed. This might mean that we need to look in unexpected places. More than anything, it requires that we cultivate an expectant mind and a heart of service, without which we risk missing out on much that God wishes to do through us.

HEART AND MIND.

Like any gift, spiritual or otherwise, those of artistry and craftsmanship can be misused or moulder unopened. The way in which God intends us to employ for the purposes of his Kingdom these or such other aptitudes as he may have granted to us might not be immediately apparent. For reasons of his choosing, there may be fallow seasons when doors are closed and opportunities limited, or times when cares and troubles press so hard upon us that faculties are dimmed and it is difficult to see a way through. At such points it may be that talents must perforce lie dormant. Yet whatever the circumstances, the starting point should be to look with excitement and expectation for what God will do in the future and to acknowledge that what is bestowed upon us is not purely for our use and enjoyment, but for furthering the work of our Father in heaven. It was ever thus. As those who had only recently been in bondage were preparing to leave Egypt, God told Moses, "Every woman is to ask her neighbour and any woman living in her house for articles of silver and gold and for clothing, which you will put on your sons and daughters. And so you will plunder the Egyptians." (Exodus 3:22). The recipients of such largesse doubtless thought that what they gained was for their adornment and beautification, fitting recompense perhaps for the ignominies of a lifetime of slavery. So careless were they about the things of heaven that later they devoted a portion of this treasure to making an object of false worship as "the people took off their earrings and brought them to Aaron. He took what they handed him and made it into an idol cast in the shape of a calf, fashioning it with a tool. Then they said, 'These are your gods, Israel, who brought you up out of Egypt.'" (Exodus 32:3-4). This was a double sacrilege, a sin of commission as well as of omission in not only failing to use gifts for godly purposes but quite deliberately opting to dedicate them to the very opposite. The issue was one of both heart and mind: of the heart since it involved yearning after what was selfish or wrong so that the whole orientation of the people was naturally towards depravity and of the mind by entailing a purposeful decision of the will in defiance of all that was known to be right and good.

As a consequence of the Israelites' short-sightedness and disobedience, what had been given to them was taken away, the Lord saying "You are a stiff-necked people. If I were to go with you even for a moment, I might destroy you. Now take off your ornaments and I will decide what to do with you." (Exodus 33:5).[150] God's ultimate aim and intention, however, was altogether different from anything the people had conceived: loot from Egypt was in fact to be used in making the tabernacle and its furnishings. That there is always a way back with God and that we are not forever cast out from his presence is emphasised by the Israelites' subsequent change of heart and the Almighty's response to it. For when the time came to build God's house, many brought gladly from what they had, to such good effect that there was an abundance, even an excess, and "Then the skilled men who were doing the work went and told Moses, 'The people are bringing more than is needed for the work which the LORD commanded to be done.'" (Exodus 36:4-5, GNT). The offerings that were made at this time were not rejected, despite what had happened earlier, for on this occasion the givers' hearts were in the right place. It was merely a case of ensuring that things did not go to waste and that anything that was not needed straightaway was reserved for future use. As always where things are given to God willingly and with joy, there was an overflow of blessing.

RADIANCE.

The inevitable consequence of making ourselves available for use by God, acting in obedience to his commands and opening ourselves to the activity of the Holy Spirit is that we will increasingly begin to glow with his radiance. Scripture repeatedly exhorts those who love the Lord to do precisely this: "Arise, shine, for your light has come" (Isaiah 60:1), "let your light shine before men" (Matthew 5:16), and "shine as stars in the universe as you hold out the word of life" (Philippians 2:15), for thereby will we in the end "shine as the sun in [our] Father's Kingdom" (Matthew 13:43, TLB). So faithfully did Moses reflect the brilliance that burned within him that it even affected his outward appearance by causing his countenance to emit rays of light.[151] The way in which this was manifest and the varying reactions to it are instructive:

The person most directly affected was not at first conscious of being outwardly changed: "When Moses came down from Mount Sinai with the two tablets of the Testimony in his hands, he was not aware that his face was radiant because he had spoken with the LORD." (Exodus 34:29). This emphasises that our own level of consciousness about how God may be working in us is not always the most reliable measure of effectiveness or degree.

Only the reaction of others caused him to realise what had happened: "When Aaron and all the Israelites saw Moses, his face was radiant and they were afraid to come near him." (Exodus 34:30). Whilst it is God to whom we should primarily look for guidance, the way in which others respond to us can be telling. The reactions and advice of fellow believers in particular deserve to be carefully weighed.

He took immediate steps to reassure, draw people to him and comfort them: "But Moses called them, and Aaron and all the leaders of the community went to him, and Moses spoke with them." (Exodus 34:31, GNT). We should be considerate in our dealings with others, for some are uneasy or fearful in the face of things spiritual. We should not remain distant from others but come close so that we can minister to them according to their needs.

He used these events as an opportunity to communicate the word of God: "Afterwards all the Israelites came near him, and he gave them all the commands the LORD had spoken on Mount Sinai." (Exodus 34:32). If we truly reflect God, people cannot fail to notice, remark on it and find it attractive. We should be alert to any opportunity this gives to proclaim the gospel.

He was considerate in his dealings with others but uncompromising in seeking closeness to the Lord: "When Moses had finished speaking with them, he put a veil over his face; but whenever he went into the Tabernacle to speak with the Lord, he removed the veil until he came out again; then he would pass on to the people whatever instructions God had given him, and the people would see his face aglow. Afterwards he would put the veil on again until he returned to speak with God." (Exodus 34:33-35, TLB). Regard for our fellow men has to be kept in proper perspective, for we should not allow others' opinions or reactions to take precedence over relationship with our Maker, nor cause us to compromise on obedience to him.

Amongst the children of Israel, Moses was one of a kind. There was none other who saw as much of God, nobody besides him who dared approach as close to the Almighty and no-one else whose face glowed in like manner with the reflected glory of his heavenly King. He was in a thoroughly unique position in his dealings with the Most High. Not surprisingly, he was and still is venerated by Jews for being the great deliverer, lawgiver, leader and prophet who remained "faithful in his work in God's house" (Hebrews 3:2, GNT). It is therefore altogether extraordinary and humbling to consider what St Paul says in comparing Old Testament and New Testament dispensations, prophet, Messiah and people: "We are not like Moses, who had to put a veil over his face so that the people of Israel would not see the brightness fade and disappear. Their minds, indeed, were closed; and to this very day their minds are covered with the same veil as they read the books of the old covenant. The veil is removed only when a person is joined to Christ. Even today, whenever they read the Law of Moses, the veil still covers their minds. But it can be removed, as the scripture says about Moses: 'His veil was removed when he turned to the Lord.' Now, 'the Lord' in this passage is the Spirit; and where the Spirit of the Lord is present, there is freedom. All of us, then, reflect the glory of the Lord with uncovered faces; and that same glory, coming from the Lord, who is the Spirit, transforms us into his likeness in an ever greater degree of glory." (2 Corinthians 3:13-18, GNT). Too seldom do we grasp the extent of the power and blessing we have been given.

PROCLAMATION.

Egypt's heretic pharaoh and those who joined with him in venerating Aten basked in the radiance of the sun. The life-enhancing power and bright shining brilliance of this star caused them to celebrate it as author and giver of life. The precise delineations of the theology that grew out of this belief and the extent to which the events recounted in Exodus might have influenced it will probably never be fully known, but it is at all events clear that (whatever he may have thought or intended) Akhenaten did not worship the God of Abraham, Isaac and Jacob. The names used for Aten oftentimes describe that deity in terms of other gods, but the One who first revealed himself to Moses in a burning bush and whose Holy Spirit subsequently came upon men with what "seemed to be tongues of fire" (Acts 2:3) would not and could not countenance anything of that kind. The Israelites were told, "You shall not make for yourself an idol in the form of anything in heaven above or on the earth beneath or in the waters below. You shall not bow down to them or worship them; for I, the LORD your God, am a jealous God, punishing the children for the sin of the fathers to the third and fourth generation of those who hate me, but showing love to a thousand generations of those who love me and keep my commandments." (Exodus 20:4-6).[152] Both the prohibition and the dire consequences of ignoring it emphasise that, although what the Lord has crafted may reflect parts of his nature or character, to show or describe him in terms of any created thing as though such were capable of encompassing or reflecting his entirety is nothing less than slander and calumny.

Nowadays we tend to be deeply uncomfortable with the idea of a jealous God. Modern sensibilities are offended by being told, "Do not worship any other god, for the LORD, whose name is Jealous, is a jealous God." (Exodus 34:14).[153] Yet it is altogether natural, right and greatly to our advantage that he who made all things should be concerned to protect his honour and reputation, for his doing so is the surest way to ensure that mankind obtains a full and proper appreciation both of who he is and what is needful if we are to come into his Kingdom. It means also that we can reach a position from which to proclaim truthfully the message which he has entrusted to us and thereby bring glory and honour to him. To honour God's name is to honour him. Hence the command, "You shall not take the name of the LORD your God in vain" (Exodus 20:7) requires that we bring no dishonour upon our Creator in terms of nature, character, reputation, attributes, deeds, laws, representatives, Word or in any other way. We should not speak of him in terms foolish or misleading, neither by our actions imply that he is anything other than he is in fact. Amongst many compelling reasons why we should take the greatest care in these matters, not least is our own self-interest, for the Lord has promised that "Wherever I cause my name to be honoured, I will come to you and bless you." (Exodus 20:24).

We have opportunities aplenty to reflect our Maker: in our own attitudes and behaviour, in the way that we speak of him and act on his behalf, and in proclaiming his name to the nations. To proclaim his name is to describe his character, attributes and deeds, as when "he passed in front of Moses, proclaiming" (Exodus 34:6; see also Exodus 33:19). This is not a matter of propaganda, manipulation or myth-making of the kind practised by countless pharaohs. It is showing whither lies "the way and the truth and the life" (John 14:6), not with the "sneer of cold command"[154] of a latter-day tyrant but the servant heart exemplified by Moses and even more so by Jesus. Any other way may deliver brief moments of acknowledgment, maybe even the adulation of men but, like the ambitions and fancies of Ozymandias, will ultimately end in "the decay of that colossal wreck". It behoves us, therefore, to ensure that our proclamation is as true and faithful as we can make it.

Conclusion.

The company we keep reflects on us, for good or ill. The people with whom we associate, the causes we espouse, the ideas we adopt, the habits we cultivate and those with whom we spend our time all say something about us.[155] We bring honour to God when what we do and say reflects well on him and on his teachings. Conversely, we do him great dishonour if we fail to abide by these principles, for then we give occasion for others to judge him and his ways on the basis of our shortcomings. When Moses pleaded for mercy after Israel's sin with the Golden Calf, he made precisely the point that God's dealings with Israel would reflect upon his reputation: "But Moses sought the favour of the LORD his God. 'O LORD,' he said, 'why should your anger burn against your people, whom you brought out of Egypt with great power and a mighty hand? Why should the Egyptians say, 'It was with evil intent that he brought them out, to kill them in the mountains and to wipe them off the face of the earth'? Turn from your fierce anger; relent and do not bring disaster on your people ...' Then the LORD relented and did not bring on his people the disaster he had threatened." (Exodus 32:11-12 and 14).[156] Since it is no less so in our day, this should cause us to consider carefully if there be anything in our speech or conduct which reflects ill on the one we purport to serve.

The Lord will make us a haven and extend our borders to the extent that we represent him fairly and honestly, to the degree that we associate with what is good and in the measure that we aim at truth, purity and holiness. There are grounds for saying that art of the Amarna period, perhaps to an extent greater than ever before in Egypt, tended to blur distinctions between deity and royalty. In Israel any such thing would have been the foulest blasphemy. The Bible repeatedly emphasises the holiness of God and his separateness from created things. Yet Scripture teaches, too, that each of us inherently reflects the God who made us by virtue of being "created ... in his own image" (Genesis 1:27). We bear a mark of great privilege, but also the responsibility that goes with it: to be as full and worthy a reflection of our Maker as we are able.

Benjamin

Whose meaning is, *son of the south*,
or, *son of my right hand*

Of whom Jacob prophesied,
"Benjamin is a ravenous wolf; in the morning he devours the prey, in the evening he divides the plunder."
(Genesis 49:27).

6. Relying on God

War and diplomacy.

"The LORD will fight for you; you need only to be still." (Exodus 14:14).

By the time Akhenaten succeeded his father Egyptians had for generations regarded Amun as "Lord of the thrones of the Two Lands" and "King of the Gods."[157] Though at first a deity local to Thebes, he grew to be associated with those royal dynasties that sprang from this city and by extension came to be the primary focus of worship for the nation as a whole. Over the years, loyalties to state, god and monarch intertwined to such an extent as to be virtually inseparable; to fight for Egypt meant following the banner of pharaoh, which in turn involved entering the lists on behalf of Amun. The latter was often shown in martial guise, a dagger strapped to his upper arm and battle axe tucked into his kilt. He it was who supposedly instituted campaigns,[158] set strategy, commanded the host and gave protection on the field of battle. When victory came, as it surely must with Amun at the head of Egypt's armies, it was thus only fit and proper that a suitable proportion of its spoils should be given to his principal temple in the sacred precinct of Thebes.[159] Little wonder that, as Egypt's empire spread and her roll call of victories lengthened, the priesthood of this cult should have become such a force in the land, its considerable spiritual authority exercised alongside an economic heft which derived from extensive landholdings and steady receipt of bequests both large and small.

Emphasis on the warlike aspects of Amun during the opening reigns of the New Kingdom reflected developments at home and abroad, themselves mirrored in changing concepts of kingship. In the latter half of the sixteenth century BC, pharaohs began more and more to espouse warrior virtues as a succession of rulers and their sons were embroiled by necessity or choice in armed conflict.[160] The need for valour in battle and the glory that resulted from victory in war fed expanded ideas of royal role, function and legitimacy; to reinforce their claims upon the throne and the love of their people, monarchs of the Eighteenth Dynasty (the first of the New Kingdom) were portrayed not only as sons of Amun and heroes in their own right but were self-consciously linked to predecessors from the end of the Second Intermediate Period, when the nation had fought to free itself of foreign domination at the hands of the reviled Hyksos.[161] In the wake of the country's deliverance from these occupiers, the flail and shepherd's crook which symbolised the ruler's time-honoured position as scourge of Egypt's enemies and saviour and protector of the common man had seldom seemed more apt.[162]

Nor was the traffic all one way. Just as earthly considerations affected how Amun was conceived, so the nature of that god and his close connection to the occupant of the throne influenced policy both domestic and overseas: deity and king were each benign, generous even, to any whose obedience and loyalty were beyond question, implacable foes to those openly hostile or whose trustworthiness was less than absolute.[163] Pitilessness towards enemies and dissidents was the order of the day as the raw power and anger (*bau*) of the One who Conceals Himself was displayed in and seen at work through his vice-regent on earth. Correspondingly, to other realms and alien peoples who remained friendly, so too were these twin protectors of the Two Lands – though it was a friendship based on servility; allies merited the word *hetepu*, which connoted peace and contentment, but was at the same time freighted with concepts of subservience or submission.[164] Egypt, whose earliest existence had been characterised by isolation behind her natural bulwarks of desert and sea, became an aggressively expansionist imperial power with an outlook and a deity to match.

Theology, political theory and everyday practicalities were consolidated and unified by adoption of the king in battle as a common topic for artists and writers. By the reign of the seventh pharaoh of the Eighteenth Dynasty, Amenhotep II (who ruled from approximately 1427 BC to 1401 BC), there was a set formula for pictorial representation of this theme, featuring images of assembling stores and troops, leaving on campaign, arrival on the battlefield, combat, triumph over the enemy, taking of booty and giving a handsome measure of these spoils to Amun. In due course two parallel forms emerged, with free-standing stelae or moderate-sized rock inscriptions for minor campaigns existing alongside carvings on temple walls (especially at Thebes) or stelae placed within religious buildings to commemorate major battles or royal presence. Victory for Egypt was portrayed as restoring right, justice and truth (*Ma'at*), bringing order out of chaos and enabling stability to supplant anarchy, dissolution and lawlessness. Defeated adversaries were caricatured as confused, disorganised and cowardly. Their troops, feeble and undisciplined, were seen tripping, fleeing or being slaughtered wholesale by the unstoppable armies of their virile and steadfast opponents. The pharaoh himself, dwarfing all other figures and with Amun alongside him as father and helper, was often pictured in hand-to-hand combat against a smaller (though still outsized) enemy leader. The outcome of this contest was a foregone conclusion; in a fight between an upstart who defied truth and the progeny of Amun, there could only be one conceivable winner.

As heroes and champions of Egypt, rulers of the early New Kingdom were the very incarnation of warrior-gods such as Baal, Seth or Montu. They stood at the apex of a warrior caste which prided itself on its prowess in feats of arms and a military which was professional, well-organised and well-equipped. The Egyptian forces, under the supreme direction of the king or his deputy, were divided into a number of armies, each corps being named after one of the principal gods[165] and comprising chariots, infantry, scouts, sappers and marines. An elaborate chain of command led from generals to battalion commanders and onwards to platoon, troop and squad leaders, with standards to identify units on the field of battle and trumpeters to enable orders to be transmitted swiftly. No longer was Egypt outclassed in terms of weaponry as when first she had faced the Hyksos, for her soldiers had composite bows, heavy bronze falchions, battle-axes and javelins every bit as good as any wielded by their opponents. Her rank and file could rest easy in the quality of the officers and NCOs set over them, for they were chosen on merit; to a greater extent than in other walks of life, a military career rewarded ability rather than birth or status, so that soldiering was the surest of means by which the enterprising though uneducated might achieve wealth or a position of importance (albeit that the very highest staff posts continued to be reserved to those who were educated and literate).

Over time, the demands of empire and of an increasingly militarised polity brought about changes in administration. Government was reorganised around professional soldiers, and bureaucracy adapted to the needs of a state geared up for war. When away from active service, the large standing army[166] was not left idle, but was used to provide labour and technical expertise for a variety of construction projects, in the process enabling government to avoid disrupting food production by taking droves of peasants away from their fields. Army units also marshalled and guarded those assorted prisoners of war, convicts and slaves who provided muscle to work the gold mines of distant Kush and Nubia or the remote copper and turquoise deposits of Sinai –activities from which derived a significant part of the wealth and prestige of the revitalised Egyptian state. In this brave new world, chariots were the elite, their crews accomplished in athletic feats, the management of horses and all the skills of a new kind of mobile warfare. Increasingly, generals were drawn from the ranks of this force,[167] these high ranking officers all the while growing closer to the monarch. The developing bond and deepening comradeship between monarch and army commanders was expressed in the titles given to the latter, which included phrases such as "of the king", "of the Lord of the Two Lands" or (in the case of the chief charioteer) "of his majesty". The influence of such men was considerable, for not only did they stand high in the esteem of their pharaoh but they also formed a sizeable proportion of the elite,[168] controlled vast reaches of territory from the north-eastern border post of Sile as far as Syria, and had at their disposal considerable reserves of manpower.

Marching out boldly.

Around the time of Akhenaten's accession, an observer of the Egyptian scene would most probably have remarked not just the pre-eminence of Amun but also the importance of that deity in providing a focus for national unity, an ideology which underpinned and legitimised empire, and a motivating force for the troops which sustained it. Evident, too, would have been the generally high regard in which the armed forces were held as guarantors of the nation's territorial integrity and international standing. Within a few years into the new reign, however, all this was turned on its head. The new pharaoh deployed his regiments to enforce closure of temples to gods other than Aten, resulting in soldiers no longer being used solely to secure Egyptian dominion overseas or reinforce prosperity at home, but as an instrument of repression against their own people.[169] This was bad enough, but for officers and men to be told simultaneously that Amun no longer merited his former place of honour must have been doubly disorientating. Quite conceivably it would have dealt a devastating blow to all that they had been brought up to fight for and believe. It would not be completely outlandish to imagine that morale and maybe even discipline suffered as a result, at a point when military capacity was being eroded in other ways. For by the reign of Akhenaten's father Amenhotep III the nation's very success abroad had begun to sow the seeds of future decline. By then the army had for many years been as likely to carry out border patrols and police actions on troublesome frontiers as take the field against an equally matched foe, and her soldiers to form labour battalions on the latest civil engineering projects as engage in set-piece battles. In such an environment combat readiness could not help but suffer and training deteriorate as the experience and stiffening presence of battle-hardened veterans was increasingly lost – a trend both reflected in and exacerbated by the growing use of mercenaries.[170]

Exodus has a great deal to say about warfare. The combat it describes is multi-layered – physical and spiritual; internal and external; past, present and future. It involves battles fought on our behalf, battles deferred, battles lost and battles won, battles in the heavenly realms and battles on earth. It describes war against a neglectful prophet (Exodus 4:18-26), a disobedient people (Exodus 32:26-35), a recalcitrant enemy (Exodus 14:13-31) and an implacable foe (Exodus 17:8-16). It takes conventions of human conflict and turns them upside down, inside out and back to front. In the process, the utter powerlessness of the strongest potentates and most malign spirits in the face of Almighty God is demonstrated beyond all argument, for he is revealed as Lord of Hosts, "victorious in battle" (Psalm 24:8, GNT) and "a strong tower against the foe"(Psalm 61:3). In terms of the Old Testament dispensation, the delivery of Israel out of bondage in Egypt marks a watershed equivalent in some degree to that which took place at the resurrection of Jesus, when "He disarmed the [spiritual] rulers and authorities [of darkness] and made a public example of them, triumphing over them in it." (Colossians 2:15, NRSV).[171] For the ills that befell Egypt at the hands of the Most High were not directed primarily at human beings but at the dark forces which held them in thrall, a fact that was stated explicitly when the High King of heaven declared, "I will bring judgment on all the gods of Egypt." (Exodus 12:12). Hence each of the Ten Plagues can be seen as directed at specific Egyptian deities,[172] whilst collectively they struck at the entire pantheon. Thus were the idols of the Two Lands shown to be exactly what the prophet Isaiah described half a millennium after the days of Moses: "gods who cannot save" (Isaiah 45:20).

BATTLES DEFERRED.

The God of Abraham, Isaac and Jacob is justly described as lover of peace and author of concord. He desires that we should "love [our] enemies and pray for those who persecute [us]" (Matthew 5:44, GNT). He yearns to bring his *shalom* into every life and that there should be reconciliation between any who are antagonistic, hence the requirement that we should "First go and be reconciled to [our] brother; then come and offer [our] gift [to God]." (Matthew 5:24). Yet he is Lion (Revelation 5:5) as well as Lamb (Revelation 5:6). He does not shy away from confronting evil, and now just as at any time in the past will "[throw] down those who [oppose him]" (Exodus 15:7). Consequently, "The LORD is a warrior; the LORD is his name" (Exodus 15:3). Though he frequently delays punishment to give a chance for repentance and offers any number of opportunities for us to relent and turn back to him, if we persist in wrongdoing and rebellion this will prove merely to be a battle deferred. So it was with Pharaoh as the Most High "unleashed [his] burning anger" (Exodus 15:7) and finally ended that king's pretensions – claims to dominion over things which are rightfully God's alone, and an overarching ruthlessness that caused "The enemy [to boast], 'I will pursue, I will overtake them. I will divide the spoils; I will gorge myself on them. I will draw my sword and my hand will destroy them.'" (Exodus 15:9).[173]

Battle may be deferred so as to give best effect to the redemption purposes of our heavenly King, but it may also be put off either as a result of or to accommodate human frailty. Since a disciple of the Lord is a soldier (see 1 Corinthians 9:7, Philippians 2:25, 2 Timothy 2:3-4 and Philemon 1:2) in his service, it follows that each must be ready to "fight the good fight" (1 Timothy 1:18 and 6:12, NRSV) as part of the army of God. Sometimes, however, there are battles in which we need to engage, but for which we are ready neither physically nor spiritually. The Israelites' struggle against the Philistines was one such.[174] This latter nation would in years to come prove to be arch enemy and frequent oppressor of Israel, confronted time and again under the Judges and when Saul and David ruled,[175] but combat is to take place according to God's timetable, not ours. Since the Lord "knows how we are formed … remembers that we are dust" (Psalm 103:14) and "created [our] inmost being" (Psalm 139:13), he is more fully aware of what we can bear and of what we are capable than we ourselves. He does not ask us to do what is beyond us. Just as he will "provide a way out so that [we] can stand up under" (1 Corinthians 10:13) whatever assails us, so too will he supply means for us to increase in stature and resources so that we can undertake things that previously seemed impossible. In similar fashion, keenly aware of his people's vulnerability, "When Pharaoh let the people go, God did not lead them on the road through the Philistine country, though that was shorter. For God said, 'If they face war, they might change their minds and return to Egypt.'" (Exodus 13:17).

By definition, an army is a collective body. If some slacken or flee then, however bravely those who remain may fight, the contest will be longer and harder than it otherwise would. To be sure, taking the field unprepared is unwise at best, potentially disastrous at worst, and the Almighty is far too good a general to compel us to engage the enemy without purpose. Yet none of this should be an excuse to shirk responsibility, nor cause us to judge results according to human standards; the Lord of Hosts does not require success as men measure such things, but he does require obedience. Some battles are not for us to fight, some can be avoided and others put off for a while, but if we abandon our post or forever defer those engagements that God has allocated to our station in the line, others will suffer for it. Sooner or later, we must take up the cudgels.

BATTLES FOUGHT ON OUR BEHALF.

The events surrounding the crossing of the Red Sea describe a battle which had to be fought, but not by Israel. When victory came, it was incontrovertibly attributable to God alone for, as Moses said whilst people panicked all around, "The LORD will fight for you; you need only to be still." (Exodus 14:14). That this should have been so was the result of a number of factors. At the most basic level it reflected the sheer inability of the fleeing and fearful Israelites at this stage in their journey to make any meaningful contribution through their own efforts.[176] With no military background or training, still unused to cooperating together as a body and operating as a cohesive group, freed from slavery only shortly beforehand and (most debilitating of all) still of weak faith, they simply did not have the psychological or spiritual strength to stand on their own two feet.[177] To build these qualities so that they would be able to meet future challenges (and so that succeeding generations should learn from their experience) it was necessary that they should see "the great power the LORD displayed against the Egyptians, [to cause them to fear] the LORD and put their trust in Moses his servant." (Exodus 14:31). Yet ultimately human weakness was not the main contributor; the essential issue came down to the Almighty's kingdom purposes. These required victory to be so incontestably his, without any hint or taint of human involvement, that by it he would "gain glory through Pharaoh and all his army, through his chariots and horsemen." (Exodus 14:17). This was not because God is in the slightest boastful or proud, but was done in order that "The Egyptians [and, by extension, the whole world] will know that I am the LORD" (Exodus 14:18). It is good to "[march] out boldly" (Exodus 14:8), and indeed often we are called to do so, "strong in the Lord and in his mighty power" (Ephesians 6:10), but there are times when this alone is not enough, when the fight is the Lord's and to him alone belongs the victory.

As with the Ten Plagues, in this final act of the great contest with Pharaoh that had smouldered and flared over the course of the preceding year, the Lord showed control over every aspect of nature and the elements. He shielded his people with "the pillar of cloud [which] ... moved from in front of them and stood behind them, coming between the armies of Egypt and Israel" (Exodus 14:19-20), brought "darkness to the one side and light to the other; so neither went near the other all night long" (Exodus 14:20), caused a storm through the blowing of "a strong east wind" (Exodus 14:21), and commanded "The waters [so that they] were divided." (Exodus 14:22). Thus were his people provided with an escape route at just the right moment and the enemy lured to their doom: "Then Moses stretched out his hand over the sea, and all that night the LORD drove the sea back with a strong east wind and turned it into dry land. The waters were divided, and the Israelites went through the sea on dry ground, with a wall of water on their right and on their left." (Exodus 14:21-22).[178] In their pride and folly, the Egyptians followed, still sure of their own abilities in spite of all that had happened. "Then the LORD said to Moses, 'Stretch out your hand over the sea so that the waters may flow back over the Egyptians and their chariots and horsemen.' Moses stretched out his hand over the sea, and at daybreak the sea went back to its place. The Egyptians were fleeing towards it, and the LORD swept them into the sea. The water flowed back and covered the chariots and horsemen – the entire army of Pharaoh that had followed the Israelites into the sea. Not one of them survived." (Exodus 14:26-28).

Pharaoh's army was deliberately brought to battle on ground carefully chosen, for "the LORD [had] said to Moses, 'Tell the Israelites to turn back and camp near Pi Hahiroth, between Migdol and the sea. They are to camp by the sea, directly opposite Baal Zephon. Pharaoh will think, 'The Israelites are wandering around the land in confusion, hemmed in by the desert.' And I will harden Pharaoh's heart, and he will pursue them.'" (Exodus 14:1-4). Like any experienced commander, God chooses when and where to fight, the tactics that will be used and the methods which will render his enemy most susceptible to defeat. With feints and counter-marches Pharaoh was lulled into a false sense of security, so that "the Egyptians pursued [the Israelites], and all Pharaoh's horses and chariots and horsemen followed them into the sea." (Exodus 14:23). Such was the pursuers' overconfidence that there was no attempt to gauge the suitability of the ground, no division held in reserve, no thought of anything other than retribution, revenge and booty. The outcome was carnage: "During the last watch of the night the LORD looked down from the pillar of fire and cloud at the Egyptian army and threw it into confusion. He made the wheels of their chariots come off so that they had difficulty driving. And the Egyptians said, 'Let's get away from the Israelites! The LORD is fighting for them against Egypt.'" (Exodus 14:24-25). Amidst the ensuing wreck, God took care of his own, for "the Israelites went through the sea on dry ground, with a wall of water on their right and on their left. That day the LORD saved Israel from the hands of the Egyptians, and Israel saw the Egyptians lying dead on the shore." (Exodus 14:29-30). Victory was complete, overwhelming, devastating.[179]

BATTLES WON.

The result was spiritual transformation. As Pharaoh's forces closed upon them the Israelites were in the grip of panic and despair, yet only a short while later they showed such steely resolve against the Amalekites that they fought "until the sun set" (Exodus 17:12, NRSV). The reason was simple: fortified by "the great power the LORD displayed" (Exodus 14:31), they gained the right frame of mind to access resources that had been available all along. Together these provided all the components for success:

Equipment: There was no lack of weaponry: "The Israelites went up out of Egypt armed for battle" (Exodus 13:18) and "overcame the Amalekite army with the sword." (Exodus 17:13). In addition to equipment that was brought with them from Egypt, armour and weapons may have been taken from Egyptian soldiers "lying dead on the shore" (Exodus 14:30) after they had drowned in the Red Sea.

People: Neither was there any shortage of troops. Whatever the precise numbers, those who left Egypt must have formed a large group, and amongst these would have been many of fighting age. Manpower seems to have been sufficiently plentiful that Moses told Joshua, "Choose [only] some of our men" (Exodus 17:8) to march against Amalek.[180]

Organisation: A basic organisational framework existed from the moment the Israelites set out from Egypt. This doubtless owed something to the Egyptians themselves, since efficient management of their huge construction projects would have required that methods of command and control be in place. Hence "Israelite foremen" (Exodus 5:14, 15 and 19) were appointed to work alongside the local "slave masters" (Exodus 1:11) and "slave drivers" (Exodus 3:7, 5:6, 5:10, 5:13 and 5:14). The foremen presumably transmitted orders and production quotas through traditional tribal, clan and family structures.[181]

Discipline: Order was carefully maintained. At the very latest, by the time the Israelites left Horeb after receiving the Ten Commandments they had a set "order of march" (Numbers 10:28, GNT), with each division "under its standard" (Numbers 10:25). High ranking officers were by then sufficiently established in their posts to be recorded by name (Numbers 10:25, 26 and 27) and there was a designated "rear guard" (Numbers 10:25).

Training: Men of the stature of Moses and Joshua are unlikely to have overlooked chances for weapons practice or rehearsing basic drill and manoeuvres.[182] Rest periods, breaks in the journey and time spent waiting for stragglers would have provided occasion for doing so. Manoeuvres could also have been tried out whilst on the march.

Leadership: Even before Moses came on the scene, there were men in positions of authority, for God told Moses, "Go, assemble the elders of Israel" (Exodus 3:16). These were, in a sense, leaders in waiting, who needed to be galvanised, encouraged and empowered for the tasks ahead, but were the raw material from which to craft a leadership structure.[183]

Morale: Morale denotes mental or moral condition, the degree of endurance and courage in bearing up under fatigue or danger. It is the great imponderable in war, and at its heart is of a spiritual nature for it concerns the soul or innermost being. After destruction of Egypt's army the one-time slaves' morale went from rock bottom to sky high, and it was this which allowed them to stand firm against unprovoked aggression as "The Amalekites came and attacked the Israelites at Rephidim." (Exodus 17:8).

The contest against the Amalekites took place over two days, with an initial defence of the "[camp] at Rephidim" (Exodus 17:1) followed by Joshua's hand-picked force taking the battle to the aggressor whilst Moses "[stood] on top of the hill with the staff of God in [his] hands." (Exodus 17:9). Each side fought manfully: "As long as Moses held up his hands, the Israelites were winning, but whenever he lowered his hands, the Amalekites were winning." (Exodus 17:11). The raising of hands indicates an attitude of prayer and supplication, signifying that heavenly as well as earthly power was at work. In confronting a ruthless and redoubtable foe, like Moses we need the help and support of others:[184] "When Moses' hands grew tired, they took a stone and put it under him and he sat on it. Aaron and Hur held his hands up – one on one side and one on the other – so that his hands remained steady till sunset. So Joshua overcame the Amalekite army with the sword." (Exodus 17:13). Against Amalek the Israelites proved that they did not lack the physical means to fight, and neither do we. Like those who marched alongside Joshua, in order to contend and prevail we need only to make proper use of what God has provided, both in the physical realm and through accessing his assistance by prayer.

BATTLES SPIRITUAL.

Doing this requires accepting that any battle is primarily spiritual in nature. The trend for our culture to insist that only things physical exist means that we too readily overlook this dimension to earthly events. At every turn, Scripture suggests an entirely different viewpoint. War between the God of Israel and the deities of Egypt was played out through the Ten Plagues.[185] For sure, these followed a logical progression that allows us to speculate as to what their proximate causes in the natural world might have been, but that does not preclude God's being their ultimate instigator, nor in any way disprove his involvement with the retribution unleashed on Egypt. What Exodus in fact makes clear is the Lord's control over Creation, the thoroughness of his planning and the perfection of his timing:

The Nile turned to blood. From July to August the Nile flooded.[186] The fertility of the lands either side of its banks was dependent on the huge quantities of rich silt and mud carried by the floodwaters. Dust and red earth washed down from the Ethiopian highlands or toxic algae encouraged by abnormally hot weather would have coloured the river red.

The plague of frogs. Whatever the precise cause of the Nile's discolouration, the ecological balance of Egypt's life-blood would have been upset, causing fish to die. Hence frogspawn that normally would have been eaten would instead have hatched. Adult frogs would have fled the noxious waters as soon as possible, but by that time many would already have been fatally poisoned and died shortly thereafter.

The plagues of gnats, flies, boils and dying livestock. Rotting piles of dead frogs and water filled with putrefying fish would have made ideal breeding grounds for insects and disease. Lice, flies and insect-born epidemics would have multiplied, killing livestock and causing people to break out in sores and boils.[187]

The plague of hail. Hailstorms are common in Egypt in February. Though what occurred was of exceptional severity, being "the worst hailstorm that has ever fallen on Egypt, from the day it was founded till now" (Exodus 9:18), it was not unseasonal.

The plague of locusts. Locusts typically arrive in January, February or March. For these to come hard on the heels of hail would thus be perfectly within the normal range of possibility. Modern research suggests that swarms can be triggered by drought, their arrival therefore being consistent with the weather patterns likely to have accompanied other plagues.[188]

The plague of darkness. Three days of darkness could have been caused by the *khamsin* (the desert wind which blows in April and May, bringing sandstorms and blizzards).

With each turn of the screw, utter defeat of the occult powers of Egypt became ever more certain, till at length died the firstborn, whom false gods could neither protect nor bring back to life.[189]

BATTLES WITHIN AND BATTLES LOST.

Time and again the unchallengeable power of Almighty God was in evidence. Yet Israel learnt that it was no foregone conclusion that the Lord would grant them victory. He "bestows his blessing" when "brothers live together in unity" (Psalm 133:1 and 3) and where there is obedience to his commands. Where rebellion and faction reign, blessing is removed. In such cases, God is ready to war against his own. He did it against a negligent prophet (Exodus 4:18-26) and a disobedient people (Exodus 32:26-35). His righteousness, justice and holiness demand no less, for God does not have one law for some and different rules for others.[190] So radical and uncompromising are the demands of the kingdom of heaven that there can be no concession in the face of those who would stand against it. The call in our day, no less than under Moses, is: "Whoever is for the LORD, come to me." (Exodus 32:26). Like the Levites of that former age, the people of God must be prepared to stand, even "against [their] own sons and brothers" (Exodus 32:29), in the fight for what is right.[191] If we are not prepared to act as vigorously as those who "rallied to [Moses]" (Exodus 32:26), vital battles will be lost.

BATTLES PAST AND FUTURE.

Moses' vision and call on Sinai were a fulfilment of promises made to Israel's forefathers and as such a reminder of battles past. They were also calls to battles present and future and a declaration of war against "the Canaanites, Hittites, Amorites, Perizzites, Hivites, and Jebusites" (Exodus 3:8, TLB). When God proclaimed, "I have come to deliver the [Israelites] from the Egyptians and to take them out of Egypt into a good land, a large land, a land 'flowing with milk and honey'" (Exodus 3:8, TLB), conflict with these tribes was assured since none of them could be expected to relinquish voluntarily the dominion they held over people or land. Wars to come were foreseen after the drowning of Pharaoh's troops in the Red Sea, when Moses sang, "In your unfailing love you will lead the people you have redeemed. In your strength you will guide them to your holy dwelling. The nations will hear and tremble; anguish will grip the people of Philistia. The chiefs of Edom will be terrified, the leaders of Moab will be seized with trembling, the people of Canaan will melt away; terror and dread will fall upon them." (Exodus 15:13-16). The "very loud trumpet blast" (Exodus 19:16) heard on Horeb just prior to the giving of the Ten Commandments was likewise a martial sound, presaging the campaigns envisaged in Exodus 23:20-32.[192]

Overturning convention.

From almost the opening sentences, Exodus pictures Israel and Egypt as mortal enemies locked in a fight to the death. Pharaohs thrice tried to destroy their foe: through enslaving her (Exodus 1:11-14), by ordering Hebrew midwives to kill all Israelite boys at birth (Exodus 1:16) and in commanding their own people that "Every boy that is born you must throw into the Nile" (Exodus 1:22). Yet these were merely the opening shots in an extended campaign.

Thereafter events developed in ways that were almost a parody of battle reliefs of the day, with:

Assembling of stores and troops: In contrast to the impressive baggage train of earthly kings, at the outset the heavenly army consisted of a solitary beast of burden, an old man, his wife and two youngsters, the latter perhaps no more than boys, as "Moses took his wife and sons, put them on a donkey and started back to Egypt." (Exodus 4:20).

Leaving for battle: Not only was this motley crew few in number, but to any casual observer they would have seemed completely unarmed. Appearances were deceptive, however, for Moses "took the staff of God in his hands." (Exodus 4:20).

Arrival on the battlefield: The troops with whom the prophet and his brother rendezvoused on arrival in Egypt were scarcely any more impressive than they in appearance: "Moses and Aaron brought together all the elders of the Israelites, and Aaron told them everything the LORD had said to Moses. He also performed the signs before the people, and they believed." (Exodus 4:29-30). These men seemingly had nothing to offer in the coming battle, but they doubtless provided moral support and prayer.

Combat: To all intents and purposes the initial engagement with the enemy seemed to end in comprehensive defeat: "When [the Israelite foremen] met Moses and Aaron waiting for them outside the palace, as they came out from their meeting with Pharaoh, they swore at them. 'May God judge you for making us stink before Pharaoh and his people,' they said, 'and for giving them an excuse to kill us.'" (Exodus 5:20-21, TLB).

Triumph over the enemy: Yet, despite all setbacks and every shortcoming, this ragtag group was utterly victorious, causing their enemy to capitulate ignominiously – to such effect that they sought to speed the former slaves on their way, whereas previously they had put every conceivable obstacle in their path: "The Egyptians urged the people to hurry and leave the country. 'For otherwise,' they said, 'we will all die!'" (Exodus 12:33).

Taking of booty: The possessions of the defeated foe were ransacked: "…the Israelites did as Moses instructed and asked the Egyptians for articles of silver and gold and for clothing. The LORD had made the Egyptians favourably disposed towards the people, and they gave them what they asked for; so they plundered the Egyptians." (Exodus 12:35-36).[193]

Distributing the spoils: In due course a large part of this booty was given to God in the form of "offerings … [made] to carry out the work of constructing the sanctuary." (Exodus 36:3).[194]

Such overturning of convention illustrates that God's ways are not ours. He does not work to human patterns, but esteems the lowly, unexpected and unprepossessing, for whereas "Man looks at the outward appearance ... the LORD looks at the heart." (1 Samuel 16:7).

Conclusion.

Exodus portrays a mixture of earthly and spiritual combat. It doing so, it shows that there are fights in which we should engage here and now, but also struggles that belong to the future or battles that we should leave to God. In determining which of these apply to our own circumstances, timing and godly wisdom are paramount. When they first left Egypt the Israelites were in high spirits and were "marching out boldly" (Exodus 14:8), but all their confidence evaporated at the first whiff of trouble. Cornered against the waters of the Red Sea, "As Pharaoh approached, the Israelites looked up, and there were the Egyptians, marching after them. They were terrified and cried out to the LORD." (Exodus 14:10). By any human reckoning, the untrained bands of former slaves would have been no match for Egypt's crack chariot divisions, and indeed God did not ask them to engage their enemy head to head. This did not mean that they were to be inactive, however. Moses gave three orders: "Do not be afraid" (Exodus 14:13), "Stand firm" (Exodus 14:13) and "be still" (Exodus 14:14). These are instructions that any commander might have issued in such a situation, but they are also matters of spiritual discipline. They apply throughout the ages and whatever the prevailing conditions. As the army of God in our own day, it follows that we need to practise allowing "perfect love [to drive] out fear" (1 John 4:18), "[taking our] stand against the devil's schemes" (Ephesians 6:11) and "Be[ing] still and know[ing] that [the LORD] is God" (Psalm 46:10).

In all our battles, the central spiritual issue is about trusting God or doubting him. Trust does not mean that there will never be questions or things we do not understand. Moses agonised, "O LORD, why have you brought trouble on this people? Ever since I went to Pharaoh to speak in your name, he has brought trouble upon this people, and you have not rescued your people at all." (Exodus 5:22-23). God allows and to a degree even encourages questioning, but this needs to take place in the right spirit. Instead of turning away from his Maker, "Moses returned to the LORD" (Exodus 5:22), putting his hopes and fears in God's hands. The prophet travelled a hard road, but over the course of many years, frequent failures and constant challenge came to rely on the Almighty in all things.[195] He "persevered because he saw him who is invisible." (Hebrews 11:27).

Judah

Whose meaning is, *praise*

Of whom Jacob prophesied,
"The sceptre will not depart from Judah, nor the ruler's staff from between his feet, until he comes to whom it belongs and the obedience of the nations is his."
(Genesis 49:10).

7. Recognising God

Meaning and allusion.

"You shall not misuse the name of the LORD your God, for the LORD will not hold anyone guiltless who misuses his name." (Exodus 20:17).

It was the sixth year of his reign before the king adopted the name Akhenaten, the change more or less overlapping with the court's move to Akhetaten and the inauguration of that place as a fully-functioning capital. Much thought clearly went into the revised title and the timing of its unveiling. In common with surrounding peoples, Egyptians loved to tinker with the complex layers of meaning to be found in names, words and images. The new moniker gave considerable scope for satisfying puns and cross-references, alliterations and similes, comparisons and allusions. Word plays in surviving texts suggest that at this time Aten was pronounced in a way that was similar to the phrase for "my father" (*iati*), conveniently emphasising not only the inviolate and sacred bond between pharaoh and god but also the relationship that ought to obtain between ruler and subject. The word *akh* (variously translated as 'beneficent one' or 'effective spirit') was similarly laden with symbolism. It brought to mind the duty that all had to observe the ancestor cult, thereby putting the pharaoh (outwardly, at least) on the side of religious orthodoxy, yet extended also to ideas of transfiguration, luminosity and a personal union with the sun god that was enacted anew each dawn. In Egyptian belief, the *akh* was one of five unseen elements of each personality.[196] It was the shining form that the spirit or soul took after the body it inhabited had died and been perfected through the rituals of mummification. Such spirits acted as intercessors between the living and the dead, to which were addressed prayers and petitions, with figures representing those who had passed away being kept in household shrines.

The monarch's new name therefore went beyond merely asserting intimate family relationship and indissoluble communion between him and Aten. It suggested that the king was in some sense united personally with the supreme deity, intimating that the divine radiance which flowed from the sun's orb was also present in the pharaoh and that the king was one of the chief means by which the god was active amongst humankind – perhaps the very embodiment of divine activity, so that to see the potentate in action was to glimpse the god at work. Furthermore, it implied that the earthly ruler spanned the boundary between this world and the realm beyond, making him a go-between through whom mere mortals might enjoy the blessings and bounty of the deity, and raising the occupant of the throne to be a natural, legitimate and indeed the sole channel through which his subjects ought to approach the ultimate source of all created things. Consistent with such grandiose claims, all of these elements appear in the religion that was practised at Akhet-aten. Clearly, the pharaoh's name was not chosen just on a whim or merely because it tripped easily from the lips; it was cleverly and carefully devised as an expression of the theology that was acted out ritually through the religious pageants that were staged in the new city and which was in turn enforced throughout the realm. Yet if this were monotheism, it was of a most curious kind, with Akhenaten, his chief wife and daughters not only praised and uplifted in a way that set them above their subjects but closely associated with and made a medium for access to the supreme god in a fashion that Moses would surely have regarded with utter horror.[197]

Nor did things end with a new designation for the king. After Akhenaten had been on the throne for about nine years, the way in which the names of Aten were written was revised. Those parts of his titles that had previously referred to the deities Ra-Harakhty and Shu were removed[198] so that he was no longer tainted by association with lesser gods. At the same time, the name of the supposed supreme creator began to be enclosed in double-bordered cartouches of a kind that had previously been reserved for pharaohs and their consorts,[199] further underlining the close link between kingship and divinity. To make this connection even more explicit, the sun disc was now shown wearing the protective cobra (uraeus), the most prestigious item of royal and divine regalia. As best can be told, these changes coincided with the point at which words and images which referred to Amun started to be removed or defaced wherever they appeared in temples and tombs or on monuments, with other words and phrases deemed unacceptable also being erased and new forms instituted in their place (although this was not done with complete consistency). Thus, for example, the word for truth (*Ma'at*) began to be spelt out phonetically instead of by using the hieroglyph for the goddess who bore that name. The same was done with the word for mother (*mut*), so avoiding use of a hieroglyph which represented an eponymous vulture goddess. Henceforth the word for god no longer appeared in the plural. The inescapable conclusion is that by this stage at the very latest the king had taken the fateful step of unambiguously recognising Aten as a god without parallel or competitor.[200]

Upward: the Revealer of Mysteries.[201]

There are several means by which we might recognise another, of which a name or title is one. This is especially true of someone whom we do not know personally, but of whom we hear at second or third hand, or of someone whom we know a little but about whom our knowledge is limited or in some degree lacking. Biblical understanding of names is that they are repositories and indicators of reputation, character, honour, fame, glory and authority. It follows that the names by which God is known are of supreme importance as a means of recognition or report, for they tell things about our Maker which we would otherwise have difficulty in discerning fully or at all – in terms of his nature, essence and activity. At given points in Scripture people are pictured discovering something about God that they did not know or truly perceive before and memorialising this by making it a title for the Most High or a description of the place where this aspect of him was encountered. Melchizedek recognised *El Gyon*, "Most High God" (Genesis 14:19-20, GNT); Hagar met *Lahai Roi*, "the Living One Who Sees Me" (Genesis 16:13-14, GNT); Abraham and Isaac experienced the bounty of *Jehovah Jireh*, the one who "will provide the lamb for the burnt offering" (Genesis 22:8); whilst Jacob celebrated *El Elohe Israel*, "God, the God of Israel" or "Mighty is the God of Israel" (Genesis 33:20). On each of these and manifold other occasions were beheld certain qualities of the Creator, particular attributes made manifest in a variety of happenings, though with no suggestion that what was conveyed was more than a limited conception of the totality.

It is therefore altogether wonderful to reflect that, not only does the Lord reveal mysteries relating to the natural world and human behaviour, but he also reveals much of himself,[202] the greatest and most unfathomable mystery of all. It is through this progressive self-revelation that God has begun the process of calling mankind back to him after the intimate knowledge of and fellowship with him that existed in the Garden of Eden was broken by human sin. To Abraham he appeared as *El Shaddai* (God Almighty)[203] when he called on the patriarch to "walk before me and be blameless" (Genesis 17:1), but deeper and fuller was the divine self-disclosure made to Moses on Horeb. As God told the prophet, "I appeared to Abraham, Isaac, and Jacob as God Almighty, but by my name 'The LORD' I did not make myself known to them." (Exodus 6:3, NRSV). Unlike his forebears, what the erstwhile prince of Egypt heard on the mountain was the personal and covenant name of the one who made heaven and earth and all they contain: "God said to Moses, 'I AM WHO I AM. This is what you are to say to the Israelites: I AM has sent me to you.'" (Exodus 3:14). The revelation given to the man who was destined to be "ruler and judge over" (Exodus 2:14) Israel emphasises that the Almighty is Redeemer and covenant Lord of the nation, the one who "will bring you out … free you … redeem you … [and] take you as my own people" (Exodus 6:6-7), but it conveys much more besides. In doing so, it speaks not only of who God is, but of who we are, since we are created "in his own image" (Genesis 1:27).

Consequently, it is well to ponder this name. It comprises three letters of the Hebrew alphabet (one of which is repeated), read right to left in the sequence *Yod heh vav heh*.[204] Together these comprise what is traditionally rendered into English as Jehovah but now more commonly expressed as Yahweh. Each of these letters carries heavy symbolic significance. The first (*yod*) is the only Hebrew letter that does not extend down to the writing line. As such, it belongs to heaven rather than to earth.[205] Its topmost point represents the primary manifestation of something out of nothingness, whilst the remainder depicts the initial impetus of creative will pointing in the direction of our world, that first "Let there be" or "Let us" (Genesis 1:3, 1:6, 1:9, 1:11, 1:14, 1:20, 1:24 and 1:26) which motivated, preceded and animated each of God's creative acts. *Yod* is associated with the masculine, whereas generally the second letter of the divine name (*heh*) denotes the feminine, both in noun and verb forms. It therefore symbolises that which enables the initial creative urge of *yod* to be directed and maintained – taking in, nurturing or sustaining that impulse so as to enable what was contemplated to come into being, in the same way that in nature we see the female giving shape, definition and form to what was initiated by the male through the implanting of seed and subsequent development of the egg.[206] The third letter (*vav*) is an extension of *yod* down to the writing line, denoting further working out of the creative force of *yod* and development of the divine will to action but standing, too, for linkage.[207] It expresses the means by which that initial expression of the divine nature which appears in *yod* and *heh* is brought to its fullest development and becomes manifest. For this to come about, there has to be a giving birth, with what was conceived in *yod* and *heh* being brought forth into the world. That process is represented by the last letter of the name, this final *heh* (feminine, for it is the female who carries what is unborn through its period of gestation and delivers it at the end of the term) denoting the *shekinah* glory of God, the means by which the divine is conveyed into and made present in Creation.[208]

The name speaks, too, of the very essence of God. Though it is nowhere explicitly stated in the Old Testament, implicit in all interaction between the Almighty and his creatures, even from before the moment that the Lord "breathed into [Adam's] nostrils the breath of life" (Genesis 2:7),[209] is that he who "called to [Moses] from within the [burning] bush" (Exodus 3:4) is three in one:

One God: whose oneness and unity is reflected in the first person singular of the name "I AM WHO I AM" (Exodus 3:14), but whose description of himself is nevertheless pregnant with the possibility that three are joined together in this whole (*yod*, *heh* and *heh* forever and indissolubly linked by *vav*);

Father: whose role in Creation and redemption involves planning and directing, alongside the sending of both Son and Holy Spirit – who does not turn his back on man but yearns to gather those of every race, tribe and nation to him as part of his heavenly family and to bless them, saying: "I have seen the deep sorrows of my people in Egypt ... I have come to deliver them from the Egyptians and to take them out of Egypt into a good land, a large land, a land 'flowing with milk and honey' – the land where the Canaanites, Hittites, Amorites, Perizzites, Hivites, and Jebusites live." (Exodus 3:7-8, TLB).[210]

Son: the "Word [who] was with God ... and was God" (John 1:1), who was "in the beginning with God" (John 1:2, NKJV) and "Through [whom] all things were made" (John 1:3) – who takes the form of man so that we may look upon him without dying and yet glimpse God himself, thereby enabling us to follow in the footsteps of Moses, who "went into the Tabernacle to speak with the Lord" (Exodus 34:34, TLB).[211]

Spirit: whose work is seen in men and in the world around: "See, I have chosen Bezalel son of Uri, the son of Hur, of the tribe of Judah, and I have filled him with the Spirit of God" (Exodus 31:2-3).[212]

Thus the very name of God describes essential elements of his nature and pictures the processes by which he works to create and thereafter to direct and order what has been created, these elements and processes together being seen (albeit only partially and imperfectly) in Creation itself. All these things are not just matters of idle theorising or speculation. They have serious implications: in terms of how we are designed to be and thus for how best we should think and act, for relationships with God and between the sexes, for the ordering of family life, for our concept of what it means to be fully human and in every part of our dealings with others. Like the Trinitarian God who made us, we are called and indeed impelled to activity and relationship in three dimensions: upwards towards our Creator, inwards towards our own moral and spiritual development and outwards to face the world. If we fail to give pay proper heed to these basic facts about ourselves, both we and the world around us will be infinitely the poorer.

Inward: being renewed day by day.[213]

Since we are made in God's image, whatever the divine name tells of our Creator must necessarily speak not just about how we should respond and relate to him but also about our own humanity. On Horeb Moses encountered someone who, in his essential self and in the deepest fibre of his being, encompasses aspects that we would term both masculine and feminine. It follows that, in order for mankind in the greatest possible degree to be image bearer of this God, men and women must in some manner be brought together. It was presumably for this reason that "male and female created he them" (Genesis 1:27, KJV) and desired that they should be "united ... [as] one flesh" (Genesis 2:24) in marriage. This does not in the slightest mean that it is wrong to be single, but it does suggest a template to be followed by those who are not.[214] Since God is Trinitarian, the logical conclusion is that the union of man and woman in marriage can only reach its fullest and most beautiful flowering as a means through which to express the divine image when its two human participants are joined by a third, namely the Holy Spirit, and when the bond thereby created is as permanent, faithful and true as that which exists between the three persons of the Trinity. In other words, only in a marriage in which man and woman invite God's active participation and maintain an exclusive union for life can the most sublime conception of matrimony and its ultimate divine purpose be realised.[215]

The aspects of God that are revealed in and through his name sit alongside his plan for mankind and the world. As disclosed and recounted in Scripture, these things are together entirely consistent with all divine activity from the first moments of Creation to the present. Time and again our nature and the dispensations which God had made in relation to mankind are seen to be the logical outgrowth of who God is, of how he acts and of what he has ordained. The words used to describe his making of the universe may appear on their face to be curious, quaint or archaic, but they are in fact of deep significance. After the broad overview of Creation presented in the opening chapter of the Bible, the second chapter of Genesis introduces its more detailed look at the creation of humankind with the phrase: "These are the generations of the heavens and of the earth when they were created, in the day that the LORD God made the earth and the heavens" (Genesis 2:4, KJV). The inverted sequence within this single sentence (heavens followed by earth, then earth by heavens) and change in verb from "create" to "make" are not simply conventional or poetic usage but indicate a deliberate switch from a perspective on creation that is male-oriented to one that is female-oriented. In so doing it underlines that both male and female impulses are at work. The female is present in the "mist" (Genesis 2:6, KJV) or "streams" (Genesis 2:6) which "came up from the earth and watered the whole surface of the ground" (Genesis 2:6) and which became part of man himself.[216] The soul (*neshamah*), placed within the body in Genesis 2:7 when God implanted his own Spirit within Adam, also represents the feminine, both in terms of Hebrew grammar and by virtue of being symbolised by the letter *heh* (see above). All this gives the lie to the fundamental spiritual nature of humanity: that we need male and female equally and that we carry both heaven and earth within us.[217]

The implications of our Maker's name in terms of the respective worth of man and woman feed into how we should approach relationships between the sexes. If male and female are together needed to reflect the divine image in the fullest manner possible, then each can be of no less value than the other. They are equally parts of the same whole, in much the same way as St Paul used the analogy of the human body for the various members of the church: "The eye can never say to the hand, 'I don't need you.' The head can't say to the feet, 'I don't need you.'"(1 Corinthians 12:21, TLB). Indeed, since the covenant name of the Most High has two female elements and only one male, it would be bold indeed to assert that the masculine is of higher import, still less that it is more exalted in the estimation or appreciation of our Creator. This being so, hardly surprising is the revolutionary and shockingly counter-cultural message which Jesus modelled with regard to the treatment of women and God's love for them.[218] In this he did no more than draw out and give an extra twist to what was already implicit in the days of Moses, when distinction by reason of sex was made neither in terms of action, for "men and women alike are to ask their neighbours for articles of silver and gold" (Exodus 11:2); nor in terms of giving to God, for this involved "men and women alike" (Exodus 35:22); nor in terms of heart for God, for the issue was solely a question of who was "willing" (Exodus 35:22, 35:26 and 35:29); nor in terms of service, for "women ... served at the entrance to the Tent" (Exodus 38:8); nor in terms of worship, to which her "sons and daughters" (Exodus 10:9) were similarly called. Indeed, the Law of Moses was unambiguous in ascribing equal value to the lives of men and women: "...if a bull gores a man or woman to death, the bull must be stoned to death, and its meat must not be eaten." (Exodus 21:28; see also 21:29-32). These things may not strike us particularly now, but they were altogether unusual for the time, and remain so in many societies up to the present day.[219]

The tendency of the natural world is to impermanence, decay and atrophy.[220] Without God, lasting and truly worthwhile achievement is impossible, and death our sure and certain end. Even Moses, whose "face was radiant" (Exodus 34:29) after he had been speaking to God, could not retain this first bright shining brilliance, for no sooner had he left the presence of the Lord than "the radiance was fading away." (2 Corinthians 3:13). We are leaky vessels, with the result that we need continual topping-up of the Holy Spirit within us (that is to say, a constant infusion of God's heavenly and holy being into our earthly and imperfect one) in order to ensure that inwardly we are indeed renewed day by day and outwardly are equipped for the tasks God has assigned to us. The key to their proper fulfilment lies ultimately in recognition – of who he is and who we are in relation to him.

Outward: reverence for the name of God.[221]

To recognise God in any meaningful sense ought to bring in its wake reverence for his name, hence the fourth commandment: "You shall not misuse the name of the LORD your God, for the LORD will not hold anyone guiltless who misuses his name." (Exodus 20:7). Recognition does not only mean recalling identity, knowing again or seeing someone for who they are or something for what it is. It also involves acknowledging existence, validity, truth, status and legitimacy. To recognise a state or ruler means giving assent to their position, influence or occupation of territory and all corresponding exercise of power and authority. This may be passive (*de facto* recognition accepts the mere fact of control) or active (*de jure* recognition acknowledges that control has, at least formally, a legitimate basis), but whichever it might be, consequences follow in terms of action. To withhold recognition implies usurpation, that there is mere pretence to a position that is not held by right, whilst to grant *de facto* recognition is a grudging acknowledgement at best. Correspondingly, recognition *de jure* implies legitimacy: that he who is in authority has the legal right to occupy the position he holds, has obtained this by due process and is entitled to such functions and privileges as follow.

In spiritual terms, these are issues of the heart, mind and will; our choice is to reject and oppose God by withholding recognition from him, to recognise him only grudgingly by not giving him what is his rightful due and failing to put his commands into practice, or to accord him full and unconditional recognition by yielding every area of our lives to him and acting accordingly. The decisions we make will affect our dealings with the world around, for "As water reflects a face, so a man's heart reflects the man." (Proverbs 27:19). With that in mind, it is instructive to consider what the attitudes and reactions of some of the people in the Exodus story have to say about our own response.

PHARAOH.

The Egyptian king is the paradigm of those who wilfully reject God, stubbornly refusing to recognise or bow the knee to him despite all evidence. He asked for a miracle, presumably to see what power, if any, stood behind Moses, but even when it was provided he still did not yield: "The LORD said to Moses and Aaron, 'When Pharaoh says to you, "Perform a wonder," then you shall say to Aaron, "Take your staff and throw it down before Pharaoh, and it will become a snake."' So Moses and Aaron went to Pharaoh and did as the LORD had commanded" (Exodus 7:8-10, NRSV).[222] Instead of embracing what was good and true, the monarch's instant recourse was to occult power, summoning "the wise men and sorcerers, and the Egyptian magicians" (Exodus 7:11).

MOSES.

By contrast, Moses embraced God wholeheartedly and willingly. With him there was no failure of recognition. Amongst the greatest of the signs and wonders that God performed before the prophet is one to which we are perhaps least likely to ascribe the name of miracle: the Almighty's revelation of himself, first in the burning bush and then on later occasions atop the same mountain after the Israelites had been delivered from bondage in Egypt. The implications of these appearances were astounding and profound, their impact on Moses so utterly transformational that he was changed outwardly as well as inwardly. His personal walk of faith marked a journey from being God's "servant" (Genesis 18:3) as Abraham had been to becoming a "friend" (Exodus 33:11), prefiguring Jesus' final discourse in which he told his closest followers, "I no longer call you servants ... Instead, I have called you friends..." (John 15:15) and pointing the way to our ultimate "adoption as sons" (Romans 8:32) of a heavenly Father. It was as a son that he went forth to battle, the war that followed the command to "go to Pharaoh to bring my people the Israelites out of Egypt" (Exodus 3:10) pitting a king who claimed descent from the gods of Egypt against a nomad born of an unknown God. The prophet was the main protagonist in what followed, but success did not depend on his efforts alone.

Moses' parents.

"Moses' parents ... were not afraid of the king's edict" (Hebrews 11:23) that "every [Israelite] boy that is born you must throw into the Nile" (Exodus 1:22).[223] This does not mean that they would have felt no degree of apprehension when they first "hid [the child] for three months" (Exodus 2:2) and then set him "among the reeds along the bank of the Nile..." (Exodus 2:3), for ignoring a decree which came from the lips of Pharaoh himself would certainly have incurred severe penalties, perhaps even a sentence of death. It would have been only natural to quail in the face of this; their fearlessness did not involve complete absence of trepidation, but determination to do right no matter what the consequences. Neither did their care for the boy end when he was placed in the "papyrus basket" (Exodus 2:3), for "Pharaoh's daughter said to [Moses' mother], 'Take this child and nurse it for me, and I will give you your wages.' So the woman took the child and nursed it." (Exodus 2:9, NRSV). We may surmise that she took every opportunity whilst the child was in her charge to impart to him knowledge of his origins and of his God.

Aaron.

Moses evidently came from a godly family. His elder brother Aaron was capable not only of hearing powerfully from God, but was prepared to obey the Lord's instructions promptly and to the letter. It could not have been straightforward or without risk for a slave to leave Egypt, but when "The LORD said to Aaron, 'Go into the desert to meet Moses...' he met Moses at the mountain of God" (Exodus 4:27). This required tremendous faith, courage and resourcefulness, each of which is evident in other aspects of Aaron's conduct. Although Scripture says that "Moses and Aaron brought together all the elders of the Israelites" (Exodus 4:29), presumably it was Aaron who was the prime mover in this since Moses had been so long abroad that many would not have known him personally. There may even have been suspicion of the returning prophet by reason of his long absence, Egyptian associations and sudden return. It would be reasonable to suppose from the fact that obstacles of this kind were overcome without too much difficulty that Aaron had both a fair degree of standing and was of good repute within the community. As a Levite, he would almost certainly have had a role in the religious life of the nation, and he was a sufficiently self-assured and persuasive speaker for God to make him Moses' mouthpiece (Exodus 7:1-2). In keeping with this, it was he who "told [the elders] everything the LORD had said to Moses [and who] also performed the [three] signs [which

God had provided on Horeb] before the people" (Exodus 4:30). Later, Aaron was alongside the prophet as together they confronted Pharaoh.[224]

All this made doubly disappointing the weakness, compromise and cowardice that Aaron displayed during the incident of the Golden Calf, when the people "gathered round [him]" (Exodus 32:1) in a way that no doubt was intimidating and menacing. Yet though there was probably some degree of threat or compulsion, he was not merely a passive observer but an active participant, for "[Aaron] took what [the people] handed him and made it into an idol cast in the shape of a calf, fashioning it with a tool." (Exodus 32:4). In fairness, Aaron may have sought to direct this eruption of paganism in ways that were less harmful, but if so his attempts were sorely misguided: "When Aaron saw this, he built an altar in front of the calf and announced, 'Tomorrow there will be a festival to the LORD.'" (Exodus 32:5). Having allowed the people to "get out of control and so become a laughing stock to their enemies" (Exodus 32:25), Aaron could not even bring himself to acknowledge responsibility when Moses demanded an explanation (Exodus 32:21). Instead, he offered the feeblest of excuses: "'Do not be angry, my lord,' Aaron answered, 'You know how prone these people are to evil. They said to me, 'Make us gods who will go before us. As for this fellow Moses who has brought us up out of Egypt, we don't know what has happened to him.' So I told them, 'Whoever has any gold jewellery, take it off.' Then they gave me the gold, and I threw it into the fire, and out came this calf!'" (Exodus 32:22-24). It would be laughable but for our own tendency to do likewise all too often.

MIRIAM.

A similar mixture of vice and virtue, strength and weakness, loyalty and unfaithfulness, standing firm on the Word of God one moment whilst trimming and temporising the next can be seen in Moses' sister, "Miriam the prophetess" (Exodus 15:20). Despite serious character flaws which led her in later life "to talk against Moses" (Numbers 12:1) and be made "leprous, like snow" (Numbers 12:10) for seven days as a punishment, in other ways she was an archetype of all that a prophetess should be:

Keeping still and waiting: When her baby brother was cast upon the Nile, she "stood some distance away" (Exodus 2:4, GNT).

Watching: All the while, she was alert "to see what would happen" (Exodus 2:4).

Speaking out as the moment required: As soon as opportunity presented itself, "the baby's sister approached the princess and asked her…" (Exodus 2:7, TLB).

Taking action in response to events: She did not leave things to chance but "the girl went [herself] and brought the baby's own mother" (Exodus 2:8, GNT).

Celebrating and worshipping in song: Responding in joy to God's activity, "Miriam ... took a tambourine in her hand" (Exodus 15:20).

Giving a lead to others: She inspired her companions to do likewise as "all the women followed her" (Exodus 15:20).

Praising and declaring the word and works of God: In words that echoed the name, power and majesty of God, "Miriam sang to them: 'Sing to the LORD, for he is highly exalted.'" (Exodus 15:21).

Announcing what God had done, was doing and would do: Reflecting the prophet's charge to tell forth and explain the activity of God as well as foretell, she recounted that "The horse and its rider he has hurled into the sea." (Exodus 15:21).

Like Aaron, Miriam is a reminder of how close we all stand to backsliding and sin, no matter how great may be our past service, nor how abundant our spiritual gifts.

JETHRO AND ZIPPORAH.

Most probably, Moses' wife and father-in-law were pagans. That Jethro said, "Now I know that the LORD is greater than all other gods," (Exodus 18:10) indicates that previously there was doubt in his mind as to whether this was so. Indeed, it could be that for him the God of Abraham, Isaac and Jacob remained just one deity amongst many, albeit more powerful than the rest.[225] Nevertheless, "Jethro was delighted to hear about all the good things the LORD had done for Israel in rescuing them from the hand of the Egyptians" (Exodus 18:9), and when he "brought a burnt offering and other sacrifices to God ... Aaron came with all the elders of Israel to eat bread with [him] in the presence of God." (Exodus 18:12). This was extraordinary indeed since, whatever his background or spiritual standing may have been, the Almighty allowed Jethro to come into his presence. The meal that was shared clearly went beyond such customary hospitality as would have been due to him by virtue of his being related to Israel's leader. It might therefore seem curious that in due course "Moses sent his father-in-law on his way, and Jethro returned to his own country" (Exodus 18:27), for it would be natural that one who had been in the presence of God would wish to go with the Israelites on their journey to the Promised Land. The sparse narrative makes it impossible to know for sure what motivated this departure. As "priest of Midian" (Exodus 2:16, NRSV) it is conceivable that Jethro remained wedded to paganism despite all he had heard and seen. Alternatively, though deeply touched and changed by what he had experienced, duty may have driven him to return whence he came.

Whatever the case may have been, Zipporah was in a position that at times must have been difficult and uncomfortable. She was the victim of racism and jealousy, for "Miriam and Aaron began to talk against Moses because of his Cushite wife" (Numbers 12:1). The fact that "Moses had sent away his wife Zipporah" (Exodus 18:2) does not necessarily imply strains between her and her husband, since "Jethro received her and her two sons" (Exodus 18:2-3), who almost certainly would have been kept with their father had there been separation or divorce. She may have been sent away for protection, more probably so that she could see her blood relations,[226] yet the fact remains that she would have had cause to smile ruefully when the Israelites were told, "Do not ill-treat an alien or oppress him, for you were aliens in Egypt." (Exodus 22:21).[227] Despite everything, however, adverse circumstances do not seem to have held her back and she was by no means a passive or background figure. Though it is conjecture, the visit to Jethro may have been akin to a diplomatic mission aimed at smoothing Israel's passage through Midianite territory. She had shown herself to be quick-thinking, resourceful and outspoken, for shortly after "Moses took his wife and sons, put them on a donkey and started back to Egypt" (Exodus 4:20) she was responsible for saving her husband's life:[228] "On the way, at a place where they spent the night, the LORD met him and tried to kill him. But Zipporah took a flint and cut off her son's foreskin, and touched Moses' feet with it, and said, 'Truly you are a bridegroom of blood to me!' So he let him alone." (Exodus 4:24-26, NRSV).[229] Without Zipporah's prompt action, the mission to deliver Israel from bondage in Egypt might have been stopped in its tracks.

THE ELDERS OF ISRAEL.

The elders played a key role in the life of the community and were the prime channel through which Moses communicated with the people. Hence "Moses went back and summoned the elders of the people and set before them all the words the LORD had commanded him to speak [following which] The people all responded together" (Exodus 19:7-8). At the start of Moses' mission, approbation and assent of the elders was vital, so "Aaron told them everything the LORD had said to Moses" (Exodus 4:30). It was presumably only once the elders had been won over and given permission that Aaron "performed the signs before the people" (Exodus 4:30), as a result of which these too "believed" and "worshipped" (Exodus 4:31). Moreover, elders accompanied Moses and Aaron to see Pharaoh, for God had said that "you and the elders are to go to the king of Egypt" (Exodus 3:18),[230] doubtless to show that Moses was not acting alone but had the backing of the whole community. Elders seem to have responded promptly to Moses' requirements regarding selection of animals for the Passover sacrifice (Exodus 12:21) and some of them were specifically called to witness the Lord's miraculous provision of water at Meribah (Exodus 17:5 and 6). Against this background of faithful service elders first ate "in the presence of God" (Exodus 18:12) and later experienced his presence in even greater fullness (Exodus 24:1 and 9-11). At a critical point, however, they were guilty of catastrophic failure of leadership, for they did nothing to prevent the Israelites' worship of the Golden Calf despite being told to "Wait here for us until we [Moses and Joshua] come back to you. Aaron and Hur are with you, and anyone involved in a dispute can go to them." (Exodus 24:14).

THE ISRAELITES.

During their sojourn in Egypt the Israelites were "fruitful" (Exodus 1:6) and "became exceedingly numerous" (Exodus 1:7), as a direct consequence of which they were "oppressed" (Exodus 1:12). It is impossible not to sympathise with the fact that after Pharaoh increased their work quotas "they did not listen to [Moses] because of their discouragement and cruel bondage" (Exodus 6:9). Likewise, we can readily picture ourselves reacting as they did in the face of Pharaoh's approaching chariots, when they were "terrified and cried out to the LORD" (Exodus 14:10). In other ways, however, their response is less easy to excuse. They would pledge fealty and obedience one minute but renege on their promises at the first sign of difficulty or discomfort, "corrupt" (Exodus 32:7) and "quick to turn away" (Exodus 32:8). Seeing "the great power the LORD displayed against the Egyptians, the people feared [him] and put their trust in him" (Exodus 14:31), yet only a short while later they showed themselves to be fractious, quarrelsome, ungrateful and cowardly: "…the Israelites quarrelled and … tested the LORD saying, 'Is the LORD among us or not?'" (Exodus 17:7), they repeatedly "grumbled" (Exodus 15:24, 16:2 and 17:3), they complained about God's miraculous provision of food, saying, "…we have lost our appetite; we never see anything but this manna!" (Numbers 11:6) and they begged Moses, "…do not have God speak with us" (Exodus 20:19). In short, they were just like us.

Conclusion.

All this sets us a challenge: to move beyond the stubborn rejection of Pharaoh and the half-hearted backsliding of the Israelites to embrace God wholeheartedly and willingly, as Moses did. The issue is one of recognition, which in turn goes hand in hand with relationship; the closer a relationship, the more ready and complete our recognition of the one to whom we are bonded. To recognise God for who he is – King of kings and Lord of lords – cannot fail both to spark praise of him and to cause a change in the direction of our lives. For the fact that "The sceptre will not depart from Judah, nor the ruler's staff from between his feet, until he comes to whom it belongs and the obedience of the nations is his" (Genesis 49:10) is not something that belongs only to the abstract. It ought to affect the way we live and our behaviour towards others. The simple truth is this: only in recognising God can we fully and properly recognise ourselves, and being honest about what we are is an essential first step down the path of becoming what our Maker always intended us to be.

Dan

Whose meaning is, *he has vindicated*

Of whom Jacob prophesied,
"Dan will provide justice for his people as one of the tribes of Israel."
(Genesis 49:16).

8. Obeying God

Law and ethics.

"Now if you obey me fully and keep my covenant, then out of all nations you will be my treasured possession." (Exodus 19:5).

Examples abound of new ideologies bringing in their wake novel ideas about morality and revolution in the norms of their host society; Christianity, Islam, Soviet communism and any number of others have each had profound impact on the cultures which adopted them. For its part, Akhenaten's rule has left few clues on this score. That is hardly to be wondered at, for the pharaoh reigned a mere seventeen years or so, scarce the blink of an eye when set against the thousands of years of ancient Egyptian history that preceded and followed. Nevertheless, hints of how the monarch might have related to his immediate family and to his subjects offer an oblique slant on the ethics he espoused and how these affected the society around him. This involves reading between the lines to some degree, but actions both public and private enable at least broad outlines to be discerned, deriving from the ruler's dealings with the world at large and with those closest to him – his chief wife Nefertiti, his several daughters[231] and putative son or sons[232] – as shown by the way in which and extent to which he permitted each of these to be represented in the art and proclamations of the day. Naturally, neither government edict nor media portrayal necessarily speaks unalloyed truth about the inner life, but that does not render them wholly valueless in terms of overall perspective. For all their obvious shortcomings they indicate the direction of official thinking and thereby shine light on underlying beliefs and motivations, the more so when comparison with other monarchs is made.

The partial unveiling of royal family relationships during the Amarna period was by any measure a radical departure from what had gone before. It is not entirely unprecedented that there should be scenes of Akhenaten and Nefertiti throwing dust on their heads and weeping in mourning for the death in childbirth of their daughter Meketaten. Other pharaohs had been and were in the future to be shown similarly. Yet depiction of the king in scenes of domestic intimacy and the use of much less formal postures than Egyptian art had countenanced up to this time were each new. On its face they might seem surprising for one who in other ways took pains to distance himself from the common run of humanity and who appears to have been just as eager to preserve the dignity, splendour and power of the crown as any monarch before or since.[233] What some have supposed by this to have been a personalisation of the ruler and his nearest blood relatives might cause us to imagine that an equally novel way of approaching relationships lay behind it. It prompted American Egyptologist James Henry Breasted (1865-1935) for one to call the instigator of these changes "the first individual in history". Yet humanised, normalised and made accessible as he might appear to modern eyes by virtue of these depictions, we have to concede that they were essentially propaganda. When set alongside his predecessors Akhenaten does not appear any less the despot. Nothing indicates that he behaved in a way that was less autocratic, nor that he lessened the stultifying court etiquette, nor that he indulged in paeans to his own majesty that were any less fulsome than those of his forebears. There is no evidence that he held a more elevated view of the dignity of his fellow men than those who had sat before him on the Throne of Horus, for he showed no reticence in ordering thousands to labour on the construction of Akhet-aten, and then in commanding that myriads more leave their homes to dwell in the new city.[234]

In another important respect, too, there seems little discernible difference between the morality to which Akhenaten's religion gave rise and that which flowed from traditional Egyptian beliefs. Seen through the prism of Judaeo-Christian values, we expect that faithfulness to a single deity should be mirrored by fidelity to one wife. Indeed, God says as much, for through his prophets he has time and again drawn an analogy between the bond that unites him to his people and that by which husband and wife cleave together.[235] Yet such a view never seems to have occurred to Akhenaten. For sure, Nefertiti was given great prominence. Throughout her husband's reign she was honoured as the king's principal wife, playing an important role on official monuments and featuring on inscriptions in a way that is consistent with her being the sovereign's trusted confidante[236] – but this did not stop the king keeping an extensive harem, its superintendent Huya being honoured with a suitably grand tomb in the hills surrounding Akhet-aten.[237] So if this were revolution it appears to have been largely public rather than private in its most obvious manifestations. Though the pharaoh eventually took his beliefs to their logical conclusion by closing temples to gods other than Aten, the overall content and structure of Egyptian law and the institutions which administered it were apparently left almost wholly untouched.

From whence the law?

In name, at least, pharaohs stood at the head of the legal system, promulgating legislation by decree, upholding justice, and maintaining law and order – that proper state of affairs which was part and parcel of what fell within the central concept of *Ma'at*.[238] In a very real sense the overarching idea of equity which this set of principles conveyed meant that Egypt's legal framework was underpinned by notions of law as objective truth instead of mere human invention. Had inhabitants of the Two Lands been minded to theorise about law, they would perhaps have described it as an attempt to replicate a standard that was mirrored in the natural order, enforcement of which was amongst the prime duties of a good king. By and large, philosophical treatment of such matters does not seem to have been their way, however. Though no legal codes from ancient Egypt survive, court documents show an essentially common-sense and pragmatic approach to both civil and criminal cases, emphasising *ad hoc* solutions to a given series of legal problems rather than strict adherence to any neat set of principles, minutely drafted statutes or intricate body of case law. Though there might sometimes be reference to precepts drawn from wisdom literature (*Sebayt*), and there was considerable emphasis on tradition and rhetorical skill, these sat alongside more everyday concerns, foremost amongst which were a recognition of the need for impartiality and the importance of social justice, for *Ma'at* required that personal gain should be set aside in pursuit of fairness and that the rich should help those who were less well off rather than exploit them.

Though often honoured as much in the breach as in the observance, these are things common to most justice systems, and were stated explicitly in the Law of Moses: "Do not deny justice to a poor person when he appears in court. Do not make false accusations, and do not put an innocent person to death, for I will condemn anyone who does such an evil thing. Do not accept a bribe, for a bribe makes people blind to what is right and ruins the cause of those who are innocent." (Exodus 23:6-8, GNT). This much Hebrew theory and practice shared with others. To begin to plumb the deeper recesses of a belief system and to understand its practical expression, however, we need to delve beyond commonality to particularity, for likenesses lie on the surface and uniqueness in the depths.[239] Amongst the things that are most striking about the legal code that was handed down "In the third month after the Israelites left Egypt" (Exodus 19:1) is a continual tension and balance, reflecting the delicate equilibrium between justice and mercy, ruler and subject, right and obligation. In this it has an orientation that makes it quite distinct from all contemporary equivalents, with twists that are often unexpected. It is no great surprise to find injunctions of the following kind: "Do not spread false reports. Do not help a wicked man by being a malicious witness. Do not follow the crowd in doing wrong." (Exodus 23:1-2).[240] It is perhaps less commonplace but not entirely out of kilter with comparable collections of rules to find the warning, "When you give testimony in a lawsuit, do not pervert justice by siding with the crowd" (Exodus 23:2), but it is altogether unusual to be told, "…do not show favouritism to a poor man in his lawsuit" (Exodus 23:3). By this the Almighty highlights that there is every bit as much danger of unfairness in erring excessively on the side of those seemingly disadvantaged as in preferring any with wealth and status. That such a command should have been given to Israel from the very first, when the need for it might not have been at all apparent, stresses the universality of what was being put in place. It is a principle to which our present society would do well to pay heed.

Such things are more than simply differences in emphasis. They point up a complete variance in the fount, foundations and moral force of those laws which were to govern Israel and those which had been instituted by every other society up to the point when "The LORD said to Moses, 'Come up to me on the mountain and stay here, and I will give you tablets of stone, with the laws and commands I have written for their instruction.'" (Exodus 24:12). When traced back to its ultimate inception, the source of each and every Israelite law was God himself, who told Moses, "These are the laws you are to set before them" (Exodus 21:1). Though surrounding nations might make extravagant claims both for themselves and their jurisprudence in terms of divine guidance and heavenly inspiration,[241] these proceeded from a wholly different theological standpoint. Whatever assertions they might make, in the final analysis the peoples of the ancient Near East were governed by the will of their rulers, upon which there was almost nothing in the way of effective restraint and whose whims were subject to neither check nor balance. By contrast, what was revealed to Moses was not merely a convenient collection of rules and regulations which happened to be useful in terms of ordering and regulating Israelite society at this particular stage in that people's move to statehood. They were instead laws divinely instituted, which sprang logically from and were a necessary outgrowth of the personality, attributes and activity of the Almighty himself, and to which all were subject regardless of rank.[242] More than that, they were inexorable consequences and flowerings of God's saving work, because a people delivered from bondage were to live according to new rules.

It was presumably at least in part for these twin reasons that the Lord presaged his giving of the Ten Commandments by a declaration of who he is and of what he had so recently done amongst and for Israel, saying: "I am the LORD your God, who brought you out of Egypt, out of the land of slavery" (Exodus 20:2) – since from these two elements (the innermost nature of our Creator and the ways in which he makes himself manifest in the world) flowed all the precepts which followed.[243] The being, creative acts, character, power, divine plan for the rescue of mankind and saving deeds of the God of Abraham, Isaac and Jacob compelled then and continue to compel certain things in terms of law and the administration of justice:

One God, Creator of the universe: There is a single person at whose behest all things were made and consequently there is a unity at the heart of Creation, not competing realities or parallel notions that are each somehow equally valid even though conflicting. It follows that there is an objective standard of truth and right conduct, set by and derived from the "Judge of all the earth" (Genesis 18:25) himself. This is why "You shall have no other gods before me" (Exodus 20:3) and "shall not make for yourself an idol" (Exodus 20:4) – not so much because they offend the dignity of our Maker (though that is crime enough) but since they go against the essential order of the universe and open us to influences that can bring nothing but ill.

A heavenly King: The Almighty is the "only Ruler, the King of kings and Lord of lords" (1 Timothy 6:15). As such, he deserves honour, praise and glory beyond anything accorded to an earthly monarch. At the barest minimum, this requires that "You shall not misuse the name of the LORD your God" (Exodus 20:7). It also means that, since dominion ultimately rests with the High King of heaven and him alone, no mere mortal should usurp his position; the model for governance of creatures which he made in his own image is therefore not autocracy (which involves elevating one above the rest and can itself be a form of idolatry) but recognition of the unique worth, essential dignity and inestimable value of every single individual, each of them formed in the likeness of their Creator.[244]

A God of order, not of chaos: Things have been put in place in ways that are ordered, and to ensure that they remain so they operate according to seasons and are subject to laws – the natural laws which govern inanimate things and those no less compelling constraints which apply to beings that are capable of thought and action. Hence our need to "Remember the Sabbath day by keeping it holy" (Exodus 20:8), for this day of rest is vital to our spiritual and physical wellbeing, being part of the rhythm in which we were designed to move.[245]

A heavenly Father who wishes to welcome us into his family: It is no mere happenstance that the pivot of the Ten Commandments, linking those that govern man's relationship with God with those that concern relations amongst men, is the injunction that relates to parenthood. Indeed, so central to a good, wholesome and fulfilling life is all that is encompassed within "[honouring] your father and mother" (Exodus 20:12) and the reciprocal obligations that parents bear towards their children by virtue of having positions of trust and oversight, that alone of the Ten Commandments it contains an explicit promise of blessing: "so that you may live long in the land the LORD your God is giving you." (Exodus 20:12).[246] Giving due weight to this commandment necessarily entails seeking to nurture healthy families forged in loving bonds between parents and offspring, recognising these ties as the fundamental building block of society.[247]

A God of compassion, justice and mercy: He is the One who proclaims himself "the compassionate and gracious God, slow to anger, abounding in love and faithfulness, maintaining his love to thousands, and forgiving wickedness, rebellion and sin" (Exodus 34:6-7) yet at the same time "does not leave the guilty unpunished" (Exodus 34:7). It follows that to the greatest extent we are able we should strive to make place within our legal systems for mercy alongside justice, forgiveness alongside retribution and compassion alongside punishment. Balance, however, is fundamental; if one element predominates at the expense of the other, sooner or later things will go awry.

A God of love: Though Scripture repeatedly emphasises that "God is love" (1 John 4:8) and that love is the uppermost motivation of all his actions towards mankind, the first explicit mentions of the Almighty feeling this emotion towards men appears only in the second book of the Bible: by his own description the Lord shows "love to a thousand generations of those who love [him]" (Exodus 20:6) and "[abounds] in love and faithfulness, maintaining love to thousands" (Exodus 34:6-7). We do not just have to rely on his word for it, however, since his deeds make clear the lengths to which he is prepared to go on behalf of rescuing fallen mankind. In the aftermath of Israel's crossing of the Red Sea, Moses saw that "in unfailing love [God] will lead the people [he has] redeemed" (Exodus 15:3). Murder, adultery, theft, lying and all kinds of covetousness are therefore all condemned (Exodus 20:13-17), because these are not acts of love towards our fellows, but the very opposite.

A God of Grace: The outrageousness of the undeserved favour which the Lord lavishes on his people should never cease to strike us. Despite all our sins, blasphemies and betrayals, in the face of all denial of him and turning from the path he has set for mankind, yet still the One who could crush us in an instant is prepared to withhold the judgment that is our due if only we will again reach out to him in sorrow and repentance for what we have done wrong. So it was that as "Moses sought the favour of the LORD his God ... Then the LORD relented and did not bring on his people the disaster he had threatened." (Exodus 32:11 and 14). This same Grace impels us to look beyond technicalities or mechanisms of law to those principles which ought to animate and inspire it: that love of God and man which Jesus identified as the things on which "hang all the Law and the prophets" (Matthew 22:40, KJV).

A God of faithfulness: Time and again the Lord has shown and continues to show that he can be trusted implicitly and that, once he has given his word, he will do as he has said.[248] Hence, when "God heard [the Israelites'] groaning ... he remembered his covenant with Abraham, with Isaac and with Jacob. So God looked on the Israelites and was concerned about them." (Exodus 2:23-25). In like manner, our word should be our bond, undertakings (contractual or otherwise) ought to be honoured and responsibilities that arise from day-to-day interactions properly discharged. This requires truthfulness in all dealings, mirrored in injunctions such as, "Do not spread false reports" (Exodus 23:1), "...do not pervert justice" (Exodus 23:2) and "Do not bear false witness" (Exodus 20:16, KJV). At the same time, there is to be a presumption that others act in good faith, with the result that on "the taking of an oath before the LORD that the neighbour did not lay hands on the other person's property ... the owner is to accept this and no restitution is required." (Exodus 22:11). There is more to this than simply codifying provisions to enable the smooth running of society. The deeper purpose of the Law of Moses was not only to create an atmosphere of trust at all levels of society, but also to highlight the underlying ethical standards and right relationships on which it was based.[249]

A God of fruitfulness: From the very first, "God blessed [Adam and Eve] and … said to them, 'Be fruitful and multiply; fill the earth and subdue it'" (Genesis 1:28, NKJV). Israel inherited this blessing, which was so powerful that even harsh persecution and enslavement could not extinguish or diminish it: "Now Joseph and all his brothers and all that generation died, but the Israelites were fruitful and multiplied greatly and became exceedingly numerous, so that the land was filled with them … the more they were oppressed, the more they multiplied and spread" (Exodus 1:6-7 and 12). If we wish to be inheritors of the self-same blessing we must behave accordingly. Blessing flows from submission to God, expressed in full and prompt obedience to his commands, a requirement that is repeatedly emphasised: first to Moses as God said, "I am the LORD. Tell the king of Egypt everything I tell you." (Exodus 6:29, GNT) and "You are to say everything I command you" (Exodus 7:2), then to Israel at large through the admonition, "Be careful to do everything I have said to you." (Exodus 23:13).[250]

A God who distinguishes and separates: A persistent theme that runs throughout the Old Testament Law is that man should not join together things which God designed to be kept separate, nor separate things that God intended to be kept together. In the same way that "the LORD makes a distinction between [his] people and [Pharaoh's] people" (Exodus 8:23), between "the livestock of Israel and that of Egypt" (Exodus 9:4) and "between Egypt and Israel" (Exodus 11:7), so there is a "distinction between clean and unclean" (Leviticus 20:25) and "between the righteous and the wicked, between those who serve God and those who do not." (Malachi 3:18).[251] We ignore such distinctions and meddle with divinely ordained separations at our peril.

A God of righteousness: amongst its many outgrowths, the Lord's righteousness translates not into the raw exercise of power but into his granting of rights to others and his desire to see those rights honoured and justice done, whatever the status, sex or nationality of those seeking equity might be.[252] Behind this we are called to recognise our common humanity, such being the spur to provisions such as, "Do not ill-treat an alien or oppress him, for you were aliens in Egypt," (Exodus 22:21) and "Do not take advantage of a widow or orphan." (Exodus 22:22). The most fundamental and inalienable rights exist by reason of our heritage as creatures made in the divine image but, as set out in Exodus 22:1-15, property is also to be respected.[253] One of the several ways in which Egypt showed her rebellion against the one true God was in her utter disregard for both person and property.[254]

A God of power: The God of Israel is not to be trifled with, for though he grants free will to his creatures his "right hand … [is] majestic in power" (Exodus 15:6) and this same "mighty hand compels" (Exodus 3:19) those who stand against him and seek to thwart his purposes. We cannot pick and choose between those of his requirements that are congenial to us and those we would rather avoid. They form a whole and are to be treated as such.[255]

A God who redeems: The Lord does not seek merely to regulate the doings of men and to mitigate their worst excesses. His aim is altogether more radical: to buy them back from slavery and thereby set them free "to have life, and have it to the full" (John 10:10) with him. The plan which he has put in place to rescue mankind from the consequences of its own sin and rebellion was seen in the Israelites' delivery from bondage in Egypt and the laws that were put in place to set proper bounds for their conduct thereafter,[256] but ultimately and most fully was made plain in the redemption brought by Christ. In like manner, we should set our faces against slavery in all its guises and proclaim in words and deeds our belief in the possibility of redemption and reform in the lives of even the most die-hard recidivists.

Unity of conception and application; recognition of human dignity and worth; correspondence with the natural order; upholding of fatherhood and family; balancing of compassion, justice and mercy; promotion of love, grace, faithfulness and fruitfulness; fostering of judicious distinctions and rightful separations; unleashing of heavenly power and opening the possibility of divine redemption: these things do not exist or apply with the same logical force in legal systems which are not undergirded by belief in the God who is revealed in the Bible. To remove all thought of him and his commands from our law is not only to take away its moral and philosophical underpinnings. It is to leave it at the mercy of expediency and the utilitarian, the whim of a pharaoh or the dictates of a malign spiritual power. That is a course fraught with the greatest of danger, the consequences of which have been seen throughout the ages in societies of every hue.

In whose charge and for what purpose the law?

Two bodies of law are commonly said to have been given on Sinai: the Ten Commandments (Exodus 20:3-17) and the Book of the Covenant (Exodus 21-23), together reflecting the cosmic order that the Almighty had put in place and transposing this to the daily life of those who had been brought out of bondage in Egypt. Israel was to be a new creation people, conforming to God's standards in spheres religious as well as secular through right conduct (righteousness) towards both their Maker and their fellow man.[257] All experience was to be subsumed under the new creation stipulations of the Law, the ultimate thrust of which was not merely to channel human behaviour in ways deemed beneficial or socially acceptable, but to mirror heaven itself and thereby enable people to learn and grow in relationship with God. This is why the Lord spoke of "the laws and commands I have written for [the people's] instruction" (Exodus 24:12) and why men were not to be passive recipients of the Law but to give active assent to it.[258] Moses presaged Israel's promise to obey the Law with "[taking] half of the blood [of sacrificed bulls] and [putting] it in bowls, and [sprinkling] the other half ... on the altar" (Exodus 24:6), the latter symbolising God's forgiveness and acceptance of the offering and the former being used to mark the people by way of confirming their solemn and binding oath.

With this in mind, those entrusted with upholding the Law were to be conscious of a wider goal than mere administration of justice. For his part, Moses was keenly aware of what was at stake when "he took his seat to serve as judge for the people" (Exodus 18:13), and it seems to have been an excess of conscientiousness in carrying out his duties rather than ambition or self-regard which caused him to "sit alone" (Exodus 18:14). Jethro saw at once that "[this] work is too heavy for you; you cannot handle it alone" (Exodus 18:18) and suggested steps to put things on a sounder footing. Whether or not he shared Moses' vision of spurring people to come before the one true God and of empowering them to live the life of faith more fully, his advice was straightforward and practical, so that "Moses listened to his father-in-law and did everything he said." (Exodus 18:24). Thenceforth, the dispensing of justice became a collective enterprise, with work divided between four tiers of tribunal made up of "able men from all over Israel [who served as] judges over the people – thousands, hundreds, fifties, and tens. They were constantly available to administer justice. They brought the hard cases to Moses but judged the smaller matters themselves." (Exodus 18:25-26, TLB). The overall impetus, however, remained the same as it had been when Moses was sole arbiter: to bring human behaviour into line with the will of God.

Then as now, this involved looking beyond any given provision of a legal code to the ethical system which underpinned it, for ultimately a just society cannot be built on jurisprudence, but comes about solely in accordance with the extent of its people's holiness, this in turn being a product of the depth of their relationship with God. Either as a result of his own insights or by virtue of echoing what was evidently on Moses' heart, Jethro therefore struck the right note in counselling, "Teach [the people] the decrees and laws and show them the way to live and the duties they are to perform." (Exodus 18:20). In other words, though charge of the Law was delegated into human hands, it nevertheless remained an essential part of God's dispensation for Israel – not simply a means by which she was to be distinguished and set apart from other nations but as a way of equipping her for the fulfilment of her destiny. As so often, this was a field of endeavour in which man was to cooperate with God, for revelation from the Most High is not unlimited or total. Quite apart from the fact that our minds are incapable of grasping the whole, if the Lord were to show us all in one fell swoop, there would be no further role for us to play. In reflecting on God's Word and commandments and in seeking how best to apply these to the circumstances that confront us, we are brought over time to glimpse more fully the meaning of what has been revealed and in the process to gain a more complete revelation.[259]

The distinction between law that comes from God and that which does not is amply illustrated by what the Israelites had left behind. The edifice of justice in Egypt was every bit as well-organised and smoothly administered as anything Moses put in place, with features that we might recognise today. Local councils of elders (known as *Kenbet* in the New Kingdom, akin to modern magistrates) handled small claims and minor disputes whilst (as in our system) serious cases would be referred to a more elevated and authoritative body: the *Great Kenbet*, presided over by vizier[260] or pharaoh. Generally, plaintiffs and defendants represented themselves, though the state might bring prosecutions. Oral evidence was given on oath, with scribes documenting complaint, testimony and verdict for future reference. Yet alongside these more or less familiar features, torture was used to extract confessions in serious criminal cases, whilst punishment even for minor crimes could range from imposition of a fine to beatings, facial mutilation, or exile, depending on the severity of the offence; murder and tomb robbery were punished by decapitation, drowning, or impaling on a stake, and penalties could also be extended to the criminal's family.[261] What truly marked Egypt out as fundamentally different from anything derived from the Judaeo-Christian tradition, however, was not such harshness (for our own nation imposed brutal sentences until the fairly recent past) but the way in which the occult intruded into every aspect of life. For, as the New Kingdom progressed, oracles came to play a major role in both civil and criminal cases; priests would bring into the court statues of gods, which would be moved back and forth between inscribed pieces of papyrus or shards of broken pottery so as to indicate the deity's decision on those issues that were put to it.[262]

The Lord's attitude towards such things is clear. The Israelites were told, "Do not allow a sorceress to live" (Exodus 22:18),[263] since in everything reliance was to be on God and him alone, with no opening being given to occult powers. Consequently, in Israel sound administration of justice was not merely a technocratic project for settling disputes and enabling wrongdoers to be brought to book. As with all other aspects of her existence, this part of national life was of essentially theological significance. Hence for Moses as judge, to "decide between the parties" (Exodus 18:16) was only possible if he were first "to seek God's will" (Exodus 18:15), and the ultimate value of doing this was to "make [the people] know the statutes of God, and his laws." (Exodus 18:16, KJV).[264] The entire apparatus of the legal system was thus designed to find out, communicate and implement divine decisions. Through these, the Law was to nurture and build a healthy spiritual environment, excluding malign influences and keeping the nation as a whole in alignment with her heavenly King. Where God's will was known in principle, applying it to particular cases could be left to trustworthy subordinates using commonly agreed rules and standards; hence Jethro's advice to "select capable men from all the people – men who fear God and hate dishonest gain – and appoint them as officials ... [to] serve as judges" (Exodus 18:21-22). However, where issues arose which fell outside these parameters and therefore needed to be referred to higher authority, Moses was to "be the people's representative before God and bring their disputes to him." (Exodus 18:19).

To whom the Law?

When reminding his people that "I ... brought you out of Egypt, out of the land of slavery" (Exodus 20:2), the Lord did not speak to them primarily as a corporate entity but as individuals, for the word "you" in this sentence is singular. Thereby were emphasised two central tenets of Judaeo-Christian belief: personal relationship to a God who saves and personal responsibility[265] on the part of each and every human being. We are to "work out [our] salvation in fear and trembling" (Philippians 2:12), and in doing so are called to be God's "fellow-workers" (1 Corinthians 3:9, NKJV) in the process of building his Kingdom. These ideas find their echo in the provisions of Mosaic Law, both through what it says and what it omits. In contrast to the practice in Egypt, there is no hint of punishment being meted out to clan members. On the contrary, bounds were set on unrestrained tribally-based retribution characteristic of the blood feud by requiring that "you are to take life for life, eye for eye, tooth for tooth, hand for hand, foot for foot, burn for burn, wound for wound, bruise for bruise." (Exodus 21:23-25).[266] Notable, too, by its absence was any need for relatives to bear debts incurred by one of their family. Yet the underlying impetus went further than any of these things, singly or collectively. Responsibility was not personal merely in the narrow or negative sense of individual compliance with rules and regulations but in the broadest positive concept of what it means to be a member of God's people, for nobody was to pass up opportunities to do right: "If you come across your enemy's ox or donkey wandering off, be sure to take it back to him. If you see the donkey of someone who hates you fallen down under its load, do not leave it there; be sure to help him with it." (Exodus 23:4-5). The aim was to create an engaged citizenry actively seeking ways to better the world around.

In this as in so much else, there is a balance to be struck between competing considerations for, whilst dealing with us as separate entities in our own right, God neither wishes nor endorses an atomised, uncaring individualism of the kind promoted and pursued in the West in recent years. Instead, individualism is to exist alongside community in such a way that neither predominates or overrides the other but each interact to mutual benefit – an idea which found its most profound and succinct expression in the concept of neighbourliness later expounded by Jesus through the parable of the Good Samaritan (Luke 10:25-37). By focussing on each man, woman and child instead of on Israel as a collective identity, at the same time the Law of Moses showed its essentially democratic and consensual nature. It was not primarily designed as a fixed body of rules imposed from on high, obedience to which was to be compelled by the armed power of the state. It was, rather, to be a prompt and a goad, causing those who pondered it to internalise the values it projected and make them their own. For this reason, the consent of the people was sought: "[Moses] took the Book of the Covenant and read it to the people. They responded, 'We will do everything the LORD has said; we will obey.'" (Exodus 24:7, largely repeating Exodus 24:3).[267] To seal this agreement, "Moses took the blood [of the animals he had sacrificed to the LORD], sprinkled it on the people and said, 'This is the blood of the covenant that the LORD has made with you in accordance with all these words.'" (Exodus 24:8).[268] This was an act of the greatest symbolic and spiritual power, re-enacting as it did the covenant which God had made with Abraham (Genesis 15) and extending the agreement that formerly had been made with one man and then with one family to cover an entire people.

Conclusion.

Obedience and faith go hand in hand for, where there is free will, full and prompt compliance can only come about through trust, acceptance and subordination of self to something greater. At root it was thus always an issue of faith when Israel "[quarrelled] with [God] and ... put the LORD to the test" (Exodus 17:2). The Almighty never compelled Israel to abide by the Law (though he often chided and punished them for failing to do so), instead saying, "I will test them and see whether they will follow my instructions." (Exodus 16:4).[269] In Exodus, failure to obey God fell into three main categories:

Rebellion and outright rejection: "Who is the LORD, that I should obey him and let Israel go? I do not know the LORD and I will not let Israel go" (Exodus 5:1) – the pride of Pharaoh.

Discouragement and enslavement: "…the Israelites did not listen to him [Moses] because of their discouragement and cruel bondage" (Exodus 6:9) – the apathy of victimhood.

Complaining and pessimism: "You are not grumbling against us, but against the LORD" (Exodus 16:8) – the sniping and cynicism of habitual naysayers.

These are traps for us no less than for those of a distant and long-vanished culture. Systems put in place by men to set laws and punish those who break them are an admission of catastrophic failure. The persistent need for such things shows that, contrary to what some have supposed, humankind is not in essence perfectible through its own endeavours. It simply is not the case that, if only we were given the right education and a more congenial environment, all social ills would disappear, for the problem of the human heart would remain. Laws therefore underscore our fallen nature and point up our essential sinfulness, as St Paul described almost two thousand years ago: "I would not have known what sin was except through the law. For I would not have known what coveting really was if the law had not said, 'Do not covet.'" (Romans 7:7). When God told his people, "Be careful to do everything I have said to you" (Exodus 23:13) he was emphasising that to break one commandment is to break the entire Law. One of Jesus' brothers said as much: "…whoever keeps the whole law and yet stumbles at just one point is guilty of breaking all of it." (James 2:10). The real point of the Law, therefore, was to emphasise our need for a sinless Saviour.

For all its pomp and circumstance, sound and fury, the religion of Akhenaten had no saviour to offer. Amongst the many conundrums of this pharaoh's reign is how and why a view of heaven and earth that caused an earthquake in the religious life of the nation should have made for surprisingly little change in the underlying ethical attitudes and behaviour of its chief proponent. It leaves us groping to understand what kind of belief system it was that could change so much externally yet still have so little apparent effect on those things that matter most. The contrast with Moses could hardly be starker. Like the judges who came from the tribe of Dan in a later age, he "[provided] justice for his people" (Genesis 49:16), but much more than that, for the system he oversaw pointed the way to someone of yet greater significance. The ultimate expression and fulfilment of the Law came with Jesus, who died that in the eyes of God we might be vindicated – exonerated of all guilt and set free.

Joseph

Whose meaning is, *may he add*

Of whom Jacob prophesied,
"Joseph is a fruitful vine, a fruitful vine near a spring, whose branches climb over a wall."
(Genesis 49:22).

9. Serving God

Monuments and prestige.

"Didn't we say to you in Egypt, 'Leave us alone; let us serve the Egyptians.'? It would have been better for us to serve the Egyptians than to die in the desert!" (Exodus 14:12).

Monuments to erstwhile greatness litter Egypt. In the desert on the western bank of the Nile, outside what once was the capital of an empire, vast but forlorn, are seated twin statues of Amenhotep III, father of Akhenaten. These so-called Colossi of Memnon[270] rear fifty feet from the surrounding plain, gazing with corroded and pitted faces on naught but emptiness. Behind them was built what is said once to have been one of the most splendid temples in all the land.[271] Centuries have passed since it was washed to nothingness by successive Nile floods, its stones recycled for use elsewhere, its sun-baked bricks ploughed into the soil. Only the giant monoliths remain as mute sentinels, a crumbling testament to the vaulting ambition of him on whom they are modelled. The ruins of his construction projects, lavished with particular care on what was then the most exalted centre of earthly dominion at Thebes, include the royal residence and palace complex that lies just to the south of present-day Medinet Habu.[272] In fitting memory of a ruler whose name became a byword for excess and self-indulgence, its varied amenities incorporated a magnificent lake, banqueting hall, extensive private suites for the king and separate apartments for his chief consort Queen Tiye, quarters for officials, servants and guests, along with a harem that is thought to have catered for over three hundred concubines.

Yet Thebes was not just about the expression and projection of human might. It was a place where the presence of the divine was keenly felt. To the ancient Egyptians the area surrounding its sacred district of Karnak was *Ipet-isut* ("the Most Select of Places"). This was hallowed ground, the focus of worship of the so-called Theban Triad, consisting of Amun, his wife Mut and their son Khons. On the site of an older sanctuary dedicated to these three, Amenhotep III rebuilt and rededicated what was to be Amun's "harem of the south". In doing so, the pharaoh was both proclaiming his own power and prestige and at the same time making explicit for a new generation the strong identification of monarchy with the cult of Egypt's great national deity. The generosity, wealth and piety of the king was celebrated in the creation of a magnificent colonnade of fourteen papyrus columns leading into a court enclosed on three sides by double rows of pillars. Meanwhile, in the Great Hypostyle Hall work started on a third pylon,[273] whilst Montu (the falcon-headed warrior god who was the original deity of Thebes) was not forgotten, for the main place of worship in his temple enclosure was also built at the command of this very same ruler. Clearly, whatever his personal beliefs might have been, the idols of Thebes were of major political importance to this potentate.

The profane uses to which theology might be put and the substantial investment of personal capital which Amenhotep III made in the cult of Amun are each amply illustrated in the Birth Room of the latter's temple at Thebes. Here are scenes which purport to describe the pharaoh's own conception. They advance claims of breathtaking hubris and daring, asserting that Amun assumed the guise of the king's earthly father Thutmose IV so as to impregnate the queen mother, Mutemuia. That this tale made one parent a cuckold and the other a dupe and unwitting adulteress seems to have been of secondary importance compared to the fact that it gave opportunity for proclaiming Amenhotep III the literal son of the supreme god in the Egyptian pantheon. So when the sovereign praised Amun, in reality he lauded himself. By elevating the deity, he cemented royal power. In spurring his people to worship, he made himself its object.[274] Cynical, self-indulgent and blasphemous it may have been, but huge resources in terms of time and money were ploughed into this mechanism for binding state and religion close. Having backed this particular horse so handsomely, the sovereign might ordinarily have been expected to stick with his choice. Yet intriguingly, on the north-west side of the Sacred Lake in this self-same temple enclosure is a huge statue of a scarab beetle dedicated to Aten.

Building to last.

Moses built no edifices in brick and stone. There were no statues made of him in his lifetime. He set no gangs of labourers to work to chisel his mausoleum. His monuments are altogether different and his prestige rests upon achievements that no pharaoh would have countenanced or deemed worthy of regard. The measure of his fruitfulness lies not in palaces or pleasure-gardens, nor in aught which celebrates his own worth. The Pentateuch is no roll-call of man's honour but of God's. It speaks not of Moses as a hero incapable of the slightest error, but as a man with flaws and weaknesses, prone to mistakes as we all are, albeit possessed too of uncommon character and ability. When the great deliverer of Israel "summoned Bezalel and Oholiab and every skilled person to whom the LORD had given ability and who was willing to come and do the work [of building the tabernacle]" (Exodus 36:2), it was for the glory of God, not the aggrandisement of his own house. The aim was to build to last: not "riches … on earth, where moths and rust destroy, and robbers break in and steal. Instead, … riches … in heaven, where moths and rust cannot destroy, and robbers cannot break in and steal." (Matthew 6:19-20, GNT). Such things can only be made with a heart of service, for "[our] heart will always be where [our] riches are." (Matthew 6:21, GNT).

To serve is by definition to put oneself last and others first. It is to act as a servant, to be subservient or subsidiary, to be in the employment of another, to be useful or render service, to supply or satisfy the needs of others, to carry out designated functions, to avail, suffice, supply or perform. Moses set an example of service and called others to serve in their turn, first listing the extravagant artistic gifts that the Lord had made available to his people and then drawing conclusions as to how these were to be used for godly purposes: "So Bezalel, Oholiab and every skilled person to whom the LORD has given skill and ability to know how to carry out all the work of constructing the sanctuary are to do the work just as the LORD commanded." (Exodus 36:1). The people's obedience to this call released a cascade of voluntary contributions as "[the workers] received from Moses all the offerings the Israelites had brought to carry out the work of constructing the sanctuary. And the people continued to bring freewill offerings morning after morning." (Exodus 36:3). In due course this brought about abundant blessing, as service with the right attitude is bound to do, for "God loves a cheerful giver" (2 Corinthians 9:7, NKJV) and says that if we "give ... it will be given to [us]" (Luke 6:38, NRSV).

Building to last means having an eye on the future, looking beyond the passing moment and taking what is valuable from the past without being shackled by it. Such a focus enables the right approach towards three of the fundamental questions of life – issues which confronted Israel in the course of her being brought out of Egypt and her subsequent wanderings, and which no less concern us today: whom do we serve, how do we serve and where (or in what manner) do we serve?

WHOM SHALL WE SERVE?

Time and again, a generation that had been in slavery in Egypt felt the pull of former things. Making an idol of the Golden Calf was a return to worshipping Egyptian gods, but even though expressions of this backward-looking tendency were not always so extreme, still ever-present were ideas and attitudes that caused the Israelites to look behind rather than ahead:

Nostalgia: To remember the past and celebrate what is good in it is important, but not if it means forsaking truth and losing all sense of proportion. When reflecting on their servitude in the land of the pharaohs, the Israelites repeatedly tended to emphasise anything that had been pleasant but forget what had been the opposite: they "[remembered] the fish [they] ate in Egypt at no cost – also the cucumbers, melons, leeks, onions and garlic" (Numbers 11:5), yet somehow overlooked "forced labour" (Exodus 1:11) and "lives [made] bitter with hard labour" (Exodus 1:14), not to mention the pogrom which resulted from Pharaoh's edict that "Every boy that is born you must throw into the Nile" (Exodus 1:22).[275] To go through life wearing rose-tinted spectacles does no-one any good in the long run. Such an approach is a recipe for skewed thinking and the making of poor choices.

Irresponsibility: Although the life of a slave is demeaning and often characterised both by brutal treatment and harsh toil, in some aspects at least it cocoons its victims from the hard decisions of everyday life since, for the slave, all is arranged and instructed. By contrast, free men must take personal responsibility for each and every part of their lives. Those who have not grown up with this expectation find it hard to assume later, hence the people's childish readiness to place everything on Moses' shoulders and then complain when things did not turn out to their liking; the plea to "Speak to us yourself and we will listen [but] do not have God speak to us or we will die" (Exodus 20:19) was prompted by sheer terror in the face of the awesome power of the Almighty, but ultimately was an abrogation of our responsibility to engage personally with the living God.[276] Worthwhile service cannot happen where such an attitude reigns.

Fear: It is by no means unreasonable to feel apprehension about stepping into the unknown or striking out in new directions. Emotions of this kind perform a valuable function in helping keep us alert and mindful of dangers or pitfalls. If they predominate to such an extent that they make us incapable of undertaking anything new or in the slightest demanding, however, they are liable to trap us in circumstances that are either bad in themselves or which belong to a stage of our journey that we must leave behind in order to grow and attain something better. In effect, they then become enemies of God's purposes. It was a monstrous thing for the Israelites to upbraid Moses by crying, "Didn't we say to you in Egypt, 'Leave us alone; let us serve the Egyptians.'? It would have been better for us to serve the Egyptians than to die in the desert!" (Exodus 14:12). Their fear of physical death had utterly blinded them to the eternal spiritual death which Egypt represented, not only preventing their proper service of the one true God but making them yearn to serve those who opposed him. We must beware of falling into the same trap.

Only by combating nostalgia, irresponsibility and fear can we clear our minds to see clearly whom to serve. The antidotes to these things are readily available. Nostalgia cannot long withstand truth: "You are truly my disciples if you live as I tell you to, and you will know the truth, and the truth will set you free." (John 8:31-32, TLB). Irresponsibility must perforce give way before the Almighty's call to service: "So now, go. I am sending you" (Exodus 3:10), whilst "Perfect love drives out fear" (1 John 4:18).[277] In each of these things as in so much else, Israel was to be an example to the world, remaining undeceived by false emotion, untouched by the lure of a life in which "slumber is more sweet than toil"[278] and free of the fond and fretful imaginings of an immature mind.

Just like the Hebrews of old, we are apt to fight shy of the challenges that freedom brings. A large part of every human being yearns at least on occasion for safety and security, even if the price of gaining these is liberty. This can be true as much on a national level as on an individual one. There is a need in arenas both public and private to reclaim an attitude of spiritual adventure and exploration, such being the antithesis of the cramped, crabbed and diminished ways of thought and behaviour that characterise slavery. Whom we serve is at root a choice: between, on the one hand, standing on our own two feet as people fully alive and, on the other, allowing ourselves to be something less than truly and most completely human. It is a question either of being forever tied to a former way of life that in the end can bring nothing but "discouragement and cruel bondage" (Exodus 6:9) or of being set upon a new path that offers both "a future and a hope" (Jeremiah 29:11, NKJV) and "life … to the full" (John 10:10). The alternatives involve competing and contrasting visions of what the goal of a life well lived should be: whether holiness or defilement, service or selfishness, health or disease, fruitfulness or barrenness, fullness to overflowing or scarcity, blessing or curse.[279] One road leads to the "unfailing love" (Exodus 15:13) of our Creator for one he has "redeemed" (Exodus 15:13). The other wends in ways beguiling but ends with "[punishment of] the children for the sins of the fathers to the third and fourth generation of those who hate [God]" (Exodus 20:5). The route we choose and the manner of following it that we adopt are matters of the will, for they concern the moral rather than the intellectual. To address these requires no great cleverness or learning, but they do demand honesty about what we are and what we have done or failed to do.[280] To submit to the purposes of God and serve him is a challenge to the conscience, not the mind; it was Pharaoh's heart (seat of the will and of the emotions in Hebrew thought) that was hard, for he set himself deliberately against the Almighty.

HOW SHALL WE SERVE?

Service is neither a preserve of the elite, nor solely the business of professionals. It requires neither extraordinary spiritual or natural gifts nor great wealth. It is the prerogative and the duty of nobles and princes no less than of commoners, the Kingdom of God being in this respect utterly democratic. The universality of the call to service is explicit in the Old Testament as in the New, encompassing those of each sex and all ages, backgrounds and aptitudes. So it was that, after hearing the Lord's requirements for building of the tabernacle and its furnishings, *"the whole Israelite community* withdrew from Moses' presence, and *everyone who was willing and whose heart moved him* came and brought an offering to the LORD for the work on the Tent of Meeting, for all its service, and for the sacred garments. *All who were willing, men and women alike*, came and brought gold jewellery of all kinds: brooches, earrings, rings and ornaments. *They all* presented their gold as a wave offering to the LORD." (Exodus 35:20-22, emphasis added).[281] As far as contributing to God's work is concerned, the Bible is clear in stating that the only determinant of the ability to serve is willingness; if a heart that is alert to the voice of the Most High prompts action, this is enough. That is not to say that there is no specialisation in or gradation of service, however. We are all made different for a purpose, with the consequence that no two are likely to be called to serve in exactly the same way.

Unsurprisingly in view of the nature of the tasks that were to be carried out following the giving of the Law, there was in the first instance a particularly important part to be played by those to whom God had given talents that were especially fitted to works of artistry, craftsmanship and construction, together with the accompanying ability of enabling others to use, improve or acquire similar skills.[282] There was a hierarchy of service, not in the sense that one was more valuable than another or that contributions from one source were indispensable and others were not, but purely so as to ensure order and the requisite management control over both concept and execution. So, under the guiding hand of God as ultimate author and designer, there emerged:

Architect: Chief amongst all those whom "the LORD [had] chosen [was] Bezalel [whom the Almighty had] ... filled ... with the Spirit of God, with skill, knowledge and ability in all kinds of crafts" (Exodus 35:30-31). His seems to have been the presiding human genius behind the work, albeit that he was ably assisted by many others.

Deputy: His right-hand man was "Oholiab ... [who in similar fashion was given] skill to do all [such] kinds of work as [did] craftsmen, designers, embroiderers ... and weavers ... master craftsmen and designers." (Exodus 35:35).

Artisans: Alongside these two worked "All the skilled workers ... to come and make everything that the LORD commanded" (Exodus 35:10, GNT). These were the labourers and journeymen whose contributions were invaluable, though no doubt less elevated in terms of artistry than those of the two specifically named.

Seamstresses: The weaving of textiles was delegated to "Every skilled woman [who] spun with her hands and brought what she had spun – blue, purple or scarlet yarn or fine linen. And all the women who were willing and had the skill spun the goat hair." (Exodus 35:25-26).

Apprentices: Those who did not already possess the requisite skill or expertise were given instruction to enable them to be useful and profitable contributors to the work, for "[The LORD had] given both [Bezalel] and Oholiab son of Ahimasach, of the tribe of Dan, the ability to teach others." (Exodus 35:34).

Suppliers: The necessary equipment and materials were provided from a variety of sources as "The leaders brought carnelians and other jewels to be set in the ephod and the breastpiece and spices and oil for the lamps, for the anointing oil, and for the sweet-smelling incense. All the people of Israel who wanted to brought their offering to the LORD for the work which he had commanded Moses to do." (Exodus 35:27-29, GNT).

Thus was accomplished a great work of God. It could not have been achieved without involvement on the part of each and every member of the community. We may expect that, were we to mobilise an entire nation in the same way, we would see things as great or greater.

This merits reflection, for it suggests there is much more we could do to help advance the Kingdom of God in our own land and further afield. Whilst we may not readily recognise ourselves as people of ability or consider that we have resources which might be of use in service of the Most High, the slightest familiarity with his Word teaches that all believers have a valuable part to play nevertheless. Lowliness of birth, want of skill or experience and lack of education are seldom the insurmountable barriers we suppose. Rather, Scripture shows that what determines whether time and talents are employed aright is whether their possessor is on fire for God, looks to him and cultivates a heart of service, for the Lord delights to employ offerings and answer prayers in ways more wonderful "than all we ask or imagine" (Ephesians 3:20). It was in exactly this way that he found an unexpected use for "the mirrors of the women who served at the entrance to the Tent of Meeting" (Exodus 38:8), from which were "made the bronze basin and its bronze stand" (Exodus 38:8), and it has been so countless times before and since. Again and again, God has declared that a servant heart is what he seeks and it is this, reflecting his own nature as one "gentle and humble in heart"(Matthew 11:29), which is of prime importance in ensuring effective deployment of our gifts in furtherance of God-given passions. It is indeed almost the overriding determinant of the extent of God's blessing on our work and hence of its success and durability, since examples from every age show that it is not the quantity of God's servants that matters so much as their quality.[283]

From all this we can expect that the Lord will make us fruitful and increase the effect of what we do in proportion to our being:

Volunteers or pressed men: The Egyptians were brought at length to acknowledge the power of God and to bow the knee before Moses as his earthly representative, just as the prophet foretold in his penultimate interview with Pharaoh: "All these officials of yours will come to me, bowing down before me and saying, 'Go, you and all the people who follow you!' After that I will leave." (Exodus 11:8). Yet they did so grudgingly, and only because compelled by the suffering brought by the Ten Plagues. How much better had they done so from the start with willing hearts!

Wholehearted or half-hearted: God desires that we serve him without let or hindrance. It is for this reason that the Israelites were told, "The first offspring of every womb belongs to me, including all the firstborn males of your livestock, whether from herd or flock" (Exodus 34:19) and "Bring the best of the firstfruits of your soil to the house of the LORD your God." (Exodus 23:19, repeated in Exodus 34:26). Offering up the very best of livestock and produce was indicative of the extent of the people's commitment to their heavenly King, no less than it had been in the days of Cain and Abel – an outward sign, but only of real value if matched by inner reality.[284]

Humble and dependent on God: True humility both requires and results from dependence on God. The humble heart of Moses and overweening pride of Pharaoh were evident from the very first moment through their contrasting reactions to the call that God placed on their lives. Moses made himself subordinate when he asked, "Who am I...?" (Exodus 3:11), whilst Pharaoh elevated himself by demanding, "Who is the LORD ...?" (Exodus 5:2). Later, it was the High King of heaven's turn to ask the questions, inquiring of the Egyptian monarch, "How long will you refuse to humble yourself before me?" (Exodus 10:3). The self-same question is directed, as it has been throughout all generations, to each man and every woman.[285]

Broken for the things which move the heart of God: The fact that the Lord is "compassionate" (Exodus 22:27 and 34:6) and that this quality is a defining characteristic of his inmost nature shows itself in his care of, regard for and thoughtfulness towards those who are oppressed, weak or helpless. The Bible does not describe a God who is distant or uninterested in our fate, but who is passionately engaged emotionally in what happens to all humanity. He was "concerned" (Exodus 2:25, 3:7 and 4:31) about the Israelites in their captivity and said that his "anger [would] be aroused" (Exodus 22:24) by mistreatment of widows and orphans. Nor did he just sit on the sidelines wringing his hands about these injustices. Instead he acted "with an outstretched arm and with mighty acts of judgment" (Exodus 5:6), not only to free his people from bondage but thereafter to institute laws for the protection of all who might be disadvantaged: unmarried women (Exodus 22:16-17), foreigners (Exodus 22:21), widows and orphans (Exodus 22:22-24), the needy (Exodus 22:25-27) and the poor (Exodus 23:6). He demands the same compassion and will to action from those who would follow him.

Obedient: True service of God demands obedience to his commands and conformity to his ways. Whilst it has justly been said that there is nothing we can do to make God love us either more or less, obedience does bring both his approbation and blessing, as it did once "The Israelites had done all the work just as the LORD had commanded Moses. Moses [then] inspected the work and saw that they had done it just as the LORD commanded. So Moses blessed them." (Exodus 39:42-43). Obedience also gladdens the heart of God, who told his faithful servant Moses, "...you have found favour with me" (Exodus 33:12) and "I am pleased with you" (Exodus 33:17). It is an act of love towards our Creator to obey him, as Jesus made clear: "If you love me, you will obey what I command." (John 14:15).

Avoid temptations and distractions: Satan tempts to make us fail and places obstacles in our way to discourage and divert. Hence Pharaoh ordered, "Make the work harder for the men so that they keep working and pay no attention to lies." (Exodus 5:9). By contrast, God tests in order to strengthen. Moses told the Israelites: "Do not be afraid. God has come to test you, so that the fear of God will be with you to keep you from sinning." (Exodus 20:20).

Much service is spontaneous, a simple matter of seeing what needs to be done and doing it, as when we might spy an "ox or donkey wandering off … [and] take it back to [its owner]" (Exodus 23:4). This requires neither hierarchy nor organisation, asking only that we keep our eyes and ears open and do what is right. There are other aspects of service, however, which necessitate our joining with others in corporate activity as the gathered people of God. These will naturally vary in complexity and scale, and hence in the degree of structure required, but at all events an appropriate chain of command is to be instituted if such ventures are to achieve their full potential, with godly leadership from those in charge and prayerful discipline on the part of those who follow.[286] The Israelites were "under the leadership of Moses" (Numbers 33:1) and when "Moses … ordered" (Exodus 17:10) or "Moses gave an order" (Exodus 36:6), usually the people obeyed, even if they often did so grudgingly. On occasion, however, proper leadership authority was not recognised and discipline broke down – in the case of the Golden Calf, to such a degree that people started "running wild and … [became] out of control" (Exodus 32:25), resulting in the Levites on God's orders going "back and forth through the camp from one end to the other, each killing his brother and friend and neighbour" (Exodus 32:27) so that "about three thousand of the people died" (Exodus 32:28).

This same episode of wanton disobedience and indiscipline caused God to reply to Moses' plea for clemency, "Whoever has sinned against me I will blot out of my book … [and] when the time comes for me to punish, I will punish them for their sin." (Exodus 32:33-34). In due course, judgment was executed in physical form as the Lord "struck [the survivors of the massacre] with a plague because of what they did with the calf Aaron had made" (Exodus 32:35). These terrible events tend to make our squeamish generation blanch, but we need to look them full in the face because they show how God feels about sin and disobedience. Such visible enactments of spiritual realities (seen in starkest relief on instituting of both Old and New Covenants)[287] took place at least in part for the instruction of succeeding generations, so that we might grasp better what is at stake should we be tempted to follow the same path as those who fell short in years gone by. When the Israelites rebelled against their God-given leader, this was not of mere political or social significance. It was a rejection of the Lord himself. The Bible shows that leadership, obedience, authority and service are interlinked. Their proper exercise and discharge are in fact nothing less than matters of life and death (spiritual, even if not in the modern era necessarily quite so dramatically physical as in the days of Moses) and we should therefore take care that our freedom as believers never veers towards licence, "For God is not a God of disorder but of peace." (1 Corinthians 14:33).

WHERE SHALL WE SERVE?

Bondage, freedom and licence encapsulate the issue of where (from what place or in what manner) we should serve. That in turn involves questions both of our physical location and our state of mind. Whatever she may have wished to do, Israel simply was not in a position to be fully open to the Lord so long as she was in slavery in Egypt. In fact, the implication of God's instruction that Moses should say on his behalf to Pharaoh, "Let my son go, so that he may worship me" (Exodus 4:23)[288] is that her oppression was then so great that she could not truly serve the Almighty at all, for it suggests that it was not possible for Israel to honour God in any meaningful degree whilst she remained under an Egyptian yoke. The Israelites were of course under external constraint in terms of bodily freedom of movement and action, yet probably the greater binding was internal – a mental, moral or spiritual confinement or restraint that had as much to do with their own mentality as with anything imposed from outside. The legacy of generations of enslavement was evident in a tendency to apathy or defeatism, so that after the apparent failure of the first attempts to liberate them, they quickly gave up all hope of rescue. It is impossible not to sympathise with their reaction, since the bitter blow of increased work quotas came on top of four hundred years of being "worked ... ruthlessly" (Exodus 1:13). Be that as it may, the result was that they were oblivious to God's promise to "free you from being slaves ... [and to] redeem you with an outstretched arm and mighty acts of judgment." (Exodus 6:6). Sunk in gloom and unable to imagine how their circumstances could possibly change, "they did not listen to [Moses] because of their discouragement and cruel bondage." (Exodus 6:9).

Clearly, their mental posture as well as their physical circumstances had to change if there were to be any possibility of genuine, deep-rooted transformation. Consequently, leaving Egypt could only ever be the first stage of their journey. To be set free from being "oppressed" (Exodus 1:12) by an outside power was a necessary though not a sufficient condition of their attaining true and complete freedom. Had they merely been delivered from the outward circumstances that accompany slavery, there would in the final analysis have been no delivery worthy of the name. They would then have been akin to someone of the type spoken of by Jesus, whose mind was set free from an evil spirit but whose "final condition is worse than the first" (Luke 11:25, substantially repeated in Matthew 12:45). The point he was making is this: if we do not fill the space which evil has vacated with the things of God, other malign influences will occupy it instead. It follows that Israel was required not merely to flee what was bad and break free of external shackles but actively to embrace what was good and be renewed mentally, morally and spiritually. She had, in short, to make a positive decision to follow her God, not by mere adherence to form or paying lip service to his commands when it happened to be convenient but by serving with every fibre of her being and throughout all aspects of national life. Tragically, although this question appeared to have been settled by the declaration, "We will obey" (Exodus 24:7), there was further backsliding, so that "The LORD's anger burned against Israel and he made them wander in the desert for forty years, until the whole generation of those who had done evil in his sight was gone." (Numbers 32:13).

Despite (or perhaps because of) this, Israel's time in the wilderness provides examples aplenty, both positive and negative, of where and how we should serve. When once the commitment to God and his service has been made, the starting point thereafter is to know when to set out and when to stay put. The Israelites learnt the hard way that unless they did things God's way according to his timing, they were likely to come to grief. They missed the chance to claim the Promised Land immediately after receiving the Law because they "treated [God] with contempt" (Numbers 14:23) by believing the bad report of Canaan and its inhabitants spread by ten of the twelve returning spies instead of relying on the promises made by the Almighty himself. Too late they repented of their waywardness and tried to make amends through their own efforts: "They rose early in the morning and went up to the heights of the hill country, saying, 'Here we are. We will go up to the place that the LORD has promised, for we have sinned.' But Moses said, 'Why do you continue to transgress the command of the LORD? That will not succeed. Do not go up, for the LORD is not with you; do not let yourselves be struck down before your enemies. For the Amalekites and the Canaanites will confront you there, and you shall fall by the sword; because you have turned back from following the LORD, the LORD will not be with you.'" (Numbers 14:40-43, NRSV). So it transpired, just as Moses had foreseen. Thenceforth they were more circumspect, so that "Whenever the cloud was taken up from above the tabernacle, the children of Israel would go onward in all their journeys. But if the cloud was not taken up, then they did not journey till the day that it was taken up. For the cloud of the LORD was above the tabernacle by day, and fire was over it by night, in the sight of all the house of Israel, throughout all their journeys." (Exodus 40:36-38, NKJV).

That in principle we should wait for the Lord's prompting before moving is a truism easy to state, the reality of discerning his will more problematic. It has to be said, however, that we are apt to make heavier weather of this than need be. It simply is not realistic to expect that we should receive direct communication from the Almighty on every day-to-day issue that might confront us, and neither is it desirable, for it would tend to make a mockery of our being free agents. To wait for divine urging at every turn is a recipe for doing nothing, a failure to recognise our responsibility as "fellow workers" (1 Corinthians 3:9, NKJV) and a form of cowardice. This is especially the case since we are in a position no less advantageous than the Israelites as they journeyed from Egypt, for daily guidance is available in Scripture and through the promptings of the Holy Spirit, these forming the modern equivalent of the fiery, cloudy pillar of old. Consequently, our overall direction of travel is clearly marked out and the principles that should govern our service stand as markers and mileposts along the way:

Serve the Lord and him only: Everyone serves something or someone, even if only their own self. We need to reflect honestly on our reaction to the command, "Take off your sandals, for the place where you are standing is holy ground" (Exodus 3:5): do we "[bow] to the ground at once and [worship]" (Exodus 34:8) or say, "I do not know the LORD" (Exodus 5:2)?

The end does not justify the means: Service must accord with God's laws and commands. The twofold recital of the need for Sabbath observance (Exodus 35:2, repeating Exodus 31:13-17; see also Exodus 35:3) was presumably to remind the Israelites that their enthusiasm to push ahead with building the tabernacle should not lead them to overlook this requirement.

Serve wholeheartedly: Nostalgia, irresponsibility and fear need to be tackled head on, and freedom exercised without straying into licence. In this way we allow God to unleash skills, gifts and talents in us, remembering that we do not work to human but heavenly standards. For generations Egypt set the benchmark for achievement, so that Solomon's wisdom was described as being "greater than of all the men of the East, and greater than all the wisdom of Egypt." (1 Kings 4:30). Yet in the face of the power of the Almighty, the magicians of Egypt "could not stand" (Exodus 9:11).

Obey fully and promptly: There are times when the acts of obedience demanded of us might not seem to make sense from a human point of view. It was probably no more immediately apparent to Moses than to us how "a piece of wood" (Exodus 15:27) could help deal with a pressing need for drinkable water after three days' travel in the desert without it. Yet when "He threw [the wood] into the water … the water became sweet." (Exodus 15:27).[289] Service worthy of the name can only spring from obedience to our Maker. Indeed, it is impossible to serve God properly without being obedient to him. God asks his people the same question now as in ages past: "How long will you refuse to keep my commands and instructions?" (Exodus 16:28).

Seek sufficiency rather than excess: The miraculous provision of manna gives a glimpse of the economics of the Kingdom of Heaven: fruitfulness and plenty, so that "Each one gathered as much as he needed" (Exodus 16:18), yet without hoarding, since "No-one is to keep any of it until morning." (Exodus 16:19).[290] The consistent message of Scripture, emphasised by Jesus in his parables of the talents (Matthew 25:14-30) and the rich fool (Luke 12:13-21), is that if we truly want to become rich, we must give away what we have. Then we will be given more. Sharing is better than laying up vast stocks that are of no productive use to anyone, just as serving is better than being served. In the end, selfishness impoverishes us – as individuals and as a society.

Be generous, according to the season: God is generous, not just in his material provision but through "abounding in love and faithfulness, maintaining love to thousands, and forgiving wickedness, rebellion and sin" (Exodus 34:6-7). He desires us to be the same, so that "No-one is to appear before me empty-handed." (Exodus 34:20). This is hardly asking too much, requiring only that we donate from what has already been given to us from the heavenly storehouse: "From what you have, take an offering for the LORD." (Exodus 35:5).[291]

When "Jethro … heard of everything God had done" (Exodus 18:1), he exclaimed, "…now I know that the LORD is greater than all other gods" (Exodus 18:11). If we serve as we ought, the works of the Almighty will be seen and many will come to the same knowledge as Moses' father-in-law.

Building with authority.

We stand under the authority of those whom our heavenly Father has set above us so that together we may give full effect to the commands of the One who made us for his glory and his service, but each and every believer is also invested with spiritual authority. Often we underestimate the extent and power of what God has delegated to us. We fail to recognise the full significance of those gifts of the Holy Spirit which either have been given to us already or are readily available if only we care to ask. That even Moses needed time to realise this is shown by the initial interchanges with his Maker on Horeb: "Then the LORD said to him, 'What is that in your hand?' 'A staff,' he replied." (Exodus 4:2). It was on its face a mundane question and an unremarkable reply, but laden with meaning. The rod in question was most likely a shepherd's crook. If so, it was a symbol of Moses' authority but also pointed to the later "Lamb of God" (John 1:29, KJV) and "great Shepherd of the sheep" (Hebrews 13:20, TLB), Jesus, who ushered in the New Covenant as Moses was God's instrument for bringing in the Old. A shepherd's crook was moreover a royal symbol, used by pharaohs to indicate their role as protector, and it therefore prefigured Christ as both "King of the ages" (Revelation 15:3)[292] and "High Priest" (Hebrews 8:1, TLB). The Almighty explained the authority he had given to Moses and Aaron thus: "See, I have made you like God to Pharaoh, and your brother Aaron will be your prophet. You are to say everything I command you, and your brother Aaron is to tell Pharaoh to let the Israelites go out of his country." (Exodus 7:1-2).[293]

We are not to treat the authority we receive from God as a passive thing. Moses was required not just to carry his staff but to use it to serve. At various points God instructed the prophet to "Throw it on the ground" (Exodus 4:3); to "Reach out your hand and take it" (Exodus 4:4); to raise it "in the presence of Pharaoh and his officials and [strike] the water of the Nile" (Exodus 7:20); and to raise it "and stretch out your hand over the sea to divide the water so that the Israelites can go through the sea on dry ground." (Exodus 14:16; see also Exodus 8:5, 9:21 and 9:33). Moses increasingly learnt to take the initiative: on first setting out on the return journey to Egypt he simply "took the staff of God in his hands" (Exodus 4:20) but by the time Israel battled the Amalekites he "[stood] on top of the hill with the staff of God in [his] hands" (Exodus 17:9), ensuring victory by keeping hands (and staff) lifted to heaven. The fact that we should use to the full the authority that has been delegated to us is shown by God's reaction when Moses cried out for help as Pharaoh's chariots closed on the fleeing Israelites: "Then the LORD said to Moses, 'Why are you crying out to me? Tell the Israelites to move on. Raise your staff and stretch out your hand over the sea to divide the water so that the Israelites can go through the sea on dry ground.'" (Exodus 14:15). Just as the High King of heaven has provided antidotes to nostalgia, irresponsibility and fear, so too has he given means to combat other barriers that we might face in using properly the authority which he has bestowed. Consequently, we have no excuse for inaction.

Conclusion.

In common with monarchs throughout the ages, pharaohs delighted to give extravagantly, as a way of simultaneously increasing their own prestige through displaying sumptuous wealth and of binding others to them. Patronage was zealously practised by the royal family and equally diligently sought by Egyptians and foreigners alike. The so-called Commemorative Scarabs issued by Amenhotep III were a case in point, forming part of a programme of lavish official keepsakes that were dispensed in the second, tenth and eleventh years of that monarch's reign. Of assorted sizes and five basic types, these variously featured bull or lion hunts, building of an artificial lake, and establishment of friendly relations with the Mitanni (sealed by the pharaoh's marriage to a princess of their blood royal)[294] or proclaimed the glory and extent of empire through praising the king's chief wife, Tiye. Distributed to those of influence and status at home and overseas, they served too as amulets, supposedly having magical powers. These beautifully crafted objects came with strings attached, however, for they were given not only in recognition of service past but in expectation of future loyalty and assistance.

God also loves to bestow gifts, albeit from a different motivation than that of earthly potentates. He does not give in order to bribe us or buy compliance. He has no need to boast of his riches or extend his field of influence. He gives for no other reason than that it is in his nature to be generous. Though power, wealth and worldly goods of every description are at his beck and call, these are never the primary focus of his generosity. He yearns instead for us to have things that no money can buy and that are beyond the ability of any man to grant. These treasures are not the inventions of a fevered brain or primitive consciousness, charms and incantations to gull the simple-minded. They are real and measurable, producing wholeness, wellbeing and plenty in the lives of those who accept them. Our response to such munificence ought necessarily to spur service, both from simple gratitude and because this is one of the ways by which we may step into the fullness of what God desires for his people. Christian service is a thing of great power: an expression of divine love for Creation and of man's love for his Maker, a means by which the Kingdom of Heaven may break into our fallen world and a form of worship. It is a means to true fruitfulness, the best and longest-lasting of monuments.

Asher

Whose meaning is, *happy*

Of whom Jacob prophesied,
"Asher's food will be rich; he will provide delicacies fit for a king."
(Genesis 49:20).

10. Remembering God

Pageant, symbolism and continuity.

"Then the LORD said to Moses, 'Write this on a scroll as something to be remembered and make sure that Joshua hears it, because I will completely blot out the memory of Amalek from under heaven.'" (Exodus 17:14).

For all that was new in Akhenaten's religion, there was also much that stayed the same. If (as seems likely) the pharaoh had at least one male offspring, the absence of sons in the art that has survived appears to show that a significant debt was still owed to time-honoured beliefs. Failure to picture princes alongside their sisters probably indicates the continued hold of one of the foundational stories of Egyptian kingship, nationhood and theology. Time out of mind, Egyptians had looked back to a mythical past when the god Osiris had been the beloved and benevolent ruler of the Two Lands. Yet though Osiris was good, his brother Seth was evil. Seth tricked Osiris into lying in a crate, which Seth locked and threw into the Nile. For a long time Isis,[295] sister and wife of Osiris, searched for her missing husband. After many trials she at last found and retrieved the crate, only for Seth to cut Osiris into fourteen pieces and scatter them far and wide. Once more the devoted Isis looked for the dead god-king, found the missing pieces of his body and put them back together, building temples to Osiris wherever one of the body parts was found. With Osiris restored to her, Isis then conceived a son, Horus, who at length confronted Seth and, after a fierce fight, slew him.[296] Every pharaoh was believed to be an incarnation of Horus, and each year the king was crowned anew to symbolise his oneness with this god and revitalise his reign. During these proceedings, a live falcon was selected from the sacred aviary, ceremoniously crowned in the temple's central court and placed in an inner chamber, where it reigned in the dark for a year as a living symbol of Horus, whose graven image was meanwhile taken annually to the roof of the temple to bathe in the rays of the sun.[297]

All this made it uncomfortable to show a living monarch and his likely successor together, for the story of Horus and Osiris suggested that the latter (as Horus incarnate) could only claim his throne through dismemberment and murder of the former (identified with Osiris). Potentially seditious in itself, this also sat awkwardly with the pharaoh's role as upholder of *Ma'at* since such an outcome was hardly calculated to honour, strengthen or preserve the existing (rightful) order, neither to promote unity and harmony in the land. Not surprisingly, Egyptians therefore chose to sidestep these unwelcome facts by devolving various liturgical functions upon the king's female progeny as long as their father reigned.[298] A number of Akhenaten's daughters by Nefertiti were accorded precisely this honour, a circumstance perhaps all the more remarkable in its faithfulness to past convention since reliefs in the rock-hewn tombs of courtiers from Akhet-aten indicate that the myth which made such conduct necessary was gradually being undermined. For it was the pharaoh who increasingly was shown taking over the role of Osiris as provider for the dead throughout the life to come: in several burial-places surrounding the new capital the illustrations of temples and estates that were the supposed sources of provender for those who had departed this world depicted places controlled by none other than the monarch himself.

Remembrance.

Akhenaten undoubtedly presided over what was by any stretch of the imagination a major rupture with the past, though this was not at the expense of all continuity, for the new set-up either adapted what already existed or even in a few cases took ideas or practices over lock, stock and barrel from what had gone before. That is in fact hardly surprising, since the changes the pharaoh made came so swiftly that there was scarce time enough for contemporaries to digest them, let alone to slough off entirely all that belonged to the old ways. In the face of wholesale alteration it would in any event have been quite understandable for people to cling to those familiar practices that were still allowed, which for many no doubt seemed islands of sanity in a stormy sea. Continuity indeed depends on such impulses, as too on a sense of connection to and an understanding of what has been. These in turn require that there be remembrance of bygone times and the giving of due weight to precedent, such often being expressed collectively through tradition, whose rituals, symbolism and ceremonies act as further aids to recall. In human hands these easily grow fossilised and hidebound, becoming then obstacles to the new departures and new growth that God desires.[299] The Creator, who called heaven and earth into being by mere words of command, is still at work and continues to delight in bringing forth what is new, which necessarily means that the old must periodically make way for the latest move of his Spirit.[300]

Yet at the same time the Lord's faithfulness requires that he should remember former things and what he has promised in years gone by, as he did when "he remembered his covenant with Abraham" (Exodus 2:24) and told Moses, "I have remembered my covenant." (Exodus 6:5). In this the High King of heaven shows not just his utter dependability but also the extent to which he is prepared to make himself vulnerable in the face of men and answerable before them.[301] Since he allows us to hold him to his word, we may legitimately call on him to remember what he has said and done in the past, not in the sense that he ever forgets but by way of indicating that there is something we want to bring to the forefront of his mind and of which we wish him to be take especial note. Moses did precisely this when seeking to deflect God's righteous anger against sinful Israel, pleading for him to "Remember your servants Abraham, Isaac and Israel [and] … Remember that this nation is your people" (Exodus 32:13 and 33:13). In this the prophet in fact did no more than follow the lead given by God himself, who in his earliest encounter with Moses on Horeb made clear that Israel had never been out of his mind or sight, that despite appearances his promises to her had not been forgotten for a moment and that these would indeed shortly be fulfilled: "I have watched over you and have seen what has been done to you in Egypt. And I have promised to bring you up out of your misery in Egypt into … a land flowing with milk and honey." (Exodus 3:16-17).[302]

God cannot be faithful without remembering, and neither can we. That our tendency to forget the past readily feeds into faithlessness is shown by the fact that when "a new king, who did not know about Joseph, came to power in Egypt" (Exodus 1:8) oppression of Joseph's descendants and kin followed close behind despite the debt that was owed to their illustrious forebear. We are therefore called to pay heed to former things and in particular to recall five essential things about our Creator:

His nature: when the Lord spoke aloud "the name by which I am to be remembered from generation to generation" (Exodus 3:15) he was not only communicating new insights about himself but at the same time issuing an injunction that these should never be forgotten. The need for us to preserve an accurate memory of God's nature is indeed amongst the reasons for the command, "You shall not misuse the name of the LORD your God, for the LORD will not hold anyone guiltless who misuses his name." (Exodus 20:7).[303]

His deeds: the instruction to "write this on a scroll as something to be remembered" (Exodus 17:14) indicates that we need to keep hold of a proper recollection and appreciation of what God has done as well as of who he is. Since his actions flow inexorably from his nature and his plan for Creation, contemplation of these should form a fundamental part of our growing in understanding of God, the role of mankind and the relationship of the one to the other. It is no mere conventional usage that leads the Almighty to presage the Ten Commandments with a statement of his saving work: "I am the LORD your God, who brought you out of Egypt, out of the land of slavery." (Exodus 20:2). Far from being just a habitual formula, this is a key to unlock the meaning of all the Lord's later interventions in human history.

His provision: By telling Moses to "Take an omer[304] of manna and keep it for the generations to come, so they can see the bread I gave you to eat in the desert when I brought you out of Egypt" (Exodus 16:32) God was doing more than simply making sure that Israel treasured a keepsake to memorialise how he "[rained] down bread from heaven" (Exodus 16:4). Manna was to be a sign of present and future provision, no less than of what had been supplied in a distant past. Beyond this, it was a foretaste of what was to find its ultimate fulfilment in the coming of Jesus, who was born in Bethlehem (meaning, *the place of bread*) and revealed as the "bread of life" (John 6:35 and 6:48) and "the bread that comes down from heaven" (John 6:41 and 6:51).

His laws: The laws of God encompass not just that body of regulations which comprise the Book of the Law and the Ten Commandments, but include the laws that order the universe and govern the innermost workings of humankind. We are told to "Remember the Sabbath day by keeping it holy" (Exodus 20:8)[305] because this is needful for the proper functioning of our species and so as to create space for relationship with our Maker.[306] This command is oft repeated in varying forms, as in the formulation, "Six days do your work, but on the seventh day do not work" (Exodus 23:12). Various reasons are given for the prohibition on Sabbath-day labour: it is to honour God, to protect the powerless and to encourage the pursuit of holiness; hence first and foremost because "the LORD blessed the Sabbath day and made it holy" (Exodus 20:11) but also "so that your ox and your donkey may rest and the slave born in your household, and the alien as well, may be refreshed" (Exodus 23:12) and as "a sign between [God and Israel] for the generations to come, so that you will know that I am the LORD, who makes you holy." (Exodus 31:13).

His motivation: The significance that we ascribe to words and deeds depends greatly on the motivation that we perceive as being behind them. It is therefore of the greatest importance that we view the things of God through the prism of his underlying motivations and do not fall into the trap of looking at these through human eyes. Since it is impossible for the Lord to go against his essential nature, the mainspring of each and every one of his actions is to be found in his fundamental characteristics. These include compassion (Exodus 22:27, 33:19 and 34:6), faithfulness (Exodus 34:6), justice (Exodus 23:2 and 23:6), forbearance (Exodus 34:6) and holiness (Exodus 15:11), but the most compelling of all and the one that comes closest to encapsulating his essence, is love (Exodus 15:13, 20:6, 34:6 and 34:7).[307] It is fatally easy to misunderstand what the Almighty does unless this is recognised. Moses was alive to the problem when trying to dissuade God from punishing Israel after her sin with the Golden Calf: "But Moses sought the favour of the LORD his God. 'O LORD,' he said, 'Why should your anger burn against your people, whom you brought out of Egypt with great power and a mighty hand? Why should the Egyptians say, "It was with evil intent that he brought them out, to kill them in the mountains and to wipe them off the face of the earth"? Turn from your fierce anger; relent and do not bring disaster on your people.'" (Exodus 32:11).

Each of the five acts of remembrance described above is important in itself, but also because such recollection brings consequences in its train.[308] As faithlessness must sooner or later bring about desertion and betrayal, so its opposite will just as surely lead to dependability and steadfastness. The same holds true in all fields of endeavour where proper and respectful remembrance of all that should be honoured and held dear competes with unseemly forgetfulness, for oblivion is not the desirable goal that some would have us believe. It is in its counterpoint of acknowledging the one "who is, and who was, and who is to come" (Revelation 1:4) that truest fulfilment is to be found. In him past, present and future can be kept in their rightful balance, and through him lies the path to integrity: the integration of all aspects of our personality into a congruent whole;[309] cohesion of thought, word and deed so as to do away with contradictions between what we think, say and do; and restored fellowship with our Creator by virtue of Christ's sacrifice removing the barrier which sin creates between us and a holy God. In ways both big and small, our integrity or lack of it will have an effect on how we think and behave, and remembering is an essential ingredient of integrity. If we omit the past from our thinking, a vital element of understanding will be missing and a crucial spur to rightful conduct (righteousness) removed.

Nowhere in the Old Testament was this seen more clearly than in the incident of the Golden Calf, which was almost a paradigm of national forgetfulness. To forget oneself is to behave unbecomingly or lose self-control, and Israel is said to have been "out of control" (Exodus 32:25) as the people "sat down to feast and drink at a wild party, followed by sexual immorality" (Exodus 32:2, TLB), mimicking Egypt's Festival of Drunkenness. These happenings cannot (or at any rate, should not) be dismissed as an irrelevance or a passing moment of madness, for they are an object lesson to our present body politic. At root this behaviour resulted from the most fatal and fundamental forgetfulness of all, since it started with forgetting God's very existence and identity, by ignoring all the things he had done and by confusing him with false gods so that those who with their own eyes had witnessed deliverance at the hand of the Almighty were nevertheless able to say of idols they had crafted themselves, "These are your gods, O Israel, who brought you up out of Egypt" (Exodus 32:4). This extraordinary exercise in self-delusion and wilful blindness was only possible by overlooking what Egypt and its gods were really like and disregarding their utter powerlessness in the face of a God who had declared, "I will bring judgment on all the gods of Egypt." (Exodus 12:12). Moreover, it utterly mischaracterised malign spiritual forces by attributing to them good things that belonged in fact to the one true God.

Lest we should be in any doubt about it, Israel's sin on this occasion shows that negligence, neglect and sin are the end results of failing to remember properly. Yet as well as avoiding negative results, rightful remembrance has a positive impact, too. Looking four-square at what God has done in the past allows us to see that nothing about him is arbitrary, inconsistent or unfair. From this we may draw firm assurance that the grace which he has displayed in bygone ages will continue throughout the present and future, so that there are indeed firm grounds for trust in his promises and hope for what is to come. The complete continuity and consistency of Scripture is but one indicator of God's trustworthiness and firmness of purpose. It shows that there has never for a single moment been a deviation in his plan to redeem mankind and restore a world that has been fatally marred by human wrongdoing. The underlying message of both Old and New Covenants is the same, for Israel had the gospel proclaimed to her under Moses no less than in the days of Christ[310] – the good news of God's personal intervention in the world so as to save, redeem and set free, to be present with his people daily throughout all trials and journeying, and thereby enable them to enjoy rest in "a good and spacious land, a land flowing with milk and honey" (Exodus 3:8).

Recollection is what binds gospel and Law together, remembrance being a goad and spur to abide by God's commandments. To the degree that Israel kept the Law, it was because she remembered the gospel of salvation. Consequently, when she forgot this fundamental truth, disobedience was not far behind. It is for this reason that God's people are so often exhorted to bring former things to mind – from a positive injunction to remember that once they "were aliens in Egypt" (Exodus 22:21) to its mirror image of not forgetting the words and works of God, culminating in Moses' heartfelt cry in what may have been one of his last sermons, "Do not forget!" (Deuteronomy 25:19).[311] This need is as keenly felt by present generations as by Israel of old. It applies not just to individuals but to entire societies. For any nation to retain collective memory, the baton must be passed on: to the people as a whole through reliable teaching and wise counsel and with an even greater measure of solicitude to those who will be their future leaders. This requires deliberation combined with understanding, insight and discernment, likewise alertness to the promptings of God coupled with astute judgment, careful selection and wise planning. Joshua, who once had been the slave Hosea, was a long time in the making as Moses' eventual successor and did not come to this role just by chance.[312] For years beforehand he was the subject of a considerable investment of time by Moses and instruction at the instigation of the Almighty, who told Moses to "…make sure that Joshua hears [the account of the battle against the Amalekites]" (Exodus 17:14) precisely since this was vital for a man whose primary role was to be a war leader.[313]

The importance which the Lord attached to Joshua's learning from the past is a reminder that great benefits can come from reflecting on what has transpired in days of yore, whether the actions and ideas that are the subject of our meditation be our own or those of another. It is in contemplating the wisdom and experiences of our forebears that we may hope to avoid at least some of their worst failures and replicate some of their successes. To see what God has done and what men and women throughout the ages have been capable of enduring, overcoming and transcending is a tremendous source of strength and encouragement, just as the less endearing traits of our species are a warning of pitfalls ahead. Yet human memory is fallible and frail. We need things to help us remember, for our attention is easily diverted and we readily lose our hold on such an intangible thing as memory. Countless studies show that remembrance is more firmly fixed if words are linked to images, even more so if these involve the engagement of all our senses and yet further when the whole takes the form of a dramatisation in which we are actors. We should thus hardly be surprised that our Maker, who knows us better than we know ourselves and who well understood these things long ago, has as a result given aids to recollection, seen in the feasts and festivals, signs and symbols of Testaments both Old and New.

Festivities.

Up to sixty festivals were held each year in Thebes alone. The largest and most important was the Beautiful Feast of the Opet, held in honour of Amun, his wife Mut and son Khonsu, which took place in *Akhet*, season of the Nile flood. With the harvest gathered in and fields under water, there was ample time for making merry; a series of processions and pageants that already extended over the course of eleven days under Hatshepsut lasted for three whole weeks by the time of Ramses II. The attendant rites celebrated fertility and rebirth as land, pharaoh, deity and the universe itself were all renewed; rich silt replenished the soil and made ready for new a new cycle of growth, the sovereign was ritually purified and crowned afresh, whilst Amun and Mut re-enacted their marriage vows and in so doing helped ensure the preservation of *Ma'at* throughout the cosmos.[314] Accompanied by the pharaoh, images of the three gods of the Theban Triad were paraded through joyful crowds from the temple of Amun-Ra at Karnak to that of Amun-Min at *Ipet Resyt* (the "Harem of the South") in Luxor and back again, uniting that deity's incarnations as creator and fertility god.[315] As so often in Egypt, the religious and political were intertwined, for in the process of the various ceremonies something of the power of Amun was thought to invest the royal *ka*. Evident, too, was the co-dependence of royalty and deity: the monarch's sacrificial offerings and performance of rituals such as the Opening of the Mouth set in motion a new cycle of creation and re-ignited the sacred spark within Amun, so that the god received from the king no less than the king from the god.

By contrast with the extravagant celebrations of the Egyptians, the annual gatherings which the Lord ordained for Israel look modest. In addition to keeping the Passover (Exodus 12:1-14) and the Day of Atonement (Leviticus 16:1-34), she was called to observe three yearly pilgrim feasts, the Lord stating that "Three times a year you are to celebrate a festival to me" (Exodus 23:14) and "Three times a year all the men are to appear before the Sovereign LORD." (Exodus 23:17).[316] In comparison with their Egyptian equivalents, even these three celebrations were of relatively short duration: the Bible specifically states that seven days – or eight if the accompanying Passover is included – were to be allowed for the Feast of Unleavened Bread (Exodus 12:15-6, 23:15 and 34:18), whilst the Feast of Weeks or Harvest (Exodus 23:16 and 34:22)[317] and Feast of Ingathering (Exodus 23:16 and 34:22) lasted a day apiece. Of the three pilgrim festivals, one was linked to Israel's deliverance from Egypt, the others to the rhythm of the agricultural year. Hence God's people were to:

"Celebrate the Feast of Unleavened Bread ... for seven days ... at the appointed time in the month of Abib, for in that month you came out of Egypt." (Exodus 23:15).[318]

"Celebrate the Feast of Harvest with the firstfruits of the crops you sow in your field." (Exodus 23:16).

"Celebrate the Feast of Ingathering at the end of the year, when you gather in your crops from the field." (Exodus 23:16).

There was nevertheless a sense in which, for Israel, all life was to be a festival to the Lord, regulated by the rhythm of the seven-day week through Sabbath, rising and falling according to the seasons of the agricultural year by means of the designated feasts, and punctuated by the thanksgiving sparked by recalling in Passover all that God had done in the national life. None of this was to be a matter of mere ritual and leaden duty, for all were to "Be joyful at your Feast" (Deuteronomy 16:14). It ought indeed to have been impossible for Israel to have felt anything other than joy in the face of what her God had done throughout the generations, and the prescribed observances were designed to keep the memory of these events before the people at all times.[319] Indeed, one of the many distinguishing features of Israelite religion was that it set ritual within the context of the history of the people and their God. Recollection of this collective experience inevitably brought in its train obligations both to the Lord and to one's fellow man, the latter being a reflection (however imperfect) of the One who made him. Consequently, feasts were also a time to share with the poor or disadvantaged. Indeed this was explicitly amongst the purposes behind instituting the Sabbath year: "For six years you are to sow your fields and harvest the crops, but during the seventh year let the land lie unploughed and unused. Then the poor among your people may get food from it, and the wild animals may eat what they leave. Do the same with your vineyard and olive grove." (Exodus 23:10-11).[320]

In keeping with their historical dimension, each festival had particular associations: Passover marked Israel's deliverance from the tenth plague; Unleavened Bread, her bitter slavery and hasty departure from Egypt, redemption by the Almighty and calling to be a holy nation; Firstfruits, redeeming of the firstborn and the bounty of the Promised Land; Weeks, the giving of the Law; Trumpets, the call for the nation to present herself before her heavenly King; Atonement, cleansing of the people from sin and purification of the Holy Place; Tabernacles, the building of the tabernacle and fruitfulness of the land. Yet as well as directing the nation's gaze backwards, they also pointed it forwards, as St Paul made clear to one of the earliest Christian communities: "don't let anyone criticize you for what you eat or drink, or for not celebrating Jewish holidays and feasts or new moon ceremonies or Sabbaths. For these were only temporary rules that ended when Christ came. They were only shadows of the real thing – of Christ himself." (Colossians 2:16-17, TLB). Thus the feasts and festivals were intended not only to help Israel cleave to the ways of the past as to something preserved in aspic, but were vibrant signs and symbols of what God was in the process of bringing about. Although these celebrations in their old form are no longer a requirement for believers, it follows that they still have a part to play in helping us to understand the Lord's purposes more fully and in illuminating the meaning of our present-day equivalents.

Signs and symbols.

The preparations which preceded the triumphal progress of sovereign and gods during the Beautiful Feast of the Opet were elaborate and meticulous, replete with symbolism. A statue of Amun-Ra, carefully bathed, arrayed in finest raiment and robes of many hues, bedecked with gold and jewels, was laid upon a gilded bower inside a model boat. Attended by his high priests, he was carried from the holy-of-holies to the temple forecourt where statues of Mut and Khonsu awaited, these having been brought from their respective temples. The pharaoh himself presided over the ceremonies that preceded departure, flanked by members of the royal family and selected worthies. With requisite preliminaries complete, shaven-headed *wab*-priests ('purifiers') then hoisted high their charges and set off for the river, joined on the way by other priests dressed in leopard skins and accompanied by fan-bearers, serenaded all the while by singers and musicians as acrobats performed. At lay-bys, set up along the way by Hatshepsut, the priests would put down their burden so a new team could take over.[321] Later practice suggests that on arrival at their destination the visiting gods would have been received with appropriate ritual and sacrifices in a large, open courtyard, following which they would be taken inside the temple itself, Mut and Khonsu to their individual shrines, the pharaoh and Amun-Ra proceeding with due ceremonial first to the Chamber of the Divine King and then on to the holy-of-holies.

The events surrounding the Beautiful Feast of the Opet were amongst other things signs of the bond between Amun and the pharaoh, the latter being king, god and personification of Egypt all in one. A sign is by definition a pointer, intended to catch the eye and direct those who read it from one place to another. The signs provided by God are designed to take us from outside to inside, edge to centre, sensory perception to faith, present to future. They are also seals of power, indicating the reality of the truth which is being preached or revealed, as when Jesus sent his disciples "into all the world … [to] preach the good news to all creation" (Mark 16:15) with the assurance that "these signs will accompany those who believe" (Mark 16:17). In the same way that signs had an important part to play in the preaching of the Kingdom of God in the age of the New Covenant, so too they performed a fundamental role in the deliverance of Israel from her bondage in Egypt and the knitting together of a new community rooted in the Old Covenant. The Lord gave Moses "two signs" (Exodus 4:9, KJV) that he was the man chosen to deliver Israel. These were provided in order to substantiate Moses' claim to be acting at divine command, so that "If they [the Israelites] will not believe you or be convinced by the first miracle, then this one will convince them." (Exodus 4:8, GNT).[322]

In due course, Moses "performed the signs before the people, and they believed." (Exodus 4:30-31). The response to the signs was belief, which is to say, faith (trust). This straightaway led, as true faith must, to gratitude and worship, and the people "bowed down and worshipped." (Exodus 4:31). The contrast with Pharaoh could hardly have been greater, as the Almighty foresaw before Moses even set foot in the king's court: "...though I multiply my miraculous signs and wonders in Egypt, he will not listen to you. Then I will lay my hand on Egypt and with mighty acts of judgment I will bring out my divisions, my people the Israelites." (Exodus 7:3).[323] So it transpired, with "miraculous signs" (Exodus 8:23 and 10:1) that caused Moses upon witnessing the emphatic and final escape from Pharaoh brought about by crossing of the Red Sea to praise his God as one "majestic in holiness, awesome in glory, working wonders" (Exodus 15:11). Later, with Israel delivered from bondage and set upon the road towards her destiny of becoming "a kingdom of priests and a holy nation" (Exodus 19:6) other marks were given to her – as tokens of things past and yet to come, as mechanisms for preserving context and continuity for future generations and as illuminators of the yet greater glory that God had ordained from long ago, not only for Israel but for the whole world. Together these signified:

Redemption – the buying back of God's chosen people from slavery and their deliverance from the destruction that ultimately awaits those who will not acknowledge the Almighty: "The blood [of the Passover lamb] will be a sign for you on the houses where you are; and when I see the blood, I will pass over you. No destructive plague will touch you when I strike Egypt." (Exodus 12:13; see also Exodus 30:12).[324]

Righteousness – the building of a people in right relationship with each other and with their Maker: "This observance [the Feast of Unleavened Bread] will be for you like a sign on your hand and a reminder on your forehead that the law of the LORD is to be on your lips. For the LORD brought you out of Egypt with his mighty hand." (Exodus 13:9).

Holiness – the setting apart and purification of believers so as to fit them for the worship and service of God for all eternity: "This [Sabbath observance] will be a sign between me and you for the generations to come, so that you may know that I am the LORD, who makes you holy." (Exodus 31:13).

Rest – establishing a healthy rhythm in this life so as to prepare for eventual entry into the Promised Land: "It [Sabbath observance] will be a sign between me and the Israelites for ever, for in six days the LORD made the heavens and the earth, and on the seventh day he abstained from work and rested." (Exodus 31:17).[325]

In the case of Passover, especially, nothing was left to chance, since even its explanation for future generations was provided: "In days to come when your son asks you, 'What does this [the Passover] mean?' say to him, 'With a mighty hand the LORD brought us out of Egypt, out of the land of slavery. When Pharaoh stubbornly refused to let us go, the LORD killed every firstborn in Egypt, both man and animal. This is why I sacrifice to the LORD the first male offspring of every womb and redeem each of my firstborn sons.' And it will be like a sign on your hand and a symbol on your forehead that the LORD brought us out of Egypt with his mighty hand." (Exodus 13:14-16).[326] In using this particular form of words the High King of heaven made it abundantly clear that remembrance of this central event in the nation's history was to govern Israel's every deed (the hand being the agent of action) and every thought (the forehead signifying the mind or brain).[327] Israel's defining ritual was thus shown to be essentially dynamic: not an excuse to look back to a golden age that no longer existed, but a call to move ahead into an ever-greater understanding of God, a deeper and more heartfelt obedience to his commands and a more urgent yearning after fulfilment of his unfolding purposes.

Signs and symbols abound in other ways, too, allowing each of the Israelites' experiences to be read as metaphors for later pilgrims' journeys of faith under the New Covenant instituted by Christ. As St Paul observed, "These things happened to them as examples and were written down as warnings for us, on whom the fulfilment of the ages has come." (1 Corinthians 10:11). There are myriad layers of meaning within both text and action, but amongst other things these highlight seven elements that form the core of the Lord's plan to save mankind and remake Creation – through life-giving power; self-sacrificial love; cleansing and rebirth; a template for right living by humankind; divine provision; heavenly guidance; spiritual gifts to enable prayer, worship and service; and God's preparation of a place where he might dwell in daily fellowship with those he made to share eternity with him:

Remembering God

LIFE-GIVING POWER.

Moses "sat down by a well" (Exodus 2:15, NKJV) from which he "drew enough water for [Jethro's daughters] and watered the flock." (Exodus 2:19, NKJV). In later times Jesus sat by a well to teach that "the water I give ... will become in him [who receives it] a spring of water welling up to eternal life" (John 4:14). The Hebrew for a well (*be'ar*) is an anagram of *bara* (meaning, *to create*), alerting us to the activity of the Creator, for a well is an access point: in literal terms, to the liquid without which life cannot continue and in metaphorical terms to the Lord's life-giving power. As such, it emphasises that man is not only to be passive in receiving from God. Just as obtaining water requires first that a well be dug and then that water be drawn from it, God's life-giving power is available to all, but we have to take hold of it. God said, "I have come down to rescue [my people]" (Exodus 3:8), but Moses' obedience in thought, word and deed was necessary if he were to receive the power that his Maker purposed to give him.

SELF-SACRIFICIAL LOVE.

Passover "is a day you are to commemorate; for the generations to come you shall celebrate it as a festival to the LORD — a lasting ordinance." (Exodus 12:14). It prefigured the self-sacrifice of "Christ, our Passover Lamb" (1 Corinthians 5:7), who "had no sin [but became] ... sin for us, so that in him we might become the righteousness of God" (2 Corinthians 5:21) and in the process "God demonstrates His own love toward us, in that while we were still sinners, Christ died for us." (Romans 5:8, NKJV). For Moses, Jethro, Aaron and "the elders of Israel to eat bread ... in the presence of God" (Exodus 18:12) was likewise a picture of the meal that Jesus commanded "in remembrance of me" (Luke 22:19, NRSV), put in place so that God might be with us and in us and so that his self-sacrificial love might inspire ours.

CLEANSING AND RENEWAL.

St Paul spoke of Israel being "baptised into Moses in the cloud and the sea" (1 Corinthians 10:2), the submission to the prophet as leader and deliverer being a foretaste of later generations' submission to Jesus as Saviour and Lord. The Israelites' passing through the waters of the Red Sea acted out the spiritual significance of baptism, a move from the slavery of sin to new life and freedom in Christ.

A TEMPLATE FOR RIGHT LIVING.

The Law of Moses required "annual atonement ... with the blood of the atoning sin offering" (Exodus 30:10), for it did not take away sin but only covered it over. Though it gave Israel a template for right living, the Law was a hard taskmaster, for sinful men defile what is holy and sin is contagious, so that "Not a hand is to be laid on him [someone who transgresses by touching the holy mountain without permission]" (Exodus 19:13). Our inherently sinful nature means "that the very commandment that was intended to bring life actually brought death" (Romans 7:10). The Law nevertheless pointed to the perfect atonement of Jesus, with "no condemnation for those who are in [him]." (Romans 8:1).

DIVINE PROVISION.

In the desert the Israelites' very survival depended on divine provision of daily necessities. At Marah, where "they could not drink its water because it was bitter ... the people grumbled ... saying, 'What are we to drink?' ... There the LORD made a decree and a law for them and there he tested them." (Exodus 15:23-24 and 26). As ever, the crux of the issue was faith: whether God, who had seen them through every difficulty up to that point, could still be trusted. After coming through this particular trial, "Then they came to Elim, where there were twelve springs and seventy palm trees, and they camped there near the water" (Exodus 15:27) – the apparently incidental details about springs and trees presumably being included because Moses saw these as an assurance of continued sustenance and divine favour, for there were twelve tribes descended from the sons of Jacob (Israel) and "the members of Jacob's family which went to Egypt, were seventy in all." (Genesis 46:27).

HEAVENLY GUIDANCE.

The lure of sin is a constant at all times and in all places, but God does not abandon his people to the vicissitudes of life or leave them without help or support. Guidance is available, in his Word and by his Spirit, as a result of the mutual commitment of the Lord and his people – an agreement sealed in blood, with Moses saying, "This is the blood of the [Old] covenant that the LORD has made with you in accordance with all these words" (Exodus 24:8), just as today believers are sanctified with Christ's "blood of the [New] covenant" (Matthew 26:28 and Mark 14:24).[328]

SPIRITUAL GIFTS FOR PRAYER, WORSHIP AND SERVICE.

The "Spirit of God ... [grants] skill, ability and knowledge" (Exodus 35:31) now just as in days of old. Such gifts are given so that we may build a tabernacle or a Temple, no longer of brick, stone or hide but a place of prayer, worship and service nevertheless, a dwelling for God in our hearts. St Paul made the point repeatedly that now we are "God's temple" (1 Corinthians 3:16) and "the temple of the living God" (2 Corinthians 6:16).

ETERNAL DWELLING-PLACE.

The ultimate goal of the Israelites' earthly wanderings was the Promised Land, where they could look forward to ease, happiness and prosperity in "a good and spacious land, a land flowing with milk and honey" (Exodus 3:8) as God shepherded them into his rest. The picture is of our heavenly home and the fellowship with our Maker that awaits believers at the end of this life's journey.

Conclusion.

Festivals are times of happiness, when we delight to consume "food [that is] rich ... delicacies fit for a king." (Genesis 49:20). They are also occasions to remember. The feasts enjoined by Scripture were to enable Israel to remember God and continue to walk in ways that would cause him to remember her (in the sense of looking kindly upon her and blessing her). When Moses prayed, "...blot me out of the book you have written" (32:32), God replied "Whoever has sinned against me, I will blot out of my book" (Exodus 32:33). Yet by the same token, one who recalls him with praise and thanksgiving, who walks in his ways and serves him all his days, such a one Jesus "will never blot out ... from the book of life, but will acknowledge his name before my Father and his angels." (Revelation 3:5).

Naphtali

Whose meaning is, *my struggle*

Of whom Jacob prophesied,
"Naphtali is a doe set free that bears beautiful fawns."
(Genesis 49:21).

11. Living for God

Life and afterlife.

"Teach them the decrees and laws, and show them the way to live and the duties they are to perform." (Exodus 18:20).

By the accession of Amenhotep III Egyptian temples had coalesced around a more or less standard design that reflected their builders' concept of the afterlife. Inside they were dark and many-pillared, with a succession of courts and passageways leading to an inner sanctum, just as the journey through the netherworld was conceived as a series of gloomy thoroughfares with many possibilities for wrong turnings, each of which might prove fatal. For after death the soul was thought to face a series of tests; failure in any one of which would mean losing the chance of eternal bliss. Every stage was watched over by terrifying guardians who barred the way to the next level. To pacify these, the dead needed to declare their names, a primitive magical technique for gaining control over and dominating the one whose name was pronounced. So, for example, on reaching the First Portal of Osiris the defunct was required to announce, 'Make way for me, for I know you, I know your name, and I know the name of the god who guards you!' Against this background a dimly lit complex with many gateways between which the visitor had to navigate and through which he had to pass was an apt illustration of what awaited the deceased. In the same way that the soul sought to overcome its travails and reach the Field of Reeds beyond,[329] so the various courtyards marked tangible progress towards the ultimate goal: the holy of holies, where a statue of the god was kept and which only suitably elevated members of the priesthood or pharaoh himself were allowed to enter.[330]

The challenges which Egyptians believed they would meet on the journey which was undertaken after death reflected those they knew in life, with boats, fishing nets and threats by desert creatures. Progress depended on displaying the requisite knowledge. The judgment of the dead, too, had its origins in the everyday. Egypt was one of the first societies to develop sophisticated legal processes, founded not on divinely inspired commandments but on correct behaviour as learned by experience and sanctified by tradition. The idea of a judgment of the dead marks a transfer of this principle to the world of the gods. Anubis would weigh a heart in the balance against the feather of *Ma'at* (truth or justice), whilst in the background lurked the monstrous devourer Ammit, part crocodile, part lion and part hippopotamus, poised and ready to swallow the heart if it belonged to one who had led a sinful life. To escape damnation and pass on to eternal happiness, ancient Egyptians believed that in the Hall of the

Two Truths they had to say aloud, 'O my heart, do not stand up as a witness against me; do not be hostile to me in the presence of the Keeper of the Balance; do not tell lies about me in the presence of the god. It is indeed well that you should hear!' Not surprisingly, the afterlife was approached with hope but also with intense trepidation, for none could know for sure whether their spells would suffice to gain them salvation.

Preserving the integrity of the earthly body was also important for giving the dead the best possible chance of success in their quest for eternal joy. Embalming and its associated rituals were therefore approached with the greatest seriousness, the entire process lasting for seventy days.[331] Following this, mourners, priests and grave goods would accompany the coffin across the Nile to one of the many necropolises on the west bank. At the door of the tomb the last rites were performed. These included the vital ceremony of the Opening of the Mouth, which was thought magically to restore living faculties to the mummified corpse so as to enable the deceased once more to eat, breathe and move. It was through this act that the spirit components of the personality were allowed to rejoin the corpse to make a fully functioning individual again. The importance of a mummy as the physical base for the spirit meant that it had to stay safe in the tomb, but equally crucial to flourishing in the afterlife was that the *Ka* should be able to leave and re-enter its body at will. A spirit which was able to do this was no longer confined to an inert collection of rags and bones but could return to the world to experience the pleasures of life and mingle with the gods under the life-renewing rays of the sun in the 'Coming Forth by Day'. For the Egyptians this was a concept so fundamental that it pervaded all spells which were put into a tomb and became the title for that entire collection of incantations which today we call the Book of the Dead.[332]

Death and rebirth.

Slavery is the antithesis of living for God in all the fullness that he wishes and intends. It is a waking death, causing deep sorrow and anguish in body, mind and spirit. It involves oppression, humiliation, unremitting toil and daily drudgery. The taking away of freedom necessarily infantilises its victims, for they must be constrained in ways that are inconsistent with adulthood. Not surprisingly, "The Israelites groaned in their slavery" (Exodus 2:23).[333] They understandably chafed under a regime whose evil was expressed in the realm of the physical, but whose guiding principles can be seen no less in the spiritual environment of the present day, for there was and were:

Insistence on labour and production as ends in themselves, with regard for neither common humanity nor the things of God: The idea of letting Israel "hold a festival to [the LORD] in the desert" (Exodus 5:1) cut no ice with Pharaoh, for "the king of

Egypt said, 'Moses and Aaron, why are you taking the people away from their labour? Get back to your work!'" (Exodus 5:4).

Threats and coercion against those who stood up for right: When Pharaoh said, "You people have become more numerous than the Egyptians. And now you want to stop working!" (Exodus 5:5, GNT) he emphasised the importance of slaves to the Egyptian economy but also echoed the previous ruler whose observation, "The Israelite people are more numerous and more powerful than we" (Exodus 1:9, NRSV) had led directly to enslavement and attempted extermination. The true import of the words was unlikely to have been lost on the two brothers, who would almost certainly have sensed the thinly veiled menace against themselves and their people.

Distractions deliberately designed to take people away from God: Pharaoh gave an order to "Make the work harder for the men so that they keep working and pay no attention to lies." (Exodus 5:9). Bread and circuses work equally well in fixing the eyes of men on appetites and transitory things of no real worth, thereby directing their gaze away from the One who made them.

Spiteful and unfair imposition of rules and regulations: The Israelites were knowingly given tasks that were almost impossible to perform, or which could only be carried out with stupendous effort: "Then the slave drivers and the foremen went out and said to the people, 'This is what Pharaoh says: 'I will not give you any more straw. Go and get your own straw wherever you can find it, but your work will not be reduced at all.'" (Exodus 5:10-12).

Division of families and communities: The inevitable consequence of increased work quotas and refusal to supply the necessary materials was that "the people scattered all over Egypt to gather stubble to use as straw." (Exodus 5:12).

False hope and misplaced trust: The Israelite foremen seem to have thought that they would get a sympathetic hearing when they "appealed to Pharaoh: 'Why have you treated your servants this way? Your servants are given no straw, yet we are told, 'Make bricks!' Your servants are being beaten, but the fault is with your own people.'" (Exodus 5:15-16). Though they were soon disabused of this notion, many continue to rely on illusory sources of help and support despite every experience and all evidence.

Injustice and an overbearing attitude on the part of those in authority: The king's response to all entreaties showed not the slightest sympathy, for "Pharaoh said, 'Lazy, that's what you are – lazy! That is why you keep saying, Let us go and sacrifice to the LORD.' Now get to work. You will not be given any straw, yet you must produce your full quota of bricks.'" (Exodus 5:17-18).

Violence, unwillingness to admit mistakes or wrongdoing, and unrestrained abuse of power by the strong against the weak: Moses and Aaron were not simply told to leave when the king abruptly ended their audience, but "were driven out of Pharaoh's presence." (Exodus 10:11). The monarch had not the slightest interest in considering the rights and wrongs of the situation, let alone of making amends for centuries of abuse.

These things are at one and the same time characteristics of the life of sin and amongst the recurring mechanisms by which Satan seeks to bind mankind to such an existence. They operate by way of the oppression of outside forces, the "Egyptian beating a Hebrew" (Exodus 2:11), but also in a far more insidious inner conflict, the "two Hebrews fighting" (Exodus 2:13) that represents the warring of like against like or of our own nature within itself. Whichever of these may be enslaving us and holding us fast, the Lord offers rebirth. He does so in his goodness and mercy, desiring the best for us and longing for us to break free of our shackles. His helping hand is the vital pre-requisite; the Israelites could not have freed themselves purely by their own efforts, and neither can we. It took a mighty move of God, who promised that "the Egyptians will know that I am the LORD when I stretch out my hand against Egypt and bring the Israelites out of it." (Exodus 7:5). Yet it also required a reaction on the part of men: to listen to "everything the LORD had said" (Exodus 4:30), to be amongst those who "believed" (Exodus 4:31) and then "bowed down and worshipped" (Exodus 4:31) in response. The Israelites were not to be passive observers who were magically transported from Egypt to Canaan without the slightest thought or effort. They had a long, hard road ahead, with trials aplenty. Their challenge was not just to be moved from one physical location to another but to cooperate with God so as to be renewed in body, mind and spirit, with new attitudes leading to new behaviour.

What was in prospect was a major work of spiritual transformation. It was not something that could be accomplished overnight – not because of any lack on the part of God but by reason of those same human frailties that plague our and every generation. Whatever our background and circumstances, we need time to leave behind the past and step into the future. That such things do not always come easily is shown by the fact that even after finally escaping the clutches of the pursuing Egyptian army and crossing the Red Sea, it was not only former slaves who remained trapped in repetitive cycles of negative thought or behaviour. On occasion even Moses, who as far as the Bible records never felt the lash of a taskmaster's whip, displayed similar tendencies.[334] Though his meeting with the Lord on Horeb, the practical support he was given by Aaron and their subsequent courageous stand before Pharaoh should by rights have put paid to any thought his having "never been eloquent" (Exodus 4:10) or being "a poor speaker, slow and hesitant" (Exodus 4:10, GNT) causing any hindrance, still twice more Moses raised the self-same issue: "If the Israelites will not listen to me, why would Pharaoh listen to me, since I speak with faltering lips?" (Exodus 6:12) and "Since I speak with faltering lips, why would Pharaoh listen to me?" (Exodus 6:30).³³⁵ In the lingering self-doubt, fear and uncertainty that lay behind these questions it is all too easy to recognise ourselves, apt (as men have ever been) to place obstacles in the way of the rebirth and new life that God makes available to those who "walk before [him] and [are] blameless" (Genesis 17:1).³³⁶

Coming alive.

Truly living for God and becoming fully alive is not a matter of elaborate ceremonies such as those contrived by the ancient Egyptians. There is no need for an Opening of the Mouth to breathe life into a mummified corpse. It is the breath of Almighty God (that is to say, the Holy Spirit) which must come upon us, not some ethereal element of our own personality. The starting point for enabling this to happen is the removal of blockages to God's activity, for all too often the Almighty would be justified in levelling at us the same accusation which Moses spoke on his behalf to Pharaoh: "You still set yourself against my people and will not let them go" (Exodus 9:17) – the one whom we will not let go being most usually ourselves. Whether we call this self-indulgence, self-centredness or self-fulfilment, the end result is the same. The cult of the self is an enemy of that self-denial and self-abnegation which is needful if we are to allow our Creator to work in us, for it is putting man before his Maker and elevating ourselves to stand in his place which lies at the heart of our rebellion against him.³³⁷ The death of the old self and rebirth into new life, which this process of letting go and dying to sin both requires and brings in its train, are symbolised by the experiences of Israel as she fought external challenges and grappled with dangers that threatened from within.

RESCUE.

The process starts with our rescue by God, of which Passover is the overarching symbol: it is a rescue writ in blood, for the Israelites were instructed to "Take a bunch of hyssop, dip it into the blood [of the sacrificed Passover lamb] in the basin and put some of the blood on the top and on both sides of the door-frame. Not one of you shall go out of the door of his house until morning." (Exodus 12:22). The power that was in the blood of the sacrifice should cause us to consider deeply, for there had in fact been no lack of blood in the Two Lands; when Moses and Aaron "struck the water of the Nile … all the water was changed into blood." (Exodus 7:20). Indeed, not just the river but also "the streams and canals … ponds and all the reservoirs" (Exodus 7:19) were each affected by the plague of blood, so that "Blood was everywhere in Egypt" (Exodus 7:21). Yet this blood had no power to protect, save or redeem. It was the blood of judgment, not of salvation. By contrast, the Lord promised that "The blood [of the Passover lamb] will be a sign for you on the houses where you are; and when I see the blood, I will pass over you. No destructive plague will touch you when I strike Egypt" (Exodus 12:13) and "the destroyer [will not] enter and strike you down." (Exodus 12:23). The importance of all these events for the future as well as the present was emphasised by the institution of a "lasting ordinance" (Exodus 12:14, 17 and 24)[338] in relation to them and the extreme sanction for any who failed to keep the resulting decrees of being "cut off" (Exodus 12:15 and 19).[339]

The immediate physical object of the Passover sacrifice was to mark Israel in an obvious way as set apart from Egypt. In the process, it pointed to the system of animal sacrifice that Moses modelled when "He got up early the next morning and built an altar at the foot of the mountain and set up twelve stone pillars representing the twelve tribes of Israel. Then ... they offered burnt offerings and sacrificed young bulls as fellowship offerings to the LORD." (Exodus 24:4-5).[340] The ultimate object which was in view through Passover, however (and the reason why it was to be a lasting ordinance even after the system of animal sacrifice based on the Jerusalem Temple had long been abandoned), was that it symbolised a far greater sacrifice. St Paul made explicit the identification with "Christ, our Passover lamb, [who] has been sacrificed" (1 Corinthians 5:7). As such, Passover was both memorial to a great saving work of God and a spur to reflect upon and take to heart that even more wonderful activity which was to come. This provides the context in which to understand what lay behind God's saying that "In the first month you are to eat bread made without yeast ... for seven days no yeast is to be found in your houses. And whoever eats anything with yeast in it must be cut off from the community of Israel, whether he is an alien or native-born. Eat nothing made with yeast. Wherever you live, you must eat unleavened bread." (Exodus 12:18-20; see also Exodus 23:18 and 34:25). For again, these things were not primarily about the past, but about the present and future, since yeast represented sin – as when Jesus told people to "Be on your guard against the yeast of the Pharisees and Sadducees" (Matthew 16:6). Once more the Lord emphasised that physical delivery from Egypt was merely to be the precursor to complete spiritual freedom.[341]

REDEMPTION, CLEANSING AND HOLINESS.

This freedom required that Israel be bought back from slavery. The image of redemption (buying back a captive out of slavery and sin) permeates every aspect of the Exodus story. It was seen most obviously in Israel's deliverance from bondage in Egypt, yet it also informed and energised the whole of the nation's life thereafter, being linked to God's blessing, protection and service. Hence "the LORD said to Moses, 'When you take a census of the Israelites to count them, each one must pay the LORD a ransom for his life at the time he is counted. Then no plague will come on them when you number them.'" (Exodus

30:11-12). Likewise, "Everyone ... must pay the required amount of money, weighed according to the official standard. ... every man twenty years old or older, is to pay me this amount. The rich man is not to pay more, nor the poor man less ... Collect this money from the people of Israel and spend it for the upkeep of the Tent of my presence. This tax will be the payment for their lives, and I will remember to protect them." (Exodus 30:13-16, GNT). The obligation on well off and indigent alike reinforced the message that Israel belonged in her entirety to God. She was to be dedicated to him in such a unique and wholehearted way that she would become "a kingdom of priests and a holy nation." (Exodus 19:6) and the consequence of her redemption was to be everlasting service of the One who had delivered her.[342]

The nation was not bought back in this way so that she might continue to live as she had formerly, and indeed could not carry on in that fashion if she were properly to fulfil God's purpose for her. It was necessary that she be cleansed of guilt and have the detritus of the past washed away, hence the requirement to "Make a bronze basin ... and put water in it. Aaron and his sons are to use the water to wash their hands and feet" (Exodus 30:18-19, GNT; see also Exodus 40:30-31). Though this is expressed as a physical act to be carried out by members of the priesthood, it was no less a spiritual need for all citizens, since God's scheme envisaged that they would each be priests in his kingdom. In much the same way, the Israelites collectively and individually were to become holy – made sacred, set apart for the service of God or other sacred use, morally pure, free from sin or sinful affections and of high spiritual excellence.[343] Amongst the ways in which holiness was to be expressed was through prayer, the bond of relationship and interaction between man and his Maker which was represented by that "fragrant blend of incense" (Exodus 30:35) the production and use of which is carefully described in Exodus 30:34-38.[344] Similarly, the injunction to pursue holiness in all things was given physical form through applying sacred anointing oil to "consecrate [the Tent of Meeting, ark of the Testimony and tabernacle furnishings] so they will be most holy, and whatever touches them will be most holy." (Exodus 30:29).[345]

READYING OURSELVES FOR WHAT LIES AHEAD.

In concept and practice holiness was to saturate the daily life of the people to such a degree that it would seep into their very pores, transforming each moment, every thought and all activity from the apparently insignificant into something of eternal worth, transmuting the mundane into an offering to God. Seen through that prism, what might to modern eyes seem like an unwarranted obsession with ritual cleanliness and purity was simply a logical outgrowth of the need for those who had been redeemed and cleansed to remain holy by avoiding defilement through contact with what might be unclean. The link with holiness is several times explicitly made, as in the statement, "You are to be my holy people.

The Egyptian Empire in the XVth Century BC

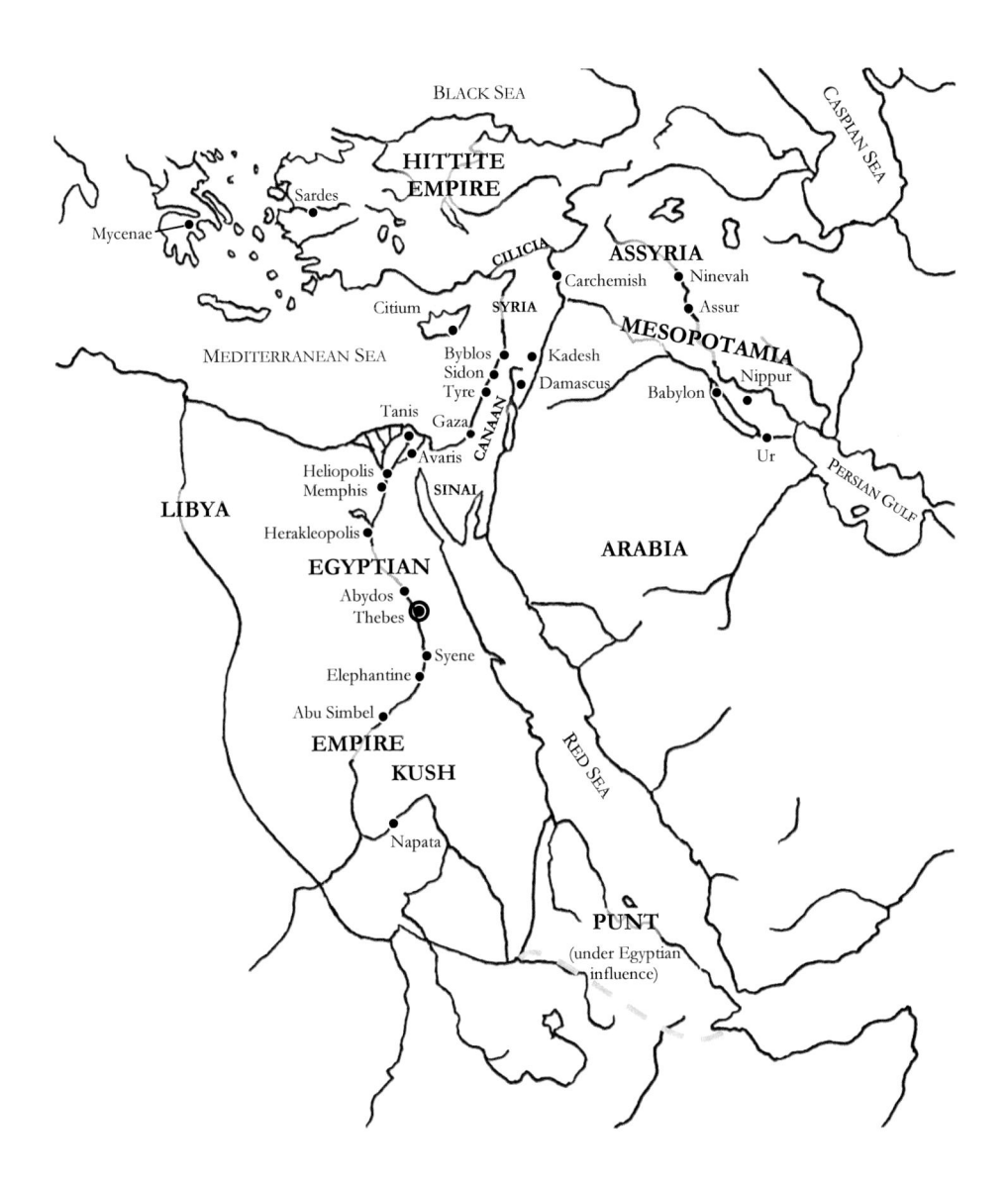

Upper and Lower Egypt

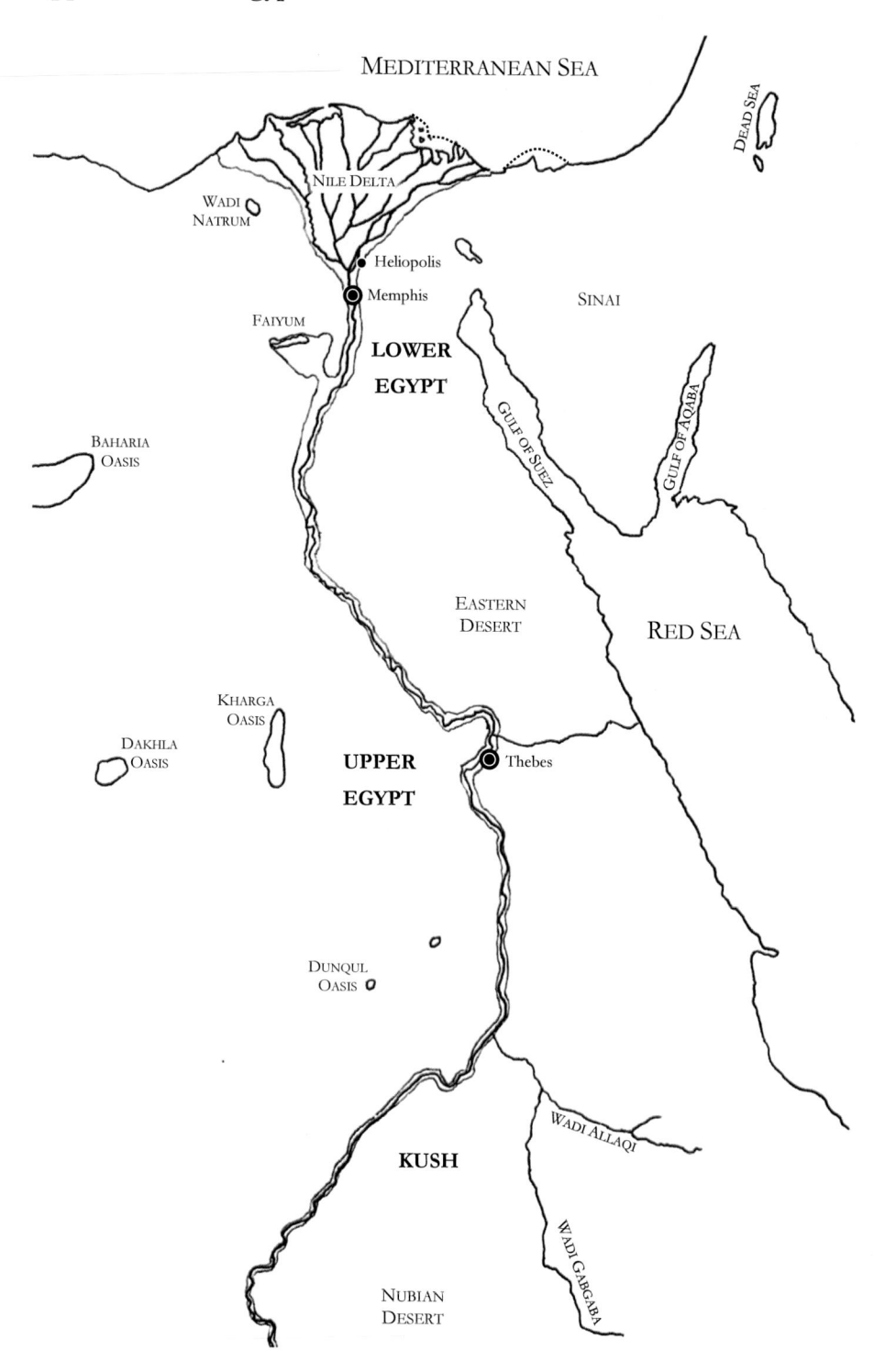

Administrative Regions of Lower Egypt

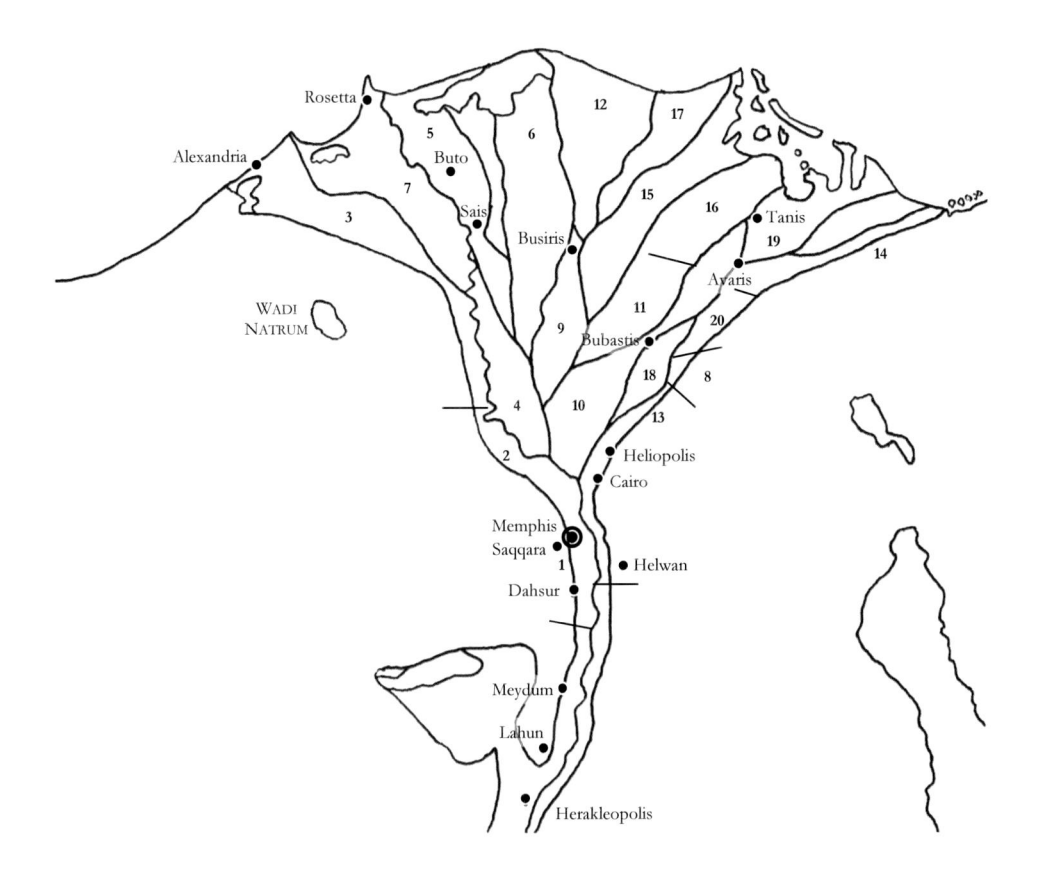

Key

Regional capitals shown in brackets.

1. Aneb-Hetch (Memphis)
2. Khensu (Letopolis)
3. Ahment (Apis)
4. Sapi-Res (Ptkheka)
5. Sap-Meh (Sais)
6. Khaset (Xois)
7. A-ment (Hermopolis Parva)
8. A-bt (Pithom)
9. Ati (Busaris)
10. Ka-khem (Athribis)
11. Ka-heseb (Leontopolis)
12. Theb-ka (Sebennytos)
13. Heq-at (Heliopolis)
14. Khent-abt (Tanis)
15. Tehut (Hermopolis Parva)
16. Kha (Mendes)
17. Semabehdet (Diospolis Inferior)
18. Am-Khent (Bubastis)
19. Am-Pehu (Leontopolis Tanis)
20. Sopdu (Per-Sopdu)

Administrative Regions of Upper Egypt

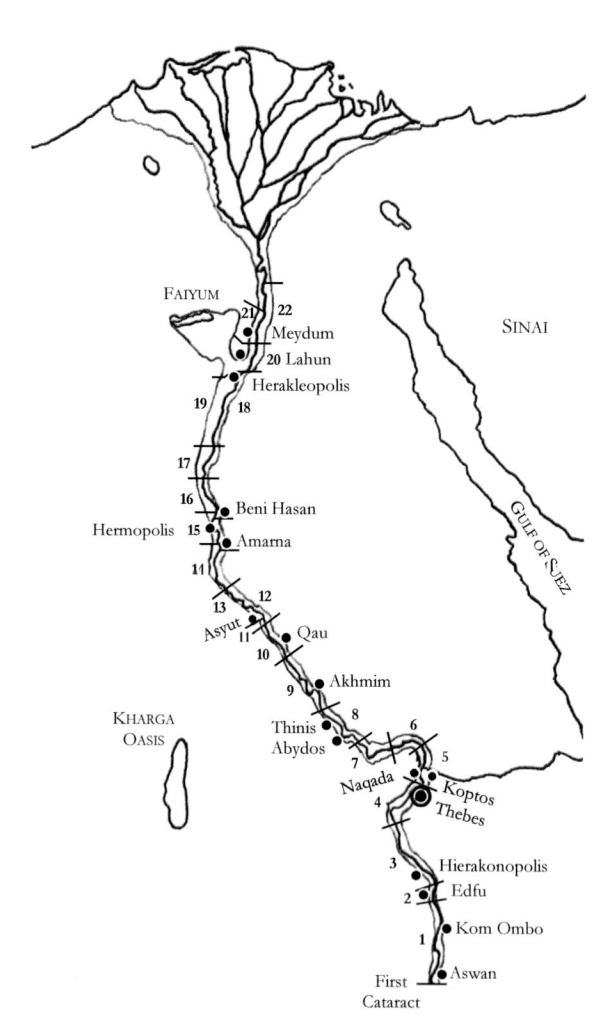

Key

Regional capitals shown in brackets.

1. Ta-Seti (Elephantine)
2. Wetjes-Hor (Appollonopolis Magna)
3. Ten (Hierakonopolis)
4. Weset (Thebes)
5. Herui (Captos)
6. Aa-ta (Tentyra)
7. Seshesh (Diapolis Parva)
8. Abju (Abydos)
9. Min (Panopolis)
10. Wadkhet (Aphroditopolis)
11. Set (Hypselis)
12. Tu-ph (Antaeopolis)
13. Atef-Khent (Lycopolis)
14. Atef-Pehu (Cusae)
15. On (Hermopolis Magna)
16. Meh-Mahetch (Hebenu)
17. Anpu (Cynopolis)
18. Sep (Alabastronopolis)
19. Uab (Oxyrhyncus)
20. Atef-Khent (Herakleopolis Magna)
21. Atef-Pehu (Crocodilopolis)
22. Maten (Aphroditopholis)

Plan of Akhet-aten

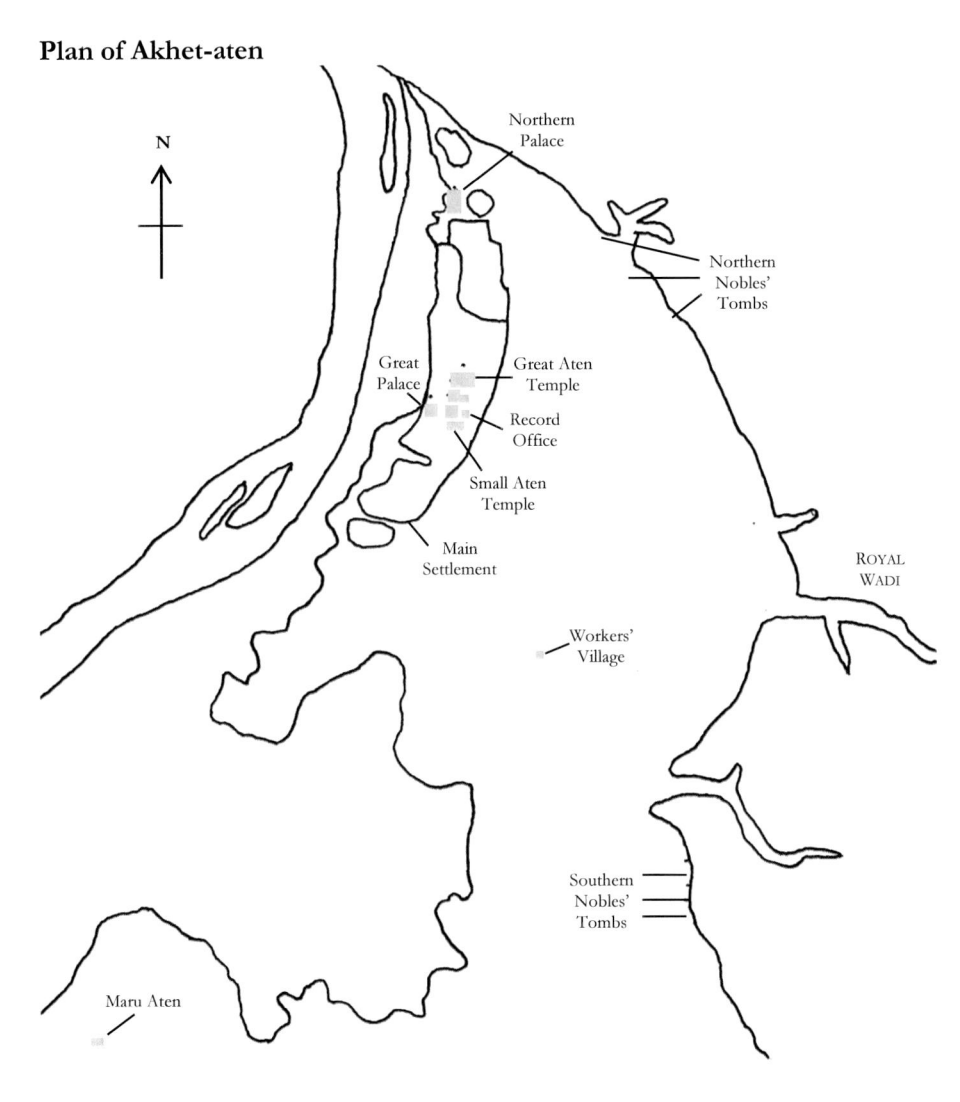

Maru Aten (Viewing Place of Aten): a palace or sun-temple built for Queen Kiya, later used by Meritaten.

Great Aten Temple (Gem-pa-Aten): the main temple, subsequently deliberately destroyed and paved over.

Small Aten Temple (Mansion of Aten): the second of the two major temples, likewise desecrated.

Royal Wadi: the burial place of royalty, Aket-aten's equivalent of the Valley of the Kings.

Great Palace and Northern Palace: ceremonial residences of the pharaoh and other royalty.

Nobles' tombs: the burial places of powerful courtiers and civil servants.

Record Office (Bureau of Correspondence of Pharaoh): storage place for official correspondence.

Areas of Settlement by the Twelve Tribes of Israel after the Conquest of Canaan

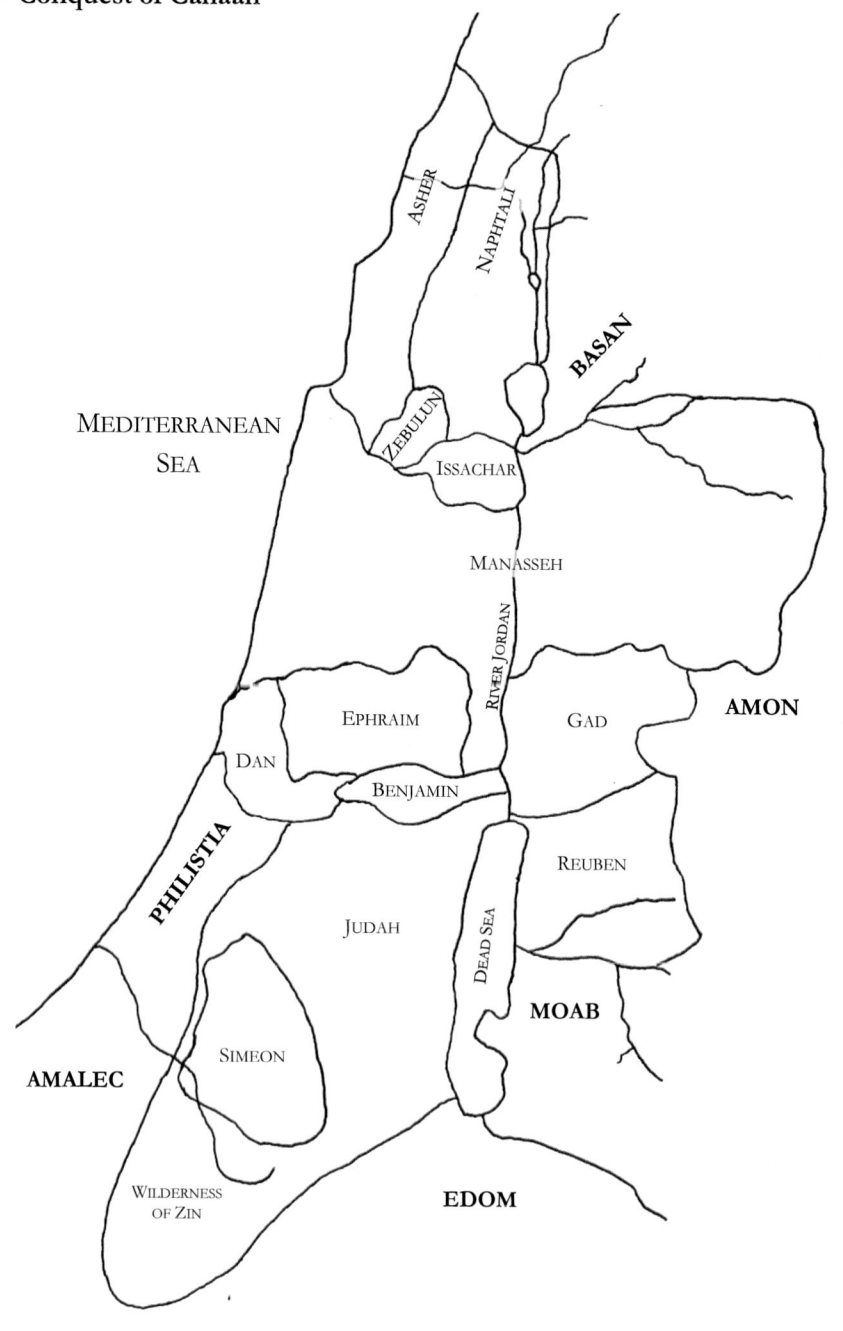

Photograph: Wikicommons

Plate IV: Colossal statue of Amenhotep III.
"Pharaoh said, 'Who is the LORD, that I should obey him and let Israel go? I do not know the LORD and I will not let Israel go.'" (Exodus 5:2).

Plate V: Bust of Amenhotep III.

"But the king of Egypt said, 'Moses and Aaron, why are you taking the people away from their labour? Get back to your work!' Then Pharaoh said, 'Look, the people of the land are now numerous, and you are stopping them from working.'" (Exodus 5:4-5).

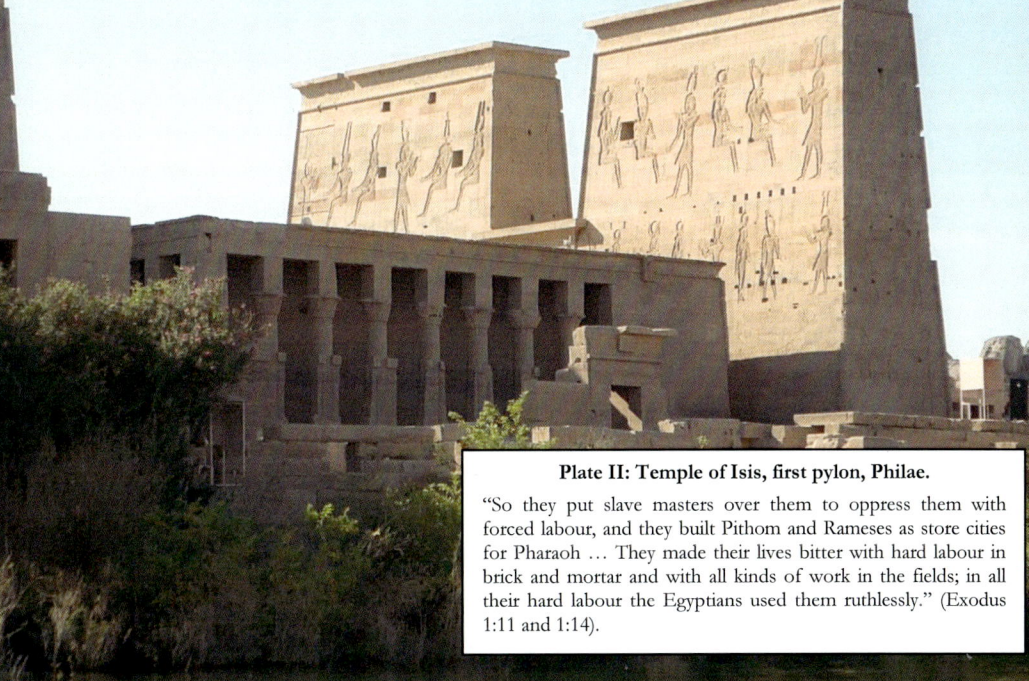

Photograph: Wikicommons

Plate I: Peristyle hall of Thutmoses IV at Thebes.

"Then a new king, who did not know about Joseph, came to power in Egypt. 'Look,' he said to his people, 'the Israelites have become much too numerous for us. Come, we must deal shrewdly with them'" (Exodus 1:8).

Photograph: Wikicommons

Plate II: Temple of Isis, first pylon, Philae.

"So they put slave masters over them to oppress them with forced labour, and they built Pithom and Rameses as store cities for Pharaoh … They made their lives bitter with hard labour in brick and mortar and with all kinds of work in the fields; in all their hard labour the Egyptians used them ruthlessly." (Exodus 1:11 and 1:14).

Photograph: Wikicommons

Plate III: Papyrus growing by the Nile.
"But when [Moses' mother] could hide him no longer, she got a papyrus basket for him and coated it with tar and pitch. Then she placed the child in it and put it among the reeds along the bank of the Nile." (Exodus 2:3).

Plate VI: Akhenaten and Nefertiti worshipping Aten in the form of the sun-disc.

"But Moses said, 'That [sacrificing to the LORD in Egypt] would not be right. The sacrifices we offer the LORD our God would be detestable to the Egyptians.' (Exodus 8:26).

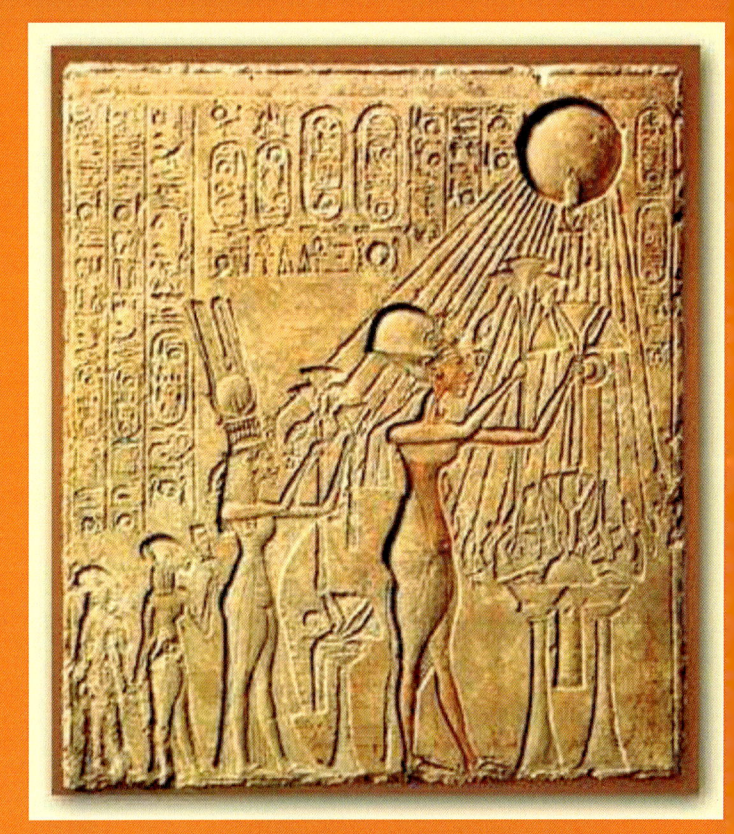

Plate VII: Desert locusts feeding.

"By morning the wind had brought the locusts; they invaded all Egypt and settled down in every area of the country in great numbers. Never before had there been such a plague of locusts, nor will there ever be again. They covered all the ground until it was black. They devoured all that was left after the hail – everything growing in the fields and the fruit on the trees. Nothing green remained on tree or plant in all the land of Egypt." (Exodus 10:13-15).

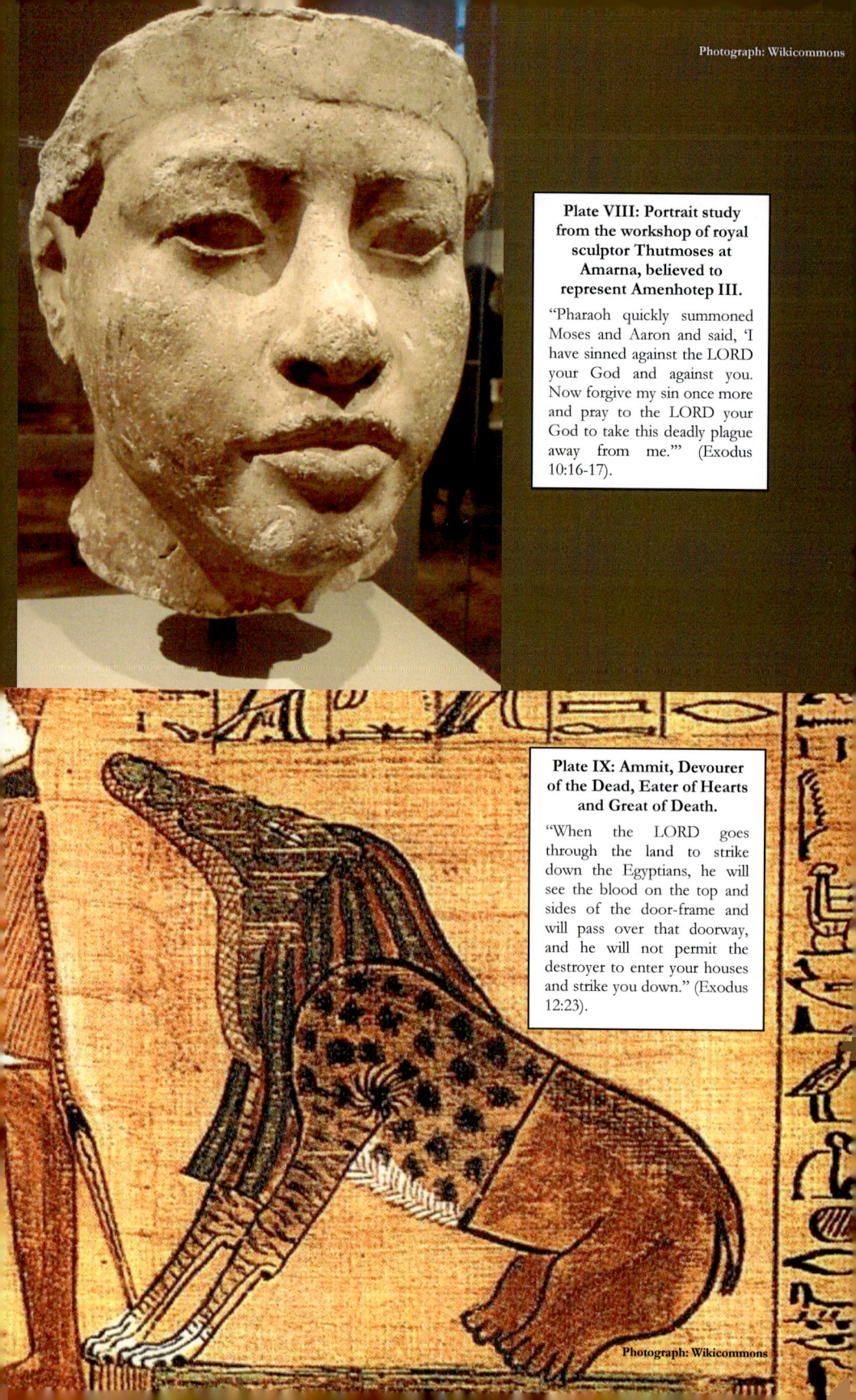

Photograph: Wikicommons

Plate VIII: Portrait study from the workshop of royal sculptor Thutmoses at Amarna, believed to represent Amenhotep III.

"Pharaoh quickly summoned Moses and Aaron and said, 'I have sinned against the LORD your God and against you. Now forgive my sin once more and pray to the LORD your God to take this deadly plague away from me.'" (Exodus 10:16-17).

Plate IX: Ammit, Devourer of the Dead, Eater of Hearts and Great of Death.

"When the LORD goes through the land to strike down the Egyptians, he will see the blood on the top and sides of the door-frame and will pass over that doorway, and he will not permit the destroyer to enter your houses and strike you down." (Exodus 12:23).

Photograph: Wikicommons

Photograph: Wikicommons

Plate X: Soufrière Hills Volcano, Montserrat 1995.
"By day the LORD went ahead of them in a pillar of cloud to guide them on their way" (Exodus 13:21).

Plate XI: Mount Galanggung, West Java, Indonesia, 1982.

"And by night [the LORD went ahead of them] in a pillar of fire to give them light, so that they could travel by day or night." (Exodus 13:21).

Photograph: Wikicommons

Plate XII: Mount Rinjani, Lombok Island, Indonesia, 1994.

"Then the angel of God, who had been travelling in front of Israel's army, withdrew and went behind them. The pillar of cloud also moved from in front and stood behind them, coming between the armies of Egypt and Israel. Throughout the night the cloud brought darkness to the one side and light to the other; so neither went near the other all night long." (Exodus 14:19-20).

Photograph: Wikicommons

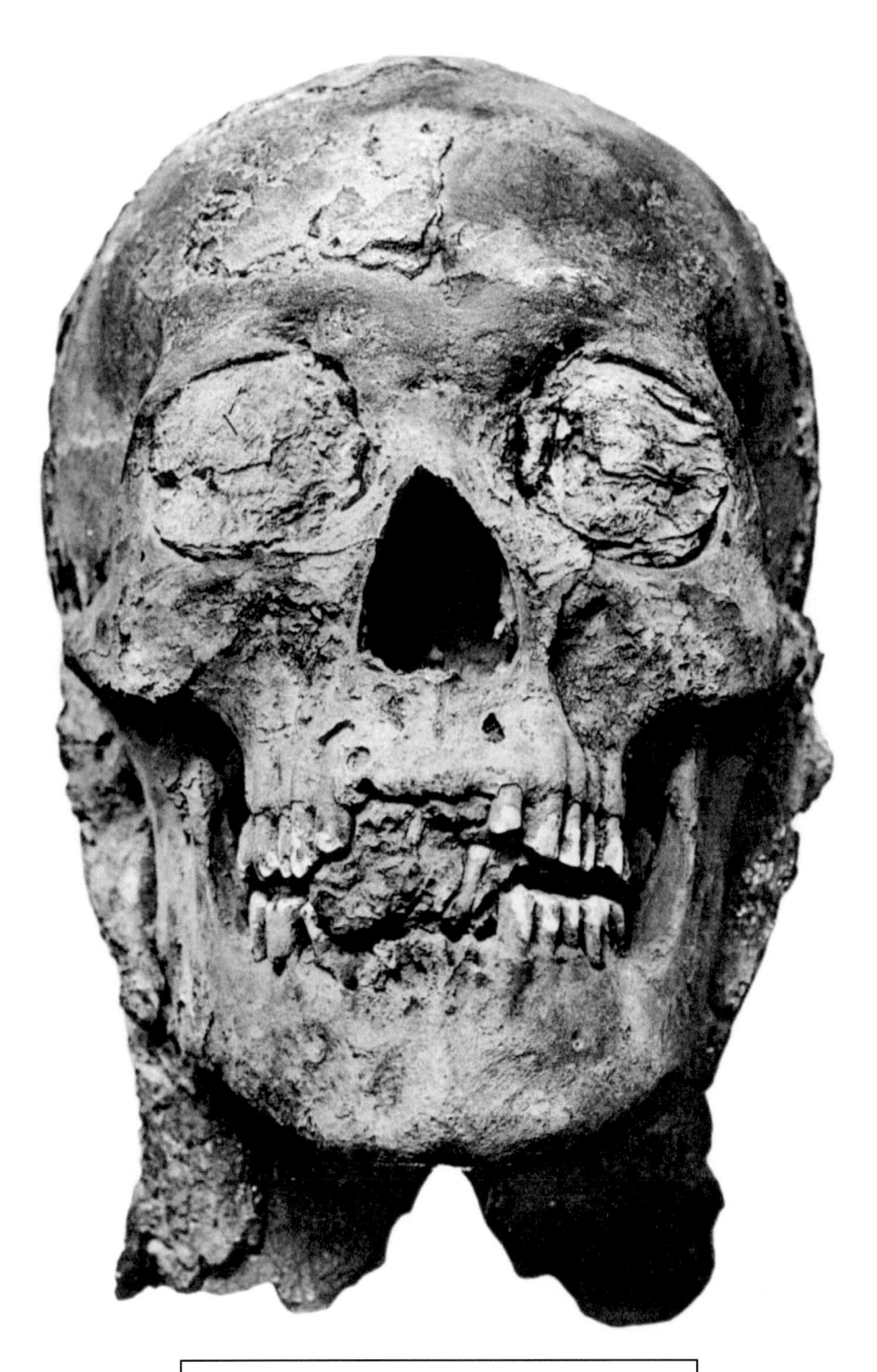

Plate XIII: Mummified head of Amenhotep III.

"Who among the gods is like you, O LORD? Who is like you – majestic in holiness, awesome in glory, working wonders? You stretched out your right hand and the earth swallowed them." (Exodus 15:11).

Plate XIV: The colossi of Memnon, fronting a now vanished temple built by Amenhotep III.

"By the power of your arm they will be still as a stone – until your people pass by, O LORD, until the people you bought pass by." (Exodus 15:16).

Plate XV: A desert oasis.

"Then Moses led Israel from the Red Sea and they went into the Desert of Shur. For three days they travelled in the desert without finding water. When they came to Marah, they could not drink its water because it was bitter. (That is why the place is called Marah.) So the people grumbled against Moses, saying, 'What are we to drink?' Then Moses cried out to the LORD, and the LORD showed him a piece of wood. He threw it into the water, and the water became sweet." (Exodus 15:22-25).

Plate XVI: Commemorative scarab of Amenhotep III.

"Then the LORD said to Moses, 'Write this on a scroll as something to be remembered'" (Exodus 17:14).

Plate XVII: Mount Sinai.

"In the third month after the Israelites left Egypt – on the very day – they came to the Desert of Sinai. After they set out from Rephidim, they entered the Desert of Sinai, and Israel camped there in the desert in front of the mountain." (Exodus 19:1-2).

Photograph: Wikicommons

Plate XVIII: Statue of Akhenaten in early Amarna style.
"Then the LORD said to Moses, 'Tell the Israelites this: 'You have seen for yourselves that I have spoken to you from heaven. Do not make any gods to be alongside me; do not make for yourselves gods of silver or gods of gold.''" (Exodus 20:22-23).

Plate XIX: Bust of Akhenaten.

"Whoever sacrifices to any god other than the LORD must be destroyed." (Exodus 22:20).

Plate XX: Bas relief portrait of Akhenaten.

"Do not take advantage of a widow or an orphan. If you do and they cry out to me, I will certainly hear their cry. My anger will be aroused, and I will kill you with the sword; your wives will become widows and your children fatherless." (Exodus 22:22).

Plate XXI: Akhenaten in the guise of the Sphinx worships Aten.

"Be careful to do everything I have said to you. Do not invoke the names of other gods; do not let them be heard on your lips." (Exodus 23:13).

Plate XXIII: Treasures from the tomb of Tutankhamun.

"Have them make a chest of acacia wood – two and a half cubits long, a cubit and a half wide, and a cubit and a half high. Overlay it with pure gold, both inside and out, and make a gold moulding around it. Cast four gold rings for it and fasten them to its four feet, with two rings on one side and two rings on the other. Then make poles of acacia wood and overlay them with gold. Insert the poles into the rings on the sides of the chest to carry it. The poles are to remain in the rings of this ark; they are not to be removed. Then put in the ark the testimony I will give you." (Exodus 25:10-16).

Plate XXII: One of the Amarna letters.

"When Moses went and told the people all the LORD's words and laws, they responded with one voice, 'Everything the LORD has said we will do.' Moses then wrote down everything the LORD had said." (Exodus 24:3-4).

Photograph: Wikicommons

Plate XXIV: Statue of the Apis bull.

"'Do not be angry, my lord,' Aaron answered, 'You know how prone these people are to evil. They said to me, "Make us gods who will go before us. As for this fellow Moses who has brought us up out of Egypt, we don't know what has happened to him." So I told them, "Whoever has any gold jewellery, take it off." Then they gave me the gold, and I threw it into the fire, and out came this calf!'" (Exodus 32:22-24).

So do not eat the meat of an animal torn by wild beasts; throw it to the dogs." (Exodus 22:31). At heart, these things are not primarily about arcane rules or arbitrary regulations; they are matters of spiritual discipline, the underlying principles of which go to keeping ourselves in the best possible state of spiritual readiness. The proper exercise of discipline requires that we "be ready" (Exodus 19:11 and 34:2), establish "limits" (Exodus 19:12 and 23), "Be careful" (Exodus 19:12, 23:13, 34:12 and 34:15), "Prepare" (Exodus 19:15) and "abstain" (Exodus 19:15). Israel was explicitly required to do each of these things before the Law was given, and subsequently she was encouraged to continue doing so through the laws and rituals that were ordained to govern daily life.[346]

Circumcision, too, addresses issues of spiritual readiness. It pointed towards setting limits, being a means by which those who were part of God's people were distinguished from those who were not and being also one of the mechanisms through which the Almighty established boundaries for Israel between sacred and profane, clean and unclean, holy and unholy.[347] It reminded the people to take care over their individual and corporate relationship with God; exposing a tender and intimate part of the anatomy was not primarily a matter of hygiene but a question of being fully open to God – a matter of the heart, not the genitals.[348] At the same time it pictured preparation, for in representing subordination of bodily comfort or desire to obedience to the commands of God and to his future service it illuminated the spiritual path that leads to mastery over physical cravings or baser instincts and which prepares those who follow it to see and do yet "greater things" (John 1:50, GNT; and 14:12, GNT). In similar vein it carried with it the idea of abstaining, symbolising a curtailing of unrestrained appetite in order that sexual desires might be channelled in accordance with the reasons for which they were given and in ways which honour the Creator who ordained them. Beyond these things, it encouraged consideration of man's purpose in this life and how best we might be "fellow workers" (1 Corinthians 3:9, NKJV) with God by encapsulating the delegation of aspects of his creative work to us. In Hebrew *milah* means both *circumcision* and *word*, linking the spawning of new life in sexual activity with the Word of God whose speech alone (Genesis 1:3, 6, 9, 11, 14, 20, 24 and 26) was capable of bringing things into being out of nothingness.

RECOGNISING REALITY.

The practice of spiritual disciplines helps keep us in a state of spiritual readiness, and in such a state we are better able to recognise reality: by separating good from bad, truth from falsehood, wisdom from foolishness, actuality from illusion. At various points the Israelites dismally failed to make these distinctions. When they complained to Moses, saying, "Was it because there were no graves in Egypt that you brought us to the desert to die? What have you done to us by bringing us out of Egypt?" (Exodus 14:11) they showed a woeful inability to see things as they really were. Confusion and lack of clarity, spurious moral equivalence and a tendency to excuse the inexcusable, cowardice and the pursuit of selfish ends, a yen for power or control rather than service, a lukewarm attitude towards the things of God and a willingness to compromise over things that should be non-negotiable – all these and more afflict us as they did them. This was not for want of information or evidence. It was not the result of inherent difficulties or obscurities. It was a matter of heart and will, not intellect. The instructions that God gave with regard to how Israel should deal with the inhabitants of Canaan are a case in point. The words are unequivocal: "Do not let them live in your land, or they will cause you to sin against me, because the worship of their gods will certainly be a snare for you." (Exodus 23:33). The Israelites shrank from their full import and application, as do we.[349]

At root, this is because in our heart of hearts we believe we can substitute the judgment and wisdom of men for the judgment and wisdom of God. We therefore adopt the wrong starting-point. Exodus shows an entirely different viewpoint and a correspondingly different reality, emphasising:

The primacy of God and his claim on man: The Israelites were told, "Do not blaspheme God or curse the ruler of your people" (Exodus 22:28) because the surpassing excellence of the Most High requires no less and to curse the ruler was to impugn the Lord himself, as when the Israelites' grumbling was seen to be "against him" (Exodus 16:8), not against Moses and Aaron. If our Maker requires something of us, it is for us to obey promptly and to the letter, whether or not we fully understand or agree with what he says.

The superlative virtue, goodness, merit and power of the Creator: The Almighty is such that any and all efforts to represent his totality are bound to fall short and, in doing so, to risk doing him grave dishonour. Hence the injunction, "Do not make cast idols" (Exodus 34:17) and the many occasions on which the Lord has made plain his horror at graven images. We can conjure up an idol in the mind as easily as craft one of metal, however. There are few idols as beguiling, insidious and damaging as believing that we know better than God.

The need to devote everything to the service of God: Wholeheartedness is to characterise the believer's service at every level. So God commands: "Do not hold back offerings from your granaries or vats. You must give me the firstborn of your sons. Do the same with your cattle and your sheep. Let them stay with their mothers for seven days, but give them to me on the eighth day." (Exodus 22:29-30).

Full and prompt obedience, a purging of the idols in our hearts and wholeheartedness in service are the challenges which follow in the wake of seeing things as they really were. The people whom Moses led out of Egypt met these with varying degrees of success. In "all the work on the tabernacle [and] the Tent of Meeting ... The Israelites did everything just as the LORD commanded Moses." (Exodus 39:32; the latter sentence substantially repeated in Exodus 39:42). The tabernacle, all its furnishings and the priestly garments were brought before Moses (Exodus 39:33-41), who "inspected the work and saw that they had done it just as the LORD had commanded. So Moses blessed them." (Exodus 39:42-43). This was a job well done, but ultimately those who had laboured on it fell short and died in the desert, when the Promised Land was theirs for the taking had they but seen clearly and done as they were told.

RESISTING TEMPTATION.

Human beings are fallen creatures. Even the saintliest have manifold faults and failings. Moses was no exception. He seems to have had a propensity to anger, as evidenced by his killing of the Egyptian (Exodus 2:11-12), his behaviour before Pharaoh (Exodus 11:8), his reaction to the Israelites' refusal to comply with the Lord's instructions relating to manna (Exodus 16:20) and to their sin with the Golden Calf (Exodus 32:19-20).[350] At times this anger was righteous, at times not. Sometimes it was expressed in godly action, though it could on occasion produce entirely the opposite result. Mostly it was kept under control, albeit here and there breaking out unexpectedly. That Moses' frustrations should intermittently have boiled over in the face of extreme provocation is entirely understandable, but the fact remains that these emotions seem to have been a source of temptation that was never entirely eradicated. The prophet was sorely tempted in other ways, too. There was the lure of trying to do God's work according to a human agenda using mortal power, which led only to murder and flight. There was the apparently sensible course of compromise and collaboration with a corrupt and corrupting regime, which could only have perpetuated enslavement. Ever-present was the danger of seeking personal glory, an easeful life and turning God's power to private advantage, which would have resulted in blessing, anointing and authority being removed. Similar challenges apply in every age. We see them in the secularism, materialism and hedonism of the present no less than in their equivalents in times gone by.

Moses' story shows that God's way to glory takes a different road. It lies in suffering, not showing off; in self-denial, not the pursuit of celebrity; in seeking the best for others, not self-promotion. To tread this path and to resist temptation as did Moses requires humility, integrity and generosity.[351]

RECONNECTING WITH GOD.

This in turn means that we need to reconnect with God. When "the LORD said to Moses, 'Set up the tabernacle, the Tent of Meeting, on the first day of the first month'" (Exodus 40:2), this represented a new beginning. In spiritual terms it was the dawn of a new age, marking a different calendar and a point of departure; it was a kind of re-creation, in much the same way that God had started afresh with Noah and his family after the Flood. It was a chance for mankind to rediscover the close bond with its Maker that had existed before the Fall of Adam and Eve. To seize this opportunity in our own lives, we need to pray, since by that means we talk to the Almighty and he speaks with us. Moses engaged in such close, clear and repeated communication with the God of his forefathers that his prayers were often answered in dramatic fashion. So, when "Moses left the king and prayed to the LORD, … the LORD did as Moses asked. The flies left the king, his officials, and his people; not one fly remained." (Exodus 8:30-31, GNT)[352] – though it is well to remember that before the prophet reached this stage in his relationship with the Most High he had to endure forty years in Midian. During that time it may well have appeared to him that God was ignoring the heartfelt prayers which the fugitive doubtless uttered, for presumably he pleaded many times to be reunited with his family and to witness the deliverance of Israel from bondage.

The fact that God made a new start for mankind did not mean that everything familiar was swept away. The Lord loves to refashion what is imperfect, to reconfigure what has been marred and to breathe new life into the old.[353] Hence in making the tabernacle, the Israelites were able to draw on architectural forms that were familiar to them. The temples of Egypt had possessed an outer court, inner court and holy of holies as the tabernacle (and later the Temple) did. The orientation of the structure was east to west like its equivalents in the Two Lands, it being specified that "On the east end, towards the sunrise, the courtyard shall also be fifty cubits wide" (Exodus 27:13) – an echo, almost of the temples of Akhenaten. There the similarities ended, though; the point was not to worship the sun, which is only a created thing, but to adore the One who "set the sun and the moon in their places [and] … set the limits of the earth" (Psalm 74:16-17, GNT). The tabernacle drew a line figuratively under the false worship of Egypt, pointing the way back to the one true God.[354]

REVOLUTIONARY GENEROSITY.

Attitudes and behaviour were similarly to be remoulded in dramatic fashion. In a fit of pique, spite and dictatorial callousness, Pharaoh withheld basic building materials from the Israelites, who were told: "You will not be given any more straw." (Exodus 5:18). The heavenly King, by contrast, is open-handed and hence the redeemed are to eschew such meanness. Their life is to be characterised by generosity of the most extravagant kind:

Generosity from God: The Almighty "gives to all generously and without reproach" (James 1:5, GNT). Exodus is replete with examples of his giving – "the wonders I have given you [Moses] power to do" (Exodus 4:21), "the bread the LORD has given" (Exodus 16:15), "the Sabbath" (Exodus 16:29), "wisdom"

(Exodus 28:3), "skill to all the craftsmen" (Exodus 31:6), "the commands ... given [to Moses]" (Exodus 34:32), the "skill and ability" of Bezalel, Oholiab and every skilled person (Exodus 35:34 and 36:1-2).[355]

Generosity in response to God: What we have been given should spark a response in us, so "No-one is to appear before me empty-handed." (Exodus 34:20). Likewise we are told, "Do not hold back offerings from your granaries or your vats." (Exodus 22:29).

Generosity to our fellow man: God's command is, "do not be hard-hearted or tight-fisted towards your poor brother ... Rather, be open-handed and freely lend him whatever he needs." (Deuteronomy 15:7-8).

Such a way of living brings in its wake wellbeing and true freedom. For obedience to God's Word and Law brings health in body, mind and spirit: "If you listen carefully to the voice of the LORD your God and do what is right in his eyes, if you pay attention to his commands and keep all his decrees, I will not bring on you any of the diseases I brought on the Egyptians, for I am the LORD, who heals you." (Exodus 15:26). There is freedom from sickness, freedom from slavery and even freedom from death, so that "When the LORD goes through the land to strike down the Egyptians, he will see the blood on the top and sides of the door-frame and will pass over that doorway, and he will not permit the destroyer to enter your houses and strike you down." (Exodus 12:23). This is the greatest generosity of all on God's part – our redemption and eternal salvation.

REACHING OUR PROMISED INHERITANCE.

The Passover promises spoken by God were to "bring out ... free ... redeem ... take you as my own people and ... be your God." (Exodus 6:6-7). He went on to say, "I am making a covenant with you. Before all your people I will do wonders never before done in any nation in all the world. The people you live among will see how awesome is the work that I, the LORD, will do for you." (Exodus 34:10). There were promises about things that the Israelites were shortly to see and receive in this world, but there were also assurances of what was to come both in the earthly realms and in the heavenly: questions of inheritance – of what will for certain sure be ours at some point, but the precise timing of the receipt of which we are not in a position to know. Amongst other things, Exodus is the story of the Israelites' journey towards this promised inheritance. Their passage through the sea on dry land symbolises progression from death to life, from one realm of existence to a higher, more spiritual one, just as their subsequent adventures mark the trials and triumphs of the life of faith. The people were beset by all manner of problems, dogged by frequent stumbles and victims of their own sinful natures. Of that entire adult generation who had been brought out of Egypt, only Joshua and Caleb lived to enter the Promised Land.

They did so because they ignored what was passing or momentary and kept their eye both on the ultimate prize and on the One who was leading them to it.

Joshua was distinguished by his eagerness for the things of heaven and his yearning to be in the presence of God, so that when "Moses would return [from the Tent of Meeting] to the camp ... his young assistant Joshua son of Nun did not leave the tent." (Exodus 33:11). This steadfastness was a characteristic that Joshua had shown from the first; when "Moses set out with Joshua his assistant, and Moses went up on the mountain of God [to receive the Ten Commandments] ... and stayed on the mountain forty days and forty nights" (Exodus 24:13 and 18), it seems that Joshua lingered on the mountainside, too – though presumably in the foothills rather than on "the top of the mountain" (Exodus 19:20) beside the prophet.[356] If we wish to be inheritors of all that God has promised, we would do well to follow that example.

SUMMARY.

This is the gospel.[357] It involves rescue, redemption, readying ourselves, recognising reality, resisting temptation, reconnecting with God, revolutionary generosity and reaching our promised inheritance. Its message is offensive, for it challenges mankind in ways that can be uncomfortable in the extreme, and hence there will always be reaction and resistance in the face of it. Wherever the Israelites went there was spiritual warfare as the opponents of God sought to thwart his purposes, exercise power for their own selfish ends and keep their fellow men in servitude. Moses had to confront those who competed with him by "secret arts" (Exodus 7:11, 7:22 and 8:7), by using surprise attack and military stratagem (Exodus 17:9-13), by setting up an object of false worship (Exodus 32:1-29) and by seeking to undermine or challenge his leadership (Exodus 15:24, 16:2 and 17:3). At every point, he prevailed.

Experiencing fullness.

To live for God in the way he wishes, we need to step into the fullness of what he has planned for us. His plan for Israel was outlined to Moses from the very first: "And this will be the sign to you that it is I who have sent you: When you have brought the people out of Egypt, you will worship God on this mountain." (Exodus 3:12). The final "you" in this sentence is plural, since it was an entire nation that was intended to take part in this worship. In the event, though, fear led the majority to reject what was offered. Although commanded to stay away from the mountain until a designated signal, the people were subsequently allowed to climb it: "Whoever touches the mountain shall surely be put to death. He shall surely be stoned or shot with arrows; not a hand is to be laid on him. Whether man or animal, he shall not be permitted to live. Only when the ram's horn sounds a long blast may they [the people] go up to the mountain." (Exodus 19:12-13). Yet such was their terror that they did not do so: "When the people saw the thunder and lightning and heard the trumpet and saw the mountain in smoke, they trembled with fear. They stayed at a distance and said to Moses, 'Speak to us yourself and we will listen. But do not have God speak to us or we will die.' Moses said to the people, 'Do not be afraid. God has come to test you, so that the fear of God will be with you to keep you from sinning.' The people remained at a distance, while Moses approached the thick darkness where God was." (Exodus 20:18-21).

Trepidation prevented the Israelites from experiencing fullness, just as it cripples many nowadays. It need not be so. Jethro stepped into fullness through hearing the gospel as "Moses told [him] about everything the LORD had done ... and how the LORD had saved them" (Exodus 18:8); by responding to it with "[delight] ... Praise ... [and a confession of faith, saying] 'Now I know that the LORD is greater than all other gods'" (Exodus 18:9-11); and by being brought as a result into "the presence of God." (Exodus 18:12). The same set of experiences is available to all who ask, for God is merciful; the ark had "an atonement cover of pure gold" (Exodus 25:17), a symbol of reconciliation between God and man, made possible through the undeserved grace by which the Almighty draws people to him and makes them at one with him. Mercy was shown time and again to Israel, as when "the LORD relented and did not bring on his people the disaster he had threatened." (Exodus 32:14). We have no reason to hang back like those who were afraid to follow Moses up the mountain. Since "Jesus Christ is the same yesterday and today and for ever" (Hebrews 13:8), the mercy that was on display in years gone by will be shown to us, too.

Conclusion.

Living for God is not always straightforward. It involves being in the world but not of it, in the same way that "Moses used to take a tent and pitch it outside the camp some distance away, calling it the 'tent of meeting'." (Exodus 33:7). It requires us not just to ascend the heights and stay there, but also to come "down from the mountain" (Exodus 32:1) to address the needs of the world, to "return to the camp" (Exodus 33:11) so as to provide help and guidance to those who have stayed behind. Nevertheless, it is not a life of unremitting toil, in contrast to what the Israelites experienced in Egypt (see Exodus 1:14, 5:4, 5:9, 5:11, 5:13, 5:18 and compare 12:16, 20:9-10, 23:12, 31:14-15, 31:17 and 35:2). It is the way to health, wellbeing and salvation, and its effect is to make us "God's temple" (1 Corinthians 3:16). As such, we are places where his Spirit dwells and consequently bearers of life to others, as it was foretold long ago: "By the power of your arm they will be still as a stone – until your people pass by, O LORD, until the people you bought pass by." (Exodus 15:16).

Issachar

Whose meaning is, *reward*

Of whom Jacob prophesied,
"When he sees how good is his resting place and how pleasant is his land, he will bend his shoulder to the burden and submit to forced labour."
(Genesis 49:15).

12. The Presence of God

Motives, reactions and legacy.

"My Presence will go with you, and I will give you rest." (Exodus 33:14).

The changes wrought during the reign of Akhenaten raise above all the question of motivation, for their most distinctive elements cannot be explained merely by extrapolation from the past. Many and various are the ideas that have been put forward, and teasing out the truth is a daunting task: much of what has been written about this pharaoh strays into the realm of fantasy and so few are the facts which can be considered incontestable that all grand theories deserve to be approached with caution. Any hypothesis needs to advance cogent reasons for steps which, to contemporaries, must have seemed baffling at first and then progressively more and more bizarre: the sovereign's change of name, itself verging on apostasy; moving the capital to a remote location which was both entirely new and in many ways utterly impractical;[358] permitting and indeed encouraging disturbing representations of royalty that diverged sharply from all precedent; allowing what look to modern eyes at least like glimpses into the private life of the monarch's family, forsaking Amun, for decades past venerated as king of the gods and protector of the ruling house; choosing Aten as chief object of worship, and doing so in such a way as to redefine the relationship between god and king; using novel forms of temple architecture; doing away with physical representations of the king's chosen god.[359] Each of these was surprising and unsettling in its own right, but beyond every precedent and in breach of all propriety was the ruler's seemingly dogmatic insistence on the worship of one deity above all others. This was a move that would probably have struck those around the king as being at one and the same time both sacrilegious and unnecessary, since in years gone by there had always been room for one more god in the pantheon.[360]

These goings-on may have had relatively little impact on ordinary people, for there is no evidence of the tax burden being greatly increased from that of previous reigns. Neither would the levies made to provide muscle for building projects necessarily have been more onerous than in the past; the projects that Akhenaten conceived were ambitious, but not substantially more so than those that came before or afterwards. Whilst forced movements of tens of thousands were needed to populate Akhet-aten, absolute monarchs in the ancient Near East were scarcely unaccustomed to relocating subjects at a whim. Large encampments habitually sprang up to provide shelter and the necessities of life for those engaged on the huge and time-consuming works which every self-proclaimed living god required in order to leave his mark. It may be that from the point of view of the labourers and artisans who lived in it, Akhet-aten differed from these not so much by reason of size or duration of occupation as by the more or less continuous personal presence of the king and the proclaimed permanence of the habitations in which the workers dwelt. Equally, although the common people were presumably conscious of monuments being defaced and inscriptions being erased, the wider significance of what was happening may well have passed them by; as little as one per cent of the population is estimated to have been literate. Even had they been told what was being done, for all we know they might have shrugged and regarded such things as a piece of silliness by lords and masters with nothing better to do with their time.

Amongst the elite, however, it is highly likely that the ruler's actions would have been seen in a very different light. Indeed, their impact for many would quite probably have been traumatic. Priests who worshipped and served the myriad traditional gods would have been doubly outraged, not only by the affront to their chosen deities but also by their own loss of purpose, prestige and livelihood.[361] The insult (and in all likelihood the economic penalty) might reasonably be supposed to have been felt almost as keenly by the towns with which such gods were associated, with particular trades suffering especial hardship.[362] Meanwhile, families who were uprooted from their homes and the accustomed easefulness of Thebes and other established centres may conceivably have nursed grievances, with even those who reacted more philosophically hankering after a return to more congenial surroundings. Officials who had basked in the pomp and circumstance of the former capital and were habituated to the conveniences, easy communications and business contacts of a long-established metropolis must have been frustrated. One way or another there is unlikely to have been an influential constituency in the land which did not feel hard done by as a result of the king's religious policies. By contrast, those who prospered under the new dispensation are likely to have been fewer in number – a single priesthood replaced many, for a start, with the king and his family assuming many of the priestly functions.

Since there are no personal diaries to give insight into the private thoughts of the people of this time, attempts to gauge their outlook can only be speculation. Whilst that does not completely invalidate conclusions drawn by analogy with equivalent circumstances or through discriminating application of human sympathy, the limitations of such an approach are obvious. Quite apart from anything else, it is always difficult to re-create the attitudes and mentality of a vanished civilisation and a bygone era. For example, there could well have been an element of self-censorship in the thoughts that a subject might permit himself to have towards a god-king. Yet when all allowance is made and every disclaimer spoken, so wanton, so inexplicable, so against all convention, order and habitual thinking were the things this pharaoh did that both nobles and commoners alike might have been forgiven for thinking him mad. Certainly, the generations which followed felt no cause to hold back, blaming this ruler for all manner of ills and dissociating themselves from every aspect of his reign. For them, there was not even a plea of diminished responsibility by reason of insanity; the architect of Akhet-aten was quite simply criminal, rebel and enemy.

Fire and cloud.

The catalyst and motivating force behind all that the book of Exodus recounts was nothing less than the presence of the Most High. It was a divine presence that "appeared to [Moses] in flames of fire from within a bush" (Exodus 3:2)[363]; which "kept vigil [on the night of Passover] to bring [Israel] out of Egypt" (Exodus 12:42); who "struck down the firstborn in Egypt" (Exodus 12:29); that went before Israel so that "Neither the pillar of cloud by day nor the pillar of fire by night left its place in front of the people" (Exodus 13:22); who "descended to the top of Mount Sinai and called Moses to the top of the mountain" (Exodus 19:20); in whose company the elders of Israel "ate and drank" (Exodus 24:11); which envisioned and empowered men by the "Spirit of God" (Exodus 31:3 and 35:31) for the making of the tabernacle and its furnishings; which "would come down and stay at the entrance [to the Tent of Meeting], while the LORD spoke with Moses" (Exodus 33:9); who "came down in the cloud and stood there with [Moses] and proclaimed his name" (Exodus 34:5); which "covered the Tent of Meeting and ... filled the tabernacle" (Exodus 40:34); and which "was ... in the sight of all the house of Israel during all their travels." (Exodus 40:38). It is the repeated, manifest presence of God with the whole nation that marks out the events of Exodus from any other part of the Old Testament. Not since the Fall of Adam and Eve, nor until the pouring out of the Holy Spirit on "everyone" (Joel 2:28, GNT; and Acts 2:17, GNT) in the New Testament era had such widespread and continuous divine dwelling with humankind been experienced, or was it again.[364]

What the former slaves witnessed was the *shekinah*, that outward expression of God's excellence which is called his glory, a bright light surrounding his presence and his revelation of himself: "To the Israelites the light looked like a fire burning on top of the mountain." (Exodus 24:17, GNT) – a phenomenon causing those in the New Testament era to agree that "Our God is a consuming fire" (Hebrews 12:29, substantially repeating Deuteronomy 4:24).[365] Little wonder that, to mark this fiery presence, "the Israelites [were] to bring ... clear oil of pressed olives for the light so that the lamps [in the Tent of Meeting] may be kept burning ... from evening till morning ... [as] a lasting ordinance." (Exodus 27:20-21).[366] Yet as well as through flame, this presence was displayed in another physical form: when quail and manna were provided for Israel in the desert, "there was the glory of the LORD appearing in the cloud" (Exodus 16:10). Later, "The LORD said to Moses, 'I am going to come to you in a dense cloud, so that people will hear me speaking with you and will always put their trust in you.'" (Exodus 19:9). Indeed, in some manner cloud and flame were linked:

"Moses went up Mount Sinai, and a cloud covered it. The dazzling light of the LORD's presence came down on the mountain. To the Israelites the light looked like a fire burning on top of the mountain. The cloud covered the mountain for six days, and on the seventh day the LORD called to Moses from the cloud. Moses went on up the mountain into the cloud. There he stayed for forty days and nights." (Exodus 24:15-18, GNT).

Such extraordinary and unprecedented events emphasise that Exodus describes the coming into being of a new age. Cain had said that "my punishment is more than I can bear … [because] I will be hidden from your [God's] presence" (Genesis 4:14), just as his parents had been "banished … from the garden [of Eden]" (Genesis 3:23) and hence were no longer able to enjoy their previous close fellowship with the Lord. Now that rupture between creature and Creator which had been caused by human sin was to be repaired as God took the initiative to draw men back to him. When he told Moses, "Do not come any closer" (Exodus 3:5),[367] this was not since he forbids any to approach him. It simply reflected the fact that Moses at that stage was not ready to go beyond a certain point – as shown by the fact that, only a relatively short while later, upon asking, "Now show me your glory" (Exodus 33:18) the prophet was welcomed as far into the presence of God as any mortal can stand. Nevertheless, a command to advance no further illustrates the inherent tension involved wherever the Lord's holiness is brought face to face with our sinfulness. When God told Moses that: "There, above the cover between the two cherubim that are over the ark of the testimony, I will meet with you" (Exodus 25:22), he was making an important point as well as designating a convenient spot for a chat. The cover of which he spoke was "the atonement cover of pure gold" (Exodus 25:17) – a symbol of reconciliation between him and mankind.

God's presence with men, in other words, came about solely at the instigation of the Almighty and only in a context where he had done something to deal with the problem of human sin and rebellion against divine authority.[368] It is against this background that the ebb and flow of divine presence with Israel needs to be seen. The Lord's wish was that he should be able to accompany his people at each stage of their journey; hence the statement of intent, "I will dwell among the Israelites and be their God. They will know that I am the LORD their God, who brought them out of Egypt so that I might dwell among them. I am the LORD their God." (Exodus 29:45-46). Nonetheless, human behaviour could cause the divine presence to depart.[369] In the aftermath of Israel's sin with the Golden Calf, the Lord announced that although "I will send an angel before you and drive out [the inhabitants of Canaan] … I will not go with you, because you are a stiff-necked people and I might destroy you on the way." (Exodus 33:2-3). As so often, it took the removal of blessing to bring about a realisation of what had been lost. Those who just a short while beforehand had been careless about the things of God grasped at least some of the import of what the withdrawal of his presence presaged and were filled with anguish: "When the people heard these distressing words, they began to mourn and no-one put on any ornaments. For the LORD had said to Moses, 'Tell the Israelites, "You are a stiff-necked people. If I were to go with you even for a moment, I might destroy you. Now take off your ornaments and I will decide what to do with you."' So the Israelites stripped off their ornaments at Mount Horeb." (Exodus 33:4-6).

Moses saw at once what this meant and his plea "but you have not let me know whom you will send with me" (Exodus 33:12) seems to have been at least in part a protest that being accompanied by a mere angel would be a poor substitute for having God himself with the people. For it is the presence of the Lord, and that alone, which inspires and transforms humankind, makes possible what formerly seemed beyond us and achieves things that no earthly influence could match. Moses had a personal assurance that "My Presence will go with you, and I will give you rest" (Exodus 33:14), but was still hungry for more. Typically, his focus was wider than what was simply of benefit to himself or his clan: "If your Presence does not go with us, do not send us up from here. How will anyone know that you are pleased with me and with your people unless you go with us? What else will distinguish me and your people from all the other people on the face of the earth?" (Exodus 33:15-16). The prophet was not interested in an individual here or there being a little bit changed. He yearned to see wholesale transformation in an entire nation so radical that they would be self-evidently, glaringly different from "all the other people on the face of the earth" (Exodus 33:15-16). This is not an alteration that can be brought about by human activity. It belongs solely to the realm of the "Lord of lords and King of kings" (Revelation 17:14). In his love and mercy, God relented in the light of his servant's plea, and so "the LORD said to Moses, 'I will do the very thing you have asked, because I am pleased with you and I know you by name.'" (Exodus 33:17).

Fear and trembling.

The Lord is indeed merciful and forgiving, yet he is also so powerful that with the mere "blast of [his] nostrils" (Exodus 15:8) he can cause the waters of the sea to part. This is a God of whom (to put it neutrally) it is right to be cautious, in the same way that we would not expect to be allowed to stray beyond proper bounds in dealing with an earthly potentate. On numerous occasions Exodus records fearful reactions to the High King of heaven and his displays of might: after coming through the Red Sea, for "when the Israelites saw the great power the LORD displayed against the Egyptians, the people feared the LORD" (Exodus 14:31); at the foot of Mount Sinai, when "Everyone in the camp trembled" (Exodus 19:16); upon the giving of the Ten Commandments, "When the people saw the thunder and lightning and heard the trumpet and saw the mountain in smoke, [they] ... trembled with fear" (Exodus 20:18). Even the presence of the Almighty experienced at second hand could be enough, so that on seeing Moses' shining face "Aaron and all the Israelites ... were afraid to come near [him]" (Exodus 34:30).[370] Though he showed great courage on many occasions, Moses was not immune to such feelings, and neither did his terror lessen over time: when he first encountered "the angel of the LORD ... in flames of fire" (Exodus 3:2) in the burning bush, he "was afraid to look on God" (Exodus 3:6) but even later, after he might have been thought to have grown used to being in the presence of his Maker, we are told that "The sight [which accompanied the handing down of the Law] was so terrifying that Moses said, 'I am trembling and afraid!'" (Hebrews 12:21, GNT).

Such responses, whether from people or leader, were by no means either irrational or excessive; there were perfectly good grounds for dread. It had been made clear that coming into the presence of the Lord without proper authorisation was punishable by death, its being explicitly stated that if "the people ... [were to] force their way through to see the LORD ... many of them [would] perish." (Exodus 19:21).[371] There are aspects of God of which we are right to be fearful. He is awesome in power and majestic in holiness. We mess with him at our peril and should "not be deceived; [for] God cannot be mocked." (Galatians 6:7). So, not surprisingly, "When the people saw the thunder and lightning and heard the trumpet and saw the mountain in smoke, they trembled with fear. They stayed at a distance and said to Moses, 'Speak to us yourself and we will listen. But do not have God speak to us or we will die.'" (Exodus 20:18-19). Moses' response to this is instructive. He "said to the people, 'Do not be afraid. God has come to test you, so that the fear of God will be with you to keep you from sinning.'" (Exodus 20:20). In other words, though he also experienced trepidation, he saw a positive side to the terror which had gripped the people and realised that God had caused this for a good purpose. His faith was such that he was prepared to put his money where his mouth was, for whilst they "remained at a distance ... Moses approached the thick darkness where God was." (Exodus 20:21).

Scripture often uses the phrase "the fear of the Lord", advises that "it is a dreadful thing to fall into the hands of the living God" (Hebrews 10:31) and says that even Moses "was afraid to look on God" (Exodus 3:6). Yet by speaking of "the fear of the Lord", the Bible does not mean that we are forever to live in terror of a wrathful and vengeful deity. It signifies rather that we should keep to the path of true religion, bearing a loving reverence for our Creator that includes submission to his lordship and to the commands of his Word. There is a positive effect to having proper regard for the holiness and power of the Almighty, as Moses recognised, for "the fear of God will be with you to keep you from sinning" (Exodus 20:20) – an aspect of divine presence that we would often prefer to ignore or avoid. It was doubtless this sense of the fear of God betokening willing submission of the heart (rather than the compulsion of a tyrant) that lay behind Moses' admonishing Pharaoh: "I know that you and your officials still do not fear the LORD God" (Exodus 9:30). Jethro, too, seems to have had a similar idea in mind when he advised his son-in-law to select "men who fear God, trustworthy men who hate dishonest gain – and appoint them as officials" (Exodus 18:21). Fear of the Lord used in this way is altogether different from an essentially physical fear of the kind that gripped the fleeing Israelites "As Pharaoh approached ... [with his chariots, when they] were terrified and cried out to the LORD" (Exodus 14:10). Nor was it the "dread" (Exodus 15:16) or "terror" (Exodus 23:27) that was to come upon the inhabitants of Canaan at the approach of Joshua's army in a succeeding generation.[372] At its deepest level it is instead based on what the preceding chapters describe: encounter, belonging, worship, knowledge, reflection, reliance, recognition, obedience, service, remembrance and the desire to live a godly life.

In speaking of such things it is important to weigh them in the light of subsequent events. Though they remain instructive, large parts of the Old Testament dispensation no longer apply as a result of Jesus dealing decisively with sin through his death and resurrection, thereby enabling man and God to be permanently reconciled. Therefore those who live under the New Covenant are reminded that, unlike Israel of old, "you have not come to a mountain that can be touched and to a blazing fire, and to darkness and gloom and whirlwind, and to the blast of a trumpet and the sound of words which sound was such that those who heard begged that no further word be spoken to them. For they could not bear the command, 'If even a beast touches the mountain, it will be stoned.' And so terrible was the sight, that Moses said, 'I am full of fear and trembling.' But you have come to Mount Zion and to the city of the living God" (Hebrews 12:18-22, GNT). In contrast to the fear and trembling that attended the giving of the Law, now there is "joyful assembly" (Hebrews 12:22) and "the sprinkled blood [of Christ] that speaks a better word than the blood of Abel." (Hebrews 12:24, NRSV). Nonetheless, we should "See that you do not refuse the one who is speaking; for if they did not escape when they refused the one who warned them on earth, how much less will we escape if we reject the one who warns from heaven!" (Hebrews 12:25).

Heaven come to earth.

The reference to one who warned on earth reminds us that God "descended" (Exodus 19:18 and 20) from heaven and chose to "come down" (Exodus 3:8, 19:11 and 33:9) to our world. He was under no compulsion to do so, but acted in order "to rescue" (Exodus 3:8) humanity, to meet with his chosen prophet "in the sight of all the people" (Exodus 19:11) and to "[speak] with Moses" (Exodus 33:9)[373] so at to "give [him] all [God's] commands for the Israelites." (Exodus 25:22). Such events took place not just with a particular moment of history or a particular ethnic group in mind but were part of a wider plan for the redemption of all mankind and the remaking of Creation. The Lord acted then, as he acts at all times and in all places, with forethought and deliberation. His deeds and his speech are neither random nor capricious. Those described in Exodus were done and said for a specific purpose: "that you may tell your children and grandchildren how I [God] dealt harshly with the Egyptians and how I performed my signs among them, and that you may know that I am the LORD." (Exodus 10:2). The four things which these verses describe encapsulate judgment for recalcitrant sinners (dealing harshly), salvation through miraculous divine intervention (performing signs), being brought into the presence of God in order to share an eternity of loving fellowship with him (knowing God not just through his deeds but personally, his covenant name being amongst other things a symbol of this) and spreading the gospel (telling others). They show aspects of God's activity in past, present and future – what he has done in days gone by, the effect of that in our own time and the hope that we can therefore have for what is to come.

However, God has so constructed the universe that his words and actions demand a corresponding response from us. We have in a sense to meet him halfway in order to experience in fullest measure what he wishes to give. As well as God's coming down, Moses thus needed to "come up" (Exodus 24:1, 24:12, 34:2). He ascended "the mountain of God" (Exodus 3:1) to commune there with the One who made heaven and earth in response to the Lord's instruction to "meet me there" (Exodus 34:2-5, GNT). The very fact that their meeting can be expressed in such a fashion tells something of what is involved in close relationship with him who made heaven and earth, for to commune is literally to be at one with another. It suggests commonality and is linguistically related to the word communication, being an essential building block of all truest and deepest interactions. When Moses climbed Horeb he symbolically "slipped the surly bonds of earth … and touched the face of God",[374] for in the instant that "The LORD descended to the top of Mount Sinai and called Moses to the top of the mountain" (Exodus 19:20), that place became heaven and earth combined, as the tabernacle was later to be.[375] That this should be so is a paradox associated with the nature and presence of the Almighty, who remarked, "You have seen that from heaven I spoke with you" (Exodus 20:22) yet was simultaneously present alongside Moses. Once again, there was a foretaste of the presence of the Creator with his creatures which was seen yet more radically in the earthly ministry of Jesus.[376]

Man must take a hand in his own spiritual elevation. He is exhorted to do so by engaging body, mind and soul in self-conscious striving towards a higher sphere: to "lift up [his] eyes" (Psalm 121:1 and 123:1, NKJV), "lift up [his] hands" (Psalm 28:2, 63:4, 91:12, 119:48 and 134:2, NKJV), "lift up his head" (Psalm 110:7, NRSV), "lift up [his] voice" (Psalm 142:1), "lift up [his] soul" (Psalm 25:1, 86:4 and 143:8, NKJV) and "lift up the cup of salvation" (Psalm 116:13). Yet at the same time he is not required to achieve everything through his own efforts. It is the presence of God, and that only, which is able to free us from the past and bring us into new life with him. In the original Hebrew the verse rendered into English as, "I am the LORD who brought you up out of

Egypt to be your God; therefore be holy, because I am holy" (Leviticus 11:45) uses the verb "raise" rather than "bring". This underlines the fact that the exodus was more than a series of physical events. Beyond the effects that were seen in the natural world, it involved acting out profoundest spiritual truths in space and time, marking God's highway to holiness for his people. The words "raise" and "yoke" share the same root (*'ayin lamed*) – a reminder that, far from being burdensome, the yoke of obedience[377] to our Maker is a means by which he will raise us up.[378] Jesus was later to say, "Take my yoke upon you and learn from me, for I am gentle and humble in heart, and you will find rest for your souls. For my yoke is easy and my burden is light." (Matthew 11:29-30).

Consistent with the onus that is on humanity to "work out [our] salvation with fear and trembling" (Philippians 2:12), the interaction of human and divine activity in bringing about the purposes of the Almighty is seen throughout Exodus. The reasons why the Lord brought the Hebrew slaves out of their captivity and moulded them into a nation, together with his intentions as regards his future dealings with them were all clearly stated: "So I will consecrate the Tent of Meeting and the altar and will consecrate Aaron and his sons *to serve me* as priests. Then *I will dwell among the Israelites and be their God*. They will know that I am the LORD their God, who brought them out of Egypt *so that I might dwell among them*. I am the LORD their God." (Exodus 29:44-46, emphasis added).[379] At the heart of this lay God's desire to be present with his people not just by way of an occasional visit but through dwelling with them permanently and removing the separation between heaven and earth.[380] In order for these things to come about and for the presence of the Almighty to come down, however, the people were required to do various things. Firstly, they had "to bring [God] an offering" (Exodus 25:1). With the raw material thus provided, they next needed to "make a sanctuary for [God, so that he would] ... dwell among them." (Exodus 25:8).[381] Only once all this had been done did the Lord do what had been on his heart from the first: "And so Moses completed the work. *Then* the cloud covered the Tent of Meeting, and the glory of the LORD filled the tabernacle." (Exodus 40:34, emphasis added). Such then was the overwhelming presence of God that even Moses, who had stood on Horeb and seen the back of the Creator of an entire universe pass by "could not enter the Tent of Meeting because the cloud had settled on it, and the glory of the LORD filled the tabernacle." (Exodus 40:35).[382]

Awe and wonder.

This was a watershed moment, of heaven come down and of God showing himself to his people.[383] The awe-inspiring sight of the glory of the Lord filling the tabernacle set the seal on all his miraculous interventions on behalf of Israel up to that point. It was a pinnacle seldom achieved again during the Old Testament era, though at length surpassed with the coming of Jesus and the inauguration of the New Covenant.[384] Yet it was but the culmination of a steadily building crescendo of manifestations of the divine presence to Moses and (in lesser degree) to those who had journeyed with him from their former homes in Egypt. For God's covenant promises were from the start premised on his being with and alongside his people. He swore:

To go with them so as to ensure their entry into the Promised Land: "I also established my covenant with them to give them the land of Canaan, where they lived as aliens ... And I will bring you to the land I swore with uplifted hand to give to Abraham, to Isaac and to Jacob. I will give it to you as a possession. I am the LORD." (Exodus 6:4 and 8).

To be with them in response to their obedience: "Whenever I cause my name to be honoured, I will come to you and bless you." (Exodus 20:24).

To fight for them through works of power: "Then the LORD said: 'I am making a covenant with you. Before all your people I will do wonders never before done in any nation in all the world. The people you live among will see how awesome is the work that I, the LORD, will do for you.'" (Exodus 34:10).

To grant access to them whenever circumstances required: "Then Moses told Aaron, 'Say to the entire Israelite community, 'Come before the LORD, for he has heard your grumbling.' While Aaron was speaking to the whole Israelite community, they looked towards the desert, and there was the glory of the LORD appearing in the cloud." (Exodus 16:9-10).

To give them guidance in the form of his laws and commandments: "Place the cover on top of the ark and put in the ark the Testimony, which I will give you. There, above the cover between the two cherubim that are over the ark of the Testimony, I will meet with you and give you all my commands for the Israelites." (Exodus 25:21-22).

To make good the mistakes of humanity and remake what our sin has damaged or destroyed: "The Lord told Moses, 'Prepare two stone tablets like the first ones, and I will write upon them the same commands that were on the tablets you broke.'" (Exodus 34:1, TLB).

To provide for their deepest needs so that "all these people will go home satisfied" (Exodus 18:23) – just as when crowds were fed by Jesus "They all ate and were satisfied" (Mark 6:42 and Luke 9:17, substantially repeating Matthew 14:20 and 15:37 and Mark 8:8), physically acting out the promises in the Sermon on the Mount and the Sermon on the Plain: of blessing for those "who hunger and thirst for righteousness, for they will be filled" (Matthew 5:6) and upon those "who hunger now, for you will be satisfied." (Luke 6:21).

These are wonderful promises, but the fact that the Lord has made these (and other) covenant commitments does not mean that he will overlook human wrongdoing or that we can safely predict (still less, control) his activity. His choices are sovereign and often he exercises them in ways that we do not expect. As on several occasions throughout Scripture, he flew in the face of all custom and every human idea of propriety by choosing the younger son above the elder, for "Moses was eighty years old and Aaron eighty-three when they spoke to Pharaoh." (Exodus 7:7)[385] – a reminder that we need to examine our own prejudices and preconceptions with regard to what God's being with us in our own age may presage.

The truth is that there are likely to be aspects of the divine presence which we will find unwelcome, uncomfortable and uncongenial. There was doubtless awe and wonder but probably disorientation and anxiety, too, as the pillar of cloud, symbolising the presence of God, "also moved from in front and stood behind them, coming between the armies of Egypt and Israel." (Exodus 14:19-20). This manoeuvre had an obvious military purpose in that it prevented the Egyptian forces closing for the kill, but on a spiritual level it was also a means by which the pure and impure were separated, a necessary precondition for the transition which Israel would shortly be required to make when she crossed the Red Sea. Physical phenomena similarly mirrored the spiritual as "Throughout the night the cloud brought darkness to the one side and light to the other; so neither went near the other all night long." (Exodus 14:20). The very thing which provided illumination for God's chosen people was a source of the exact opposite for those who remained in opposition to him, as it has ever been, "For the message of the cross is foolishness to those who are perishing, but to us who are being saved it is the power of God. For it is written: 'I will destroy the wisdom of the wise, And bring to nothing the understanding of the prudent.'" (1 Corinthians 1:18-19, NKJV). The manifest presence of God, made most plain in the coming of Jesus, is often the greatest stumbling block to those whose minds are darkened.

This should challenge us. Too often we overlook the divine presence because it does not come in the way or at the time we want. Miracles are routinely disregarded and instead we credit blind forces of nature or human activity so that scepticism replaces the wonderment that should attend such works of God. Exodus provides an entirely different perspective. It demonstrates over and over again that the splendours of man pale beside those of his Maker. This is seen in the progressive demolition of each pillar of the Egyptian state: the occult practices of "the wise men and sorcerers" (Exodus 7:11); reliance on the Nile, lifeblood of the two Lands, which was "changed into blood" (Exodus 7:20) and spewed forth frogs which "covered the land" (Exodus 8:6); the health and wellbeing of both man and beast, afflicted in turn by "gnats [which] came upon men and animals" (Exodus 8:17), "swarms of flies" (Exodus 8:21), "a terrible plague on ... livestock" (Exodus 9:3) and "festering boils" (Exodus 9:9); utter devastation of agriculture, the mainstay of the economy, first by "hail [that] struck everything in the fields" (Exodus 9:25), then by locusts which "devoured all that was left after the hail" (Exodus 10:15); the sun itself, supreme object of worship, which was blotted out by "total darkness" (Exodus 10:22); the continuance of the family line, fatally ruptured as "the LORD struck down all the firstborn in Egypt" (Exodus 12:29); and at length even the army, whose crack divisions were left "dead on the shore" (Exodus 14:30).

These things show God's presence in the negative, a stern Old Testament judge of caricature, who "does not leave the guilty unpunished ... [and] punishes the children and their children for the sin of the fathers to the third and fourth generation." (Exodus 34:7).[386] They are only one side of the coin, however. This same deity is "The LORD, the LORD, the compassionate and gracious God, slow to anger, abounding in love and faithfulness, maintaining love to thousands, and forgiving wickedness, rebellion and sin." (Exodus 24:6-7). We cannot have one aspect of divine presence without the other, for otherwise we would be asking God to deny his very nature. Scripture discloses that the character of the Almighty both involves and demands a tension between justice and mercy, a balance between truth and love, an overarching harmony and proportion in all his words and works that is at one and the same time coupled with surpassing power exercised in gentleness and moderation.[387] For such a God to be present with men would necessarily involve overturning many of our most cherished ideas and traditions. To be in the throne room of such a heavenly King would be an awesome sight indeed. It was something of this kind that was experienced by the "seventy elders of Israel [who] went up [Mount Sinai] and saw the God of Israel. Under his feet was something like a pavement made of sapphire, clear as the sky itself. But God did not raise his hand against these leaders of the Israelites; they saw God, and they ate and drank." (Exodus 24:9-11).[388]

Conclusion.

The pretensions of earthly potentates are writ large in the character of Pharaoh. All that Exodus describes of this man is consistent with what the historical record discloses about the god-kings of Egypt. They claimed for themselves things that belong to the Most High alone: not just their subjects' loyalty, but their worship; unfettered power of life and death; the right to enslave and oppress their fellow creatures; dominion over heaven and earth. Their grandiose projects were undertaken out of pride, designed to impress and overawe, to "[reach] the sky, so that [they could] make a name for [themselves]" (Genesis 11:4, GNT). As though in pale imitation of the "pavement made of sapphire ... [where the elders] ate and drank" (Exodus 24:9-11) the floor of the banqueting suite of Amenhotep III's palace at Malqata (a complex covering over seven acres) was plastered and painted to represent the Nile, with fish and birds shown playing in its waters so that the monarch had the created order beneath his feet.[389] A pharaoh might not be the equal of one of the great gods in the heavens, yet he was still a divine representative, a mediator of the presence of the deity. His person and his insignia could not be touched by ordinary mortals, whilst those who appeared before him were required to prostrate themselves seven times on the front and seven times on the back.[390] Such was the man before whom Moses stood – a great king and a fearsome adversary, but just a man, all the same.

The prophet also stood in the presence of another, more worthy. His presence was in cloud (Exodus 13:21, 16:10 and 19:9) and fire (Exodus 3:2)[391], in tabernacle (Exodus 40:34-35) and Tent of Meeting (Exodus 29:11 and 33:9), on "the mountain of God" (Exodus 3:1) and in "the bread of the Presence" (Exodus 25:30 and 39:36). It was evident in "wonders never before done in any nation in all the world." (Exodus 34:10). Though Moses had once been "driven out of Pharaoh's presence" (Exodus 10:11), he was never driven from the presence of this heavenly King. Instead, he was welcomed, as all are welcomed, to sit and eat with him (Exodus 18:12 and 24:9-11), to share fellowship with him (Exodus 33:7-11, 33:12-23 and 34:4-9) and to travel with him along the highways and byways of life's journey (Exodus 40:36-38). The God spoken of in Exodus is "the same yesterday and today and for ever." (Hebrews 13:8). In contemplating his Word and works, our relationship to him and how best we might serve him, we could do worse than ask two questions that once were posed by Moses: "If your Presence does not go with us, do not send us up from here. For how will anyone know that you are pleased with me and with your people unless you go with us? What else will distinguish me and your people from all the other people on the face of the earth?" (Exodus 33:15-16).

Epilogue

Ephraim and Manasseh

Whose meanings are,
double fruitfulness **and**
forgetting [our troubles]

To whom Jacob
"reached out his right hand and put it on Ephraim's head, though he was the younger, and crossing his arms, he put his left hand on Manasseh's head, even though Manasseh was the firstborn."
(Genesis 48:14).

Epilogue

Past, present and future.

"Therefore, say to the Israelites, 'I am the LORD, *and I will bring you out from under the yoke of the Egyptians. I will free you from being slaves to them, and I will redeem you with an outstretched arm and with mighty acts of judgment.'" (Exodus 6:6).*

At roughly the same time that Moses exhorted Pharaoh on behalf of the Almighty to "Let my people go" (Exodus 5:1, 7:16, 8:1, 8:20, 9:1, 9:13 and 10:3), a new form of bondage was being put in place a thousand leagues away. The Hindu caste system, instituted more than three millennia ago, still traps almost a third of a billion Dalits.[392] By dint of nothing more than accident of birth they are denied the most basic freedoms, lacking choice over where to live, work and worship. Sadly, they are not alone, for in every land there are slaves of one kind or another – trafficked and exploited, downtrodden or ignored, sick and weak, addicted and careworn, unaware that there is a God who loves them. Were we ever in doubt as to the relevance of the Exodus story for the present, such facts should dispel any lingering ambivalence; in relating God's rescue, God's Law and God's presence, in foreshadowing the New Covenant that is in Christ Jesus and in pointing to a new hope, this is no fanciful tale of a distant past but the story of numberless lives and countless longings. The greater part of the world remains in shackles, from which it cannot escape without the help of the God who is described in Scripture. A clarion is therefore sounded to those whom he has placed in positions of influence: to make known his name, to tell of his deeds and to take a stand against those who would say, "I do not know the LORD and I will not let Israel go." (Exodus 5:2).

In doing so, we can be confident that the Exodus story is about real people and real events. So great are the uncertainties which surround ancient Egyptian history that it is tempting to conclude that we cannot know anything much about it with any degree of reliability: neither precisely who ruled at a particular point, nor how large was its population, nor even when many significant events occurred. Yet in every respect Exodus fits with what is known of the generalities of the New Kingdom period. Its incidental details, from the "attendants [of Pharaoh's daughter] ... walking along the river bank" (Exodus 2:5) to "dough ... carried ... on [the fleeing slaves'] shoulders in kneading troughs wrapped in clothing" (Exodus 12:34) bear the hallmarks of an eyewitness account.[393] Moreover, if to such pieces of circumstantial evidence are added the particularities of the reign of Amenhotep III and his son and successor Akhenaten, the congruities are striking indeed. It then becomes possible to discern the outlines of a convincing psychological explanation for why the so-called heretic pharaoh should have pursued the curious religious policies of his reign – an explanation which otherwise is lacking. For, although those who have venerated the sun and its manifestations have seldom shown reluctance to worship other deities as well, Akhenaten seems to have been fundamentally different.[394] From the very first, he appears to have rejected the cults of other gods and to have moved increasingly in the direction of outright monotheism as his reign progressed.[395]

If Akhenaten's father were the Pharaoh of the exodus, none of this should cause surprise. The young prince could either have seen as a boy or heard later from those who had themselves been present of the terrible calamities which befell his nation in the days of Moses.[396] For someone of honesty and questing intelligence, there would have been only one conclusion to be drawn: that the myriad idols of Egypt had been vanquished by the one true God of the Hebrews.[397] It is no wonder that he should then have turned his back on the old deities and sought a single object of worship. Since the One the Israelites called LORD had revealed himself in fire – first in the blaze of the burning bush and then in that great column which led Israel and stood between her and her enemies – it is wholly believable that the future monarch should have alighted on a divinity whose symbol was the huge ball of flame which passed each day across the heavens.[398] As desert locations seemed in some manner special to the Semitic God (Exodus 3:18, 5:1, 5:3, 7:16, 8:27-28 and 13:18), it was logical for the king to search in similar places to find a suitable home for his new capital. If he had been familiar (even at second or third hand) with songs of praise or lament that the one-time slaves had sung as they worked, how readily their language, ideas and sentiments might have been imported into the hymns he penned to Aten. Had he borne the burden of knowing that the throne had devolved upon him only because "the LORD struck down all the firstborn in Egypt" (Exodus 12:29), how might this have weighed upon him as the years passed and caused untold convolutions in his mind.[399]

Ultimately, these things are matters of speculation.[400] The evidence is such that one theory does not yet stand head and shoulders above another as the only reasonable interpretation of the facts. The historical suppositions which underlie this work may therefore be of more than passing interest, but in the final analysis they do not bear on the truth or otherwise of what the Bible recounts. In relation to the far more fundamental issue of whether there is a God at all and, if so, whether he is correctly described in Scripture, the same does not apply. As to those issues, clear-sighted investigation and dispassionate analysis leave no sensible alternative but to conclude that the universe did not bring itself into being out of nothing, that it had a beginning just as it will have an end, and that the nature and personality of the Creator who revealed himself to Moses is precisely what we would expect of the One who has ordered the natural world in the way we observe. As to the reasoning process that leads to this result, an analogy is provided by the English legal system, with its two standards of proof.

To be convicted of a crime, an accused must be proven guilty beyond reasonable doubt, but in civil cases a lesser standard applies – proof on the balance of probabilities, that is to say, whether it is more likely than not that a certain thing is the case. God has so structured the cosmos that some element of doubt is apt to remain until a step of faith is taken, for only once we respond to him in this way does he come to live in us by His Spirit and we experience the reality of His presence.

By contrast, proof on a balance of probabilities is readily available to any who follow diligently and without preconception where the evidence leads – in the same way that Moses "[went] over ... [to] see this strange sight – why the bush does not burn up." (Exodus 3:3). Mature reflection leaves no honest or sensible option but to conclude that divine activity was needed to create the universe and that if we cannot know the truth of what the Bible says, we cannot know the truth of anything. The question then becomes what we should do with this knowledge; and here again Exodus has much to teach us. On the most obvious of levels ancient Egypt is a place deeply foreign, separated from our own age not just by the passage of time and steady accretion of technical expertise but by a system of beliefs that is utterly alien. Scratch the surface, however, and there are parallels aplenty. The time in which we live does not want for idols and false gods, has no lack of tyrants, is no less susceptible to expediency and the utilitarian. In such a world, the challenges for us are not so very different from the ones Moses and Akhenaten faced, in varied ways and with entirely opposite results. The latter built on sand,[401] whereas the message of the former has resonated across centuries, pointing the way to the coming of the ultimate Redeemer of all mankind, Jesus Christ.

We should therefore compare and contrast. Whatever name we give to the Pharaoh of Exodus, one thing is certain: his legacy was disastrous for the Egyptian state and its people. This was true not just of those drowned charioteers about whom Moses sang, "The deep waters have covered them; they sank to the depths like a stone ... [God] stretched out [his] right hand and the earth swallowed them" (Exodus 15:5 and 12). It applied to countless thousands more who mourned not only those men but also the firstborn of their families and the wreckage of a devastated land. These things resulted from human choices, freely made. They were not the malign actions of a deity who happened to prefer one nation to another. Far from it: the Bible confirms the land and people of Egypt to be of greatest importance historically and spiritually, both in the past and for the future. Not only was the nation of Israel birthed from out of the Two Lands, but Egypt has a special role as a place of refuge. It was so in the days of Abraham when "there was a famine in the land" (Genesis 12:10), for a second time when "all the countries came to Egypt to buy grain from Joseph, because the famine was severe in all the world" (Genesis 41:57) and most significantly when Jesus' family "stayed [in Egypt] until Herod died. This was

Epilogue

done to make come true what the Lord had said through the prophet, 'I called my Son out of Egypt.'" (Matthew 2:15, GNT).[402]

The tribes and sub-tribes of Israel bear the names of good fortune, hearing, attachment, excellence, honour, plunder, praise, justice, fruitfulness, happiness, freedom, reward, double fruitfulness and forgetting our troubles. Those things are exemplified in Exodus, for one of the functions of Israel is to act as a demonstration. Through their trials and tribulations we see that to encounter God brings undeserved good fortune; to belong to him needs us to act on what we hear; to worship him means making a decision to attach ourselves to him; to know him involves perceiving at least a part of his excellence; to reflect him does honour to him and to us; to rely on him enables our enemies to be plundered; to recognise him brings forth our praise; to obey him allows his justice to reign; to serve him ushers in fruitfulness; to remember him allows the greatest happiness; to live for him is perfect freedom; to be in his presence, to experience the highest reward. The sum of all these is double fruitfulness and being enabled to put our troubles behind us. The experiences of the Hebrew slaves in Egypt and their growth to nationhood after being freed from bondage were neither chance happenings nor random meanderings. Exodus shows that history is purposeful and an expression of God's will – the ultimate goal of which is salvation for all who embrace that most wonderful of gifts, freely offered to the whole world through the coming of a sinless Saviour. Holding fast to that assurance, we need only to "Stand firm and [we] will see the deliverance the LORD will bring [us] today." (Exodus 14:13).

Moses and Pharaoh

Appendix I

Dating methodology.

Uncertainty surrounds many events in ancient Egyptian history, causing leading twentieth century Egyptologist Cyril Aldred to observe: "...the problem of finding out what exactly happened in ancient Egypt is truly formidable, and is not lessened by the uneven wealth of records, which often tend to confuse the picture with intractable detail in some areas, and to obscure it altogether with an entire absence of data in others." The problem of incomplete, misleading or abstruse literary sources is compounded by the fact that such information as is available through the archaeological record is often fragmentary and susceptible of subjective interpretation. Claims to absolute precision in all particulars are thus spurious and to pretend otherwise would be disingenuous. There are some things of which one can be relatively sure, but much is in the realm of probability and likelihood. Against a background of conjecture, inference and supposition, incontrovertible proof is always likely to be elusive.

The events of the book of Exodus have commonly been dated either to 1446 BC during the reign of Amenhotep II or to the reign of Ramses II some one hundred and sixty years later. The former view is based on using time periods stated in the Bible to work back from the date of Solomon's dedication of the Temple in Jerusalem. The latter points amongst other things to the statement in Exodus that Israelite slaves were used to build store cities called Pithom and Rameses. Archaeological evidence can be cited in favour of each approach, but in neither case does this comprehensively disprove the other hypothesis (and nor does it close the door to other possibilities within this envelope of eight score years or so). The position taken in this work is that the events described in Exodus 2:1-20 took place during the reign of Thutmose IV and the Israelites' departure from Egypt in the immediately succeeding reign (under Amenhotep III, the father of Akhenaten).[403] This dates the flight of God's people to a little over half a century later than 1446 BC – in around 1390 BC or thereabouts – a determination which it is submitted is capable of reconciling the competing traditional viewpoints whilst remaining faithful to Scripture and dovetailing with Egyptian sources. The considerations which bear upon this conclusion and the facts which underpin it are set out below.

Contemporary counting methods.

The ancient Egyptians did not reckon time from a single datum. Up to the end of the Old Kingdom, events were fixed by reference to biennial censuses of cattle or happenings which were especially memorable, such as the accession of a king or victory in battle. From the Middle Kingdom onwards, chroniclers looked to the number of years the reigning king had been on the throne. The uncertainty and potential for mishap inherent in these approaches is compounded by the fact that:

There was a tendency for some pharaohs to have a period of co-regency with their chosen successor, allowing the possibility of overlapping periods.

Often there is doubt as to whether co-regency occurred, Akhenaten and his father Amenhotep III being a case in point.

The exact lengths of a reign have been preserved in only a very few instances.

It is not certain that we have a full list of kings and their proper order of succession.

There exists both a so-called High Chronology and Low Chronology,[404] the latter giving a date up to twenty-five years later than the former.

There is a possibility of dynasties overlapping at certain periods, as political fragmentation led to parallel (and sometimes competing) royal lines based in different power centres.

In light of the above, modern scholars have generally worked forwards or backwards from a small number of more or less fixed points determined by references in Egyptian records to astronomical events, the dates of which can (or so it was generally held until recently) be set independently. Yet even in such a relative handful of cases, absolute precision has proven elusive. For example, the heliacal rising of the star Sirius[405] in the ninth year of Amenhotep I's reign has traditionally been used to fix the date of that monarch's accession, but only within a span of twenty-six years since it is not known whether the sighting was made from Heliopolis or Thebes, some 450 miles away – and some now doubt even this degree of reliability. So, whilst astronomical data in ancient texts enable cross-checking to some extent, a degree of caution remains in order when approaching any of the dates commonly ascribed to happenings in ancient Egypt. Though techniques such as carbon dating can often help flesh out the picture, even these are seldom able to give complete certainty.[406] Nowadays it is more or less universally acknowledged that the years of reigns and dynasties, and even the span of entire epochs such as the Third Intermediate Period, are only approximate prior to accession of the Twenty-fifth Dynasty Kushite pharaoh Taharqo (Taharka) in 690 BC.

Further cause for circumspection in trying to marry the biblical narrative with Egyptian records and ancient remains results from the fact that it was not uncommon for people in the ancient Near East to adopt schematic or aggregate figures to express long stretches of time. Often, schematic figures might be premised on the passing of a certain number of generations, each generation habitually being ascribed a putative forty-year span, whilst an aggregate figure might lump together a number of subsidiary periods which were in fact partly concurrent. Both these techniques seem to have been used at various points by biblical writers, and there is every possibility that the ancient Egyptians did likewise. Certainly, aggregation of concurrent periods is a practice attested in both Mesopotamia and Egypt at the relevant times.[407]

Dates in the Bible.

No Egyptian record has come to light which refers uncontrovertibly to the Exodus events.[408] This in itself is hardly surprising, given pharaohs' habit of expunging unflattering references or inconvenient facts. A prime example of precisely that kind of behaviour is provided by the treatment of Akhenaten after his death. As described in chapter 1, there was a policy of deliberate forgetfulness in reaction to the deep trauma caused by his reign, with the monarch's name being expunged from the king lists, his capital at Akhet-aten abandoned by officialdom,[409] personal names that referred to Amun being substituted for those that honoured Aten,[410] temples to the old gods being reopened, the recently deceased ruler's monuments being defaced and his most distinctive policies swiftly reversed. There is no reason to suppose that the misery, humiliation and despair brought about by the Ten Plagues, the escape of large numbers of slaves and the loss of a pursuing chariot force would have elicited a different response. It follows that lack of written corroboration from Egyptian sources cannot of itself be taken to disprove the biblical account.

The Bible has various reference points that bear upon dating of the exodus, these being (1) the years spent in Egypt by the Israelites from their first migration to that land in the days of Joseph, (2) the invasion of Canaan under Joshua, (3) the length of time that Israelites are recorded as having been in possession of various Canaanite towns during the days of the judges, (4) the reigns of King Saul and King David and (5) the dedication of Solomon's Temple. Taking these in reverse order:

DEDICATION OF SOLOMON'S TEMPLE.

"In the four hundred and eightieth year after the Israelites had come out of Egypt, in the fourth year of Solomon's reign over Israel, in the month of Ziv, the second month, [Solomon] began to build the temple of the LORD." (1 Kings 6:1). The fourth year of Solomon's reign can be fixed with reasonable certainty around 966 BC by synchronising events in the reigns of later Israelite kings with Assyrian records. It follows that if the dates given in the Bible are correct, the events described in the second book of Moses cannot have occurred earlier than 1446 BC. However, placing the exodus somewhat more recently than this might still be consistent with the date given for the dedication of Solomon's Temple if the four hundred and eighty years referred to in 1 Kings 6:1 were a schematic or aggregate figure. If so, then the time period given in 1 Kings 6:1 might cover a span of some decades less than four hundred and eighty years – though differences between our methods of calculation and those used by the author of 1 Kings would almost certainly not be enough to account for the one hundred and sixty years or thereabouts needed to bring the Exodus events into the reign of Ramses II.

SAUL AND DAVID.

If the Temple in Jerusalem were dedicated in 966 BC and this was "the fourth year of Solomon's reign over Israel" (1 Kings 6:1), it follows that Solomon came to the throne in or about 970 BC. Before him "David was thirty years old when he came to the throne, and he reigned for forty years." (2 Samuel 5:4), giving a date for his accession of roughly 1010 BC. Since David's predecessor and Israel's first king "Saul was thirty years old when he became king, and he reigned over Israel for forty two years." (1 Samuel 13:1), this would put Saul's accession at 1052 BC or thereabouts.

THE RULE OF THE JUDGES.

After conquering Canaan the Israelites occupied parts of the land for at least three hundred years prior to the anointing of Saul as first king of Israel: "Jephthah again sent messengers to the king of the people of Ammon [saying,] … '…Israel dwelt in Heshbon and its villages, in Aroer and its villages, and in all the cities along the banks of the Arnon, for three hundred years…'" (Judges 11:14 and 26, NKJV).[411] Working back from the date on which Saul came to the throne (1052 BC), this would give a date for Israel's first entry into the Promised Land of around 1352 BC. Adding to this forty years to take account of the tribes' desert wandering between leaving Egypt and arriving in Canaan would give a date for the exodus of 1392 BC, with this almost certainly taking place during the early years of Amenhotep III's reign. Though archaeological evidence from the time of the judges to support this supposition is slight, that is hardly surprising given the events that the Bible records during this period, for much of which Israelite tribes were subjugated by surrounding nations and living a hand to mouth existence.[412] For example, we are told that "the power of the Midianites was so oppressive [that] the Israelites prepared shelters for themselves in mountain clefts, caves and strongholds" (Judges 6:2) and Gideon was to be found "threshing some wheat secretly in a wine press, so that the Midianites would not see him." (Judges 6:11, GNT). Far from disproving the biblical account, lack of remains from this era is of a piece with "The Midianites [having] so impoverished the Israelites that they cried out to the LORD for help." (Judges 6:6).

It is noteworthy that the book of Judges makes no direct mention of Egypt or Egyptians. At first blush this might seem curious. For example, if the Israelites had indeed conquered large parts of Canaan almost a century before Ramses II came to the throne, that pharaoh might have been expected to encounter them when he marched his army north in the fourth and fifth years of his reign in order to confront the Hittites. Yet whilst it is conceivable that the writer of Judges simply did not consider this event worthy of recording on the basis that it did not impinge on the redemption history of Israel, it is equally possible that the pharaoh's route might not have taken him through Israelite territory. For each of these campaigns, Ramses II left Egypt at the border fortress of Tharu, which lay close to the Mediterranean shoreline at the outer extent of Egypt's north-eastern territories. From thence the Egyptian divisions proceeded along the road known as the Way of Horus or Via Maris, which wound along the coast as far as present-day Lebanon. Most probably their columns kept to this route until they reached the valley of the River Eleutheros, which wends more or less due east from the centre of Lebanon to Kadesh in modern Syria.[413] If so, they could well have avoided contact with Israel; the littoral immediately north of the Egyptian border was by this time within Philistine territory, and it is feasible that resurgent Canaanite forces controlled the remainder as far as Lebanon.[414] This indeed seems precisely the import of the fact that "The Amorites confined the Danites to the hill country, not allowing them to come down into the plain." (Judges 1:34).

Some kind of contact between Egypt and Israel evidently took place in a later generation, however. A stele or commemorative stone erected by Merneptah (son of Ramses II), usually dated to about 1225 BC, contains the first known Egyptian reference to Israel. Its inscriptions record the political circumstances obtaining in the lands bordering Egypt during this king's reign, stating that "Canaan is the victim of all sorts of calamities … Israel is destroyed, her seed [or perhaps, grain] is no more."[415] A wide range of theories have been put forward about the historical events to which this might refer (not least being the possibility that it records Israel's subjection by foreigners during the time when the judges ruled), though in truth the wording is so ambiguous as to be capable of being made to fit all kinds of events. On the present state of our knowledge, it is hard to see that this stele advances the issue of dating with any degree of precision. What can be said, though, is that its claims do not sit comfortably with Ramses II's being the Pharaoh either of the oppression or of the exodus. Had either been the case, it would have made an assertion in the reign of that pharaoh's immediate successor that "Israel is destroyed, her seed is no more" either so nonsensical or so contrary to facts which were within the recent personal knowledge of the greater part of Egypt's population as to be impossible to make without inviting ridicule or worse. Although propagandists down the centuries have shown scant embarrassment about making false and even preposterous claims, the grievous Egyptian suffering caused by the Exodus events and the fact that these things were so fresh in the memory would surely have given even the most megalomaniac and insensitive pharaoh pause.

Ramses II and his son are thought to have reigned for seventy-four years between them (sixty-three years for Ramses II and eleven for Merneptah). The Ten Plagues of Egypt may have lasted anything from six months to a year, Israel wandered forty years in the wilderness, and Joshua's campaigns of conquest in Canaan must have taken at least a further thirty years (see below). In other words, even if the exodus took place in the early years of Ramses II's rule, for the claims made on this stele to be anywhere near the truth Israel's position in Canaan would need to have changed from dominance at the death of Joshua to that of being "destroyed" within as little as three years. Stranger things have happened, but it seems unlikely.[416]

JOSHUA AND THE CONQUEST OF CANAAN.

The Bible affirms that the Israelites wandered forty years in the wilderness under the leadership of Moses (see, for example, Numbers 32:13 and Acts 13:18). After his death, Joshua is said to have led the tribes across the Jordan to conquer Canaan (Joshua 1:1-2). Scripture does not state in terms how soon after Moses' demise this happened, but there is nothing to indicate a long delay. It would be entirely reasonable to assume that a short time elapsed between the two events. Likewise there is a sense of immediacy about Moses' return to Egypt after God told him that "all the men who wanted to kill you are dead." (Exodus 4:19). In the absence of anything stated to the contrary, there is no reason to assume that Moses was dilatory in doing as he was commanded.

Joshua "died at the age of a hundred and ten" (Joshua 24:29). He was unlikely to have been much older than eighty when he began the assault on Jericho. The process of Israelite conquest of Canaan under his leadership must therefore have lasted at least thirty years (and may conceivably have taken longer).[417] If thirty years is added to the forty that Israel wandered in the wilderness after coming out of Egypt (and taking the supposition that Moses led Israel out of Egypt in or around 1390 BC) this would give a date of 1320 BC or thereabouts for Joshua's death. Applying these assumptions to the conjecture that underlies this work (and taking for the sake of argument the dates commonly ascribed to the reigns of the pharaohs in question), the result would be as follows:

Moses fled Egypt at some point during the reign of Thutmose IV.[418]

He returned to the land of his birth early in the reign of Amenhotep III[419] and set about fulfilling the commission that God had given him more or less straight away.

The plagues which God sent upon Egypt would in total probably have lasted no more than a year.

It would thus still have been in the first part of Amenhotep III's reign that the Israelites left Egypt.

Since Amenhotep III is thought to have ruled for something in the order of thirty-eight years, the Hebrew tribes' wandering in the desert would have been complete by the early years of Akhenaten's kingship.

Akhenaten is thought to have ruled for seventeen years, during which time the Israelites' conquest of Canaan would have been in progress.

A number of clay tablets containing diplomatic correspondence (the so-called Amarna Letters) have been preserved from Akhenaten's reign.[420] Some of these comprise reports from Egyptian allies and vassals in Canaan, seeking urgent military help against an invader and reporting disasters that have befallen them. One of them (EA 256), written by Mutbaal, king of Pella (a city lying just east of the Jordan between Lake Galilee and the Dead Sea), in the course of asserting that its author has done as his Egyptian overlord might wish, prays in aid the witness of third parties, saying, "Ask Benenima [Benjamin]. Ask Tadua. Ask Yishuya [Joshua]." That the name of Joshua, Israel's political leader and commander-in-chief, should appear is striking. So, too, is the reference to Benjamin, for this tribe had the honour of leading Israelite armies into battle.[421] Whilst Tadua does not appear in the Bible it might conceivably be an inaccurate attempt to render the name or title of another prominent Israelite or of an identifiable group amongst the invaders.[422] In similar vein, two letters (EA 79 and EA 122) from Rib-Adda of Gebal[423] speak of the "sons of Ebed-Ashera", which might plausibly refer to the tribe of Asher and its sub-clan of Heber (see Genesis 46:17 and Numbers 26:45) since Gebal fell within the territorial allotment of Asher (see Joshua 19:24-31).

Letter EA 228 from Abdi-Tirsi of Hazura (Hazor) reads: "I protect Hazor with all its cities for the king, my lord. Let the king, my lord think of all that is done against Hazor." According to Scripture Jabin of Hazor bore the title "king" (Joshua 11:1), which is consistent with his holding sway over more than just that one city and fits with Abdi-Tirsi's claim to be acting on behalf of Hazor "and all its cities". That Jabin and Abdi-Tirsi were one and the same is perfectly possible, since the former is more likely to have been a title or honorific than a personal name (see note 420). At all events, the power and influence of Hazor must have been considerable, for the Bible confirms that "Hazor had at one time been the capital of the federation of all those kingdoms [named in verses 1-3]" (Joshua

11:10, TLB). The eventual fate of this city was a grisly one, as "Joshua then turned back, captured Hazor and killed its king. ... They put everyone there to death; no one was left alive, and the city was burned." (Joshua 11:10-11, GNT). British archaeologist John Garstang found evidence of destruction by fire during his excavation of the ruins of Hazor during the early twentieth century, together with pottery evidence that dated the first observable level of destruction to around 1400 BC.

The overall picture of Canaan conveyed by the Amarna Letters as a whole is of a region ablaze, with banditry, opportunism and score-settling by those native to the area, treachery on every side and armed incursions from within and without. There are fearful references to groups of *Habiru* or *Apiru* (also sometimes known as *Sa-Gaz* from the equivalent cuneiform logograms),[424] who are said to be threatening the cities of Canaan and spreading terror amongst the populace. Pleas for aid from the pharaoh become ever more despairing, as in EA 286 from Abdu-Heba of Jerusalem: "The Habiru are capturing our fortresses ... taking our cities ... destroying our rulers ... plundering all the country of the king. May the king send soldiers quickly. If no troops come this year the whole country is lost to the king." The urgency of the situation is palpable, as is Egyptian inertia and loss of prestige. Letter EA 109 almost drips with contempt: "Previously, on seeing a man from Egypt, the kings of Canaan fled before him, but now the sons of Abdi-Ashirta [ruler of Amurru] make men from Egypt prowl about like dogs." Clearly, pharaoh's influence was on the wane and those who had previously relied on him were in a precarious position, facing an existential threat, unable to be sure of the support of neighbouring rulers and believing their own resources inadequate for mounting a coherent defence. Scripture records ample reason for the terror and panic revealed in the correspondence, as Joshua "captured all [the Canaanites'] kings and struck them down, putting them to death." (Joshua 11:17).[425]

JOSEPH.

The Israelites spent just over four centuries in Egypt after Joseph persuaded his father and brothers to settle in Goshen, the fertile area which straddles the eastern Nile delta: "Now the length of time the Israelite people lived in Egypt was 430 years. At the end of the 430 years, to the very day, all the LORD's divisions left Egypt." (Exodus 12:40-41; and see also Genesis 47:1-12).[426] If Amenhotep III were indeed the Pharaoh of the exodus, the ruler of Egypt in Joseph's day would almost certainly have been the Twelfth Dynasty ruler Amenemhet III, who is commonly thought to have occupied the throne for forty-five years from 1842 BC to 1797 BC. The events of this king's reign, often regarded as the high point of the Middle Kingdom, are suggestive of what the Bible tells of Joseph.[427] It seems to be during this period that the so-called Hyksos (a Semitic people of unknown origin) came to settle in the delta area, and indeed skeletal remains in Avaris indicate that long-haired sheep were introduced into the Nile delta at around this time. Though an identification of Hyksos with Hebrews cannot be made with anything approaching certainty, Scripture records that Jacob and his sons "took with them their livestock" (Genesis 46:6).

Joseph correctly interpreted two dreams of pharaoh which each predicted that "seven years of great abundance are coming throughout the land of Egypt, but seven years of famine will follow them." (Genesis 41:29-30). Carvings discovered by the German archaeologist Richard Lepsius in 1844 in the narrow gorge where the Nile passes by the Egyptian border fortress of Semna appear to show a series of unusually high Nile floods during the first decades of Amenemhat III's reign. Initially these are at a level that would have been beneficial to agriculture in Egypt, but in subsequent years the floodwaters rose to heights more likely to have been catastrophic for the livelihoods of those further downstream. Bringing with them three of four times the volume of water and debris associated with a normal inundation, they would most probably have caused such devastation and dislocation that famine would have been a genuine threat, since floodwaters that took longer than usual to recede might have severely limited the acreage that could be planted in time for the next harvest season. Unsurprisingly, all possible attempts seem to have been made to propitiate Sobek, the crocodile god which was closely associated with the Nile; Amenemhat III's daughter was even called Sobekkare Sobekneferure ('Sobek is the spirit of Ra' and 'Sobek is the perfect form of Ra'), and Sobekhotep ('Sobek is satisfied') was one of the commonest names in the generation born to those living at the time Amenhotep III ruled.

In addition, the priorities of Amenemhet III's reign appear consistent with a time of famine or its anticipation.[428] There seems to have been little in the way of large-scale military activity,[429] whilst great emphasis was placed on worship of the goddess of harvest. Administration was reorganised so that local officials no longer possessed the extensive authority of former years, when some of the greater magnates had exercised almost vice-regal powers. This fits with the Bible's confirmation that Joseph centralised grain storage and distribution, "[collecting] all the food produced in those seven years of abundance in Egypt and [storing] it in the cities. In each city he put the food grown in the fields surrounding it." (Genesis 41:48-49). The result was that, when the threatened famine came, the monarch's grip over both economy and people was greatly strengthened: "So Joseph bought all the land of Egypt for Pharaoh; all the Egyptians sold him their fields because the famine was so severe. And the land became Pharaoh's. Thus all the people of Egypt became Pharaoh's serfs. The only land he didn't buy was that belonging to the priests, for they were assigned food from Pharaoh and didn't need to sell." (Genesis 47:20-22, TLB; and see also Genesis 47:26).[430]

Meanwhile, it seems Amenemhet III took a personal interest in agricultural affairs and was prepared to sink huge resources into projects designed to improve the availability or productivity of farmland or increase crop yields. Under him were built the great waterwheels of the Al-Fayoum oasis[431] southwest of modern Cairo, used to regulate the flow of the Nile's waters into the lake known as Birket Karun. By draining nearby marshes, this irrigation system and its related overflow canal resulted in 153,000 acres being reclaimed for planting. The overflow canal is called the Bahr Yousef. The Arabic name for Joseph is Yousef.[432]

Execration and oppression.

Yet in due course the debt that was owed to the family of Jacob was forgotten, for "a new king, who did not know about Joseph, came to power in Egypt ... So [the Egyptians] put slave masters over [the Israelites] to oppress them with forced labour" (Exodus 1:8 and 11). Evidence for this oppression of Israel is hard to pin down, but the so-called Execration Texts are a potential link. These comprise the names of people or places written on pottery which was then deliberately smashed – presumably as a kind of magic spell designed to bring about the destruction of those named on the broken object or to render them powerless. There are two series of Execration Texts, one ascribed with reasonable confidence to the Thirteenth Dynasty (which would allow a suitable length of time after the reign of Amenemhat III for a new king to come to power who did not know about Joseph), the other perhaps belonging earlier.[433] Amongst the names which appear in the texts are ones that are undoubtedly of Semitic rather than Egyptian origin, with two in particular standing out: Yakkub (Jacob) and Yaseph (Joseph) – borne by Israelites whom their oppressors might be thought to have had especial cause to revile, being respectively the progenitor of the race and the one responsible for their settlement in Egypt. It has to be said that the evidence is slender, but the Execration Texts could conceivably have been part of a process of cursing and then enslaving Israel.

The store cities.

The Israelites "built Pithom and Rameses as store cities for Pharaoh." (Exodus 1:11). Ruins thought to be those of Pithom were excavated by French archaeologist Edouard Naville in 1883 and again by the American Melvin Grove Kyle in 1908. They each found buildings whose lower courses were made of bricks formed with a plentiful mix of good chopped straw, middle courses whose brickwork had a smaller amount of stubble in which roots could still clearly be seen and upper courses constructed of pure clay, with no straw at all. Whether or not the place was correctly identified as Pithom,[434] the curious and otherwise inexplicable fact of bricks made without straw confirms the Bible narrative:[435] "That same day Pharaoh gave this order to the slave drivers and foremen in charge of the people: 'You are no longer to supply the people with straw for making bricks; let them go and gather their own straw. But require them to make the same number of bricks as before; don't reduce the quota...' So the people scattered all over Egypt to gather stubble to use for straw." (Exodus 5:6-8 and 12).

Dating the cities of Pithom and Rameses to the reign of Ramses II (and therefore placing the exodus at that time) seems relatively straightforward on its face, but rather less so on further investigation. On one side of the equation are the facts that during his excavations Naville found an inscription of Ramses II which declared, "I built Pithom at the mouth of the East," together with a long rectangular building with unusually thick walls, whose bricks were stamped with this pharaoh's name; that monuments of Ramses II have been found in what are thought to be the sites of these ancient cities; that one store city bears Ramses' name; and that in 1915 the American archaeologist Clarence Fisher found a stele of Ramses II at Beth Shan which asserts that this king "built Rameses with Asiatic [that is, Semitic] slaves". Things are more complex on closer inspection, however:

Ancient Egyptians valued continuity with the past so highly that, when new cities were built, they tended to bring old statues and other monuments from elsewhere to give a sense of lineage.

By the same token, statues and monuments might be brought to a place to signify new use or ownership. Materials were frequently re-used or recycled. This trend was exacerbated by the fact that some materials (wood, in particular) were in short supply.[436] Older materials might thus be incorporated into younger archaeological deposits, whilst the long re-use, revisiting and robbing of some monuments could lead to later material being discovered in earlier contexts.

Ramses II's claims to have built Pithom and Rameses need to be treated with circumspection. They might mean no more than that he had existing cities rebuilt or enlarged. Equally, given his proven readiness in several other instances to take credit for the achievements of others, the claims might be false.

Though it seems that Ramses II made Pi-Rameses a staging post for military operations in the Levant during the early years of his reign, the exact meaning of the Hebrew phrase that is translated as "store cities" is not entirely clear.

There is room for doubt as to whether the place the Bible calls Rameses was that which the Ramesside pharaohs made their capital, for whilst it is not inconceivable that a store city and the centre of government were part of the same metropolis, the latter was invariably called Pi-Rameses.[437]

Very few ancient Egyptian cities can be excavated because modern dwellings have been built on top of old ones. This naturally limits the information that can be gleaned from the archaeological record.

References to Asiatic [Semitic] slaves do not mean that these were necessarily Hebrews. They could equally well have been prisoners of war taken in Ramses II's military campaigns in the regions surrounding Israel.

Ramses means, *born of Ra*, or, *son of Ra*, the "meses" component of the name being the same as the name Moses. Each pharaoh was considered to be descended from Ra (sun god of Heliopolis and lord of the dead). Hence Ramses might be used generically to speak of a royal personage or royal land, rather than designating a pharaoh with that particular throne name. From a literary point of view, it is a neat stylistic device for the author of Exodus to pit a king born of Ra against someone about whose origins the Egyptians were so unsure that they called him simply Moses ("born").[438]

From the fifth dynasty (approximately 2300 BC) the name of Ra was included in the title of all pharaohs. Each pharaoh had five names,[439] including a throne name and a "son of Ra" name. There was thus a sense in which every pharaoh from this time onwards might be called Ramses.

The name Rameses in Exodus 1:11 and 12:37 and Numbers 33:3 and 33:5 may have been a later editorial updating or simply have reflected the terminology with which Moses was familiar. Something of this kind seems to explain the reference in Genesis to a "district of Rameses", for neither Ramses I nor Ramses II ruled when "Joseph settled his father and his brothers in Egypt, giving them property in the best of the land near the city of Rameses, as the king had commanded." (Genesis 47:11, GNT).[440]

Excavations at Hazor have revealed three levels of destruction. Those who see Ramses II as the Pharaoh of the exodus cite the third and latest level, which has been dated to around 1230 BC, but the first level of destruction could equally have been that caused by Joshua's forces. As already mentioned, this has been dated to around 1400 BC.

Consequently it does no violence to Scripture to conclude that Ramses II was not the Pharaoh of the exodus. By contrast, if Ramses II were ruler at the time of Moses, it is on its face difficult to account both for the three hundred year period referred to in Judges 11:26 and the timing of Solomon's dedication of the Temple described in 1 Kings 6:1. Neither is it easy to reconcile what the Bible says about the loss of chariots in the Red Sea with Ramses II's proven ability to field a large chariot force in the early years of his reign (see below). None of the alternatives that have been proposed to address these issues are entirely satisfactory. Since archaeological evidence can be read either way, it makes sense to choose the alternative which fits best with the Bible.

Pharaoh's daughter.

If the suppositions made above are correct, Thutmose IV (who also bore the name Menkheperure) can stake a reasonable claim to being the Pharaoh whose attempts to extinguish Israel are described in Exodus 2:1-20. He had at least four daughters: Tiaa, Pyikhia (or Petepihu), Amenemopet and Tentamun.[441] There is no direct evidence as to whether any of these ever married. Given our lack of knowledge, any speculation concerning them should be treated with the greatest caution. It may simply be that details of their marriages and children have not survived. By the same token, however, it is not beyond the bounds of possibility that a perceived dearth of suitable spouses led to some or all of them spending their lives languishing in the House of the Royal Children.[442] Alternatively, it is conceivable that one or more of them may have wed their own father according to time-honoured customs of Egyptian royalty and as a consequence have been consigned to the Royal Harem. At all events, it is not difficult to imagine circumstances in which an Egyptian princess, unmarried or for other reasons childless, might have wanted to adopt a baby in the manner described in Exodus 2:8-10.[443]

Death and disease.

Archaeologists have uncovered over seven hundred statues erected by Amenhotep III to Sekhmet, the lioness-headed goddess of Memphis and chief companion of its god Ptah – more than there are statues of the pharaoh himself and all other gods combined. This female deity, whose name means, *The Powerful One*, was associated with pestilence and was often represented as an avenger who revelled in the slaughter of humans, having an insatiable and uncontrollable lust for their blood. The daughter of Ra, she was "the spreader of terror" and an instrument of the sun god's wrath, so that in battle pharaohs would associate themselves with the "rage of Sekhmet". Legend had it that she was sent by the gods to destroy mankind. That Egyptians felt a need to propitiate this fearsome creature on such a scale is consistent with a time of plague, famine, disease, strife, hardship and distress – precisely the things that Egypt would have experienced during Amenhotep III's reign if he were the Pharaoh of the exodus.[444] Indeed, excavations at Avaris have uncovered graves with multiple bodies, and at Thebes a mass burial of royal children was discovered in the mid-nineteenth century by Scots archaeologist A. Henry Rhind. It is not currently possible to say for sure whether these evidence the aftermath of the Tenth Plague, though they are an unusual form of burial for ancient Egypt, normally associated with some kind of trauma, such as war or famine. They would of course be precisely what one would expect to find if there had been widespread and sudden death of the sort described in Exodus 12:29-30, for mortality on that scale over a short time period usually overwhelms any ability to follow the funeral customs which obtain in kinder times.

The king's family were not insulated from the misfortunes that befell their fellow countrymen, for royalty did not escape the killing of Egyptian firstborn: "At midnight the LORD struck down all the firstborn in Egypt, from the firstborn of Pharaoh, who sat on the throne, to the firstborn of the prisoner, who was in the dungeon, and the firstborn of the livestock as well. Pharaoh and all his officials and all the Egyptians got up during the night, and there was loud wailing in Egypt, for there was not a house without someone dead." (Exodus 12:29-30).[445] As to be expected if the Exodus account and hypothesis behind this work are correct, Crown Prince Thutmose, firstborn son of Amenhotep III and elder brother of Akhenaten, died unexpectedly whilst still a child.[446] To add to an overall aura of severe dislocation in national life at this time, there is an unexplained gap in official records between the twelfth and nineteenth years of Amenhotep III's rule – an utter absence of documentation in a reign otherwise notable for its abundance.[447] This hiatus appears to mark a watershed, with the king showing significant changes in attitude and behaviour thereafter. Amongst other things, there is a suggestion that from this point of rupture onwards he quite deliberately chose to shut himself away; when he again travelled south to Thebes after a period residing in the north, he seems purposefully to have moved as far from its hustle and bustle as possible, having a new palace built some distance off at the edge of the western mountains. It is almost reminiscent of the behaviour of a grief-stricken Queen Victoria following the death of her beloved husband Prince Albert.

There is no reason to suppose that Egypt's suffering would automatically have been at an end the moment that Pharaoh's chariots were lost in the Red Sea, for the aftershocks of the afflictions that had plagued her must have been felt for many years, with ramifications far beyond the borders of The Two Lands. Traces of bubonic plague have been found at Akhet-aten, and during the latter part of Akhenaten's reign sickness seems to have been widespread in the Near East. The king of Alashia (tentatively identified with the island of Cyprus) reported that Nergal, local god of pestilence, was abroad in his land, preventing production of the planned quota of copper ingots for pharaoh. Plague is also recorded at Byblos and Sumura. Later it spread from the Amqa region of Lebanon into the Hittite lands of modern Turkey, where it killed King Suppiluliuma I. Grist is added to the mill of those who seek a link with the Tenth Plague by the fact that the disease which brought about the death of this monarch seems to have been carried by Egyptian prisoners of war taken during a campaign conducted by the dead man's son, Hittite Crown Prince Amuwanda.[448]

Appendix I

Terminology.

Vocabulary and terminology often reflect contact with foreigners or unusual customs and hence can be an indication of the extent of Egyptian exposure to and knowledge of Hebrews and the God of Israel at various points. Ancient Egyptian records contain six terms which bear particularly on this:

Inscriptions which Thutmose III caused to be made at Thebes to boast of victories in Canaan contain the names Ya'kobh-el and Yoseph-el, these being composites of Jacob and Joseph with *El*, the Semitic word for the creator God.

The name Asher (son of Jacob by Leah's servant Zilpah – Genesis 30:13) also appears, though in this case without the suffix *El*.

The temple of Amun in Soleb (Nubia) has a topographical list from the time of Amenhotep III in which is written 't3 ssw yhw3', meaning, *Yahweh of the land of the Shasu*,[449] this being the first clear extra-biblical evidence of the name "Yahweh".

Shasu was a generic word used by the ancient Egyptians to describe any Bedouin who lived east of the Nile delta, including the Midianites amongst whom Moses dwelt for forty years. Mount Horeb, the "mountain of God" (Exodus 3:1) is traditionally thought to have been in Midianite territory at the southern end of the Sinai Peninsula. In all likelihood Egyptians would have regarded Yahweh as a desert God (see note 69).

The designations *Habiru* or *Apiru* have been noted above.

Comparing the occurrence of these words across the reigns of five Egyptian monarchs produces just the distribution one would expect if Amenhotep III were the Pharaoh of the exodus:

Names	Tuthmose III (reigned 1479-1425 BC)	Amenhotep II (reigned 1427-1401 BC)[450]	Amenhotep III (reigned 1388-1351 BC)	Seti I (reigned 1290-1279 BC)	Ramses II (reigned 1279-1213 BC)
Jacob-El	yes				yes
Joseph-El	yes		yes		
Asher			yes	yes	yes
Yahweh			yes		yes
Shasu		Yes	yes	yes	yes
Habiru		Yes		yes	

There seems to have been a rediscovery of the names of Jacob and Joseph by the time of Thutmose III, though at some point earlier "a new king, who did not know about Joseph, [had come] to power in Egypt" (Exodus 1:8). At all events, knowledge of Joseph's name in the reign of Amenhotep III is not surprising, since the Israelites made a point of taking his remains: "Moses took the bones of Joseph with him because Joseph had made the sons of Israel swear an oath. He had said, 'God will surely come to your aid, and then you must carry my bones up with you from this place.'" (Exodus 13:19).

The name of Asher (representing one of the twelve tribes of Israel) would have been unlikely to elicit much attention whilst Israelites formed only an amorphous body of slaves. With their emergence as a political force and ultimately as a nation with its own territory, Egyptians are likely to have become more discriminating. Upon conquest of Canaan, Asher was allotted the coastal area as far north as Sidon in Phoenicia and as far south as Mount Carmel (see Joshua 19:24-31). As such, their lands lay hard by areas of Egyptian control or influence around Byblos in modern Lebanon. Moreover, they straddled routes that could have brought them into contact with Egyptian troops or traders heading north into Lebanon and Syria, though (as already observed) for at least part of the time during the period of the judges Israelite forces were driven back into the hills by Canaanite opposition. A possible reference to Asher in the Amarna Letters is noted above.

References to Yahweh would not be expected before the reign of Amenhotep III since this name was almost certainly only pronounced to humankind for the first time before Moses on Horeb. On that occasion "God also spoke to Moses and said to him: 'I am the LORD. I appeared to Abraham, Isaac, and Jacob as God Almighty, but by my name "The LORD" I did not make myself known to them.'" (Exodus 6:2-3, NRSV). There is nothing inconsistent with the ebb and flow of events in the ancient Near East for this name to have been forgotten or overlooked by the Egyptians for a while and then rediscovered during the reign of Ramses II.

It is noteworthy that there are no references to *Habiru* or *Apiru* during the reign of Amenhotep III, although they appear in preceding and succeeding reigns. Whilst it would be wrong to read too much into this, it is of a piece with official attempts to gloss over awkward facts relating to the Exodus events.

Pharaoh's chariots.

There is no evidence that any of the pleas for assistance that the Amarna Letters record Akhenaten's receiving from Palestine ever led to practical help being given. Although various speculations have been advanced as to why this should have been so, no entirely convincing explanation exists for the paralysis that seems to have gripped Egyptian foreign policy at this time. There is a conundrum of both capacity and motivation, for although it is sometimes said that the pharaoh may have been too preoccupied with matters theological to heed more practical concerns, this hardly seems to fit easily with the self-conscious attempts that seem to have been made to use religious reforms to cement, enhance or project royal power. Though dogmatic assertion is impossible, the son of the Pharaoh of the exodus would clearly have had reasons both military and psychological for not sending troops: militarily because the requisite capability either did not exist at all or was being used at home to police a restive population, and psychologically because he would have been unlikely to risk a further trial of strength with Israel's God so soon after previous bruising encounters.[451]

The Bible records that when Pharaoh changed his mind and decided to pursue the fleeing Israelites "he had his chariot made ready and took his army with him. He took six hundred of the best chariots, along with all the other chariots of Egypt, with officers over all of them." (Exodus 14:6-7).[452] Whilst this battle group was attempting to chase the renegades through the parted waters of the Red Sea "the LORD swept them into the sea. The water flowed back and covered the chariots and horsemen – the entire army of Pharaoh that had followed the Israelites into the sea. Not one of them survived." (Exodus 14:27-28).[453] Akin in some respects to a modern armoured division, chariots were the elite of the Egyptian forces and their primary offensive arm. They were expensive to build, equip and maintain, affordable only by wealthier families. Destruction of the greater proportion of the nation's chariots would inevitably have involved decimation of the nobility who manned them. Making good such losses was the work of a generation or more. Even then, lack of virtually all the best and most experienced officers is likely to have hindered the ability to rebuild a force as accomplished as that of former years. These men would have been sorely missed, not only for the sake of their personal experience and abilities but because they carried with them a corporate memory from the days of their country's military greatness. Time and again we see that, once any organisation suffers such a complete rupture with its past, recovering what has been lost is tremendously difficult, sometimes impossible. Egypt's apparent reticence to engage in foreign ventures during Akhenaten's reign may simply have reflected an absence of means.[454]

Loss of a sizeable chariot force shortly after coming to the throne is not easy to square with the intensive military activity of Ramses II's early years as pharaoh.[455] After dealing with coastal raids by the piratical Sherden in the second year of his reign, in the fourth and fifth years he undertook major campaigns in Syria, culminating in the battle of Kadesh against the Hittites under King Muwatallis in 1274 BC, but with campaigns almost bi-annually for about fifteen years thereafter. One estimate puts the number of Egyptian chariots at Kadesh as high as 2,000, though it is fair to say that others have produced considerably lower figures. Yet whatever the precise size of the force, if Ramses II had been pharaoh at the time of the Ten Plagues, the problem for Egypt would have been acute: the implication of pharaoh's taking "all the other chariots of Egypt" (Exodus 14:6-7) and that "Not one of them survived" (Exodus 14:27-28) is that the entire Egyptian chariot arm had effectively ceased to exist. To conclude that so soon after this disastrous pursuit Egypt could equip and train a sufficient body of men to be able to withstand a foe as fearsome as the Hittites requires ambitious claims for manpower and resources. Whilst not impossible, the likelihood is against it.

As would be expected given the losses Egypt had suffered, there is evidence of foreign mercenaries playing an increasingly important part in her armed forces. By Amenhotep III's time even prisoners of war were being drafted into the Egyptian forces, and so winning eventual freedom – a stela from the Amarna period goes so far as to show a Syrian mercenary being waited on by a native Egyptian (something that would have been unthinkable in bygone years).[456] From Amenhotep III's reign onwards the Egyptian armies were manned more and more by foreigners, including Libyans, Sudanis, Sherden and other Sea Peoples, and finally by Carian, Ionian and Greek mercenaries. By the Ramesside era many of these had risen to high rank, with attendant wealth and status.

Cataclysm, confusion and crisis.

Other factors may have been at play in Egypt's failure to intervene in Canaan during Akhenaten's reign. It is reasonable to suppose that in the aftermath of the Exodus events there would have been confusion in Egypt, followed by a painful period of adjustment. The nation would have suffered the severe economic dislocation of losing a significant source of manpower with the departure of its Hebrew slaves – and this at a time when harvests had failed, flocks and herds fallen prey to disease and a significant proportion of her population had died, including those whose skills could not easily be replaced.[457] During the latter years of Amenhotep III's reign there was a decline in the number of certain kinds of luxury goods, a sharp drop in quantity and quality of artwork, an apparent shortage of tomb painters and perhaps even of priests. It seems that stonemasons and quarrymen also were in short supply, for the only series of colossal statues produced for Akhenaten was not made from scratch but adapted from what had originally been statues of his father. The picture is of skilled and unskilled labour in short supply, but on top of this, many of those marked by birth and upbringing for positions of secular or military leadership would have perished in the Red Sea. To rebuild the nation in the face such calamity would have tested the most resilient of societies. In such circumstances, to imagine that Egypt could swiftly thereafter mount any sustained military campaign against serious opposition seems far-fetched.

There is tangential evidence that Amenhotep III may have sought to mitigate some of these effects by putting in place measures to increase population. In the thirtieth year of his reign he issued a decree exempting certain classes of women from taxes, perhaps with the intent of making marriage and child-rearing more affordable. Yet where the father seemingly at least tried to do something to address one aspect of the crisis, the son pursued policies which would most probably have greatly exacerbated it. On top of the already heavy burdens on the realm Akhenaten's profligate use of resources for building his new city and for sustaining the lavish daily offerings which accompanied worship of Aten must have come as body blows. In the straitened circumstances in which Egypt found herself after the exodus, the pharaoh's demands are most unlikely to have provided economic stimulus, for the problem was not that of an economy suffering an aggregate lack of demand. The more probable consequence of his actions was that the state would have arrogated scarce labour and materials to itself, to the detriment of other parts of society. Indeed, there are signs that the ambitious nature of the ruler's projects strained the nation to breaking point. Amongst the indications of a land groaning under and then progressively overwhelmed by the harsh burdens placed on it is the fact that Akhenaten failed to provide supplies of gold that had been promised to his ally, the king of the Mitanni – an unheard-of event for Egypt, whose plentiful stores of bullion were proverbial. In Akhet-aten itself only two of the tombs that the king lavished on his followers were fully cut and decorated. Even the heretic pharaoh's own final resting place was unfinished.

The economic cost to Egypt of all these upheavals is likely to have been considerable, but the human impact of change, disorientation and exhaustion of the treasury must have been yet greater. Many of those who survived the Ten Plagues or who avoided the disaster in the Red Sea would still have faced a miserable existence – certainly, conditions in the workmen's village at Akhet-aten appear to have been squalid, with mice and rats, bed bugs, maggots and fleas all commonplace. The likelihood is that there was a weakening of the state brought about by the disruption and discontent which accompanied unpopular religious reforms, leading the king to keep such troops as were available on police duty at home rather than send them overseas. There is some evidence for this in the way that revenue from the temple estates was dealt with: not only were temples to gods other than Aten forcibly shut by Akhenaten but their extensive property portfolios and income were expropriated or even (like the granary of the temple at Thebes) destroyed. The many local temple officials who had hitherto handled these affairs were no longer trusted to do so, leaving the army as the only body capable of performing the task.[458] In consequence, corruption and malpractice seem to have taken root, causing subsequent rulers serious problems when the former system of administration was restored.[459] Horemheb (who ruled after Akhenaten's short-lived successors Tutankhamun and Ay) was amongst those who bore down severely on those suspected of wrongdoing.

Psychological impact.

Akhenaten became pharaoh by virtue of his elder brother's death. If the hypothesis behind this work is correct, he can hardly have been ignorant of the circumstances that caused the throne to devolve upon him.[460] He would have been unusual indeed had this not affected him. To place the exodus and the events leading up to it during his father's reign both makes sense of Akhenaten's later actions and provides a convincing psychological explanation for them. Without some such impetus, there is nothing to account for why he behaved as he did. As explored in chapter 1, the wholesale changes that this pharaoh instituted in a traditional society in the face of all that he would have been brought up to believe and defend were so radical and so different from all that went before that they would have been almost impossible to conceive without the most extraordinary catalyst. Likewise, the new theology which Akhenaten imposed was (in its most developed manifestations, at any rate) so utterly alien to all traditions from which the monarch and those around him sprang that something beyond the usual run of events is needed to explain such a fundamental departure. Whilst there may have been an element of building on the past, at least at the start of the reign, significant chunks of the beliefs and forms of worship which Akhenaten instituted thereafter have no obvious root in previous Egyptian examples. Yet we can readily conceive that a man who had experienced or heard about the God of Israel's interactions with Egypt and reflected diligently on what was known in the Two Lands about that God could well have hit upon ideas of the kind that this pharaoh espoused.[461] More to the point, he would have had ample reason to turn his back on the traditional deities of his ancestors.

That there was something deep and dark in Egypt's past, an event so terrible as to be unmentionable by name, is attested by one of the boundary stelae from Akhet-aten. Threatening dire consequences if the king and various others were not buried in that city, it says that "[these consequences] shall be worse than what I heard in Year 4 … worse than what I heard in Year 3 … worse than what I heard in Year 1 … worse than what [my father Amenhotep III] heard … worse than what [my grandfather Thutmose IV] heard…" Further evidence of disasters that afflicted the land comes from parts of a speech recorded on a wall of one of the earliest buildings of Akhenaten's reign at Thebes, which refers to temples falling into ruin and the statues of gods being toppled.[462] There is every indication that these events weighed heavily on the mind of the king.

Ancient writings.

It tends to be accepted as a commonplace that ancient historians do not always approach their topic with the same rigour as their modern equivalents, but

Appendix I

even if true that does not automatically mean that they reveal nothing worthwhile. However circumspect and discriminating we may need to be in adopting wholesale the assertions of any given writer, it would be wrong to assume that everything they say is pure invention. There may be nuggets to be had or trails of enquiry to be followed which provide insights into the past, for almost certainly these men had access to sources or traditions now lost. Caution is always in order, but the idea of some form of connection between Moses on the one hand and Amenhotep III and Akhenaten on the other appears, albeit hazily, in a number of ways. For instance, the *Aegyptiaca*, a history of Egypt written in the third century BC by the priest Manetho records: "The eighteenth dynasty consisted of fourteen kings at Thebes ... Achencheres ruled for sixteen years. In his time Moses became leader of the Jews in their exodus from Egypt."[463] The name Achencheres is generally taken to refer to Akhenaten.

Manetho also told a story about a pharaoh called Amenophis, by whom he is commonly supposed to have meant Amenhotep III. The tale goes that this ruler wanted to see a vision of the gods and to that end sought help from a mystic, Amenophis son of Paapis.[464] The latter indicated that this royal wish would be granted if the monarch cleansed the land of lepers and others who were unclean, as a result of which a delighted king gathered together 80,000 such souls and forced them to toil in stone quarries to the east of the Nile. The necessary preconditions having been met, the seer proceeded to predict thirteen years of disaster in Egypt. So horrified was he by what he had to tell that having recounted it he promptly killed himself. The entire episode might of course just be a folk tale, but to the extent that it represents a recollection of actual events, it seems likely that a number of different elements are jumbled together. Disasters befalling Egypt under Amenhotep III would certainly be compatible with the events of Exodus taking place in that potentate's reign, and although the Ten Plagues themselves probably took place within a relatively short period, their effects would certainly have been felt for years to come. On the other hand, whilst a large displacement of people could perhaps be connected with the Israelites' departure from Goshen, the reference to a site later abandoned would seem to fit better either (in terms of numbers)[465] with the creation and later forsaking of a new capital at Akhet-aten or (in terms of location and the name given by Manetho to the pharaoh in his story) with Amenhotep III's reopening early in his reign of previously abandoned limestone quarries at Tura (Ainu).

Like Manetho, first century AD Jewish writer T. Flavius Josephus made contemporaries of Moses and Akhenaten in *Against Apion*.[466] Josephus was born at Jerusalem in AD 37, wrote *The Jewish War*[467] and *Antiquities of the Jews* and is generally considered a reliable historical source. His ideas or the tradition on which he drew perhaps influenced Sigmund Freud, whose last published work, *Moses and monotheism*, contended that the religion of Akhenaten influenced the development of Jewish monotheism under Moses. For the reasons given above, it is submitted that it fits better with the facts to say that it was the other way round.[468]

Biblical consistency.

Some contend that the accounts contained in the books of Joshua and Judges are inconsistent, in that the former by and large supports the idea of a sudden and largely successful Israelite incursion into the entire land of Canaan, whereas the latter pictures piecemeal conquest alongside frequent setbacks and periodic oppression of Israel by surrounding peoples. There is in truth no difficulty in holding both accounts correct. Military history provides countless examples of initial success subsequently undone by insurgency, infiltration and a resurgent foe. The Israelites suffered in later generations precisely because under Joshua they failed to carry out to the letter the instructions which God gave: they fell short by making an unauthorised treaty of peace and friendship with the men of Gibeon (Joshua 9:14-15) and by omitting to take those "very large areas of land" (Joshua 13:1) described in Joshua 13:2-7. The failure to subdue "all the territory of the Philistines and … the five lords of the Philistines – the Gazites, the Ashdodites, the Ashkelonites, the Gittites, and the Ekronites" (Joshua 13:2-3, NKJV) was a particularly serious oversight since this nation proved a thorn in Israel's side for generations to come.

Cultural influences.

The so-called hymns to Aten which are generally thought to have been composed by Akhenaten are said by some to be the inspiration behind Psalm 104:16-23. Whilst it is true that both the eulogies to the Egyptian god and the Psalm are extended outpourings of praise which picture a divine Creator at work in the natural world, the claim that the former influenced the latter is ambitious. The Psalms in their present form are commonly dated to the time of Israel's monarchy,[469] whose inception under King Saul was in 1052 BC or thereabouts, three hundred years after Akhenaten ruled. To the extent that earlier oral traditions are preserved in the Psalter, there is no obvious reason to conclude that cultural influence flowed only one way. Although subservient cultures often borrow from those that are dominant, there is also a flow in the other direction; it is not beyond the bounds of possibility that songs (perhaps sung by slaves as they worked) were heard and taken up by the Egyptians, in the same way that Negro Spirituals influenced a wider musical canon. Once a chance of that happening is admitted, so too should be the likelihood of Hebrew theology informing the beliefs of a pharaoh who was traumatised by the events of his father's reign and all that these demonstrated about the superiority of Israel's God over every deity of Egypt.

Appendix I

The appointed time.

So extensive and lavish were the building projects of Amenhotep III's reign that he was given the nickname *menwy*, the man of monuments. In many ways this period might be seen as the apogee of Egyptian power and influence, a time of almost unparalleled artistic achievement, of increasing luxury and growth in both production and consumption, a pinnacle from which the superiority of the Two Lands and its gods might have seemed self-evident. As the double crown was placed on this pharaoh's head for the first time there was peace and political stability, with Egypt respected and feared abroad in equal measure, the might of her armed forces confirmed by a litany of victories stretching back over many generations, her empire seemingly held secure. The names adopted by the new king reflected this self-confidence. Their overweening self-regard pointed also to the pagan worldview which the monarch was pledged to uphold, seeking to set another in the place which only the High King of heaven should occupy: as arbiter of right and wrong (the Horus name: "Mighty bull appearing in truth"); as fount of law and peace (the Two Ladies name: "He who establishes laws and pacifies the Two Lands"); as Lord of Hosts (the Golden Horus name: "Great of strength, Hammer of the Asiatics"); as the source of all that is good and true (the throne name: "Ra is Lord of Truth"); as object of worship and fount of approbation (the Son of Ra name: "Amun is content"). It was this pharaoh who first consistently authorised gods' statues to be made with his own countenance, a practice that was rare before his accession but routine thereafter.

In *Akhenaten, King of Egypt* Cyril Aldred describes the reign of Amenhotep III as "a climax in the belief of the divinity of the Pharaoh." It seems that there was an increasing tendency at this time to express the power and wealth of the ruling dynasty theologically, harking back almost a thousand years to the days of the Old Kingdom. That had been the era of pyramid-building, when later generations supposed pharaohs to have had uncontested status as living gods with no earthly competitors. In the days of Amenhotep III pharaoh once again set himself up as a deity in opposition to the one true God, styling himself not just king of kings but Ra of kings and using the title "the good god" with an enthusiasm unparalleled in previous reigns. Temples and statues were raised in honour of Amenhotep III himself, so that he was seen to be not merely an earthly representative of the gods but in every respect their equal. The man who did these things was no paragon. Rather, he seems to have been something of a voluptuary, writing to Milkilu of Gezer in Canaan that he would pay forty shekels apiece for "extremely beautiful cup-bearers in whom there is no defect" and receiving gifts of women from various rulers keen to keep on the right side of him – his penchant for tribute of this kind presumably being well known. Taken together with the Egyptians' oppressive treatment of the Israelites, the result of all this was to provide a perfect moment for the Almighty to step decisively into history by showing that true dominion is his and by bringing judgment on those who had meted out such harsh treatment to others. Scripture affirms that there is an "appointed time" (Romans 9:9) for all things. The Lord delays judgment until that moment – because he is merciful and since "he is patient with [us], because he does not want anyone to be destroyed, but wants all to turn away from their sins." (2 Peter 3:9, GNT). Hence he acts in judgment only when "sin ... has reached its full measure" (Genesis 15:16). All that we know suggests that the early years of Amenhotep III's reign were just such an instant.

Summary.

In conclusion:

The date given in the first book of Kings for Solomon's dedication of the Temple in Jerusalem makes it impossible for the exodus to have taken place earlier than 1446 BC. Nevertheless, it could have occurred some decades later.

The date ascribed to the escape from Egypt must allow for at least three hundred years of Israelite occupation of Canaan between the death of Joshua and the crowning of King Saul.

Neither of these facts sits readily with the exodus happening as late as the reign of Ramses II. The Bible's reference to a store city called Rameses is not conclusive as regards attribution of the Exodus events to the reign of this pharaoh.

On balance, the preponderance of evidence is against Ramses II having been on the throne when Moses returned from Midian. Amongst other things, if that had been the case it would be hard to account for Ramses II's ability to mount major campaigns early in his reign given the severe military losses described in Exodus 14.

Archaeological evidence can be read either way. It should thus be treated as corroborative rather than determinative. The absence of conclusive Egyptian records relating to the flight of Israelite slaves does not advance the issue one way or the other.

Albeit largely circumstantial, there is evidence to suggest Amenhotep III was on the throne when the exodus took place:

- Manetho's reference to great disasters coming upon Egypt during the reign of a king called Amenophis fits with the Ten Plagues occurring at this time.
- The extravagant homage paid to Sekhmet, goddess of pestilence, under Amenhotep III is consistent with this reign being a time of death and disease on an unusual scale.

- The fact that otherwise unknown towns and villages are listed on statues of Sekhmet suggests depopulation on a large scale.
- That the first reference in Egyptian records to Israel's God Yahweh should occur in the reign of Amenhotep III is logical if the exodus took place at that time.
- Amenhotep III's arrogation to himself of divinity and the circumstances surrounding his reign fit with the time appointed by God to deliver Israel.
- Evidence suggests a watershed during this reign, with a major disruptive event or series of events leading to a shortage of key workers, a reduction in quality and quantity of artistic production, straitened economic circumstances and a change in outlook on the part of the king.
- Placing the exodus at the time of Amenhotep III would result in Joseph's living during the reign of Amenemhet III. Evidence from that period is consistent with what the Bible says about the years of famine then experienced by Egypt.
- The Execration Texts appear to fit this schema as part of a process of cursing, enslaving and oppressing Israel.

Though again largely circumstantial, there is evidence to suggest that Akhenaten ruled at the time of Joshua's conquest of Canaan:

- The writings of Manetho and Josephus form part of an overall pattern that points to Akhenaten's father being the Pharaoh of the exodus.
- However corrupted it might be, a tradition has been preserved in these writings of a connection between Moses and Akhenaten.
- The premature death of Akhenaten's elder brother Crown Prince Thutmose is not in and of itself conclusive one way or the other since the elder brother of Ramses II for one also predeceased him. Yet if Crown Prince Thutmose were indeed one of the slain Egyptian firstborn the circumstances of his demise would provide the psychological background to explain his sibling's actions once he became pharaoh.
- It is difficult to build a truly satisfying picture of the motivations and inspirations behind Akhenaten's religious reforms without identifying a trigger for them which goes beyond mere extrapolation from existing Egyptian ideas and beliefs. By contrast, they can readily be understood if he were a younger son of the Pharaoh who confronted Moses.
- The Amarna Letters are consistent with Israelite attacks on Canaan at this time.

- The paralysis that seems to have gripped Egyptian policy in and around Canaan under Akhenaten can be easily apprehended if the pharaoh feared a further encounter with the God who had shown his power when delivering Israel from slavery.
- Likewise Egypt's failure to intervene in Canaan or to provide support to its vassals in that region may have reflected lack of military capability following loss of the chariot force which pursued the Israelites into the Red Sea.
- Exhaustion brought about by a combination of the Exodus events and their aftermath on the one hand and Akhenaten's profligate use of depleted resources for building his new city at Akhet-aten on the other may also have been a factor in Egyptian inactivity.
- In addition, disruption and discontent brought about by the imposition of unpopular religious reforms might have weakened the state and persuaded Akhenaten to keep troops at home rather than send them overseas.

Like much else, population figures are problematic and uncertain. Nevertheless, such broad trends as can be discerned appear consistent with a substantial increase in the population of ancient Egypt up to somewhere in the region of 1300 BC, followed thereafter by a significant fall.[470] It would be wrong to make exaggerated claims on the back of this but, to put it at its lowest, there is a respectable case that population figures are consistent with what the Bible says.

None of the above amounts to proof beyond reasonable doubt, but on a balance of probabilities there is a strong likelihood that Akhenaten's father was on the throne when the exodus took place.

In sum: Freud was right in seeing a link between Moses and Akhenaten, but had things the wrong way round. It was the prophet who influenced the pharaoh.

Appendix II

Population figures.

Israel.

Whilst in Egypt "the Israelites ... were fruitful and increased greatly in number" (Genesis 47:27) and "were fruitful and multiplied greatly and became exceedingly numerous" (Exodus 1:7).[471] So much so that Pharaoh feared insurrection: "He told his people, 'These Israelis are becoming dangerous to us because there are so many of them. Let's figure out a way to put an end to this. If we don't, and war breaks out, they will join our enemies and fight against us and escape out of the country.'" (Exodus 1:9-10, TLB). Whatever precise numbers may have been, it therefore follows that by the time that Moses was born Hebrew slaves were a significant proportion of the total population of the Two Lands.[472] Given the paucity of data, exactly how numerous they were at any given point and what percentage of the whole they accounted for can only be guesswork but, by way of analogy, it is estimated that by AD 1 slaves may have been anything between 25% and 40% of the population of the city of Rome (albeit a much lower proportion elsewhere in the Roman Empire).[473] Remains in those parts of the Nile Delta which the Bible indicates were the areas of heaviest Israelite settlement (Goshen) point towards fairly large-scale occupation by a Semitic culture which was distinct from that of the surrounding Egyptians. These have not yet been irrefutably identified as belonging to the Israelites, but an avenue of enquiry certainly exists.

A census of the whole Israelite community in the second year after they left Egypt "counted, twenty years old or more, a total of 603,550 men." (Exodus 38:26; see also Exodus 12:37 and Numbers 1:21-46 and 2:4-31). On its face the precision of this number, its consistency wherever it appears and the statement that it was arrived at by counting "clans and families, listing every man by name, one by one" (Numbers 1:2) requires that it be taken literally.[474] Yet even this understates overall numbers, since "The families of the tribe of Levi, however, were not counted along with the others" (Numbers 1:47) and it seems that the "Many other people [who] went up with [the Israelites]" (Exodus 12:38) when they left Egypt might have been omitted from the count altogether (see Exodus 12:37-38).

Bearing this in mind, and given that the census described in Numbers reckons only men of military age, it points to an overall Israelite population of at least two million and quite possible substantially more. Many regard this as inherently unlikely or even impossible. Impossibility is said to lie in the fact that this number is so large in comparison with what otherwise are thought to have been the populations of Canaan and Egypt at this time, as well as in the difficulties in provisioning such a multitude during forty years of desert wandering. The Bible is of course quite clear that the Israelites were only able to survive in the wilderness through repeated miracles – manna (Exodus 16:1-35), quail (Exodus 16:13) and water from the rock (Exodus 17:1-7). Whilst we may speculate as to the means by which God brought these miracles about, they are by their nature incapable of empirical analysis. By contrast, the probable size of the Israelite population can be tested by examining whether the population of Egypt was such that the proportion of it accounted for by Hebrew slaves might provide a figure approaching that given in the Bible; by considering whether the overall level of settlement in Canaan was sufficiently great as to be consistent with the Bible's account of that region's later conquest by Joshua; and by considering the practicalities of shepherding such a multitude across the Red Sea.

Egypt.

Numerous attempts have been made to estimate the population of ancient Egypt, with widely varying results. It is more or less generally agreed that there was a period of demographic expansion from somewhere in the region of 1500 BC, with a high point being reached later in the New Kingdom (perhaps around 1300 BC or thereabouts). It then seems that decline set in at some point during the latter part of the Eighteenth Dynasty and that this period of lower population continued into the Twentieth Dynasty before numbers rose again. The devil, however, is in the detail. The middle range of estimates is that some two million inhabitants lived in all of the land in 1500 BC, increasing by 50% to some three million by about 1300 BC before falling and then climbing again so that around 1200 BC (at the time of Seti I and Ramses II) the population of Egypt was in the region of 2.9 million. Some estimates, though, hazard that at its New Kingdom peak the population may have grown to as much as four million or even higher.[475]

It has to be acknowledged at the outset that all figures and dates mentioned above are speculative. Both the estimates themselves and the data and methodology by which they are arrived at are to some degree at least problematic. Given the inherent uncertainties and incomplete data, dogmatic assertions one way or the other would clearly be unwise. The broad trend is nevertheless intriguing since a significant loss of population in the late Eighteenth Dynasty[476] would on its face be consistent with the departure of Israelite slaves at this time, whilst the higher population estimates for the period prior to this sudden fall reach an order of magnitude that begin to make less unbelievable the census figures given in Numbers 1:21-46. That the higher population estimates need not be regarded as altogether fanciful is shown by comparison with later ages, which provide a yardstick against which to measure:

Appendix II

After a long period of decline, the population of Egypt levelled off at about 1.7 million in the tenth and eleventh centuries AD, rising thereafter so that by the time the Turks took over in the sixteenth century AD the population was in the region of 3.15 to 3.6 million.

Prior to the tenth century AD, the population had been considerably greater. It is generally thought to have reached a high point of about 4.5 to 4.75 million in the first century AD, after which numbers declined by around a third through to the fourth century AD.[477]

The decline during this period did not reflect inability of the land to support such numbers, but was a consequence of wider political and economic factors, not least barbarian invasions, civil disorder, dislocation of trade and a fall in productivity that were mirrored throughout the Roman Empire over the same time span.

There is much to suggest that in the first century AD Egypt could have supported even greater numbers than then lived in the land. Along with the rest of the Roman provinces in North Africa she was at that point widely regarded as the bread-basket of the Empire, producing substantial grain surpluses for export.[478]

Roman society in the first century AD was notably well organised, but agricultural methods and technology were not so far ahead of those in ancient Egypt as to suggest that the latter would have been incapable of supporting broadly similar numbers at the time of the New Kingdom (albeit that in doing so she may no longer have had a grain surplus for export).[479]

Taken together, these factors suggest that it is by no means beyond the bounds of possibility for Egypt during the New Kingdom to have had a population of five million or even more.

If so, then even if Israelites formed only the same proportion of the total population as slaves did in the Confederate States in 1860, the census figures recorded in Numbers start to look achievable.[480]

Canaan.

Widely varying estimates have been produced for the Bronze Age population of Canaan. At one end of the spectrum, the figure for the whole region has been put as low as 100,000. At the other, it is claimed that the city of Hazor alone had as many as 40,000 inhabitants.[481] Given such fundamental disagreement, clues must be sought elsewhere:

In *The Jewish Revolt* Josephus claims that between 600,000 and 1,300,000 were killed when the Romans destroyed the second Temple and sacked Jerusalem in AD 70.

In his eighty-volume *Historia Romana* Cassius Dio says that a further 580,000 Jews were killed during the bar Kochba uprising of AD 132-135.

It is right to approach these figures with a degree of scepticism. They are round numbers with no indication as to how they were arrived at, and although Josephus was an active participant in the revolt of AD 70, Cassius Dio wrote over a century after the Bar Kochba uprising.

Yet this does not mean that these writers should be ignored altogether. The likelihood is that educated public figures such as Josephus and Cassius Dio would have been aware and taken account of the results of Roman censuses,[482] which allowed a fairly accurate picture of overall population. Consequently their evidence should not be dismissed out of hand.

Killing on anything like the scale related by Josephus and Cassius Dio suggests an overall level of settlement greater than the number of casualties by some order of magnitude. Even if the Romans had killed a third of the entire population of their province of Palestine during the Jewish revolt, on Josephus' figures this would mean that anything between 1.8 million and 3.9 million people had lived there before the conflict began.

Account needs to be taken of the extra productivity (and concomitant population growth) resulting from Roman organisational and technical achievements. Similarly, allowance has to be made for the possibility of higher population in Roman times resulting from improved sanitation and from food imports on a scale not seen in earlier epochs.

All those factors would suggest that the population which Canaan was capable of sustaining may have been greater in the first centuries BC and AD than at the time when the Israelites began their conquest, but not necessarily by a huge amount.

The Bible says that the northern Canaanite kingdoms which united under the leadership of Hazor were able to field a substantial force: "a huge army, as numerous as the sand on the seashore" (Joshua 11:4).[483] The tenor of the biblical narrative is that this enemy was not substantially inferior in numbers to the Israelites.

When all is said and done, we are forced to admit that time and again ancient societies have surprised by their achievements, sophistication and scale. In that regard, the arguments that once raged about the size or even the existence of the ancient city of Nineveh should give us pause.[484]

As things presently stand, it is not possible to make definitive claims about the population of Bronze Age Canaan. There is no incontrovertible proof that population figures which the Bible gives are right, but by the same token neither is the opposite the case. In view of the accuracy of other aspects of the biblical narrative, the population figures given in Scripture deserve a respectful hearing.

Crossing the Red Sea.

Population figures have a bearing on the logistics of moving the Israelites through the Red Sea in the face of Pharaoh's advancing chariot divisions. The operation was undoubtedly challenging, but looks eminently achievable. Naturally, exactly what was involved would have been a function both of the dimensions of the gap through which the people passed and of the numbers who needed to make the transit, and these are things which now can only be matters of conjecture. Nonetheless, the reliability of the biblical account can be gauged by general observations set against suppositions that fit the overall context. If we were to assume for the sake of argument a crossing point two miles long and three miles wide,[485] then even a total Israelite population in the order of three million[486] can be seen to have required surprisingly little time to pass from one side to the other:

There are 1,760 yards in a mile, so the width of such a crossing point would be equal to 5,280 yards and its length 3,520 yards, giving an area of 18,585,600 square yards.

Assuming three square yards per person would allow up to 6,195,200 people to occupy this space.[487]

Since the Israelites brought with them their "flocks and herds … [with] Not a hoof … left behind" (Exodus 10:25-26, TLB), and had treasure "plundered [from] the Egyptians" (Exodus 12:36), we might conjecture that even though the tribes numbered considerably less than the area could hold, in fact the whole of it was needed to accommodate man, beast and baggage train together.

A reasonably fit man might expect to make two and a half miles per hour over hilly or difficult terrain. The ground the Israelites were required to cross would have been flat (albeit possibly broken),[488] but they had with them infants, the aged and infirm as well as those in the prime of life.

Needing to drive flocks and herds before them and encumbered by baggage, their speed is thus unlikely to have been much more than two miles per hour and could have been lower.

If they were only able to make one mile an hour, the first to enter the crossing point would have exited two hours later, at which point the rearguard would have been just about to start their transit, with a two-hour crossing still ahead of them.

Even with some fairly harsh assumptions in terms of numbers, speed and available space, this suggests that all could have been across in four hours from jumping-off (the likelihood being that they probably managed the transit faster than that, perhaps in as little as half the time).

The Bible says that "all that night the LORD drove the sea back with a strong east wind and turned it into dry land ... and at daybreak the sea went back into its place" (Exodus 14:21 and 14:27), whilst it was "During the last watch of the night [that] the LORD looked down from the pillar of fire and cloud at the Egyptian army and threw it into confusion. He made the wheels of the chariots come off so they had difficulty driving." (Exodus 14:24-25).

The Jews had three watches during the night: from sunset to 10.00 pm, 10.00 pm to 2.00 am and 2.00 am to sunrise, so confusion was sown amongst the Egyptians somewhere between 2.00 am and daybreak, with the rear elements of the Israelite tribes still being in the course of crossing the sea during this time.[489]

The Egyptians could not have begun their pursuit until the Israelite rearguard had already gone some way across the sea, since otherwise there would have been contact between Pharaoh's forces and their erstwhile slaves – the Bible does not report this happening, and surely would have done so had it occurred.

The rearguard must in fact have kept some way ahead of the pursuing chariots, for the pillar of cloud ensured that "neither [Israelites nor Egyptians] went near the other all night long" (Exodus 14:20).

If the Israelites started their crossing at 3.00 am at an average speed of two miles per hour, they would all have been across by daybreak at 5.00 am;

On that hypothesis, the Egyptians would have started their pursuit through the sea maybe half an hour or so after 4.00 am, the rearguard then being about thirty minutes ahead of them and halfway across the sea.

The Egyptians might have made good speed for a while but their progress was soon hampered, as God "threw [the Egyptian army] into confusion. He made the wheels of their chariots come off so that they had difficulty driving." (Exodus 14:25).

It was in those circumstances that "Moses stretched out his hand over the sea, and at daybreak the sea went back to its place ... [so that] The water flowed back and covered the [Egyptian] chariots and horsemen" (Exodus 14:27-28).

Whatever we might now think of them, the sequence and timing of events described in Scripture is certainly internally consistent. The journey details which appear in Exodus 13:20, 14:2 and 19:2 and Numbers 33:1-49 and elsewhere lend authenticity to the account, since they bear all the hallmarks of being based on information supplied by eyewitnesses. Though the repeatability demanded by modern science will always be out of our grasp, it is once again possible to imagine circumstances which allowed God to work the miracles recounted in Exodus without breaking any laws of nature. Consequently, unless and until compelling evidence to the contrary is produced, the biblical account deserves to be taken at face value.

Appendix III

The inhabitants of Canaan.

Though little is known for sure about the origins of the Philistines, they are believed to have been seafaring folk of Indo-European stock who were amongst the so-called Sea Peoples which invaded Egypt early in the twelfth century BC.[490] After being driven out, it seems either that they migrated in considerable numbers to south-west Canaan or that they were deliberately settled in that region by the Egyptians. Their territory centred on the cities of Gath, Gaza, Ekron, Askelon and Ashdod but at various points extended more widely throughout southern Canaan.[491] The Bible lists ten peoples which were present in Canaan at the time of Abraham: "the Kenites, the Kenizzites, the Kadmonites, the Hittites, the Perizzites, the Rephaim, the Amorites, the Canaanites, the Girgashites, and the Jebusites." (Genesis 15:19-21, GNT). Although Philistines do not figure in this list, Abraham at one point is said to have "stayed in the land of the Philistines" (Genesis 21:34), whilst Isaac "went to the king of the Philistines in Gerar" (Genesis 26:1) and there are references to Philistines in Genesis 26:8, 26:14-15 and 26:18. These references suggest that Philistines were to be found in Canaan at this point, though in neither such numbers nor such concentrations that they counted amongst the major political forces of that region.

By the time of Moses, the demographic make-up of Canaan had changed. Four tribes which were noted in Abraham's day (the Kenites, Kenizzites, Kadmonites and Rephaites) were no longer deemed worthy of mention, and a new tribe (the Hivites) had come on the scene. Hence God told Moses that he would drive "out before you many nations – the Hittites, Girgashites, Amorites, Canaanites, Perizzites, Hivites and Jebusites, seven nations larger and stronger than you" (Deuteronomy 7:1 and 20:17). Although once again the Philistines are not listed, they appear to have been in Canaan or its vicinity: the Bible says that, "When Pharaoh let the people go, God did not lead them on the road through the Philistine country, though that was shorter. For God said, 'If they face war, they might change their minds and return to Egypt.'" (Exodus 13:17). Certainly, the Philistines seem to have been firmly established in their five main power centres at the latest by the end of Joshua's life. Shortly before his death, God reminded Joshua that land which had been allotted to Israel but was as yet untaken included "all the territory of the Philistines and ... the five lords of the Philistines – the Gazites, the Ashdodites, the Ashkelonites, the Gittites, and the Ekronites" (Joshua 13:2-3, NKJV).

The biblical account is consistent with Philistines having been in Canaan from long before Moses and Joshua, though perhaps not in large numbers. There was apparently an increase in Philistine power and influence over the course of time, leading to consolidation of territory in south-west Canaan. It would be reasonable to expect that there was an accompanying growth in Philistine population, though whether this reflected immigration on the part of those who had previously settled in Egypt it is presently impossible to say for sure. Whatever may have been the case, references to Philistines in Genesis and Exodus are neither inconsistent nor anachronistic.

Appendix IV

Gods and goddesses of ancient Egypt.

The list below gives a flavour of the extreme polytheism of ancient Egypt. Difficulty in analysing its religion leaves the total number of deities uncertain, though there were at least eighty and by some reckonings as many as two thousand, the ones appearing in this Appendix being those most generally accepted. Pharaohs, the majority of living creatures and large numbers of inanimate objects were thought divine.

Aker (aka Akar)	9	Banebdjedet		Haroeris	
Amaunet	12	Bast (aka	9	Harpocrates	
Ammit (aka Ammut, Ahemait)	10	Bastet, Basthet, Ubasti and Pasht)		Harsaphes	
				Harsomtus	
Amset (aka Imset)				Hathor	5, 7, 10
		Bat		Hatmehit	
Amun (aka Amon, Amen)	4, 5, 8, 9, 10, 11, 12	Behdety		Hauhet	
		Bes	10	Hauron	
		Buchis		Heka	
Amun-Ra	9	Duamutef		Hemsut	
Anat		Duau		Heqat (aka Heqt, Heqet, Hekit)	2
Anedjti		Esye			
Anhuret		Ha			
Anubis	10	Hah (aka Huh, Heh, Hauh, Huah and Hahuh)		Herishef	
Anuket	1			Herwer	
Apis				Hesat	
Apopis				Horus	9
Arensnuphis		Hapi (god of the Nile flood)	1, 2	Horus the Child	
Ash				Hu	
Astarte				Iati	
Atem (aka Atum)	9	Hapi (son of Horus)		Ihy	
Aten	9	Harakhte (aka Herakhte)	9	Imhotep	6
Ayebt				Imsety	
Baal	11			Isfet	

Isis	7, 10, 12	Nefertum (aka Nerfertem)	9	Set (aka Seth, Sukhet)	7, 11
Kadesh		Neith	11	Seven Hathors	
Kebhsenuf		Nekhbet		Shed	
Kek		Nepri		Shentayet	
Khenti-amenti		Nemty		Shesemtet	
Khenti-kheti		Nephthys		Shu	7, 9
Khepri	9, 10	Nun		Sia	
Kherty		Nut	7	Sobek (aka Sukhos)	1, 3, 7, 9
Khnum	1, 9, 10	Onuris			
		Osiris	1, 10	Sokar (aka Seker)	9, 10
Khons	9	Pakhet			
Lah (aka Yah)		Panebtawy		Sopdet (aka Sothis)	
Ma'at	9	Ptah	5, 9		
Mafdet		Raet (aka Rattawy)		Sopdu	9
Mandulis				Tait	
Marul		Re (aka Ra)	9	Ta-bitjet	
Mehet-uret		Ra-Harakhte	9	Tatenen	
Mehit		Reshef		Taweret	
Menhyt		Satet (aka Sati, Satis)	1	Tefnut	7
Menkeret				Thoth (Djeheuty)	
Menqet		Seb (aka Geb, Gebb, Keb, Kebb)	3		
Meret				Two Ladies Triad	
Meretseger					
Meskhenet		Sekhet		Uatchit	4
Mihos		Sekhmet (aka Sakhmet)	6, 10	Upuaut (aka Wepwawet)	
Min (aka Menu, Amsu)					
		Selket (aka Selkis)	10	Uto	
Mnevis	5			Wadjet	
Montu (aka Mentu)	11	Sematawy		Waset	
		Sepa		Wennofer	
Mut		Serapia	8		
Naunet		Serapis	6		
Nebet-ihi		Seshat			
Nebetu					

Appendix IV

The Lord declared, "On all the gods of Egypt I will bring judgment" (Exodus 12:12):[492]

1. *August:* The plague which turned the Nile to blood (Exodus 7:14-25) targeted Khnum (guardian of the river's source), Hapi (god of the Nile flood), Anuket and Satet (dispensers of cool water), Osiris (whose bloodstream was formed of the river) and Sobek, a fourfold deity representing the four elemental gods (Ra of fire, Shu of sky, Geb of earth and Osiris of water).

2. *September:* The plague of frogs (Exodus 8:1-15) targeted Hapi and Heqt (the latter being a frog goddess, both related to fertility).

3. *October:* The plague of dust and gnats (Exodus 8:16-19) targeted Seb and Sobek (earth gods).

4. *November:* The plague of flies (Exodus 8:20-32) targeted Uatchit, the fly god, and Amun (as ruler of the air).[493]

5. *December:* The plague on domestic animals (Exodus 9:1-7) targeted Ptah, Hathor, Mnevis and Amun, all of whom were associated with cows or bulls. Amun was symbolised (amongst other things) by a ram.

6. *January:* The plague of boils (Exodus 9:8-12) targeted Sekhmet (goddess of epidemics), Serapis and Imhotep (gods of healing and medicine).

7. *February:* The plague of hail and fire (Exodus 9:13-35) targeted Nut (the sky goddess), Isis and Seth (who were agricultural deities), Shu and Sobek (gods of the sky or atmosphere), Hathor (a sky goddess) and Tefnut (goddess of moisture and clouds).

8. *March:* The plague of locusts (Exodus 10:1-20) targeted Serapia (a goddess thought to give protection against these insects). Since "an east wind [which God made] blow across the land … brought the locusts" (Exodus 10:13-14), it also targeted Amun (god of the wind).

9. *April:* The plague of darkness (Exodus 10:21-29) targeted Ra, Amun-Ra, Aten, Atum, Bastet, Harakhte, Horus, Khepri, Khnum, Nefertum, Ptah, Ra, Ra-Harakhte, Sekhmet, Sobek and Sopdu (all of whom were associated in greater or lesser degree with the sun),[494] Khons and Thoth (moon gods), Sokar (god of light) and Aker (god of the horizon and of the border between day and night). Ma'at and Shu were also considered part of the solar cult.

10. *May:* The plague of death of the firstborn (Exodus 12:29-30) targeted all the gods of Egypt, most especially Amun (in his role as king of the gods) and Pharaoh himself (as god-king and earthly representative of

the gods) but also Bes (protector of children), Osiris (god of the dead), Hathor (goddess of the dead), Isis (who was protector of Horus during his childhood and responsible for helping Osiris return to life), Sekhmet and Selket (respectively protectors of the righteous and of those stung by scorpions), Khnum and Khepri (creator gods whom this plague showed to be incapable of bringing the dead back to life), Sokar (god of the underworld), Ammit (a funerary deity known as the Devourer of the Dead) and Anubis (supposedly the inventor of embalming).

11 *June:* Parting of the Red Sea (Exodus 14:21-22) targeted Amun, god of the wind who was said to calm the sea for sailors, whilst destruction of the pursuing Egyptian army (Exodus 14:23-28) targeted Amun, Seth, Baal, Montu and Neith, each of whom was a war god.

12 The swallowing of the serpents which the Egyptian magicians conjured by the snake that came from the staff Aaron threw down (Exodus 7:10 and 7:12) targeted Amun (who was a snake in his incarnation as Kematef), Amaunet (portrayed as a snake or snake-head, on which rested the crown of Lower Egypt) and Isis (supposedly the most powerful magician in the universe, having learnt the secret name of Ra).

Unsurprisingly given his position as chief amongst the Egyptian gods, Amun was frequently a specific target of these judgements, though ultimately they all struck at his authority since as the highest god he bore supreme responsibility for protection of that land and its people. The same charge could in some degree be levelled against Ma'at since each plague upset the natural and proper order, which that goddess represented and was supposed to uphold. Whatever the precise details, the plagues clearly demonstrated the superior power of the God of Israel.

Appendix V

Location of Horeb.

Exodus does not initially say anything to specify the location of Mount Horeb, the "mountain of God" (Exodus 3:1 and 4:27)[495] beyond stating that it lay on "the far side of the desert" (Exodus 3:1) or "the west side of the wilderness" (Exodus 3:1, RSV). The lands of Midian both encompassed and were surrounded by deserts; the Pentateuch mentions by name those of Shur (Exodus 15:22), Paran (Numbers 10:12, 12:16, 13:3 and 13:26), Etham (Numbers 33:8), Kedemoth (Deuteronomy 2:26), Sin (Exodus 17:1), Zin (Numbers 13:21, 20:1, 27:14, 33:36, 34:3 and 34:4) and Sinai (Exodus 16:1, 19:1-2). The Desert of Shur (Exodus 15:22) was in the Negev on the immediate north-eastern border of Egypt, but the location of all the others is uncertain. Add to that the possibility of another desert which is not specifically mentioned in the Books of Moses and clearly a statement that Horeb lay on "the far side of the desert" (Exodus 3:1) does not take us very far, especially since the wilderness concerned need not necessarily have been fully within uncontested Midianite territory.[496] Though reference to "the desert of Sinai" (Exodus 19:1) might be thought at least to help fix the location of Horeb in the Sinai Peninsula, this begs a number of questions: as to whether the Horeb of Exodus 3:1 and the Sinai of Exodus 19:2 are one and the same; if they are, why different names should be used for them; and as to whether the places which the Bible calls the Desert of Sinai and Mount Sinai are identical to those to which we now give these names. On its face, there is nothing in the first biblical mention of Horeb[497] to say that it might not have been anywhere in the Sinai Peninsula, the Arabian Peninsula or even in the lands of Moab (those relatively fertile regions which lay immediately to the east of the southern River Jordan and Dead Sea).[498]

Distances and journey times are of limited help in fixing the location of Horeb more precisely. Moses' repeated request for Pharaoh to "let us take a three-day journey into the desert to offer sacrifices to the LORD our God" (Exodus 3:18, 5:3 and 8:27) does not seem relevant since all the peaks that have been suggested as candidates for being the biblical Horeb are easily more than three days' travel from Egypt. Encumbered as they were by flocks and herds as well as by the very young and the aged, it is highly unlikely that a large and disparate body such as the Israelites could have covered much more than fifteen miles a day. In harsh and unfamiliar terrain, even that is likely to have been pushing it, and it is implicit in the Exodus account that there were periods when the tribes rested in one place for days at a time.[499] It is therefore entirely understandable that "The whole Israelite community ... came to the desert of Sin, which is between Elim and Sinai, [only] on the fifteenth day of the second month after they had come out of Egypt" (Exodus 16:1).[500] In the course of their journey, the tribes not only had to cope with the demands of keeping people and animals together on a trek through country where food and water were scarce, but had also needed to battle against the Amalekites (see Exodus 17:8-13).[501] Thus it was not until the "third month after the Israelites left Egypt – on the very day – [that] they came to the desert of Sinai [and] ... camped there in the desert in front of the mountain." (Exodus 19:1-2).

Moreover, journey times and stages recorded in Exodus, Numbers and Deuteronomy do not allow even the likely radius within which the Israelites travelled to be fixed with any degree of certainty since their speed and exact point of departure are not known with sufficient accuracy. The Bible measures the time taken to reach the mountain from when "the Israelites left Egypt" (Exodus 19:1-2), but this could refer just as easily to when they first started out from Goshen as to the moment of finally crossing the Egyptian frontier. Given that the westernmost part of Goshen lay upwards of fifty miles from the nearest border post and that soon after their departure the Lord told Moses to "turn back .... [to give Pharaoh the impression of] wandering around the land in confusion" (Exodus 14:2-3), the potential for error is obvious, with uncertainty over the precise direction of travel an additional complication. About the best that can be said is that a radius from the Egyptian border that allowed the Israelites to reach the far south of the Sinai Peninsula would also take in the southern reaches of Moab and at a pinch might also extend to a narrow stretch of land in the Arabian Peninsula east of the Gulf of Aqaba. For an amorphous group of former slaves to have reached the outer edge of this radius in the eleven stages recorded in Numbers 33:3-15 is demanding, but achievable. By contrast, to have travelled much beyond it looks immensely challenging. Consequently, candidates beyond this radius deserve to be treated with the greatest caution.

Like Moses when he wrote Exodus, later generations seem to have treated Mount Horeb and Mount Sinai as synonymous, hence the statement that "Nothing was in the ark except the two tablets of stone which Moses put there at Horeb, when the LORD made a covenant with the children of Israel, when they came out of the land of Egypt." (1 Kings 8:9 and 2 Chronicles 5:10, NKJV; see also 1 Kings 19:8, Psalm 106:19 and Malachi 4:4). This might be thought to sit uneasily with the fact that the tribes reached "the Desert of Sin" (Numbers 33:12) four distinct journey stages before they came to "the Desert of Sinai" (Numbers 33:15)[502] and three stages before they reached Rephidim (Numbers 33:14), where "there was no water for the people to drink" (Exodus 17:1). It was at Rephidim that the Lord told Moses to "Walk on ahead of the people ... I will stand there before you by the rock at Horeb. Strike the rock, and water will come out of it to drink." (Exodus 17:5-6). On a casual reading this suggests that Horeb was reached before Sinai, for it was only "After they set out from Rephidim [that] they entered the Desert of Sinai, and Israel camped there in the desert in front of the mountain" (Exodus 19:2). More careful analysis discloses two possibilities. The first is that Mount Horeb and Mount Sinai are indeed separate places (though they were evidently not a huge distance apart and may have formed part of the same mountain chain). The second is that they are one and the same, and when Moses "[walked] on ahead of the people" (Exodus 17:5) he came to the spot which Numbers records as having been the next stage of Israel's itinerary.[503] Since there is no reason to assume that Moses misremembered or made a mistake when he wrote these things down, the latter is the preferable interpretation. It is consistent with the various biblical references which indicate that Mount Horeb and Mount Sinai are interchangeable.

As to different names being used for the same location, there are many examples of such a practice, reflecting different linguistic influences or different usages within the same language group.[504] Since he was familiar with Egyptian, Hebrew and Midianite, Moses might readily have switched from one to the other. Given the care that he took in crafting the Pentateuch, however, it would be surprising if he had done this in a way that was altogether random. It is notable that Horeb appears only three times in Exodus but is used throughout Deuteronomy with the exception of one verse that uses the name Sinai instead.[505] The likelihood therefore is that there was a self-conscious literary purpose in the choice of one term rather than the other. If Horeb were the usual Midianite name, for example, it would clearly be appropriate to use in Exodus 3:1 since this is the first occasion the mountain is mentioned and Moses was then living in Midian. Likewise God's promise that he would "stand there before you by the rock at Horeb" (Exodus 17:6) may have deliberately been expressed in terms that caused Moses to think back to his first encounter with the Almighty on the self-same mountain. In similar vein, saying that "the Israelites stripped off their ornaments at Horeb" (Exodus 33:6) could be making a spiritual point by causing the reader to reflect on the time when Moses was told, "Take off your sandals, for the place where you are standing is holy ground." (Exodus 3:5). The etymology of Horeb (see note 25) would also make it the right term to support the theological statements to be found in Deuteronomy. By emphasising heartfelt worship of God and complete obedience to his commands, this echoes the time when "the angel of the LORD appeared to [Moses] in flames of fire from within a bush." (Exodus 3:2). To that end, the people were specifically reminded of the fact that "the LORD spoke to you at Horeb out of the fire." (Deuteronomy 4:15)

By the time of Christ, the name Horeb seems to have fallen out of use, since it does not appear at all in the New Testament. In his final speech to the Sanhedrin before being martyred, Stephen called the place where Moses saw the burning bush and received the Ten Commandments "Mount Sinai" (Acts 7:30 and 7:38, NKJV). Similarly, when St Paul talked of the "covenant from ... Mount Sinai" (Galatians 4:24), he clearly meant the Old Testament covenant mediated through Moses. Again, there appears to be a clear and distinct identification of Mount Horeb with Mount Sinai. The issue then is whether what Stephen and Paul had in mind was the same peak to which we now give the name Sinai. At first sight this may seem doubtful since St Paul speaks of "Mount Sinai in Arabia" (Galatians 4:25, NKJV) and in the present day Arabia usually means the lands of the Arabian Peninsula (essentially modern Saudi Arabia, Yemen and Oman). In St Paul's time, however, this was not so.[506] After his conversion on the road to Damascus he "went immediately into Arabia" (Galatians 1:17) by which he almost certainly meant that he entered the Nabatean kingdom which then stretched from the borders of Damascus south-west to Suez and into the Sinai Peninsula. Though this kingdom also extended into the north of Saudi Arabia, St Paul's reference to Mount Sinai's being in Arabia thus simply leaves open all the possibilities inherent in the Old Testament. Of itself it does not require the traditional identification with the Sinai Peninsula to be overturned.[507]

In sum, it seems safe to conclude that Mount Horeb and Mount Sinai are one and the same. On the basis of the itinerary given in the Bible, a case can be made for locating this peak elsewhere than in the Sinai Peninsula. As the evidence presently stands, however, the burden of proof on those who would advance such a case has not been discharged.

Appendix VI

The Hebrew Alphabet.

Alef	Bet	Gimel	Dalet	He	Vav	Zayin	Het	Tet	Yod	Kaf
א	ב	ג	ד	ה	ו	ז	ח	ט	י	כ ך

Lamed	Mem	Nun	Samekh	Ayin	Pe	Tsadi	Qof	Resh	Shin	Tav
ל	מ ם	נ ן	ס	ע	פ ף	צ ץ	ק	ר	ש	ת

Though opinions differ as to its exact origins and the time of its birth, early forms of Hebrew script are certainly of great age. Hard by the temple of the goddess Hathor, close to what were once the Egyptian copper and turquoise mines of Serabit el-Khadim in south-western Sinai, preserved by the dry conditions of that region, are somewhat less than thirty graffiti in a so-called proto-Sinaitic script. In appearance these are rather similar to Egyptian hieratic, the writing which developed at more or less the same time as hieroglyphics but was less elaborate and thought less sacred. Easier to write and speedier to form, the cursive characters of hieratic were used for everyday purposes such as record-keeping, accounts and letters. Until the latter half of the twentieth century it was generally accepted that the tongue which the Serabit el-Khadim graffiti transcribed was Semitic, that the script in which these were written was essentially a development of hieratic and that this was a forerunner of later Semitic alphabets. Nowadays there is greater circumspection about each of these claims, not least since far less progress than originally hoped has been made in deciphering the full text of the graffiti.[508] Nevertheless, the original hypothesis is far from being disproved. Taken in the round, such evidence as exists (admittedly circumstantial) suggests that a language and script of Semitic origin are indeed the most likely possibilities:

The mines at Serabit el-Khadim are of ancient foundation. Pharaoh Sneferu of the Fourth Dynasty (who reigned roughly from 2613 BC to 2589 BC, the immediate predecessor of Cheops) was the first Egyptian ruler to send expeditions to Sinai in search of turquoise. The discovery of rich deposits not only of that mineral but of copper, too, led to centuries of workings, interrupted or lessened from time to time by the vagaries of Egyptian politics but continuing nonetheless for over two thousand years.[509]

The first proper temple at this location was built during the Middle Kingdom. The earliest part of the main rock-cut temple to Hathor (which is perhaps the first Egyptian temple built outside the Nile valley) dates from the Twelfth Dynasty and was most probably founded by Amenemhat III at a time when the mines were particularly active.

Though it is difficult to ascribe precise dates to the Serabit el-Khadim graffiti, these facts suggest that it is perfectly within the bounds of possibility that they date from before the exodus.

It would not be surprising to find that people from Canaan worked at Serabit el-Khadim. Amenemhat III (1842-1794 BC) and Amenemhat IV (1798-1785 BC) each sent a number of expeditions to the mines of Sinai at a time when Egypt had close links with Canaanite city-states. Asiatic (that is to say, Semitic) migration into Egypt was a recurring theme at several points in Egyptian history.

Taken together with other archaeological findings at the Serabit el-Khadim site, this has led some to conclude that Asiatics were a regular part of the workforce at these mines, where they lived and worked alongside Egyptians as paid workers rather than slaves.

Whether or not this was so, it appears that at various stages the mines were also worked by prisoners-of-war from southwest Asia,[510] a region which included Canaan and the lands that bordered it. There would seem no reason in principle to exclude the possibility of Hebrew slaves also being sent to Serabit el-Khadim from time to time.[511]

Either way, it is entirely logical that the language and script of the Serabit el-Khadim graffiti should be Semitic.

This has a bearing on the reliability of the Exodus account since it has in the past been suggested that Hebrews possessed no written script at the time of their departure from Egypt. Consequently, it is asserted that the biblical narrative cannot be contemporaneous with the events it describes. As to this:

Evidence suggests that Egyptian kings were literate from earliest times.[512] The Bible says that "Moses was educated in all the wisdom of the Egyptians" (Acts

7:22). Since he was raised as a prince, if is thus highly probable that he was taught to read and write.[513]

It is overwhelmingly likely that Moses made the effort to use a language and script which would have been readily understood by succeeding generations, since his entire purpose in writing was to create a record for their benefit.

There is no telling whether Moses might have come across the proto-Sinaitic script or known those who were familiar with it. The possibilities are legion. He may have personally visited Serabit el-Khadim, either whilst still living as a prince in Egypt – the economic importance of the mines was such that they may well have been thought to warrant royal supervision – or during his time in Midian. He might have spoken with men who had formerly worked in the mines, perhaps runaway slaves who sought refuge amongst the Sinai Bedouin or later joined the Israelites in their desert wanderings.

These are matters of speculation, but it is not difficult to conceive ways in which Moses may have come across the proto-Sinaitic script. Equally possible is that this was a form of writing already in use among the Hebrews, so that the prophet merely adopted the script which his people knew.[514]

Alternatively, Moses' familiarity with hieroglyphics and hieratic could have enabled him to craft an alphabet that was suited both to the Hebrew tongue and to the concepts that he wished to convey through it. This is less far-fetched than might at first appear: the Cyrillic alphabet built in similar fashion on the work of St Cyril and St Methodius, enabling the Bible to be rendered into Slav languages.[515]

In light of the above, there is no compelling basis to conclude that Exodus cannot be contemporary with the events it describes because Israelites of that time did not possess writing. On the contrary, there is reason to believe that Moses could write, that scripts were readily available for him to use or adapt as needed[516] and that the necessary writing materials were to hand. The command that Moses should "Write on a scroll" (Exodus 17:14) suggests that the prophet has access to papyrus[517] and ink, presumably brought with him from Egypt.

Glossary

The names of cities are given below in the commonly used Greek form, with the Egyptian variant in brackets. The reverse procedure is adopted for the names of pharaohs, dates for whose reigns are approximate only.

Abydos (*Abodu, This* or *Thinis*), seat of the principal sanctuary of Osiris (q.v.), said to contain the preserved head of that god and to be birthplace of the first pharaohs. At least once in their lives every Egyptian was supposed to make a pilgrimage to Abydos.

Akhenaten (reigned from approximately 1353-1335 BC), tenth pharaoh of the Eighteenth Dynasty, younger son of Amenhotep III (q.v.). Originally named Amenhotep IV (*Amenophis IV*), he was the so-called heretic pharaoh who ordered the construction of a new capital at Akhet-aten (q.v.), closed temples to the old gods and compelled worship of his favoured deity, Aten (q.v.).

Akhet-aten, a new capital built at the command of Akhenaten (q. v.) on virgin land beside the Nile more or less halfway between Memphis (q.v.) and Thebes (q.v.). It was largely abandoned after the death of its creator.

Aldred, Cyril, (1914-1991) English Egyptologist, art historian and author.

Amarna, Tell el, modern name for the ruins of Akhet-aten (q.v.).

Amarna Letters, diplomatic correspondence between Egypt and foreign powers preserved on clay tablets found in the Record Office (Bureau of Correspondence of Pharaoh) at Akhet-aten (q.v.).

Amarna period, the years during which Akhenaten (q.v.) ruled at Akhet-aten (q.v.).

Amenhotep II (*Amenophis II*) (reigned from approximately 1427-1401 BC), pharaoh of the Eighteenth Dynasty.

Amenhotep III (*Amenophis III*) (reigned from approximately 1388-1351 BC), pharaoh of the Eighteenth Dynasty, father of Akhenaten (q.v.).

Amenti, the underworld, where spirits of the dead were gathered, judged and prepared either for torment or paradise. The former went to a fiery pit in which the damned were hacked to pieces by demonic beings such as the Commander of Fire and the Eater of Entrails.

Amka, a city-state in northern Canaan which was an Egyptian ally in the mid-fourteenth century BC.

Ammit (aka **Ammut** or **Ahemait**), a female demon who lurked in Duat (q.v.) near the scales of justice. Part lion, part crocodile and part hippopotamus, she was Devourer of the Dead, Eater of Hearts and Great of Death. After weighing by Anubis (q.v.) hearts heavy with sin were fed to her, causing the soul of those to whom they belonged to die a second time and become restless forever.

Amun, originally a deity local to Thebes (q.v.) who became chief god of Egypt during the New Kingdom (q.v.), being "Lord of the thrones of the Two Lands" and "King of the Gods."

Amurru, a region roughly equivalent to modern Lebanon.

Anubis, jackal-headed god of the afterlife who oversaw the process of mummification and weighed the heart of the dead to determine whether they would attain everlasting bliss or be condemned to eternal wandering or destruction.

Apis bull of Memphis, a bull deity sacred to Osiris (q.v.), worshipped in Memphis (q.v.) and the surrounding region. These important cult animals were said to be the offspring of a cow struck by lightning from heaven, believed to be incarnations of the god Ptah (q.v.) and manifestations of the River Nile and Hapi, god of the yearly flood. Symbols of fertility, strength and kingship, they were one of three animal embodiments of a pharaoh (others being the falcon and the lion). The priests of Memphis identified an Apis bull by its markings: black all over, save for a distinctive white diamond on the forehead, a sun disc between the horns, the image of an eagle on the back and a scarab on the tongue. During their lives mother and calf were kept in the temple of Ptah and worshipped as deities. At their death Apis bulls were embalmed, carried on an alabaster bed to the underground galleries of the Serapeum at Saqqara and placed in a huge sarcophagus. The remains of twenty-five mummified bulls have been found there.

Aten, favoured deity of Akhenaten (q.v.), pictured as the visible disc of the sun, which represented the power of the god made manifest in the world.

Atum, a god thought to have appeared spontaneously from Nun (q.v.) and thereafter to have given birth to parts of the universe.

Avaris (*Hut-waret*), a city which, according to Manetho (q.v.), was originally an armed camp built by the Hyksos (q.v.) to overawe their Egyptian subjects. It is a possible site for the store city of Rameses (q.v.). Avaris lies just to the south (and became a district of) the subsequently constructed city of Pi-Rameses.

Ba, the impersonal life force thought to be present in all living things.

Baal, meaning, *Lord*, one of the principal Canaanite gods, also worshipped in Egypt. In later years Israelites parodied his title *Baalzebul* (Lord of Lords) by turning it into *Baalzebub* (Lord of the Flies).

Beautiful Feast of the Opet, a celebration held each year in Thebes (q.v.) to celebrate the union between pharaoh and Amun (q.v.), whose son he was considered to be.

Book of the Dead, the name now given to a series of funerary texts which gave instructions to a deceased on how to navigate the series of tests he would face after death.

Breasted, James Henry (1865-1935), American Egyptologist and founder of the Oriental Institute at the University of Chicago who coined the term "fertile crescent" and helped Howard Carter decipher seals recovered from the tomb of Tutankhamun (q.v.).

Buchis bull of Hermonthis (*Iuny*), a representation of the gods Ra (q.v.) and Osiris (q.v.), linked also with Montu (q.v.), god of war. Like Apis bulls (q.v.), they had distinctive markings: a black face with a white body. The centre of the Buchis cult was Hermonthis (Armant, *Iuny*). Mummified Buchis bulls and their mothers were buried in a designated cemetery, called the Bucheum, fastened to wooden boards with metal staples that held the forelegs and hind legs in place.

Buto (*Per-Wadjet*), city of the cobra goddess Edjo (*Wadjet*), patroness deity of Lower Egypt. The city lay some fifty miles east of Alexandria in the Nile Delta.

Byblos (*Kepen*), a port in Phoenicia (modern Lebanon) with close political and cultural ties to Egypt.

Canaan, the Promised Land whose widest boundaries are described in Exodus 23:31. Canaan (like the Greek term Phoenicia) means, *Land of Purple*, a reference to the purple dye which was one of the most distinctive products of its coastal regions. The dye was derived from shellfish of a kind then to be found in profusion in the north-east Mediterranean.

Cartouche, an oval-shaped loop used in the hieroglyphs of ancient Egypt to enclose the names of gods and royalty.

Cassius Dio (Lucius Cassius Dio Cocceianus) (approximately AD 150-235), Roman historian. His 80-volume *Historia Romana*, written in Greek, told the story of Rome from her foundation. Despite its being the fruit of 22 years' work and detailed research, only fragments now remain.

Djahy, the Egyptian designation for southern Retennu (q.v.). Djahy was the land which lay between the city of Ascalon in south-west Canaan to the borders of Lebanon in the north and as far inland as Galilee.

Duat (also called **Tuat** and **Tuaut**), the underworld, a vast area under the earth connected with *Nun* (q.v.). It was the realm of Osiris (q.v.) and also the region through which the sun god travelled east to west each night. Duat was envisioned as an idealised form of Egypt.

Dunand, Maurice, (1898-1987), French archaeologist who excavated at Byblos (q.v.) between 1924 and 1975.

Fisher, Clarence Stanley, American archaeologist (1876-1941) who excavated in Egypt, conducted the first American excavation in Palestine and co-developed the Reisner-Fisher Method which for some decades was the official procedure of digging and recording in Palestine.

Freud, Sigmund, (1856-1939) Austrian physician and founder of psychoanalysis, author of *Moses and monotheism* (first published in German in 1937).

Garstang, John, (1876-1956) British archaeologist who excavated at Hazor in 1926.

Gezer, a Canaanite city lying halfway between Jerusalem and the Mediterranean coast. Its inscribed boundary stones allow positive identification of the remains with the city mentioned in the Bible.

Goshen (***Kessan***), also called the Land of Zoan (q.v.) or Land of Rameses (q.v.), a region straddling part of the Nile delta which was settled by Jacob's sons. It became the area where Hebrew slaves were concentrated most heavily.

Harem of the South (***Ipet Resyt***), a temple of Amun at Luxor thought to occupy the primeval mound of creation, hence belonging to Amun (q.v.) in his guise as fertility god Amun-Min.

Hathor, goddess originally thought to be of Semitic origin, perhaps linked with the Mesopotamian Ishtar, Assyrian Astarte, Canaanite Ashtoreth and Greek Aphrodite, adopted in Egypt after the end of the Old Kingdom. Though primarily a fertility goddess, she was also nursemaid and wife of Horus and the "Lady of the Turquoise", patron goddess of miners and wayfarers, often depicted as a cow.

Hatshepsut, (reigned from approximately 1479 BC to 1458 BC), daughter of Thutmose I and wife of her half-brother Thutmose II. She ruled in her own right on her husband's death, sponsoring wide-ranging trade missions and extensive building projects. Though usually judged by posterity to have been a successful ruler, her successor Thutmose III made strenuous efforts to expunge her memory, with monuments and inscriptions being defaced so as to remove all reference to her.

Heliopolis (meaning, *City of the Sun*, in Greek; in Egyptian **Awanu** or **Iunu**, meaning, *Place of Pillars*), principal seat of sun worship to Ra-Atum (Atum-Ra), a composite of the gods Atum (q.v.) and Ra (q.v.). Here Akhenaten (q.v.) built a temple called *Wetjes Aten* (meaning, *Elevating Aten*).

Hermopolis (***Khemnu***, meaning, *Eight-town*, a name derived from the eight primeval gods present in the waters of Chaos). Nowadays known as Ashmunein, it was later a centre of worship for the moon god Thoth.

Hierakonpolis (***Nekhen***), home of the vulture goddess Nekhebet (*She of Nekheb*), who came to be regarded as the presiding genius of the whole of Upper Egypt. She is frequently associated with her counterpart, the cobra goddess Edjo of Buto (q.v.) and Lower Egypt.

Hieroglyph, one of the pictorial characters on which the writing system of ancient Egypt was based.

Hittites or **Hatti**, people of Asia Minor who controlled a powerful empire between the fifteenth and thirteenth centuries BC. They increasingly vied with Egypt for control in Syria and Canaan. The most famous battle between the two powers took place at Kadesh (q. v.) in the reign of Ramses II (q.v.).

Horus, son of Osiris (q.v.) and Isis (q.v.), opponent of the evil god Seth (q.v.), who was his uncle.

Hyksos (***Hikau khasut***), invaders and subsequently rulers of Egypt during the so-called Second Intermediate Period (q.v.), credited with introducing the wheel and the chariot to the Nile valley. Paintings on the walls of cemeteries at Beni Hasan in Middle Egypt show a group of *Hikau khasut* (clad in coats of many colours like those described in Genesis 37:3) being received on behalf of Twelfth Dynasty pharaoh Sesotris II by Khnumhotep, Governor of the Eastern Desert – an event likely to have taken place about 1890 BC, perhaps a hundred years before the time of Joseph.

Isis, sister and wife of Osiris (q.v.), mother of Horus (q.v.). She was considered greatest of goddesses, venerated as an ideal wife and mother.

Jericho, a city lying on the western bank of the River Jordan. One of the earliest known sites of continuous settlement, it is thought to have been inhabited from as early as 9000 BC. It was the first Canaanite city west of the Jordan captured by the Israelites under Joshua.

Josephus, T. Flavius, (born **Joseph ben Matthias**) (AD 37-100) Jewish leader and historian, author of *Against Apion*, *The Jewish War* and *Antiquities of the Jews*. He reluctantly took part in a Jewish revolt against Roman rule in AD 70 but later found favour with Emperor Vespasian and settled in Rome.

Ka, a spirit double thought to be created at birth which resembled its owner physically.

Kadesh (modern **Tell Nebi Mend**), a strategically located city on the Orontes River in Syria, site of a major battle between the Hittites and the Egyptians under Ramses II, traditionally dated to 1274 BC.

Karnak (*Ipet-esut*), village standing on part of the site occupied by ancient Thebes (q.v.).

Kiya, a secondary queen of Akhenaten, possibly of foreign birth.

Kochba, Simon bar (died AD 135), leader of a Jewish revolt against Rome in AD 132. For three years he ruled an independent state until twelve Roman legions completed a bloody reconquest.

Kyle, Melvin Grove (1858-1933), American archaeologist who excavated at the supposed site of Pithom in 1908.

Lepsius, Karl Richard (1810-1884), German archaeologist, considered the father of Egyptology.

Luxor (*Weset*), village standing on part of the site occupied by ancient Thebes (q.v.).

Ma'at, goddess of harmony, justice and truth but also the ancient Egyptian concept of truth, order, balance, morality, law and justice. This came to encompass all aspects of existence, including the basic equilibrium of the universe, the relationship between its constituent parts, the cycle of the seasons, heavenly movements, religious observations and fair dealings, honesty and truthfulness in social interactions. The preservation of *Ma'at* was amongst the most important duties of a pharaoh.

Macalister, Robert Alexander Stewart (1870-1950), Irish archaeologist who excavated at Gezer from 1902-1909.

Manetho, priest of Sebennytos (modern Samannud), third century BC Egyptian historian and author of the *Aegyptiaca*.

Megiddo, city-state of northern Canaan, strategically sited to control trade routes from Egypt to the north. It is of ancient foundation, excavations having unearthed twenty-six layers of ruins.

Memphis (*Menufer*), one-time capital of Egypt founded by Menes in about 3100 BC. Material from its ruins was used in building modern Cairo.

Meritaten (aka Merytaten or Meryetaten), eldest daughter of Akhenaten (q.v.) by Nefertiti (q.v.), she is frequently depicted in Amarna art and mentioned in diplomatic correspondence.

Middle Kingdom, period from approximately 2040 BC to 1640 BC, encompassing the Eleventh, Twelfth and Thirteenth Dynasties.

Mitanni, a Hurrian-speaking state in northern Syria and south-eastern Anatolia which existed from roughly 1500 to 1300 BC. Though initially rivals of the pharaohs, the Mitanni subsequently allied with Egypt in an attempt to contain rising Hittite power.

Mnevis (*Mer-wer*) bull of Heliopolis, an aspect of the god Atum-Ra of Heliopolis (q.v.), this creature was considered a divine herald and earthly intermediary of the sun god Ra (q.v.). A bull having the required markings was taken to a designated temple, where it was worshipped and its movements treated as an oracle. In the fifth year of his reign Akhenaten (q.v.) ordered the Mnevis bull to be buried in the hills to the east of Akhet-aten (q.v.).

Montu, god of Thebes (q.v.). Originally regarded as an aspect of the sun, he later became known as a war god but was also seen as guardian of a happy family life. He was one of those who protected Ra (q.v.) during his nightly journey through the underworld, where Montu battled Apep, the serpent of chaos.

Naville, Edouard, Swiss archaeologist (1844-1926) who excavated at Tell el Mashkuta (a possible site of ancient Pithom) in 1883.

Nefertiti, chief wife and queen of Akhenaten (q.v.). She bore the title Great Royal Wife and after her husband's death is believed by some to have reigned briefly as Neferneferuaten immediately before the accession of Tutankhamun.

New Kingdom, period from approximately 1550 BC to 1070 BC, encompassing the Eighteenth, Nineteenth and Twentieth Dynasties.

Nome (*sepat*), an administrative division of ancient Egypt, dating from pre-dynastic times (prior to 3,100 BC or thereabouts) but remaining in place throughout the Old, Middle and New Kingdoms. Lower Egypt was divided into twenty nomes, Upper Egypt into twenty-two.

Nubia, region of the Upper Nile south of Aswan, lying largely within modern Sudan. The name most probably derives from the ancient Egyptian *nub*, meaning, *gold*. It was a source both of that precious metal and of hard stone, especially granite. Its inhabitants were often the cause of trouble on the southern border of Egypt.

Nun, the waters of the primordial abyss thought to have existed before creation of the world.

Opet festival (the Beautiful Feast of Opet), celebrated each year in Thebes (q.v.) from the time of the New Kingdom (q.v.) onwards, it symbolised rebirth.

Statues of the Theban Triad (q.v.) processed ceremonially from the temple of Amun (q.v.) in Karnak (q.v.) and the pharaoh was crowned anew.

Osiris, ruler of the underworld, brother and husband of Isis (q.v.), father of Horus (q.v.).

Pharaoh, title of Egyptian kings from the New Kingdom onwards. It derives from *per-aa*, meaning, *great house*, and was originally used to refer to the royal palace.

Philo of Byblos (Herennius Philon) (approximately AD 64-141), a Hellenised Jew, author of various grammatical and historical works, of which only fragments or quotations in other sources survive.

Pithom, one of the "store cities" built for Pharaoh by Israelite slaves. Its identification is uncertain: though commonly thought to be the modern Tell al-Maskhuta, it may perhaps have been Heliopolis (On), sometimes referred to be the Egyptians as Pi-Atum (the estate of the god Atum).

Ptah, creator god of Memphis (q.v.), husband of Sekhmet and father of Nefertem.

Ra, god of the sun with a major cult centre at Heliopolis (q.v.), believed to rule in all parts of the created world – earth, sky and underworld. In dynastic times Ra was merged first with Horus (q.v.) as Ra-Harakty and then with Amun (q.v.) as Amun-Ra. His worship was suppressed under Akhenaten (q.v.) but revived after that pharaoh's death.

Rameses, the second of the "store cities" built by Israelite slaves during the Oppression described in Exodus 1. Its identity is uncertain, but Avaris (q. v.) is a likely candidate.

Ramses I, (reigned approximately from 1292-1290 BC) the founder of the Nineteenth Dynasty, formerly a general under Horemheb.

Ramses II (reigned approximately from 1290-1224 BC), powerful pharaoh of the Nineteenth Dynasty.

Rhind, Alexander Henry, Scottish archaeologist (1833-63), author of *Thebes, its Tombs and their Tenants*. Amongst other materials he acquired the Rhind Papyrus, a mathematical treatise which shows that the ancient Egyptians computed the value of pi as 3.1605, a margin of error of less than one percent.

Scarab (dung beetle or *Scarabaeus sacer*), believed to be a manifestation of the sun god and thus used as amulets, as well as for ritual or administrative purposes. A large number of commemorative scarabs were produced in the early years of the reign of Amenhotep III (q.v.).

Second Intermediate Period, term used to designate the period between the Middle Kingdom and the New Kingdom. It roughly spans the years 1640-1550 BC and comprises three dynasties: the Fourteenth (of which almost nothing is known), the Fifteenth (the so-called Hyksos kings) and the Sixteenth (under whom Egyptian rule was restored).

Sed festival, a jubilee celebrated by a king who had been thirty years on the throne, involving ritual renewal of the monarch.

Semna Despatches, Egyptian military bulletins commonly dated to the reign of Amenemhet III (reigned approximately 1842-1797 BC), dealing with surveillance of the habitually troublesome southern border with Nubia (q.v.). They report routine patrols and checks on population movements rather than large-scale campaigns.

Seth, god associated with evil, the brother and murderer of Osiris (q.v.). Seth was eventually slain in battle by Horus (q.v.), the son of Osiris and Isis (q.v.).

Siculus, Diodorus, Greek historian who wrote between approximately 60 BC and 30 BC. His 40-book historical work, *Bibliotheca Historica*, identifies several ancient authors on whom he drew but whose work is now lost. The *Bibliotheca Historica* itself does not survive in full.

Solon, (639-559 BC), Athenian lawgiver, counted as one of the Seven Sages. Made first archon (chief magistrate) of Athens at a time of acute economic distress, he wrote a new constitution and legal code for the city.

Stele, an inscribed stone marker or memorial, either free-standing or cut into walls and cliffs, used as memorials to the dead, to commemorate events and to record decrees.

Strabo, (63 BC - AD 20), Greek geographer and historian. His *Geographica* is well regarded, but of his *History*, covering the period from 146 BC to the death of Julius Caesar, only fragments survive.

Tacitus, Cornelius, (AD 55-120), Roman historian whose *Annals* and *Histories* (his major works) exist only in fragmentary form.

Talatat, standardised stone blocks used during the reign of Akhenaten (q.v.) for building temples to Aten (q.v.) at Thebes (q.v.) and Akhet-aten (q.v.). They measured roughly 11 inches x 11 inches x 22 inches but do not seem to have been an unqualified success since their use was abandoned at the end of the Amarna period (q.v.).

Tanis (*Djanet*), a city in the north-eastern Nile delta which became the northern capital of Egypt in the Twenty-First Dynasty, considered by some to be the place where Moses was found among the bulrushes by Pharaoh's daughter. Earlier identifications of Tanis with the "store city" of Rameses (q. v.) are no longer generally accepted, however.

Theban Triad, the three principal gods of Thebes (q.v.), comprising Amun (q.v.), his consort Mut and their son Khonsu.

Thebes (***Weset***), former capital of Egypt, on the site of which now stand the villages of Luxor (q.v.) and Karnak (q.v.). Thebes is a Greek corruption of the Egyptian *ta'ipe*, meaning, *The Sanctuary*.

Thutmose IV (**Thutmosis IV**) (reigned from approximately 1401-1391 BC), pharaoh of the Eighteenth Dynasty, younger son and successor to Amenhotep II (q.v.). He commissioned the so-called Dream Stele, which recounts a dream in which the Sphinx promised the future pharaoh the succession if he would restore its statue at Giza, then almost entirely submerged under drifting sand.

Tutankhamen originally named Tutankhaten, short-lived successor to Akhenaten (q.v.) and one of the last pharaohs of the Eighteenth Dynasty. His precise familial relationship to Akhenaten is a matter of debate, though possibly he was his son.

Ur of the Chaldeans, original home of Abraham and one of the earliest cities, lying close to the mouth of the Euphrates at the western end of the Persian Gulf. In 1923, just four miles west of Ur at 'Obeid, archaeologist C. L. Wooley (q.v.) found the so-called Foundation Tablet of Annipadda, remarkable not just because of its age but since it is the first document known to us which records events contemporary with its creation.

Uraeus, symbol of royalty and deity, a diadem in the shape of a rearing cobra's head which was thought to protect the king by spitting fire at any who sought to harm him.

Valley of the Kings, the royal necropolis on the west bank of the Nile at Thebes (q.v.) in which lie buried numerous pharaohs, in particular, those of the New Kingdom (q.v.).

Wooley, Charles Leonard (**1880-1960**), British archaeologist and expert in Mesopotamian studies best known for the important finds he made whilst excavating royal tombs in Ur (q.v.).

Zoan (***Djanet***), the name used in the Bible for a city in the north-western Nile Delta which became Egypt's capital during the Twenty-Fifth Dynasty. It may possibly be the same place as Tanis (q.v.), though the identification is uncertain.

Bibliography

Aldred, Cyril, *Akhenaten, King of Egypt*, Thames and Hudson 1996.

Aldred, Cyril, *The Egyptians*, Thames and Hudson 1987.

Behe, Michael J, *Darwin's Black Box: the biochemical challenge to evolution*, The Free Press 2006.

Blanchard, John, *Does God believe in Atheists?*, Evangelical Press 2000.

Bowker, John, *The Complete Bible Handbook*, Dorling Kindersley 1998.

Carpiceci, Alberto Carlo, *Art and History of Egypt*, Casa Editrice Bonechi 1994.

Cole, R. Alan, *Tyndale Old Testament Commentaries, volume 2: Exodus*, Inter-Varsity Press 2008.

Fields, Nic, *Soldier of the Pharaoh*, Osprey 2007.

Gonen, Rivka, *Urban Canaan in the Late Bronze Period*, BASOR 253 (Winter 1984), 61-73.

Halley, Henry H., *Halley's Bible handbook*, Zondervan 1965.

Harper, Michael, *Jesus the Healer*, Highland Books 1992.

Hart, George, *Egyptian Myths*, British Museum Press 1993.

Hobson, Christine, *Exploring the world of the Pharaohs*, Thames and Hudson 1991.

John, J, *Ten: living the Ten Commandments in the twenty-first century*, Kingsway Publications 2003.

Kozloff, Arielle P, *Amenhotep III: Egypt's radiant pharaoh*, Cambridge University Press 2012.

Lancaster, Brian, *The Elements of Judaism*, Element Books Limited 1993.

Montserrat, Dominic, *Akhenaten: history, fantasy and ancient Egypt*, Routledge 2003.

Naaman, Nadav, *Four Notes on the Size of Late Bronze Canaan*, BASOR 313 (Feb 1999), 31-37.

Ramsay, Christopher Bronk et al, *Radiocarbon-based Chronology for Dynastic Egypt*, Science, 18 June 2010.

Rohl, David, *Pharaohs and Kings: a biblical quest*, Crown Publications 1997.

Romer, John, *A History of Ancient Egypt from the first farmers to the Great Pyramid*, Allen Lane 2012.

Shaw, Ian, *The Oxford History of Ancient Egypt*, Oxford University Press 2003.

Shiloh, Yigal, *The Population of Iron Age Palestine in the Light of a Sample Analysis of Urban Plans, Areas, and Population Density*, BASOR 239 (Summer, 1980), 25-35.

Schroeder, Dr Gerald L., *Genesis and the Big Bang*, Bantam Doubleday Dell 1996.

Spalinger, Anthony J, *War in Ancient Egypt*, Blackwell Publishing 2005.

Vercoutter, Jean, *The search for ancient Egypt*, Thames and Hudson 1995.

Webber, Robert E., *Worship Old and New*, Zondervan 1994.

Wenham, Gordon J., *Exploring the Old Testament (Volume 1): the Pentateuch*, SPCK 2003.

Wilkinson, Bruce H. (executive editor), *Your Daily Walk*, Zondervan 1991.

Notes

1 The Egyptian state is usually thought to have been formed around 3100 BC. The first documented dynasty in China was the Shang, which dates from about 1523 BC. The name Egypt derives via Greek from *Hewet-ka-Ptah* (meaning *Mansion of the Spirit of Ptah*), Ptah being one of the principal gods of Memphis.

2 The title Pharaoh comes from the phrase *per-aa*, meaning "great house." It was originally used to refer to the royal palace rather than to the king, to whom it was not applied until the time of the New Kingdom.

3 Unsurprisingly, for the Sinai Peninsula covers 22,671 square miles and a tent-dwelling people would scarce be expected to leave readily discernible imprints. The Sinai region was by no means unknown to Egypt. From earliest times it had been the location both of extensive workings for copper and of turquoise mines at Wadi Maghara and Serabit el-Khadim in the south-west. Regular donkey caravans took supplies to the labourers and brought back the results of their excavations, with port facilities nearby and Egyptian garrisons posted at various border crossings. In the sixteenth century BC Egyptians built the Way of Shur, a highway across northern Sinai to Beersheba, whilst the *Via Maris* (also known as the Way of Horus) hugged the Mediterranean coast through Canaan and onwards to Mesopotamia. Trade routes crossed the upper part of the peninsula from Arabia. The desert of Shur (meaning an enclosure or wall) formed a natural barrier on the north-eastern border of Egypt, which the Israelites had to cross on their way to Horeb (see Exodus 15:22).

4 It was found by Italian archaeologists excavating the classical theatre at Caesarea. Until this discovery there was no contemporary evidence outside the Bible for the existence of Pilate, although Tacitus, Josephus and Philo all wrote about him. Coins dating from Pilate's time as governor of Judea have also since come to light.

5 The ancient Egyptians referred to the country they inhabited as *Ta-Mery* (meaning *The Beautiful Land*). An alternative description was *Kemet* or *Black Land*, contrasting the dark, fertile soil of the Nile flood plain with *Deshret*, the *Red Land* of the desert. Upper and Lower Egypt were respectively Ta-Sheme'aw (*Sedgeland*, because of the prevalence of papyrus, a type of sedge) and Ta-Mehew (*Northland*). Together these comprised the territory unified by King Narmer of Upper Egypt in around 3120 BC to create the realm its people called The Two Lands. From that time onwards those who ruled over the unified nation wore what the Greeks called the *Pschent* and the Egyptians the *Sekhemti* (meaning, *the Two Powerful Ones*), a double crown incorporating both the red diadem of Lower Egypt and the white of Upper Egypt.

6 Although Rome had de facto control of Egypt after the victory of Octavian (the future Augustus Caesar) at the battle of Actium in 31 BC, the Thirty-second Dynasty did not end until the death of Cleopatra VII in AD 395. Thereafter Egypt was under the heel of Rome or her successor Byzantium until the Arab conquest in AD 641.

7 The Great Pyramid was the world's tallest building from completion in 2580 BC until AD 1548, when the central tower of Lincoln cathedral overtook it. It covers about thirteen acres, measuring 768 feet square, and is estimated to have contained 2,300,000

stones of an average thickness of three feet each and an average weight of two and a half tons. Some 40,000 paid workers (not slaves) are thought to have been engaged in quarrying the required 5.5 million tons of rock. Over their entire length the four baselines of this structure deviate only seven inches from true.

[8] The new city, Akhet-aten (meaning *Horizon of Aten*), was built at a place now called Tell el Amarna. The time during which it was the capital is thus known as the Amarna period.

[9] The word translated as criminal (*kheru*) was habitually used to describe the defeated rulers of foreign enemies. To use it of the pharaoh implied that he was a traitor and not a proper king of Egypt.

[10] Akhenaten was not the only ruler to be treated thus, for inscriptions of former rulers were often defaced or removed by a successor. This happened, for example, in the case of Queen Hatshepsut (who ruled from approximately 1479 BC to 1458 BC) when she was succeeded by Thutmose III, the great-great grandfather of Akhenaten. One might reasonably suppose a similar fate to have befallen such references to Moses as appeared in Egyptian records and on their monuments.

[11] Akhenaten (meaning *Effective spirit of Aten*) originally bore the Son of Ra name Amunhotep (meaning *Amun is content* or *Amun is satisfied*).

[12] The phrase "finger of God" appears in the Bible on only three other occasions. The stone tablets containing the Ten Commandments are said to have been "inscribed by the finger of God" (Exodus 31:18 and Deuteronomy 9:10). Jesus said, "But if I drive out demons by the finger of God, then the kingdom of God has come to you." (Luke 11:20).

[13] He is in good company. Both King David and the apostle Paul were murderers by virtue of being complicit in the deaths of others. David deliberately had Uriah the Hittite placed in the front rank of battle so that he would be killed and David could continue his affair with Uriah's wife, Bathsheba (2 Samuel 11:15). Paul held the cloaks of those who stoned Stephen, the first Christian martyr, and looked with approval on what they did (Acts 7:58 and 8:1).

[14] Moses is thought to have been appointed to high office in the government of Egypt. Jewish historian T. Flavius Josephus says that the future prophet led an Egyptian army in the south. If so, this experience of administration and of commanding large bodies of men would have been invaluable later.

[15] God told Aaron and Miriam: "When there are prophets among you, I reveal myself to them in visions and speak to them in dreams. It is different when I speak with my servant Moses; I have put him in charge of all my people Israel. So I speak to him face-to-face, clearly and not in riddles; he has even seen my form!" (Numbers 12:6-8, GNT). Even leaving aside the major encounters on Horeb, there are many examples of this, including Exodus 6:1-8, 10-11 and 28, 7:1-5 and 8, 9:22, 11:1, 25:2.

[16] Not only does God "knit [us] together in [our] mother's womb" (Psalm 139:13) but "Before [He] formed [us] in the womb [He] knew [us]." (Jeremiah 1:5, NKJV). The perfection of God's arrangements is shown amongst other things in the fact of Moses'

brother escaping Egypt at just the right moment: "Meanwhile the LORD had said to Aaron, 'Go into the desert to meet Moses.' So he went to meet him at the holy mountain; and when he met him, he kissed him. Then Moses told Aaron everything that the LORD had said when he told him to return to Egypt; he also told him about the miracles which the LORD had ordered him to perform." (Exodus 4:27-28, GNT).

17 Shiphrah means 'fair' or 'beautiful'. Puah is variously rendered 'splendid' or 'lass, little girl'. These two "feared God and didn't obey the king – they let the boys live" (Exodus 1:17, TLB). In this they behaved as did the apostles of later centuries, who affirmed: "We must obey God rather than men!" (Acts 5:29). The two midwives remained resolute under questioning so that when Pharaoh demanded, "Why have you disobeyed my command and let the baby boys live?" (Exodus 1:18, TLB), they had a ready answer (see Exodus 1:19). They illustrate courage of the kind that the Bible commends: neither rashness, foolhardiness, lack of instinct for self-preservation nor absence of any degree of apprehension but the ability to subordinate all to the will of the Almighty and his calling on our lives. It might have been in the former sense that "Moses was afraid" (Exodus 2:14) but the latter in which "By faith he left Egypt, not fearing the king's anger; he persevered because he saw him who is invisible." (Hebrews 11:27).

18 It seems that Moses was conscious not just of the fact that the Hebrews were "his own people" (Exodus 2:11) but also of owing allegiance to the God of Israel. The Bible does not say exactly how long he remained under his mother's tutelage, nor to what degree she may have retained contact with him in later life, merely that "When the child grew older, she took him to Pharaoh's daughter and he became her son" (Exodus 2:10), perhaps through formal legal adoption.

19 As Jesus observed when speaking of John the Baptist, we should not look for prophets in luxurious surroundings: "When you went out to John in the desert, what did you expect to see? A blade of grass bending in the wind? What did you go out to see? A man dressed up in fancy clothes? People who dress like that live in palaces! Tell me, what did you go out to see? A prophet? Yes indeed, but you saw much more than a prophet." (Matthew 11:7-9, GNT).

20 Reuel means "friend of God". In Exodus 3:1 and throughout the remainder of the book he is called Jethro, this probably being a title meaning "His Excellency". The circumstances which led Moses "to stay with the man, who gave his daughter Zipporah to Moses in marriage" (Exodus 2:21) not only once again show Moses' keen sense of justice but also foreshadow the role that God had in mind for him. As befitting the future lawgiver, deliverer and shepherd of Israel, "Moses got up and came to [the] rescue [of Jethro's seven daughters] and watered their flocks" (Exodus 2:17) when "shepherds came along and drove [the women] away" (Exodus 2:17). In the same way that Moses was drawn out of the Nile in Exodus 2:5-6, he later was responsible for drawing out – first water from the well of Midian (Exodus 2:19) and in due course Israel from Egypt. The encounter by a well leading to betrothal which is described in Exodus 2:15-21 echoes events in the lives of Isaac and Rebekah (Genesis 24) and Jacob and Rachel (Genesis 29). For the symbolic significance of wells, see chapter 10.

21 Moses also sought help from his Midianite brother-in-law Hobab: "Please do not leave us. You know where we should camp in the desert, and you can be our eyes." (Numbers 10:31). The Midianites were kin to Israel, being descended from Abraham by his wife Keturah (see Genesis 25:1-2).

22 Scripture records that "when [Moses] was forty years old, it came into his heart to visit his brethren, the children of Israel. And seeing one of them suffer wrong, he defended and avenged him who was oppressed, and struck down the Egyptian." (Acts 7:23-24, NKJV). It was only "when [a further] forty years had passed" (Acts 7:30, NKJV) that God spoke on Mount Horeb. Like King David hundreds of years later, Moses was called from tending flocks to become shepherd of Israel (see 2 Samuel 7:8).

23 Moses failed in his first attempt to help his fellow Israelites because he sought to act in his own strength, independently of God. Worse, it seems that his motives included a spirit of vengeance: "[he] avenged [the Israelite who had been ill-treated by an Egyptian] by killing the Egyptian." (Acts 7:23-24). The prophet later recognised that this was wrong, for the Lord says that "it is [his] to avenge, [he] will repay." (Deuteronomy 32:25, quoted in Romans 12:19). The Law of Moses specifically addresses unbridled vengeance. Its widely misunderstood injunction to take "life for life, eye for eye, tooth for tooth, hand for hand, foot for foot, burn for burn, wound for wound, bruise for bruise" (Exodus 21:24; see also Leviticus 24:20) was designed to ensure that the punishment fitted the crime and was not excessive, preventing disproportionate retribution of the kind described in Genesis 34. Jesus' application of the principles which underlie the injunction is described in Matthew 5:38-42. Proportionality in penalties both civil and criminal can be seen in Exodus 21:18-22 and 33-36.

24 Though his knowledge apparently was sketchy enough that when he went to Jethro to seek permission to leave for Egypt he asked, "Let me go back to my own people in Egypt to see if any of them are still alive." (Exodus 4:18). Doubtless the people he had in mind when asking this question were his immediate blood relations.

25 Various meanings are suggested for Horeb, from *dried-up ground*, *desert* or *desolation* to *glowing* or *heat*. It is related to Hebrew words for *bush* and *sword*. Though commonly identified with Mount Sinai, nowadays called Jebel Musa (meaning *The Mountain of Moses* in Arabic), its location is in fact uncertain. See Appendix 5 for further detail.

26 Akhenaten was not the first to give prominence to Aten. His father Amenhotep III had a barge called "Aten dazzles" and one of his favourite epithets was "the dazzling sun-disc" (*aten tjehen*). Aten was first mentioned as a divinity as early as the Twelfth Dynasty, which lasted from approximately 1938 BC to 1759 BC.

27 Jesus encouraged reflection on the spiritual lessons to be had from the natural world when he said, "Consider the ravens" (Luke 12:24) and "Consider how the lilies grow." (Luke 12:27).

28 The Lord's voice is not restricted to what is audible to the ears. He speaks in a variety of other ways, one of which is through Creation. This is why the apostle Paul says that "since the creation of the world God's invisible qualities – his eternal power and divine

nature – have been clearly seen, being understood from what has been made, so that men are without excuse." (Romans 1:20). On his triumphal entry into Jerusalem, Jesus observed that "if they [his disciples] keep quiet, the stones will cry out." (Luke 19:40). Nevertheless, if we were reliant on Creation alone for our understanding of the Almighty, our concept of him would be sorely lacking. We need his own revelation of himself, which was provided most completely in the life, death and resurrection of Jesus Christ.

29 Like Moses, Elijah had a revelation of God on Horeb (see 1 Kings 19:12-18). When Jesus was transfigured, these same two prophets (who had seen him in symbols centuries earlier) appeared alongside him (see Matthew 17:1-8 and Mark 9:1-8).

30 At various points the Bible also shows people discovering something about God which they had not known before and marking this by giving him a new title. Examples include Abraham's recognition of God as provider (traditionally rendered as *Jehovah jireh*) in Genesis 22:8.

31 It may nevertheless be that something of the name Yahweh (or Jehovah) was known in Israel before this time, albeit perhaps not in the degree which God revealed to Moses on Horeb. Yochebed, the woman who "bore … Aaron and Moses" (Exodus 6:20, GNT), seems to mean "the LORD [Yahweh] is glory." (Though Exodus 6:20 can be read to mean that Amram was Moses' father and Yochebed his mother, the context of the genealogy in Exodus 6:14-19 makes it more likely that the latter "bore" Moses in the sense of being a female forebear. Exodus 2:1-2 does not name Moses' parents, saying only that "a man of the house of Levi married a Levite woman and she became pregnant and gave birth to a son.")

32 For further discussion of the significance of the divine name, see chapter 3.

33 The question was not merely academic since it essentially reflected what had happened the last time Moses had tried to help his people. In demanding, "Who made you ruler and judge over us?" (Exodus 2:14) the Israelite who had been hitting his fellow denied that Moses had God's authority. It was equally reasonable to say, "If I go to the people of Israel and tell them that their fathers' God has sent me, they will ask, 'Which God are you talking about?' What shall I tell them?" (Exodus 3:13, TLB).

34 To be fair to Moses, it may be that his becoming "powerful in speech and action" (Acts 7:22) lay in the future and that at this point in his life he was indeed as he described. It is also conceivable that he spoke Egyptian more fluently than Hebrew since presumably he would have had limited contact with his compatriots from the moment that his mother "took him to Pharaoh's daughter and he became her son." (Exodus 2:10). The language of Exodus lends support to this supposition, for many of the terms it uses seem to be borrowed from Egyptian: words such as basket, bulrushes, pitch, reeds and river.

35 The Lord did not commend Moses for humility when the prophet protested his inadequacy for the task to which he was called, despite the signs and wonders that the Lord had performed in front of him. This was not self-abasement, for being humble does not mean denying our strengths but being honest about our weaknesses. Moses' response was in fact the product of self-centredness and a form of pride, portraying his

shortcomings as more important than the sufficiency of God. In truth, human competence (or lack of it) is seldom the issue where service of the Almighty is concerned since he chooses us by reason of our availability, not our abilities, which in any case are given by God. The Lord's answer to Moses' question, "Who am I, that I should go to Pharaoh and bring the Israelites out of Egypt?" (Exodus 3:11) was simply, "I will be with you." (Exodus 3:12), though he also dealt with the practicalities: "[Aaron] can speak well. He is already on his way to meet you and his heart will be glad when he sees you. You shall speak to him and put words in his mouth. I will help both of you speak and will teach you what to do. He will speak to the people for you, and it will be as if he were your mouth and as if you were God to him." (Exodus 4:14-16).

[36] Quite apart from any religious connotations, for Akhenaten to reject the name given to him by his father would have been a highly charged act in a patriarchal society. The title he chose was entirely novel, there being no other bearer of it before or since. (Amunhotep had been used by three preceding monarchs, though after Akhenaten it was never again to be the name of a pharaoh.)

[37] The New Kingdom began around 1550 BC, more than sixteen decades before Akhenaten ruled.

[38] To choose a name for another denoted the taking of dominion, just as Adam had done by the act of naming the birds and the beasts: "He [God] brought them to the man to see what he would name them; and whatever the man called each living creature, that was its name." (Genesis 2:19).

[39] The name can alternatively be rendered as *"Beneficent one of (or for) Aten"*.

[40] The lament of the priests is audible in the litany of ills and misfortunes that were laid at Akhenaten's door after his death. Although the so-called Restoration Stele raised in the Hypostyle Hall of the temple at Karnak by Tutankhamun in the early years of his reign avoids mentioning Akhenaten by name, it is unsparing in criticising that ruler's neglect of the traditional gods and attributing to this the disasters that had lately come upon Egypt: "Now when His Majesty was crowned king the temples and the estates of the gods and goddesses from Elephantine as far as the swamps of Lower Egypt had fallen into ruin. Their shrines had fallen down, turned into piles of rubble and overgrown with weeds. Their sanctuaries were as if they had never existed at all. The world was in chaos and the gods had turned their backs on this land. If an army was sent to Djahy [roughly the area from Egypt's north-eastern border as far as Lebanon] to extend the frontiers of Egypt, it met with no success; if one prayed to a god to ask something from him, he did not come at all and if one spoke to a goddess likewise she did not attend. Hearts were faint in bodies because everything that had been was destroyed."

[41] Such decisions confront each human being in every time and place. They go back to the earliest days of mankind. Hence Cain, in danger of being tripped up by unrighteous anger, feelings of rejection and a (totally unjustified) sense of having been treated unfairly was warned by God that "[sin] wants to rule you, but you must overcome it." (Genesis 4:6-7, GNT). Cain then had a choice: to give in to his feelings or to do "the right thing" (Genesis 4:7, GNT) by using his God-given capacities to overcome his baser instincts.

The issue is one of wilfulness or willingness: to be wilful by following the devices and desires of our own hearts, no matter what, or to be willing by doing things God's way, following him wholeheartedly and holding nothing back.

42 The timeless nature of the contest is apparent in its echoes of the serpent's temptation of Adam and Eve in the Garden of Eden (Genesis 3). Then as now, men confronted the lures and entanglements of hedonism, materialism and rejection of God. Moses faced the same challenges (see chapter 11). Intriguingly, there was an overt link between Amun and snakes: a statue of the god would regularly be brought to the sanctuary at present-day Medinet Habu (Thebes) with the sole purpose of meeting his supposed ancestor, a primeval form of himself imagined as the snake Kem-atef (meaning, *The one who has completed his moment*), this being the form in which Amun was said to have been manifest at the creation of the world.

43 Surviving texts show that the ancient Egyptians were skilled doctors and excellent mathematicians, being familiar with the main principles of trigonometry, some types of fractions, and the calculation of surfaces and volumes. They understood the basics of hydraulics, invented a water clock, and their astronomical studies led them to devise a 365-day calendar. They knew how to levy and deploy a large labour force, using surveyors to work out the men and materials needed for vast construction projects which included amongst other things levelling ground, excavating canals, building dykes, dams and bridges, and putting in place mechanisms to lift and regulate the flow of water. For this to have been possible almost three thousand years before Christ whilst many other peoples were still living in rudimentary conditions was extraordinary.

44 *Pace* Californian labour leader Denis Kearney, from a speech given at San Francisco in 1878.

45 Upper and Lower Egypt were symbolised respectively by a lily and a papyrus flower, each betokening life and growth. However, they also had symbols with connotations of death and destruction: Wadjet, the rearing cobra with inflated hood (associated with the goddess Edjo) for the latter and Nekhbet, the vulture goddess, for the former. These were guardians of the pharaohs and associated with royal and divine births. A poison-spitting serpent and a fearsome carrion bird were apt representations of the occult powers that ancient Egypt worshipped. Pharaohs likewise bore symbols of both benevolence and malevolence: a shepherd's crook to betoken care for their subjects and a flail to show that as well as being protectors of their people they were also scourge of their enemies.

46 The names of the magicians were evidently preserved in Jewish tradition. St Paul referred to these sorcerers to warn of those who stand against the will of God: "Just as Jannes and Jambres opposed Moses, so also these teachers oppose the truth. They are men of depraved minds, who, as far as the faith is concerned, are rejected. But they will not get very far because, as in the case of those men, their folly will be clear to everyone." (2 Timothy 3:8-9, GNT). Jambres means "He who opposes".

⁴⁷ Jesus remarked that it would not be possible to drive out demons using power which was in itself demonic. "If Satan drives out Satan, he is divided against himself. How then can his kingdom stand?" (Matthew 12:26).

⁴⁸ One of the temples at Karnak has a stone over its entrance which is forty feet long and weighs 150 tons. Its Hypostyle Hall contains 134 columns, the twelve central ones each being 78 ft high and 11.5 ft in diameter. It has been claimed that one hundred men could stand on the top of one of these columns.

⁴⁹Eve struck the right note when she said, "By the LORD's help I have gotten a son" (Genesis 4:1, GNT), thereby recognising that she and her husband were only agents in the creation of new life and it was God who brought that life into being. The issue is one of acknowledging God for who he is and giving him credit for what he does, rather than seeking glory for ourselves or others, or ascribing God's activity to impersonal forces of nature.

⁵⁰ The artistic, engineering and philosophical achievements of the ancient world are not the only things that should cause us to re-examine our attitudes in this regard. The so-called Antikythera Mechanism, a mechanical computer designed to calculate astronomical positions and predict eclipses, has been dated to the first century BC.

⁵¹ Archaeological finds confirm the biblical account. Excavations carried out at Gezer by R A Stewart Macalister over five years from 1904 disclosed many jars containing the remains of children who had been sacrificed to the Canaanite god Baal. Also found at Gezer, Megiddo, Jericho and elsewhere were so-called foundation sacrifices, where a child would be killed and its body encased in the wall of a newly built house to bring good luck to the occupants.

⁵² St Paul says that "when the Holy Spirit controls our lives he will produce this kind of fruit in us: love, joy, peace, patience, kindness, goodness, faithfulness, gentleness and self-control" (Galatians 5:22-23, TLB).

⁵³ Given the qualities he displayed, it is hardly surprising that "Moses himself was highly regarded in Egypt by Pharaoh's officials and by the people." (Exodus 11:3). The honour accorded to him was based neither on rank nor on the fact that he had been "educated in all the wisdom of the Egyptians." (Acts 7:22). It simply recognised godly character.

⁵⁴ The first nine plagues are organised in sets of three, with a warning being given before the first plague in each set (see Exodus 7:14-20, 8:20-21 and 9:13-15). Exodus 4:22-23 suggests that a warning was also given before the tenth, final plague.

⁵⁵ Egypt lacked cash crops and summer cereals. The wheat and barley cycle ended by the beginning of April (wheat being harvested about one month later than barley) and sowing began at the start of October for wheat and at the start of December for barley. A failure of the spring harvest would lead to people going hungry until the next crops ripened unless supplies could be brought in from overseas – though it was usually Egypt who supplied surplus foodstuffs for foreigners in danger of famine rather than vice versa.

56 The killing of the firstborn was not the vengeful act of a pagan deity, but a proportionate response long delayed so as to give maximum opportunity for repentance. Paradoxical as it may at first seem, it in fact displayed mercy on the part of God since it did not do to Egypt as she had done: Israel had been "enslaved and ill-treated four hundred years" (Genesis 15:13), and Pharaoh had sought the killing of all Hebrew boys, not just the firstborn (see Exodus 1:15-22). The aim of this policy was doubtless to bring an end to the Hebrew race by ensuring that the surviving women intermarried with Egyptians.

57 There are also four instances where "Pharaoh's heart became [or was] hard" (Exodus 7:13, 7:22, 8:19 and 9:35) and another where "his heart was unyielding" (Exodus 9:7) without its being said whether God or Pharaoh was the cause of this. The heart is used in the Bible to describe the centre of our being, encompassing mind, will and emotions. The element of choice is emphasised by use of the word "if" in Exodus 8:2, 8:21, 9:2 and 10:4.

58 The reaction of the common people is more difficult to discern from the biblical account. As well as holding Moses in high regard, the Lord "[made] the Egyptians favourably disposed towards [the Israelites]" (Exodus 3:21), though whether this resulted purely from fear or included more positive emotions is not stated. It is notable, however, that "The Egyptians urged the [Israelites] to hurry and leave the country. 'For otherwise,' they said, 'we will all die!'" (Exodus 12:33).

59 For more than three and a half millennia attitudes towards and treatment of Israel have been amongst the great spiritual touchstones (see Exodus 1:15-22, Esther 3:13-14 and Matthew 2:16). As God said to Abraham, "I will bless those who bless you, and the one who curses you I will curse; and in you all the families of the earth shall be blessed." (Genesis 12:3, NRSV). During the desert wanderings of Israel this was restated by the pagan seer Balaam, who against his will pronounced, "May those who bless you be blessed and those who curse you be cursed!" (Numbers 24:9). Josephus remarks that "The Egyptians began the slanders against us [the Jews]."

60 Nevertheless, the Bible is history, not myth or hagiography. Moses' faults and mistakes are recounted alongside the episodes that do him honour. Unlike the legendary heroes of other nations, there is nothing miraculous in the manner of his conception and birth, as emphasised by the genealogy which appears in Exodus 6:14-27.

61 The climax of this battle is related in the last book of the Bible: "And war broke out in heaven; Michael and his angels fought against the dragon. The dragon and his angels fought back, but they were defeated, and there was no longer any place for them in heaven. The great dragon was thrown down, that ancient serpent, who is called the Devil and Satan, the deceiver of the whole world – he was thrown down to the earth, and his angels were thrown down with him." (Revelation 12:7-9, NRSV). Then "He [an angel] seized the dragon, that ancient serpent, who is the devil, or Satan, and bound him for a thousand years." (Revelation 20:2). At last "the devil, who deceived them, was thrown into the lake of burning sulphur, where the beast and the false prophet had been thrown. They will be tormented day and night for ever and ever." (Revelation 20:10).

⁶² The words translated "divided" in Exodus 14:21 and "separate" in Genesis 1:6 are from the same Hebrew root.

⁶³ The first six commands concern construction of the tabernacle. The seventh relates to keeping of the Sabbath. This mimics the six days of creative activity and the seventh day of rest in Genesis 1.

⁶⁴ By contrast, the plagues of Egypt were a progressive undoing of Creation and removal of its blessings. Six days of creative activity are mirrored in six occasions on which Pharaoh was told to let the people go (see Exodus 5:1, 7:16, 8:1, 8:20, 9:1 and 9:13) before eventually he complied after the seventh and final call (see Exodus 10:3).

⁶⁵ God told Israel to "Consecrate to me every firstborn male. The first offering of every womb among the Israelites belongs to me." (Exodus 13:1-2), though in practice he accepted the Levites in lieu (Numbers 3:12). Pharaoh's wish to have Israelite boys killed was not merely morally depraved, but involved seeking to steal from God what was rightfully his.

⁶⁶ The king stayed at Akhet-aten in year six of his reign and by year eight it had become the main royal residence. The city's ruins lie 175 miles south of Giza and 220 miles north of Thebes, stretching in a band along the Nile for about nine miles. At its widest point the city is a little less than a fifth of its length, giving a total urban area in the region of thirteen to fifteen square miles. Although yet to be fully excavated, enough has been uncovered to show that the layout of the main body of the city differed significantly from the habitual Egyptian pattern of a grid within a square, for generally the residential areas of the city appear to have grown organically rather than to have been the result of an overall plan. (The workman's village which was built between the city and its necropolis in the eastern hills, however, follows the traditional arrangement.)

⁶⁷ The hills which stood to the east and west of the plain on which the city was built were proxies for Bakhu and Manu, the twin mountains between which the sun god was deemed to rise each day to shine upon his temple and bring life to it. The Egyptians believed there were four pillars holding up the sky, of which Bakhu and Manu probably formed two.

⁶⁸ The landscape may have possessed further significance for the pharaoh by virtue of being untouched by human hand, in the same way as God had said to Moses, "If you make an altar of stones for me, do not build it with dressed stones, for you will defile it if you use a tool on it." (Exodus 20:25). In the context of defilement, see also Exodus 20:26 and 28:42-43.

⁶⁹ There may conceivably have been another factor in the choice of site for Akhet-aten. Moses thrice asked Pharaoh to "let us take a three-day journey into the desert to offer sacrifices to the LORD our God" (Exodus 3:18, 5:3 and 8:27), on one occasion adding "or he may strike us with plagues or with the sword." (Exodus 5:3). From this repeated request Egyptians might have concluded that Israel's God set particular store by desert environs. Spiritually, going into the desert reflects the need for holiness, separation from sin and a decisive break with worldly desires and temptations. Although the Israelites

were taken literally into the wilderness their journey was also a spiritual one as "Moses led Israel from the Red Sea and they went into the Desert of Shur. For three days they travelled in the desert without finding water." (Exodus 15:22).

70 Gem-pa-Aten means *"Aten is found"* or *"He has found Aten"*. The first major building project of Akhenaten's reign was the building of another Gem-pa-Aten to the east of the ritual site at Karnak (Thebes). This is orientated east towards the rising sun, rather than to the west like the rest of the Karnak shrines. From the first Akhenaten's religion thus turned its back both literally and metaphorically on the worship of Amun. Thebes was known in the Egyptian language from the end of the New Kingdom as *niwt-imn* (the city of Amun). Akhet-aten was therefore conceived linguistically and spatially to be the antithesis of Thebes.

71 Such as the Radiant Festival of the Valley or the Beautiful Feast of the Opet, held at Thebes in honour of Amun (see chapter 10).

72 There were at least four palaces in the city, which vary considerably in form. On the plain near the river massive temples to Aten were constructed. These were open to the sky and the rays of the sun and were probably influenced by the design of much earlier solar temples dedicated to the cult of Ra. Other sites of religious importance are located on the edges of the desert plain.

73 Nefertiti means *"The radiant one has come"*. As well as meaning "radiant," the word *nefer* has connotations of beauty, completeness and vitality. It carried particular significance in the cult of Aten.

74 The close relationship between Aten and the royal family was emphasised by depictions of the god as a sun disc whose rays terminate in hands which reach out to the king, queen and their children, sometimes offering the hieroglyphic sign for life (the *ankh*) as they do so.

75 The sections dealing with the giving of the Law (chapters 19-24) might in a sense also be included within the concept of worship, since the purpose of the Law was to enable Israel to be dedicated wholly to the service of God and made holy so that he might dwell with them. If these are included, well over half of Exodus directly concerns issues relating to worship.

76 See the genealogy in Exodus 6:16-25.

77 The Levites remained central to worship at the Jerusalem Temple (see 2 Chronicles 31:2 and Nehemiah 12:27).

78 Doubtless Pharaoh had in mind that the women and children would effectively be hostages if they remained behind, hence his unwillingness to let them accompany their men-folk.

79 As the Westminster Larger Catechism (question 1) has it, "Man's chief and highest end is to glorify God, and fully to enjoy him forever." The worship that all Creation will offer in heaven is described in the last book of the Bible: "Then I heard every creature in heaven and on earth and under the earth and on the sea, and all that is in them, singing:

'To him who sits on the throne and to the Lamb be praise and honour and glory and power, for ever and ever!'" (Revelation 5:13). Worship and obedience go hand in hand, as shown by the Israelites' later reaction when "the people bowed down and worshipped [and] did just what the LORD commanded Moses and Aaron." (Exodus 12:27-28).

80 The steps which Moses took in worship were at first tentative. Though reverential, a large part of his reaction appears (quite understandably) to have been sheer terror, for "At this, Moses hid his face, because he was afraid to look at God." (Exodus 3:6). We may presume that he did as he was told when commanded to "take off your sandals, for the place where you are standing is holy ground." (Exodus 3:5). Later, there was no mistaking his zeal and prompt obedience as "Moses bowed to the ground at once and worshipped." (Exodus 34:8).

81 Just as the sacrifice of Jesus on the cross has led to our being "bought at a price; [and therefore we should] not become slaves of men." (1 Corinthians 7:23). Similarly, "we should no longer be the slaves of sin" (Romans 6:6, GNT) since the dearest wish of our Heavenly Father is that we be "brought into the glorious freedom of the children of God." (Romans 8:21).

82 However, the parallels should not be taken too far, since "The Holy Spirit was showing by this [the furnishings and arrangements for worship in the tabernacle] that the way into the Most Holy Place had not yet been disclosed as long as the first tabernacle was still standing. This is an illustration for the present time, indicating that the gifts and sacrifices being offered were not able to clear the conscience of the worshipper. They are only a matter of food and drink and various ceremonial washings – external regulations applying until the time of the new order." (Hebrews 9:8-10).

83 Undrinkable water was also made potable: "Then Moses cried out to the LORD, and the LORD showed him a piece of wood. He threw it into the water, and the water became sweet" (Exodus 15:25). Furthermore, the Lord ensured victory over the Amalekites (see Exodus 17:8-16).

84 With Pharaoh's forces in hot pursuit, the Israelites "camped by the Red Sea near Pi Hahiroth and Baal Zephon." (Exodus 14:9, GNT). Pi Hahiroth means "the Mouth of Freedom", the sea marking a division between the realm of the Egyptians and the wilderness beyond which beckoned Israel to Horeb and thereafter to the Promised Land.

85 The activity of the Almighty is seen in his "making a way in the desert and streams in the wasteland." (Isaiah 43:19). As recognised in the song which "Moses and the Israelites sang to the LORD" (Exodus 15:1) after crossing the Red Sea, God "will lead the people [he has] redeemed [and] … will guide them to his holy dwelling." (Exodus 15:13).

86 This is not meaningless ritual or an elaborate game; the ever-present risk of untimely death in approaching holy places unprepared is emphasised in Exodus 19:21, 28:35 and 30:20-21. That an equivalent danger exists in the New Testament era is demonstrated in Acts 5:1-11. Earthly rulers have always been jealous of their dignity and honour and we should hardly expect the High King of Heaven to be otherwise, though his grace and forbearance contrasts with the prickliness of humans who wield only a fraction of the

power; under Xerxes, for example, it was the case that "[for] any man or woman who approaches the king in the inner court without being summoned the king has but one law: that he be put to death." (Esther 4:11).

87 In the same way, the later Temple of Jerusalem was called the house (*bayit*) of God and declared to be sacred only after the Lord's presence entered it: "when Solomon had finished building the house of the LORD ... the LORD appeared to Solomon the second time... And the LORD said to him: 'I have heard your prayer and your supplication that you have made before Me; I have consecrated this house which you have built to put My name there forever, and My eyes and My heart will be there perpetually.'" (1 Kings 9:1-3, NKJV). In older translations of the Bible God is recorded as saying that he will 'tabernacle' (dwell) with his people.

88 When Jesus died, "the curtain of the temple was torn in two" (Matthew 27:51, Mark 15:38 and Luke 23:45), symbolising the taking away of the barrier that hitherto had existed between man and God by reason of our sin. The universal value placed on thread of the kind used by the Israelites is shown by Tokugawa's Kei'an Laws of 1648-9, which prevented the Japanese lower classes from using red or blue cloth.

89 On a seventy-two-year span, this flowering would come at age twelve, the traditional coming of age for Jewish youths. In contrast to the flowering of childhood, that of adulthood requires establishing a foundation in terms of occupation (flower-cup) and one's own household (flower-bowl). The seven branches of the menorah may be seen as choices of future direction in life.

90 An added dimension to the meaning of the menorah is provided by the golden lamp-stands mentioned in the final book of the Bible, these representing seven archetypical churches, together with God's power and authority present in and at work through them (see Revelation 1:12, 2:1 and 2:5).

91 The Bible uses a number of different Hebrew words to express the idea of worship: (1) *shachah*, meaning to bow down or prostrate oneself as a subject before a king, pointing to inner and outer homage in token of awe and surrender; (2) *'avad*, meaning to serve, not only by way of an inner heartfelt response of thanksgiving but also through totally committed action; (3) *yare'*, meaning to fear, revere and respect, encompassing being obedient to God's voice, walking in his ways, keeping his commandments, turning away from evil, and approaching him as befits his majesty; and (4) *hodah*, meaning both to give thanks and to make confession.

92 Sabbath and the sacrificial system were thus as much an aid to worship and coming into the presence of God as was the tabernacle. Again, language emphasises that relationship with God was of the essence; the Hebrew for sacrifice (*korban*) derives from a root meaning "to draw near", the intention of sacrifice being to enable man to come nigh to God by bridging heaven and earth and covering over sin, which lies at the root of separation between man and his Maker. Yet sin was only ever covered over by animal sacrifice. It was not dealt with finally until "God made [Jesus] who had no sin to be sin for us, so that in him we might become the righteousness of God." (2 Corinthians 5:21).

93 The Hebrew for sign (*'ot*) combines the first letter of the alphabet (*'alef*, standing for the heavenly or spiritual) with the last (*tav*, standing for the earthly or material), linked by the connective 'and' (*vav*). It thereby pictures the higher (*'alef*) linking with the lower (*tav*) to embody heavenly truth on earth. At its heart and in its essence lie both holiness and eternity: holiness by virtue of one day in seven being set apart and eternity through representing that realm beyond the confines of time and outside the daily striving of mortals which belongs to God rather than to man. The Hebrew word for holy (*kadosh*) comes from a root meaning "to set apart". Thus Sabbath is to be a day set apart from regular time, which Jews mark by ceremonies involving fire and wine both at its start (*kidddush*) and at its end (*havdalah*).

94 In Heliopolis the so-called Mnervis bull was believed to be a herald of Ra and an earthly intermediary of that god, whilst the goddess Hathor was often depicted as a cow. The other major cults were those of the Apis and Buchis bulls, centred respectively on Memphis and Hermonthis. Akhenaten had the Mnervis bull brought to Akhet-aten for burial, presumably for one or more of the following reasons: (1) to prevent its veneration rivalling that of Aten; (2) to illustrate the primacy of Aten and those who served him; (3) to allow some of the reflected glory of the Heliopolis cult to rub off on the new religion; or (4) to deconsecrate Heliopolis, making the new capital the unequivocal centre of sun-worship.

95 Akhenaten was the younger son of Amenhotep III's chief wife Tiye. This couple's elder son, Crown Prince Thutmose, died young. Besides the boy who became Akhenaten, they had at least four other children who survived to maturity: princesses Satamun, Isis, Henuttaunebu and Nebetah. It is not known whether a further princess called Baketaten, whom Amarna period material connects with Amenhotep III and Tiye, was one of these four princesses under another name, or someone entirely separate.

96 Anubis placed the heart on one side of a set of scales and a feather representing truth (as worn by Ma'at, goddess of truth) on the other. If the scales balanced, the person went to eternal joy. If the heart was heavy with sin, the monster Ammit, Devourer of the Dead and Eater of Hearts, gobbled it up.

97 Amun was also depicted in human form with two lofty feathers on his head.

98 There seems to have been a distinction between Aten and Amun in this respect. The visibility of the sun disc in the sky made a pointed contrast with Amun, sometimes described as god of the wind, whose name means "He who is hidden" or "the one who conceals himself". The essence of Amun was considered both imperceptible and inexplicable, such that he could not be called by a name that hinted at his inner nature. His identity was supposedly so secret that none of the other gods knew his real name. Amun was described as "too great to enquire into and too powerful to know", both "beyond the sky and deeper than the underworld" (Papyrus Leiden I 350).

99 Ra-Harakhte (Ra-Horus of the horizon) was an amalgam of the sun god Ra and the god of heaven, Horus. Ra-Harakhte had his solar component in common with Ra, but derived from Horus the character of a youth. The composite deity thus represented the newly born sun at daybreak.

¹⁰⁰ The hymns comprise an extended outpouring of praise that some have likened to Psalm 104:16-23. Though each speaks of the natural world waking and sleeping under the beneficent eye of a supreme Creator, there are nevertheless distinct differences between the two, not least in terms of the political statements made in Akhenaten's schema. In particular, the hymns to Aten assert an exclusive relationship between deity and one man (the pharaoh) of a kind which neither Psalm 104 nor any other part of Scripture countenances. For example, the former says that "You [Aten] are in my heart and there is none who knows you but your son [Akhenaten] alone", the latter making no equivalent assertion.

¹⁰¹ The names are difficult to translate in ways that adequately render their theological import and their puns on the names of other gods. The form in use from years three to nine of Akhenaten's reign roughly equates to "Ra-Harakhy who rejoices in his name as Shu-who-is-from-Aten". The form used from regnal years nine to seventeen might be rendered as "Ra-ruler-of-the-twin-horizons, who rejoices in the horizon in his name as Ra-the-father-who-returns-as-Aten". The hieroglyph which renders the earlier version is particularly striking since it shows Akhenaten in the guise of the god Shu, flanked both by his own titles and those of Nefertiti, lifting high the twin cartouches of Aten. As Shu stood for illumination and was thought to occupy the space between heaven and earth, by adopting his likeness the pharaoh seems to have been claiming for himself both superhuman enlightenment and a mediating role in bringing knowledge of Aten to a wider audience.

¹⁰² The First Prophet or High Priest of Amun at Thebes had hitherto been the pharaoh's principal adviser on spiritual matters. Before Akhenaten came to the throne there had increasingly developed a practice that the Second Prophet of Amun at Thebes should be a close relation of the king or his chief queen. This nevertheless seems to have amounted to somewhat less than the outright royal control over matters theological which Akhenaten apparently sought.

¹⁰³ Though as St Paul observes, "since the creation of the world God's invisible qualities – his eternal power and divine nature – have been clearly seen, being understood from what has been made, so that men are without excuse." (Romans 1:20). In contrast to Amun, the one true God conceals neither himself nor his intentions from his people, for "Surely the Sovereign LORD does nothing without revealing his plan to his servants the prophets." (Amos 3:7). Furthermore, he makes it clear that "you will seek me and you will find me when you seek me with all your heart" (Jeremiah 29:13) and we have only to "Ask, and you will be given what you ask for. Seek, and you will find. Knock, and the door will be opened. For everyone who asks, receives. Anyone who seeks, finds. If only you will knock, the door will open." (Matthew 7:7, TLB, with a similar wording in Luke 11:9).

¹⁰⁴ He told Jethro that "the people come to me to seek God's will. Whenever they have a dispute, it is brought to me, and I decide between the parties and inform them of God's decrees and laws." (Exodus 18:15-16).

105 This involved considerable trust on Moses' part since for all he knew he might still have been a wanted man in Egypt, despite God's saying that "all the men who wanted to kill you are dead." (Exodus 4:19). The request Moses made of Jethro is couched in a way which might perhaps seem curious at first sight, though presumably Exodus records only a fraction of what might well have been a lengthy exchange between the two. It could be that at this point Moses was shy of recounting his meeting with God on Horeb (or at least the full extent of the charge laid upon him) or that the question he eventually asked his father-in-law was the one which was hardest to refuse in a society that esteemed family ties so highly.

106 Similar unfounded complaints are recounted later: "In the desert the whole community grumbled against Moses and Aaron." (Exodus 16:2) and "They camped at Rephidim but there was no water for the people to drink. So they quarrelled with Moses and said, 'Give us water to drink.'" (Exodus 17:1-2). Other instances appear elsewhere in the Pentateuch.

107 It is by a similar process that believers "are being transformed into [Christ's] likeness with ever-increasing glory, which comes from the Lord, who is the Spirit." (2 Corinthians 3:18).

108 One was so grave as to exclude him from the Promised Land: "But the LORD said to Moses and Aaron, 'Because you did not trust in me enough to honour me as holy in the sight of the Israelites, you will not bring this community into the land I give them.'" (Numbers 20:12). Moses' fault lay in disobedience, lack of trust and misrepresentation of God; he was told to "Speak to that rock before [the Israelites'] eyes and it will pour out its water" (Numbers 20:8) but instead "Moses raised his arm and struck the rock twice with his staff." (Numbers 20:11). As God's earthly agent he therefore portrayed his heavenly principal as acting in anger when this was not God's wish or intention, and furthermore implied that the authority of God's word was somehow not enough. There was a distinction between this event and the earlier miraculous provision of water from rock at Meribah, where Moses was specifically told to "Strike the rock" (Exodus 17:6). See also chapter 11.

109 Pharaoh's arrogant posturing and likening of himself to God are evident in his threat to Moses that "The day you see my face you will die." (Exodus 10:28). Prophetically, Moses retorted, "Just as you say ... I will never appear before you again." (Exodus 10:29).

110 Though this quest will continue for an eternity in heaven, there will always be aspects of God that are unknown and unknowable by man by reason of our human limitations. An imperfect analogy is provided by pi, the symbol representing the ratio of the circumference of a circle to its diameter: there can be constantly increasing precision in calculating its value without ever expressing it definitively. The prophet Isaiah records the Almighty as saying, "As the heavens are higher than the earth, so are my ways higher than your ways and my thoughts higher than your thoughts" (Isaiah 55:9).

111 There are many specific references in the Pentateuch either to Moses doing so, having done so or being told by God to do so: (1) "Then the LORD said to Moses, 'Write this on

a scroll as something to be remembered ..."' (Exodus 17:14); (2) "Moses then wrote down everything the LORD had said." (Exodus 24:4); (3) "Then the LORD said to Moses, 'Write down these words, for in accordance with these words I have made a covenant with you and with Israel.'" (Exodus 34:27); (4) "At the LORD's command, Moses recorded the stages in [the Israelites'] journey." (Numbers 33:2); (5) "If you do not carefully follow all the words of this law, which are written in this book ..." (Deuteronomy 28:58); (6) "every curse that is written in this book ... according to all the curses of the covenant that are written in this Book of the Law ... every curse that is written in this book." (Deuteronomy 29:20-21 and 27, NKJV); (7) "if you obey the LORD your God and keep his commands and decrees that are written in this Book of the Law ..."(Deuteronomy 30:10); (8) "So Moses wrote down this law" (Deuteronomy 31:9); (9) "Now write down for yourselves this song and teach it to the Israelites and make them sing it , so that it may be a witness for me against them." (Deuteronomy 31:19); (10) "So Moses wrote down this song that day" (Deuteronomy 31:22); and (11) "After Moses finished writing in a book the words of this law from beginning to end, he [commanded the Levites] 'Take this Book of the Law and place it beside the ark of the covenant of the LORD your God. There it will remain as a witness against you ...'" (Deuteronomy 31:24). There seems little basis for the assertion that there was no kind of Hebrew writing at the time of the exodus (see appendix 6 for details of early Hebrew script).

112 He "used to take a tent and pitch it outside the camp some distance away, calling it 'the tent of meeting' [and there] ... the LORD would speak to Moses face to face, as a man speaks with his friend." (Exodus 33:7 and 11).

113 Subsequent meetings between God and Moses on Horeb occurred after the events recounted in Exodus 33 and 34: as he had in rage broken the first set of tablets containing the Ten Commandments (see Exodus 32:19), Moses had to go back up the mountain to receive the replacements which God graciously provided (see Exodus 34:1).

114 "Moses, Aaron, Nadab, Abihu, and seventy of the elders of Israel went up into the mountain. And they saw the God of Israel; under his feet there seemed to be a pavement of brilliant sapphire stones, as clear as the heavens." (Exodus 24:9-10, TLB). Extraordinary and awe-inspiring as this sight must have been, it is nevertheless clear that those who came before God on this occasion did not see the glory of the Lord in the degree of fullness that was later granted to Moses, nor experience the intimate relationship that he had with his Maker; though "they saw God, and they ate and drank" (Exodus 24:11) they were only allowed to "worship at a distance" (Exodus 24:1) whilst God instructed that "Moses alone is to approach the LORD; the others must not come near. And the people may not come up with him." (Exodus 24:2).

115 Though Jacob called the place where he "wrestled ... till daybreak" (Genesis 32:24) with a heavenly being in the form of a man Peniel "because I saw God face to face, and yet my life was spared" (Genesis 32:30), this does not mean that he saw the face of God in the sense in which that word is used in Exodus 33:20. The dictionary definition of the expression "face to face" is being in the immediate presence of another, clearly, without anything interposed.

[116] In Matthew's version it is their mother who voices the request, but since she "came to Jesus with her sons" (Matthew 20:20) the likelihood is that all three had something to say on the matter.

[117] To the list of divine character traits might be added the knowledge, perseverance and brotherly kindness mentioned in 2 Peter 1:5-7, plus many more.

[118] Though the Egyptians eventually felt the full force of judgment, God had nevertheless been merciful to them (see note 56).

[119] These words mirror those which God spoke to Moses when he next climbed Horeb to receive new stone tablets. On that occasion the Almighty "passed in front of Moses, proclaiming, 'The LORD, the LORD, the compassionate and gracious God, slow to anger, abounding in love and faithfulness, maintaining love to thousands and forgiving wickedness, rebellion and sin. Yet he does not leave the guilty unpunished; he punishes the children and their children for the sin of the fathers to the third and fourth generation.'" (Exodus 34:6-7).

[120] Jesus himself asserted that he was "written about ... in the Law of Moses" (Luke 24:44).

[121] The words "I am he" reflect part of the divine name revealed to Moses when God first appeared to him on Horeb in the burning bush (Exodus 3:14; see chapter 1 and the seven "I am" statements to be found in John 6:35, 8:12, 10:7, 10:11 and 14, 11:25, 14:6 and 15:1).

[122] Even the mere reflection of a small part of it was such that Moses' face became "aglow" (Exodus 34:35, TLB). At his Transfiguration, "[Jesus'] face shone like the sun" (Matthew 17:2).

[123] Without God miraculously sustaining him, Moses would have died. Humans can survive in the order of seven to eight weeks without food but only eight to fourteen days without water.

[124] After loss of their pursuing chariot force in the Red Sea, at best pharaohs are likely thereafter to have received only garbled and intermittent intelligence about the activities of their former slaves.

[125] Until the Amarna period artists worked on a grid of eighteen vertical squares. A hand's breadth was equal to the height of one square, a standing human figure occupying eighteen squares from the sole of the feet to the hairline; the face from hairline to base of neck, two squares; the chest from shoulders to waist, five squares; the legs from knees to the sole of the foot, six squares. An arm was equal to the width of one square and a central vertical line running past the front of the ear divided the body into two halves. Some (though by no means all) distortion of the human form during the Amarna period is accounted for by the fact that the standard grid at this time was extended to a height of twenty squares.

[126] After the end of the Amarna period the old grid was reinstated, but the resulting representations were poor shadows of former glories. In consequence, a new grid of

twenty-one squares was adopted during the nineteenth dynasty, which produced the elongated body shapes characteristic of this later period.

127 Fröhlich's Syndrome is a glandular disorder which causes ballooning of the skull, obesity, and feminine deposits of fat around thighs and buttocks. All these are seen in representations of Akhenaten. However, it also renders sufferers infertile, which Akhenaten was not. Marfan's Syndrome is an inherited disorder whose sufferers are often unusually tall, with long faces, chest deformities and fingers extended by the stretching of the connective tissues. Again, such traits are apparently evident in representations of Akhenaten, who also suffered from a cleft palate and scoliosis.

128 Whereas traditional Egyptian art had tended to focus on the eternal, that of the Amarna period often portrays those everyday activities which could only be enjoyed because of the lifegiving power of the sun.

129 A computer tomography (CT) scan performed on Tutankhamun's skeleton in 2005 revealed a distended skull similar to that shown in pictures of Akhenaten. That there was a close family connection between Tutankhamun and Akhenaten is now generally accepted, the present consensus being that Tutankhamun was Akhenaten's son by a secondary wife, Kiya. The extent to which other bodily distortions shown in depictions of Akhenaten are a result of naturalist representation remains uncertain.

130 Busts of the dead were kept in houses, to which surviving family members would pray. Consequently, the word *akh* was linked to ancestor-worship and concepts of religious duty.

131 It is noteworthy that after Akhenaten's reign, Egyptian art seems to have lost some of its former pagan delight in the world and its joys, having thenceforth more sombre preoccupations such as funerary scenes and magic rites. Whilst there may be a number of reasons for this, including the influence of decoration in royal tombs in the later period, it is consistent with a change of mood occasioned not just by recognition of Egypt's diminished stature in the world and the aftermath of the Amarna experiment but also with the trauma of the Exodus events.

132 American architect Louis Sullivan (1856-1924) stated that "form ever follows function" in his 1896 article *The Tall Office Building Artistically Considered*. Sullivan developed the concept of the steel skyscraper in late nineteenth century Chicago at a point when changes in taste and economic developments came together with technological progress in such a way as to make traditional forms seem outmoded. His protégé Frank Lloyd Wright adopted similar principles.

133 Hume's discussion of miracles appears in *An Enquiry concerning Human Understanding* (1748).

134 This is so throughout Scripture and remains the case in the present. Hence whilst God reminded Moses, "…see that you perform before Pharaoh all the wonders I have given you power to do" (Exodus 4:21), there was no doubt about who was their ultimate source. Earlier, the Lord had specifically said, "So I will stretch out my hand and strike the Egyptians with all the wonders that I will perform among them." (Exodus 3:20).

Likewise he said, "Now you will see what I will do to Pharaoh: Because of my mighty hand he will let them go ... [and] drive them out of his country." (Exodus 6:1).

[135] Some examples are given in chapter 6. It is important to emphasise that to envisage ways of accounting for the Exodus events in this manner does not in any way lessen their miraculous nature; it merely gives a context in which to understand better the mechanisms which God might have used in bringing about what Exodus describes.

[136] As Moses pointed out, "You are not grumbling against us [Moses and Aaron], but against the LORD." (Exodus 16:8). This was not pure assertion, for God said, "This [the planting of Aaron's staff in front of the Testimony] will put an end to their grumbling against me" (Numbers 17:5 and 17:10).

[137] For example, mathematician and physicist Roger Penrose has calculated the odds of the Big Bang creating an ordered rather than disordered universe as one in 10 to the power of 10^{123}, a number so vast that it is said to contain more zeros than there are particles in the cosmos. In terms of probability, it is difficult to conceive of something that comes closer to expressing the impossible. The fine-tuning of Creation is evident in the largest and the smallest: if gravity were altered by as little as one in 10^{40}, neither sun nor planets would exist, whilst the slightest of changes to the ratio which the mass of a proton bears to that of an electron would result in the atomic nuclei necessary to produce the elements which make up the universe being unable to form.

[138] To take just one example, the average heart beats in the order of 100,000 times a day, pumping blood through 80,000 miles of blood vessels. Each day blood cells travel an aggregate distance of 168 million miles. The heart beats over 2,500 million times over a life span of three score years and ten.

[139] There is order in separation of one from another (Genesis 1:3, 6 and 18); structure in one being gathered to another (Genesis 1:9 and 10); fruitfulness in land, sea and creatures (Genesis 1:11-12, 1:20-22 and 1:28); harmony in that each was according to its kind yet part of the whole (Genesis 1:21 and 25); a benign world bathed in light and well watered (Genesis 1:14-18 and 2:10-14); a pleasant world whose creatures were blessed by God (Genesis 1:22 and 28); and a beautiful world, good in every particular and very good in its whole (Genesis 1:3, 10, 12, 18, 21, 25 and 31).

[140] The idea of a template does not extend only to objects. St Paul described the first man Adam as being "a pattern of the one who was to come" (Romans 5:14), namely Jesus, and advised his readers to "take note of those who live according to the pattern we gave you." (Philippians 3:17). His protégé Timothy was likewise told, "What you have heard from me, keep as the pattern of sound teaching, with faith and love in Christ Jesus." (2 Timothy 1:13).

[141] He could of course have created everything in an instant, but elected to work through imperfect mankind since in his wisdom and mercy he has chosen to make us "fellow workers" (1 Corinthians 3:9, NKJV) as well as "joint heirs" (Romans 8:17, NKJV).

[142] There are echoes in this of the spiritual gifts described by St Paul when he said that "[God] Himself gave some to be apostles, some prophets, some evangelists, and some

pastors and teachers, for the equipping of the saints for the work of ministry, for the edifying of the body of Christ," (Ephesians 4:11-12, NKJV). In New Testament terms Moses might be considered to have fulfilled something of all these roles, though others were at various times alongside him. Miriam was a "prophetess" (Exodus 15:20); in his function as High Priest (Exodus 40:13) Aaron was to be shepherd (pastor) to Israel; and God gave "[Bezalel] and Oholiab son of Ahimasach, of the tribe of Dan, the ability to teach others." (Exodus 35:34).

[143] Other instances of precise measurement in both design and construction appear in Exodus 25:23, 26:2, 26:8, 26:16, 27:1, 27:9, 27:11, 27:12, 27:13-16, 27:18, 30:2, 36:9, 36:15, 36:21, 37:1, 37:6, 37:10, 37:25, 38:1, 38:9, 38:11-15 and 38:18.

[144] See chapter 3 for discussion of some of the significance of these things.

[145] The requirement that things should be "of one piece" was repeated in respect of the cherubim and the cover of the ark (Exodus 25:19 and 37:8); the lampstand and its decorative features (Exodus 25:31, 25:36, 37:17 and 37:22); and the altar and its horns (Exodus 27:2, 30:2, 37:25 and 38:2).

[146] These four things together in both their physical and spiritual aspects convey only part of the wealth of meaning in the Hebrew word *shalom* (usually rendered into English as 'peace'). It is *shalom* which God told Aaron and his descendants to pronounce by way of blessing when he provided the formula: "The LORD bless you and keep you; The LORD make His face shine upon you, And be gracious to you; The LORD lift up His countenance upon you, And give you peace." (Numbers 6:24-26, NKJV). Amongst other things, this blessing was to enable Israel to reflect God more fully, since in this way "[the priests] will put my name on the Israelites, and I will bless them." (Numbers 6:27). To bear God's name was indicative of belonging to him and being a means of reflecting him to the world at large.

[147] Such dualism has at various times influenced Christian thinking. It is still to be found in the Olympic ideal (the cult of the body) and the ascetic principle (which regards all matter as tainted).

[148] Integrity is linguistically related to the words 'integral' and 'integration'. To practise integrity therefore involves the very opposite of compartmentalising our lives. To reserve godliness and worship only for one day a week is a failure of integrity.

[149] Though the Holy Spirit was mightily at work from the very first, for at the earliest moments of Creation "the Spirit of God was hovering over the waters [of the newly created earth]" (Genesis 1:2). Adam was literally inspired by the Holy Spirit when God "breathed into his nostrils the breath of life, and the man became a living being." (Genesis 2:7).

[150] In the parables of the talents (Matthew 25:14-30) and of the ten minas (Luke 19:11-27), Jesus has harsh words for those who do not use their gifts from God properly. The apostle Peter told his readers that "Each one should use whatever gift he has received to serve others, faithfully administering God's grace in its various forms."

(1 Peter 4:10). Israel's mistake was later redeemed in generous giving, as recorded in the careful list of donations for the tabernacle in Exodus 38:21-31.

[151] The Hebrew for "was radiant" is related to the Hebrew noun for "horn". The Vulgate (the Latin translation of the Bible made by St Jerome in the fourth century) consequently rendered Exodus 34:29 wrongly, and thus European Mediaeval art often showed horns sprouting from Moses' head. This casts an interesting light on depictions of Satan as having horns, for Lucifer was originally the "morning star, son of the dawn" (Isaiah 14:12) who even now "masquerades as an angel of light" (2 Corinthians 11:14).

[152] Reference to the heaven above, earth beneath and water under the earth echoes the language of creation (see Genesis 1:1 and elsewhere), in the process emphasising that God's essential being is different from any created thing.

[153] Alongside jealousy sits righteous anger. Though Moses was denied the honour of leading Israel into the Promised Land because he misrepresented God by striking a rock in temper to bring forth water, neither punishment nor reprimand was issued when "his anger burned and he threw the tablets [carved with the Ten Commandments] out of his hands, breaking them to pieces at the foot of the mountain. And he took the calf they had made and burned it in the fire; then he ground it to powder, scattered it on the water and made the Israelites drink it." (Exodus 32:19-20). Moses' initial fury and the cold rage that followed were not only entirely justified, but presumably also properly reflected the way that God himself felt.

[154] Both quotations are from the poem *Ozymandias* by Percy Bysshe Shelley, a reflection on the fleeting nature of earthly dominion inspired by hearing of a huge statue of Ramses II lying toppled in the dust. Ozymandias is a Greek form of Usermare (meaning, *Justice of Ra is powerful*), one of the names of Ramses II.

[155] They also tend to influence us. Hence the Israelites were instructed, "Be sure that you do not mix with the heathen people still remaining in [Canaan after the conquest]" (Joshua 23:7, TLB).

[156] Moses' argument as to why the Lord should stay his hand was fourfold: (1) the Israelites were his people (Exodus 32:11); (2) to destroy them would undo the miraculous work of delivering them from Egypt (Exodus 32:11); (3) killing them would give the Egyptians cause to mischaracterise God and misrepresent his actions (Exodus 32:12); and (4) God was bound by the sworn covenant he had made with Abraham, Isaac and Jacob (Exodus 32:13).

[157] The description "King of the Gods" is used, for example, in the jubilee chapel of Senusret I, who is thought to have reigned from 1965 BC to 1920 BC.

[158] Before a campaign the pharaoh consulted a war council of staff officers and senior state officials, amongst whom were high-ranking representatives of the cult of Amun.

[159] In accordance with age-old practice, captured enemy leaders would be ritually killed. Lesser prisoners of war would be used as slaves, either within the temple of Amun at Thebes or on one of its other properties elsewhere in the empire.

160 Instances include Pharaoh Seqenenre II Tao (Seventeenth Dynasty, Second Intermediate Period, who reigned for a short time around 1558 BC) and two of his sons: Kamose (Seventeenth Dynasty, Second Intermediate Period, who reigned from approximately 1555 to 1550 BC) and Ahmose (Eighteenth Dynasty, New Kingdom, who reigned from approximately 1550 to 1525 BC). All three led armies in battle, as did Eighteenth Dynasty Prince Wadjmose, son of Thutmose I (who reigned from about 1506 to 1493 BC).

161 The Hyksos ruled large parts of Egypt for just under a century before their expulsion in about 1550 BC. Egyptians called the tribal chiefs of those Semitic peoples who migrated to the Nile Delta during the First Intermediate Period *Hikau Khasut* (meaning *Princes of Desert Uplands*). The Greek historian Manetho mistranslated this as *Hyksos* (meaning *Shepherd Kings*), a name which not only stuck but is now applied to the entire immigrant group rather than merely to their leaders.

162 The monarch was "good shepherd" to his people, a phrase first used of him in the Middle Kingdom and later extended both to Amun and other major gods.

163 The harshness shown to the Israelites whom Pharaoh feared in the event of war would "join our enemies and fight against us and escape out of the country" (Exodus 1:10, TLB) was an aspect of this. In his beneficent aspect the king was connected to the cat goddess Bastet, but when violently aggressive to enemies he was identified with the lion goddess Sekhmet; New Kingdom scenes and texts depict the latter's consuming rage (*nesert*) as fire blazing from the uraeus. Such dualism was not new, for similar ideas are found in the Twelfth Dynasty. Tension between love (connected to Bastet) and fear (linked to Sekhmet) was fundamental to Egyptian ideas about the world.

164 Egypt kept her allies on a tight leash. To ensure loyalty, from the reign of Thutmose III (who ruled from about 1479 BC to 1425 BC) onwards pharaohs took not only an oath from rulers of the city-states to the north-east but also hostages in the form of the ruler's sons or brothers. These would be sent to Egypt and kept there as a guarantee of good conduct.

165 The number of army corps varied over time. At Kadesh in 1274 BC Ramses II's forces were organised into the Amun, Seth, Ra, and Ptah divisions, the latter apparently being newly formed.

166 Estimates of the size of the Egyptian army vary greatly. At the battle of Kadesh in 1274 BC or thereabouts, Ramses II is thought to have deployed anything between 50 chariots and 5,000 soldiers at the lower end of the scale to a sum total of 20,000 to 25,000 troops at the higher end. The total size of the Egyptian army at this time has been reckoned at no more than 40,000 and probably nearer 30,000. Egyptian records of the battle trumpet victory for Ramses II, though his opponent King Muwatalli of the Hittites proclaimed the same with rather more justification.

167 This seems to have been commonplace at least by the time of Amenhotep II (New Kingdom, Eighteenth Dynasty, who ruled from approximately 1427 BC to 1401 BC). Chariots had been unknown in Egypt prior to the Hyksos incursions which began around

1650 BC, and their lack initially put Egyptian forces at a considerable disadvantage against these invaders. Gradual mastery of chariot warfare using vehicles copied from their enemies at length enabled the Egyptians to turn the tables. It is generally thought that the wheel only reached Egypt with the Hyksos.

[168] On one estimate the upper echelons of the military accounted for 17.3% of the elite as a whole (warrior class, civilian officials and priests) under Ramses II and 15.9% under Ramses III (or 25% and 22.5% respectively if the viceroy of Nubia and his underlings are included). That the proportion should have been so high is not altogether surprising, for this was an age of heroes; individual strength, daring and skill in war being highly prized in Bronze Age societies. The New Kingdom period was roughly contiguous with the Minoan civilisation of Crete and its Mycenaean equivalent on the Greek mainland, from which were drawn inspiration for the feats immortalised by Homer and in the myths and legends of ancient Greece.

[169] Though mercenaries were increasingly used throughout the army, it is noteworthy that Akhenaten's bodyguard seems to have consisted largely of foreigners such as Syrians, Libyans and Nubians. Whether this reflected doubt as to the skill or reliability of local troops, ferment caused by the pharaoh's religious and political innovations, or was the result of other factors it is impossible now to say.

[170] Such developments came to a head at a dangerous time, as a new contender for the position of regional superpower emerged in the form of the Hittites. From their Anatolian heartlands this vigorous, warlike nation spread east and south, their empire approaching its zenith as Akhenaten came to the throne. Under him, Egypt lost both influence and allies in the north to this ambitious rival.

[171] In similar fashion, there are a number of instances in Exodus where God almost seems to be mocking those who sought to stand against him and making a public spectacle of them. For example, the mechanisms which he used to ensure that Moses survived infancy are an ironic comment on the inability of anyone, no matter how powerful, to stand in the way of divine purposes. The king was repeatedly outwitted and his plans frustrated by a series of resourceful women, which would have been considered utterly humiliating for a man in the societies of the ancient Near East. To add insult to injury, the baby survived precisely what Pharaoh had ordered should happen to all Hebrew boys, namely being "[thrown] into the Nile" (Exodus 1:22). For this to become the route by which the future prophet was brought to safety was extraordinary, for the waterways held many dangers. When "Pharaoh's daughter went down to the river to bathe … her attendants were walking along the river bank" (Exodus 2:5), presumably on the lookout for crocodiles, hippopotami and other hazards. Likewise the false gods of Egypt were shown one by one to be utterly powerless before the High King of heaven.

[172] See Appendix 4.

[173] The hardness of heart which the Bible frequently attributes to Pharaoh and those around him was evident not merely in unwillingness to acknowledge the one true God and do his bidding, but also in the lack of fellow-feeling, gentleness, mercy, pity,

compassion and kindness that characterised their dealings with those over whom they had power.

174 Under Moses Israel was called to fight physical battles. By contrast, in the New Testament era St Paul counsels that "The weapons we use in our fight are not the world's weapons but God's powerful weapons, which we use to destroy strongholds. We destroy false arguments; we pull down every proud obstacle that is raised against the knowledge of God; we take every thought captive and make it obey Christ." (2 Corinthians 10:4-5, GNT). Jesus told Pilate, "My kingdom is not of this world. If it were, my servants would fight to prevent my arrest by the Jews. But now my kingdom is from another place." (John 18:36).

175 The Philistines early on showed their vindictive nature, for "[they] envied [Isaac, and as a result] ... all the wells ... dug in the time of ... Abraham, the Philistines stopped up, filling them with earth." (Genesis 26:15). They were an ungodly people, worshipping idols such as "Dagon their god" (Judges 16:23) and "[practising] divination" (Isaiah 2:6). Later conflict with this tribe came about because the Israelites neglected to carry out the Lord's commands to the letter, for "all the regions of the Philistines" (Joshua 13:2) were amongst those "very large areas of land [still] to be taken over" (Joshua 13:1) at the death of Joshua. As a result of this failure, subsequent generations suffered grievously.

176 It is never God's desire that his people should be helpless in the face of adversity, for he wishes us to use the abilities and resources he has given, not throw up our hands in despair. He chided Moses, "Why are you crying out to me? Tell the Israelites to move on. Raise your staff and stretch out your hand over the sea to divide the water so that the Israelites can go through the sea on dry ground." (Exodus 14:23). The Lord had told the prophet at the outset of his mission to "take this staff in your hand so that you can perform miraculous signs with it." (Exodus 4:17). Moses' obedience to this command and the miraculous happenings which resulted are often in evidence elsewhere (see for example Exodus 10:13-15 and 22-23) so perhaps on this occasion he simply forgot himself in the heat of the moment.

177 Despite these shortcomings, they were still an army even at this point, for they are called the Lord's divisions (see Exodus 6:26, 7:4, 12:17, 12:41 and 12:51) and "Israel's army" (Exodus 14:19; and see also Deuteronomy 20:1, 20:2, 20:5 and 20:9). Israel's faintness of heart on this occasion was redeemed by her courage in confronting the Amalekites (Exodus 17:8-16).

178 Computer modelling by scientists at the National Center for Atmospheric Research in Boulder, Colorado suggests that a powerful wind could have divided the stretch of water that the Israelites crossed. They concluded that the event was likely to have taken place at a spot in the Nile delta. Analysis of archaeological records, satellite data and maps allowed estimates of water flow and depth at the site three thousand years ago. A computer programme then simulated the effect of strong overnight winds in such an environment, showing that an easterly wind of 63mph blowing for twelve hours over waters six feet deep would have driven these back in two directions, creating a land

bridge about two miles long and three miles wide. The sea would indeed have been parted, with barriers of water raised on either side of newly exposed mud flats.

[179] Exodus 14 shows human choices freely made intersecting with the settled purposes of God. Pharaoh was far from being a victim of an uncaring deity making cynical use of human beings to prove a point. The king acted without let or hindrance, unconstrained by outside force, but his rashness, imperviousness to every demonstration of the sovereignty and power of Israel's God, readiness to ignore all moral restraint and conviction of easy victory against civilians or untrained levies made sure his army's destruction.

[180] See Appendix 2 for discussion of population figures. In the choice of a select few rather than all able-bodied men, there are echoes of Gideon, who took only three hundred against the entire host of Midian (see Judges 7:1-22).

[181] Such as the "thousands, hundreds, fifties and tens" (Exodus 18:21) over whom Jethro advised Moses to appoint officials.

[182] It does not strain credibility to imagine that this was within the wit and ability of those involved. Fairly recent history provides a parallel to the career of Joshua for, like him, the "Black Napoleon" Toussaint L'Ouverture (1743-1803) was a former slave with no military training who proved a natural general. His campaigns won freedom for the slaves of Saint Domingue (a French colony on the Caribbean island of Hispaniola) and led ultimately to creation of Haiti as an independent state. Moses' probable experience before quitting Egypt in peril of his life at the age of forty is described in note 14.

[183] Once again the sureness of God's provision and timing is evident. The months during which Egypt was racked by the Ten Plagues would have provided an opportunity for the Israelites to organise and prepare for their coming freedom.

[184] Rephidim means spreading or support. Moses' hands were spread in prayer and supported by Aaron and Hur.

[185] Ten Plagues mirror Ten Commandments, ten being a number of completeness or perfection. The fact that such horrors were visited on Egypt was neither disproportionate nor unfair (see note 56). As to the cause of such happenings, the sceptic cannot have it both ways; it is illogical to deny miracles as David Hume did on the basis that they involve "transgression of a law of nature by a particular volition of the Deity, or by the interposition of some invisible agent" whilst at the same time asserting that there was no miracle because no natural law was broken. Whatever means God used to bring them about, that they were miracles is stressed by the extreme nature even of those that might have seemed most natural in origin and the repeated exemption of Israel from harm (see Exodus 8:2-4, 14, 16-17 and 21-22, 9:18 and 23-26, 10:4-6 and 21).

[186] The Egyptian year was divided into three four-month phases: Akhet (from June 15 to October 15), the season of flood; Peret (from October 15 to February 15), the season for sowing; and Shemu (from February 15 to June 15, the end of the Egyptian year), the season of harvest, also known as the season of the great heat. There is any number of natural events that might cause abnormally high temperatures. Volcanic explosions, for

example, are well known for disrupting usual weather patterns, the massive eruptions on Iceland in 1783 being but one example.

[187] For example, the Tumbu fly (prevalent in much of sub-Saharan Africa and occasionally found further north) causes painful boils on humans and can bring about death in animals. It lays its eggs in sandy soil.

[188] The insects usually avoid each other, but harsh circumstances (such as drought) can trigger swarms by causing a sharp increase in levels of the neurotransmitter serotonin in their bodies.

[189] Some conjecture that the killing of the firstborn resulted from harvested grain being stored wet and contaminated with locust droppings, making it fertile ground for the growing of toxic bacteria. The supposition is that only the firstborn would have been killed since the bacteria would have affected just the upper level of the granary and the eldest would have been fed first. The solution is neat, but perhaps too much so. Whatever the mechanism that may have been used, Scripture says that the killing was carried out by a "destroyer" (Exodus 12:23) or "band of destroying angels" (Psalm 78:49). It has been suggested that "firstborn" in this context would be better rendered as "the chosen [or, the flower] of Egypt" (see note 445).

[190] The military consequences of God's blessing being removed are seen in the second confrontation with the Amalekites that is described in Numbers 14:43-45 and in the ill-fated attempt to enter the Promised Land without divine authorisation recounted in Numbers 14:39-45.

[191] Jesus made the same point when he said that "Whoever does God's will is my brother and sister and mother" (Mark 3:35) and "He who is not with me is against me." (Luke 11:23).

[192] These verses contain promises of assistance and blessing but are also a call from God as Israel's commander for military discipline. Hence the need to "Pay attention" (await orders), "Do not rebel" (avoid mutiny) and "listen carefully" (obey all commands). If Israel does these things, then God "will be an enemy to your enemies and will oppose those who oppose you." (Exodus 23:22). For fuller discussion of these verses, see chapter 17 of *Redeeming a Nation* by this author.

[193] This plundering of the enemy was so important that God twice reminded Moses about it (see Exodus 3:21-22 and 11:2-3). It was necessary both to complete the humiliation of the Egyptian gods and to provide resources that would be needed to build the tabernacle and its accoutrements, as well as to provide for the Israelites in their desert wanderings.

[194] Abraham set the example of devoting a proportion of the spoils of battle to the Lord's service after he rescued Lot and "gave [the priest Melchizedek] ... a tenth of all" (Genesis 14:20, GNT) he had taken from the enemy.

[195] This does not mean that he was never assailed by doubt. One of his sons "was named Gershom, for Moses said, 'I have become an alien in a foreign land'" (Exodus 18:4), suggesting a spiritual low point when this boy was born. Neither of his children's names

referred to YHWH, for at the time they were born Moses had not yet encountered God on Horeb.

[196] The remaining four were (1) the *Ka*, a spirit double created at birth which resembled its owner physically; (2) the *Ba*, representing the impersonal life force in all living things; (3) the Shadow, without which in a land of brilliant sunshine no man could exist, and was thus deemed to have an existence of its own; and (4) the Name, remembrance and repetition of which ensured that the life of the deceased would be perpetuated.

[197] Far from putting himself on anything approaching a par with God, Moses was constantly at pains to downplay the role which he and his family played. Scripture shows repeatedly that he was punctilious about relaying God's commands to the people accurately (see for example Exodus 11:4-6, 13:3-16, 19:14-15 and 25, and 35:1-35). He was thus thoroughly justified in telling the disgruntled Israelites, "In the evening you will know that it was the LORD who brought you out of Egypt, and in the morning you will see the glory of the LORD, because he has heard your grumbling against him. Who are we, that you should grumble against us? … Who are we? You are not grumbling against us but against the LORD." (Exodus 16:6-8).

[198] The later form of Aten's name translates as something like "Ra, ruler of the twin horizons, who rejoices in the horizon in his name as Ra the father who returns as Aten."

[199] A cartouche is an oval-shaped loop that hitherto had been used exclusively to encircle royal names.

[200] Doubt as to whether Akhenaten was an out and out monotheist reflects conflicting evidence, though suppression of the plural form of the word for god is a strange step to take if he were not. The same applies to replacement of the kingly title "the Good God" (which had been used in previous reigns) with "the Good Ruler". Only a compelling theological motivation would seem to provide the incentive for this to be done by someone who otherwise was so keen to stress royal dignity.

[201] A description given to the Almighty in Daniel 2:29 and 2:47, on the first occasion by the prophet and then by the pagan king Nebuchadnezzar. The latter was brought to exclaim, "Surely your God is the God of gods and the Lord of kings and a revealer of mysteries, for you were able to reveal this mystery." (Daniel 2:47).

[202] In this he is the very antithesis of Amun, the One Who Conceals Himself. The Lord has no time for "Satan's so-called deep secrets." (Revelation 2:24). At the end of time there will be "nothing concealed that will not be disclosed, or hidden that will not be made known." (Matthew 10:26, Mark 4:22, Luke 8:17 and Luke 12:2). Then there will be renewed human fellowship with our Maker, when "the dwelling of God is with men, and he will live with them." (Revelation 21:3).

[203] *El Shaddai* might perhaps also be rendered as, "God, the Mountain One", an appellation that both ascribes loftiness and power and at the same time reflects the fact that mountains are the symbolic home of God. Many biblical events of great spiritual importance occur on mountains. These represent a halfway point between heaven and earth and as such are an interface between divine and corporeal, sacred and profane,

mortal and immortal, created and uncreated. Happenings of special significance include the aborted sacrifice of Isaac on Mount Moriah (Genesis 22), the revelation of God's name to Moses (Exodus 3:6), the giving of the Ten Commandments (Exodus 20:1-19), Elijah's stand against the 450 prophets of Baal (1 Kings 18:16-46), his later encounter with God in a "gentle whisper" (1 Kings 19:12), the Sermon on the Mount (Matthew 5-7) and the Transfiguration of Jesus (Matthew 17:1-13 and Mark 9:1-13).

204 Yahweh, the personal name of the God of Abraham, Isaac and Jacob, is represented in Hebrew by the tetragrammaton ("four letters") יהוה *(Yod Heh Vav Heh)*, transliterated into Roman script as *Y H W H* and seemingly connected with the old Semitic root הוה *(hawah)* meaning "to be" or "to become". Since Jews had such a high view of the majesty of God and were wary of inadvertently committing blasphemy by misusing his name, in place of Yahweh they used *Adonai*, meaning Lord. The four letters of the divine name were only written and never spoken, except by the High Priest once a year on the Day of Atonement, resulting in the original pronunciation being lost.

205 *Yod* stands for the transcendent: that divine inspiration which, though always above the physical world, does not keep aloof from Creation. It carries with it at the same time ideas of engagement and activation, since its cognate *yad* (meaning "hand") intimates expression of the will and thought turned to deed. The divine name thus pictures God as being by nature not static, but active. *Yod* is used for the male (third person singular) imperfect verbal form, thereby indicating its role as initiator, since classical Jewish thinking regards the male as the instigator of action.

206 In Hebrew *heh* is the definite article ("the"), this being a determiner that restricts or particularises a noun. In doing so it mirrors the function of the female element in creation, taking the creative impetus and channelling it towards a given form or means of expression. Scripture hints at the maternal aspects of God on several occasions, for he tells his people, "Can a woman forget her nursing child, And not have compassion on the son of her womb? Surely they may forget, Yet I will not forget you." (Isaiah 49:15, NKJV) and promises that "As a mother comforts her child, so will I comfort you" (Isaiah 66:13). Jesus likewise exclaimed, "O Jerusalem, Jerusalem, you who kill the prophets and stone those sent to you, how often I have longed to gather your children together, as a hen gathers her chicks under her wings, but you were not willing." (Matthew 23:37 and Luke 13:34).

207 The word *vav* means "a hook" and the letter *vav* is used as the conjunctive "and".

208 Though the shape of the letters in the Jewish alphabet has changed somewhat over time, the grammatical association of particular letters with masculine or feminine is a constant. Changes in form could in any event be seen as representing a better or fuller understanding, just as our concept of God has developed between Old and New Testament times.

209 It is the Spirit of God that animates and gives life to man, as language itself emphasises, for the Hebrew word for breath (*ruach*) is the same as that used for the Spirit of God. Language also alludes to the Trinitarian nature of our Creator, for the plural

"we" is used on the first occasion in the Bible on which the Almighty speaks of himself: "Then God said, 'Let us make man in our image, in our likeness'" (Genesis 1:26).

210 We may surmise that the initial moment of Creation was preceded by aeons of consideration, discussion and planning amongst the three persons of the Trinity, between whom there has always been and forever will be an eternity of loving fellowship. This period is symbolised by *alef*, the (silent) first letter of the Hebrew alphabet. (The first word of the Bible in Hebrew is *bereshith*, meaning "in the beginning". It starts with *bet*, the second letter of the Hebrew alphabet, suggesting that *aleph* must have come before it. The fact that aleph is silent reinforces the idea that God is primarily to be found in silence – hence the "sound of sheer silence" – 1 Kings 19:12, NRSV – encountered by Elijah and the need to "search [our] hearts and be silent" – Psalm 4:4.)

211 The appearance of three visitors to Abraham (Genesis 18) seems to have involved his seeing the second person of the Trinity. The same might also be said of the occasion when Jacob wrestled with God (Genesis 32:22-32).

212 The activity of the Trinity is seen in the work of Creation itself. God the Father spoke the creative words which brought the universe into being (Genesis 1:3, 6, 9, 11, 14, 20, 24 and 26), God the Son carried out these creative decrees (John 1:3) and the Holy Spirit sustained and manifested the presence of God in Creation (Genesis 1:2). The role of the second person of the Trinity in this process is hinted at in the opening letter *bet* of the Hebrew Bible. This may be translated as "in" but might also be rendered as "with" or "by means of" – hence "in the beginning" but equally "by means of a beginning".

213 Scripture says that "inwardly we are being renewed day by day" (2 Corinthians 4:16).

214 St Paul seems to be speaking of celibacy when he said, "I would prefer that all of you were as I am" (1 Corinthians 7:7, GNT). Be that as it may, that men and women are complimentary rather than designed to be entirely separate is emphasised by the fact that the Lord "made a woman from the rib he had taken out of [Adam]" (Genesis 2:22).

215 The depth of significance in lifelong faithful union of man and woman in marriage is further emphasised by the fact that the Church (the worldwide fellowship of believers) is the Bride of Christ. St Paul addresses precisely this: "(None of us ever hate our own bodies. Instead, we feed them, and take care of them, just as Christ does the church; for we are members of his body.) As the scripture says, 'For this reason a man will leave his father and mother and unite with his wife, and the two will become one.' There is a deep secret truth revealed in this scripture, which I understand as applying to Christ and the church." (Ephesians 5:29-32, GNT).

216 The Hebrew for mist (*'aid*) is composed of the first two letters of the word for man (*adam*). To transform *'aid* to *adam* involves adding the letter *mem*, which symbolises water. *Mem* also conveys the number forty, which stands for purification and subsequent renewal in a higher state. The number forty is of great significance in the Bible: before the Flood it rained for forty days and forty nights (Genesis 7:12); Moses was forty years old when he killed the Egyptian and fled to Midian (Acts 7:23-24) and a further forty years passed before God called him to return and free his people from bondage (Acts

7:30); Joshua was forty when Moses sent him to spy out the land of Canaan (Joshua 14:7); God miraculously provided for Israel through forty years of desert wandering (Exodus 16:1-35); Jesus fasted for forty days and nights in the wilderness (Matthew 4:2) and ascended to heaven forty days after his resurrection (Acts 1:3 and 9). There are many other examples.

217 Genesis 1 repeats the phrases, "And God said" and "Let there be …" or its variant "Let the …" (Genesis 1:3, 6, 9, 11, 14, 20 and 24). These are biblical ways of expressing the active male orientation, conveying the idea of creation out of nothing and depicting the initial dynamism of the creative imperative and its development through discrete stages (days). Genesis 1 focuses on the concrete nature of things and their outer form, whereas Genesis 2 emphasises inner qualities and potential. The pivot between the two viewpoints is the statement, "This is the account of the heavens and the earth when they were created." (Genesis 2:4). In Hebrew the phrase "when they were created" (Genesis 2:4) is *be-hibar'am*, an anagram of the name *'Avraham* (Abraham). When God told the patriarch, "No longer will you be called Abram; your name will be Abraham" (Genesis 17:5), this required addition of the (feminine) letter *heh*. To make Abraham whole and enable him to reach his full potential, God had to put his own (feminine) presence in him.

218 John Bunyan observed, "I read not that ever any man did give unto Christ so much as one groat, but the women followed him and ministered to him of their substance. 'Twas a woman that washed his feet with tears, and a woman that anointed his body to the burial. They were women that wept when he was going to the cross; and women that followed him from the cross and that sat by his sepulchre when he was buried. They were women that were first with him at his resurrection-morn; and women that brought tidings first to his disciples that he was risen from the dead. Women therefore are highly favoured …" (*Pilgrim's Progress from this world to the next*).

219 Islam takes a very different stance towards women. Amongst other things, it requires evidence from two women to equal that from one man, thereby implying that a female has only half the worth of a male.

220 The Second Law of Thermodynamics states that any physical system becomes less ordered and more random over time.

221 The last book of the Bible speaks of a "time [that] has come for judging the dead, and for rewarding [God's] servants the prophets and [his] saints and those who reverence [his] name, both small and great" (Revelation 11:18). The importance of reverence in all our outward actions is emphasised by St Paul; it should lead to our "perfecting holiness out of reverence for God" (2 Corinthians 7:1), "submitting to one another in the fear of God" (Ephesians 5:21, NKJV) and "obey[ing our] earthly masters … with sincerity of heart and reverence for the Lord" (Colossians 3:22).

222 This is the first time the word 'miracle' occurs in the Bible, though by no means the first occasion that God's miraculous activity is seen amongst men. The implication of the king of Egypt's approach is that miracles evidence God's presence and activity and thus are a way by which he may be recognised. This is true as far as it goes, since God can and

assuredly does work miracles, but needs to be treated with caution for two reasons: firstly because "A wicked and adulterous generation asks for a miraculous sign" (Matthew 12:39) in ways that amount to putting God to the test; and secondly because of the "counterfeit miracles, signs and wonders" (2 Thessalonians 2:9) which Satan is capable of producing, counterfeit in this context meaning not bogus but producing false impressions.

[223] Whilst it is Moses' mother who appears as the prime actor in the unfolding drama, her husband could not have failed to know what was going on, and would certainly have risked punishment for aiding and abetting her crime.

[224] "Now the LORD spoke to Moses and Aaron about the Israelites and Pharaoh king of Egypt, and he commanded them to bring the Israelites out of Egypt … They were the ones who spoke to Pharaoh king of Egypt about bringing the Israelites out of Egypt. It was the same Moses and Aaron [as mentioned in the immediately preceding genealogy]." (Exodus 6:13 and 27).

[225] It is difficult to know if it was merely a conventional expression when Jethro said, "Praise be to the LORD, who rescued you from the hand of the Egyptians and of Pharaoh, and who rescued the people from the hand of the Egyptians" (Exodus 18:10). Moses certainly gave him grounds to be genuine in glorifying the one true God, for "Jethro … heard of everything God had done for Moses and for his people Israel, and how the LORD had brought Israel out of Egypt." (Exodus 18:1).

[226] Later she returned to her husband, for "Jethro … together with Moses' sons and wife, came to him in the desert … Jethro sent word to him, 'I, your father-in-law Jethro, am coming to you with your wife and her two sons." (Exodus 18:5-6). Relations at that stage seem to have been perfectly cordial, for "Moses went out to meet his father-in-law and bowed down and kissed him. They greeted each other and then went into the tent." (Exodus 18:7). Ancient Near Eastern conventions of hospitality and propriety are on display here (as in Exodus 2:18 and 20), but there seems also to have been genuine warmth between the men, as evidenced by Jethro's enthusiastic response to what Moses told him.

[227] Similar injunctions towards fair and equal treatment of outsiders are often repeated throughout Scripture, a testament to our readiness to take advantage of those who are different or subordinate. The Israelites were told, "Do not oppress an alien; you yourselves know how it feels to be aliens, because you were aliens in Egypt" (Exodus 23:9) and "Six days do your work, but on the seventh day do not work, so that your ox and your donkey may rest and the slave born in your household, and the alien as well, may be refreshed." (Exodus 23:12).

[228] Or perhaps the life of one her sons (most probably the firstborn, Gershom); the grammar of the original Hebrew means that it is not possible to say for sure whether "him" in Exodus 4:24 and 26 refers to Moses or his son.

[229] This passage is significant, but obscure. That there is more to it than meets the eye is clear from the statement that "At that time [Zipporah] said 'bridegroom of blood',

referring to circumcision" (Exodus 4:26), implying that a more profound meaning later became evident. Comparison with the Lord's later warning to Israel that "you are a stiff-necked people and I might destroy you on the way" (Exodus 33:3) brings to mind God's holiness in the face of our unrighteousness, but Moses and his son were perhaps also a prefiguring of the coming Passover. The importance of circumcision and its relationship to Passover is repeatedly emphasised: "If a foreigner has settled among you and wants to celebrate Passover to honor the LORD, you must first circumcise all the males of his household. He is then to be treated like a native-born Israelite and may join in the festival. The same regulations apply to native-born Israelites and to foreigners who settle among you." (Exodus 12:48-49, GNT). Passover in turn points to the atoning sacrifice of Jesus. If the Church is the Bride of Christ, then he is the Bridegroom – a bridegroom of blood indeed.

[230] Although the elders' presence during the interview with Pharaoh is not specifically mentioned, they must have been there since "Moses and Aaron did just as the LORD commanded them" (Exodus 7:6, 10 and 20).

[231] Akhenaten and Nefertiti had at least six daughters who survived beyond infancy, these being Meritaten (*Beloved by Aten*), Meketaten (*Protected by Aten*), Ankhesenpaaten (*She lives through Aten*), Neferneferuaten (*Perfection of Aten*), Neferneferue (*Perfection of Ra*) and Setepenre (*Chosen of Ra*).

[232] The fact that sons were not featured in carvings and inscriptions of the Amarna period does not necessarily mean that Akhenaten had none. The relationship of a pharaoh to his male progeny was theologically awkward because the living king was identified with Horus, who could only claim his throne from the dead king, identified with Osiris (see chapter 10). As a result, though daughters were often shown assisting at festivals and religious ceremonies, sons were deliberately kept out of the limelight.

[233] It sits oddly with the pharaoh at the same time being shown in a body that is so unusual, if the intention behind this was to display a creature that was otherworldly.

[234] The dislocation this involved must have been massive. If 60,000 were moved to the new city, this would represent 2% of a population of 3,000,000, proportionally equivalent to shifting over a million people in modern Britain. They would have needed to start their lives from scratch in a previously uninhabited area that offered poor prospects compared to regions with existing infrastructure. Population figures are discussed in Appendix 2.

[235] For example, God says, "Judah has desecrated the sanctuary the LORD loves, by marrying the daughter of a foreign god." (Malachi 2:11). He then draws a parallel with the way in which men should treat their earthly wives: "...the LORD is acting as the witness between you and the wife of your youth, because you have broken faith with her, though she is your partner, the wife of your marriage covenant ... So guard yourself in your spirit, and do not break faith with the wife of your youth." (Malachi 2:14-15).

[236] This is not entirely without precedent. Akhenaten's mother, Queen Tiye, had figured more prominently on monuments than any previous queen or consort bar Hatshepsut (who had ruled as pharaoh in her own right).

[237] At least one of Akhenaten's co-wives (Kiya) is mentioned in official inscriptions. In addition to his having a multiplicity of wives and concubines, there is unproven speculation that this monarch indulged another immoral custom of his ancestors by taking to wife his eldest daughter, Meritaten. Egypt's royal line was traced through the female branch, and several of its deities provided examples of incestuous relationships: the goddess Hathor was both mother and wife of Ra, whilst Isis was sister and wife of Osiris. Pharaohs were thus encouraged to emulate these gods, in the process increasing their chances of having royal offspring and helping maintain the purity of their blood lineage.

[238] *Ma'at* was the opposite of *Isfet* (which stood for chaos, lies and violence). It bound all things in indestructible unity – the natural world, the state and the citizen each being part of a wider order generated by *Ma'at*. Convinced that human behaviour had a direct impact on all existence, ancient Egyptians sought to ensure cosmic harmony and balance through proper conduct in public and religious life. Upsetting *Ma'at* was believed to have consequences for the nation (through natural disaster, defeat in war or other misfortunes) no less than for individuals.

[239] *Pace* Rebecca West in *Black Lamb, Grey Falcon*.

[240] Similar ideas can be found, for example, in the Code of Hammurabi (dating from around 1772 BC, promulgated by the sixth king of Babylon). A stone engraved with Hammurabi's laws was found amongst the ruins of Susa in 1902 by French archaeologist M. J. de Morgan. It is now in the Louvre.

[241] The Code of Hammurabi, for example, depicted that king as receiving laws from the sun-god Shamash.

[242] Scripture shows Moses, Aaron, Miriam and Aaron's sons all receiving some degree of censure or punishment.

[243] The "I AM" (Exodus 3:14) of the Almighty's name is echoed in the statement, "I am the LORD your God who brought you up out of Egypt" (Exodus 20:1), emphasising that God's Law proceeds from his very essence.

[244] The Lord's wish was that he should be King of Israel, which was why the nation was originally ruled by judges and not by earthly potentates. When the elders of Israel asked the ageing Samuel, "…appoint a king to rule over us, so that we will have a king, as other countries have" (1 Samuel 8:5, GNT), God told the prophet, "…You are not the one they have rejected; I am the one they have rejected as their king … give them strict warnings and explain how their kings will treat them." (1 Samuel 8:7-9, GNT). The resulting admonishment neatly summarises the despotic behaviour of kings throughout the ages (see 1 Samuel 8:10-18).

[245] Sabbath observance nevertheless needs to be approached with a sense of proportion. As Jesus observed, "the Sabbath was made to benefit man, and not man to benefit the Sabbath." (Mark 2:27, TLB).

246 The fact that blessing follows obedience is frequently emphasised: "There [by the waters of Elim] the LORD made a decree and a law for them, and there he tested them. He said, 'If you listen carefully to the voice of the LORD your God and do what is right in his eyes, if you pay attention to his commands and keep all his decrees, I will not bring on you any of the diseases I brought on the Egyptians, for I am the LORD, who heals you.'" (Exodus 15:25-26).

247 This is of such importance that "Anyone who attacks his father or his mother must be put to death" (Exodus 21:15) and "Anyone who curses their father or mother must be put to death." (Exodus 21:17).

248 Throughout the four centuries of Israel's sojourn in Egypt the Lord never ceased to be mindful of the promise made "on oath to you and your forefathers" (Exodus 13:11) regarding the "land I promised on oath to Abraham, Isaac and Jacob" (Exodus 33:1). His failure to deliver Israel from bondage earlier reflected neither untrustworthiness nor inattention nor lack of concern, but mercy: before being dispossessed and destroyed, the Amorites were given ample opportunity to repent and change their ways, until eventually "[their] sin … reached its full measure" (Genesis 15:16) and the Lord would stay his hand no longer.

249 In doing so, it emphasised two things: (1) the radical demands of a just and righteous God that his people should also "be holy, because I am holy" (Leviticus 11:44-45, GNT) and "be perfect, even as your heavenly Father is perfect" (Matthew 5:48); and (2) the inability of mankind to meet God's standards through their own efforts, hence their need for a sinless Saviour. Jesus repeatedly drew out the true meaning of the Law, most notably in the Sermon on the Mount (see Matthew 5:17-7:6).

250 There was similar emphasis on thorough compliance in making the tabernacle and its furnishings, with instructions carried out to the letter: as regards ark (Exodus 25:10-20 and 37:1-9), table (Exodus 25:23-29 and 37:10-16), lampstand (Exodus 25:31-39 and 37:17-24), tabernacle (Exodus 26:1-37 and 36:8-38), altar (Exodus 27:1-8 and 38:1-7), courtyard (Exodus 27:9-19 and 38:9-20) and priestly garments (Exodus 28:2-42 and 39:1-31). Just as "Moses and Aaron did as the LORD commanded them" (Exodus 7:6) when they appeared before Pharaoh, so Scripture carefully records that Moses did "as the LORD commanded" (Exodus 40:19, 21, 23, 24, 27, 29 and 32, KJV) at each stage of construction. Sevenfold repetition of this phrase indicates total obedience (seven being the biblical number of completeness or perfection), which gave rise to extraordinary blessing: "And so Moses completed the work. *Then* the cloud covered the Tent of Meeting, and the glory of the LORD filled the tabernacle." (Exodus 40:34, emphasis added).

251 Explaining that "It was only because your hearts were hard that Moses [allowed divorce]" (Mark 10:5), Jesus continued, "No human being must separate, then, what God has joined together." (Mark 10:9, GNT). Correspondingly, the importance of keeping divinely ordained distinctions is emphasised by severe penalties for not doing so. Hence "Anyone who has sexual relations with an animal must be put to death" (Exodus 22:19)

and "Do not mate different kinds of animals. Do not plant your field with two kinds of seeds. Do not wear clothing woven of two kinds of material." (Leviticus 19:19).

[252] To be righteous is to be just, upright and morally good, living in right relationship with others.

[253] The laws relating to property principally involve making restitution (Exodus 22:3, 5, 6, 11, 12 and 14), though in grave cases the wrongdoer was required to "pay back double" (Exodus 22:4, 7 and 9). As well as being a crime against humanity, enslavement of Israel must have involved expropriation, since "the Israelites ... acquired property [in the region of Goshen]" (Genesis 47:27). Compensation or reparation was made at least to some (necessarily inadequate) degree as the Israelites "plundered the Egyptians" (Exodus 12:36) on their eventual departure from the Two Lands.

[254] Those such as the Diggers who argue that Scripture requires the abolition of private property ignore the fact that the command "You shall not steal" (Exodus 20:15) cannot make sense unless there is ownership. Nevertheless, amongst the first Christians, "No-one claimed that any of his possessions were his own, but they shared everything they had" (Acts 4:32), emphasising the radical new standards of behaviour that apply under the New Covenant of love for those who are in Christ and thus are free of the Law.

[255] The requirement for prompt and absolute submission to the will of the one who made us is a necessary result of his being the Creator, the supreme judge and the arbiter of what is right and wrong. Since the call to obey is an outgrowth of such things, declaration of the Almighty's name is a logical starting point from which to demand the dutiful compliance of men, hence: "I am the LORD. Tell the king of Egypt everything I tell you." (Exodus 6:29, GNT). Obedience of God's people is vital in enabling his kingdom purposes to be realised; Abraham was told that "through your offspring all nations on earth will be blessed, *because you have obeyed me.*" (Genesis 22:18, emphasis added, repeated in substantially similar form to Isaac in Genesis 26:4-5).

[256] For example, the Law of Moses makes it clear that none are to be enslaved against their will for generation upon generation (see Exodus 21:2-11).

[257] When Jesus "was transfigured ... there appeared to them Elijah with Moses, who were talking with Jesus." (Mark 9:2 and 9:4, NRSV). Since the latter represented the Law and the former the prophets, presumably they were discussing the ways in which each of these had paved the way for the saving work of Christ.

[258] To a degree Jews look upon the Torah as Christians might view Jesus or the Holy Spirit: as reflecting the face of God on earth, as the blueprint which God used to guide Creation itself, as the agent by which God maintains Creation, as God's revelation to mankind, as a handbook to a spiritually and socially viable society and as the means by which the essence of God's thought is made manifest through human endeavour. This gives an interesting perspective on the fact that "in the beginning was the Word and the Word was with God and the Word was God." (John 1:1). It was this Word who "became flesh and made his dwelling among us" (John 1:14) and Christ "[sustains] all things by his powerful word" (Hebrews 1:3).

259 Torah derives from the Hebrew root *yrh*, meaning to shoot [an arrow] or to teach. This conveys a sense of the Law as a projectile loosed into the distance, pointing beyond immediate horizons and directing man to search whither it leads. Jews see the statement that "God spoke *all* these words" (Exodus 20:1) as indicating that the Almighty also in a sense spoke the answers to future questions about the meaning and application of the Law.

260 Vizier is the modern term for the Seal-bearer of the King (*Khetenu-bity*), the highest-ranking official in the land. From the Fifth Dynasty (c. 2510-2370 BC) onwards the vizier responsible for justice was called the *Priest of Ma'at*, and in later periods judges wore images of the goddess of that name. In addition to their judicial functions, viziers oversaw day-to-day running of the country, kept trade records and supervised regional governors, the civil service, tax collectors, scribes and royal security. Two long-serving viziers each built careers under Amenhotep III and Akhenaten: Aperel (aka Aperia) was Vizier of the North and commander of chariots (bearing the title, *God's Father*), whilst Ramose combined the posts of Vizier of the South and Governor of Thebes. The latter was one of the earliest public figures to convert to the cult of Aten.

261 Though imprisonment was an option, this seems to have been "the place where the king's prisoners were confined" (Genesis 39:20) and thus used sparingly.

262 Spiritually this is quite different from Mediaeval trial by fire or trial by combat, barbarous though these might have been, for there was no attempt in those cases to refer judgment to occult powers. The capricious nature of the Egyptian justice system even in an earlier age is illustrated by the fact that the cupbearer and baker with whom Joseph was incarcerated were imprisoned simply because they had "offended their master, the king of Egypt [and] Pharaoh was angry with [these] two officials" (Genesis 40:1-2). The Bible gives no explanation of why the former was eventually "restored to his position" (Genesis 40:21) whilst the latter was "hanged" (Genesis 40:22, KJV), leaving open the possibility that this, too, was mere whim on the ruler's part.

263 Both the injunction and the reasons for it are expanded on elsewhere: "Don't sacrifice your children in the fires on your altars; and don't let your people practice divination or look for omens or use spells or charms, and don't let them consult the spirits of the dead. The LORD your God hates people who do these disgusting things, and that is why he is driving those nations out of the land as you advance." (Deuteronomy 18:10-12, GNT).

264 Moses' desire to teach in this way was laudable, though the way in which he first went about it was counter-productive. Keeping the people "[standing] round from morning till evening" (Exodus 18:13) whilst he dealt with every case personally was bad for him and for them, as Jethro immediately recognised: "What you are doing is not good. You and these people who come to you will only wear yourselves out." (Exodus 18:18).

265 Even under the Old Covenant of the Law, with its hundreds of burdensome commandments, each person was required both to know and to obey the voice of the Lord (see Exodus 15:26 and 19:5-6 and Deuteronomy 4:29-30, 8:20 and 9:23). The Old Testament contains 613 divine commandments (*mitzvoth*) to Israel.

266 This part of the Law has been oft misunderstood. That it was meant simply to ensure punishment fitted the crime and did not overstep all bounds is shown by Jesus' subsequent clarification in the Sermon on the Mount (see Matthew 5:38-42). The evil which these provisions were designed to address is demonstrated by the reaction of Dinah's brothers to her rape, when they "entered the city without opposition, and slaughtered every man there, … plundered the city … confiscated all the flocks and herds and donkeys … both inside the city and outside in the fields, and took all the women and children, and wealth of every kind." (Genesis 34:25-29, TLB).

267 Since the verb translated as "obey" literally means "hear", the sense of this interchange is that the people commit both to acting in accordance with the will of God and also to studying his Word so as to understand and give effect to it. Through studying Torah, Jews believe that they enter into the very process of creation and revelation.

268 Moses' words were echoed by Jesus when he spoke of "my blood of the covenant" (Matthew 26:28, Mark 14:24) and "the new covenant in my blood" (Luke 22:20).

269 That the issue was one of faith is supported by God's saying, "For this commandment which I command you today is not too mysterious for you, nor is it far off. It is not in heaven, that you should say, 'Who will ascend into heaven for us and bring it to us, that we may hear it and do it?' Nor is it beyond the sea, that you should say, 'Who will go over the sea for us and bring it to us, that we may hear it and do it?' But the word is very near you, in your mouth and in your heart, that you may do it." (Deuteronomy 30:11-14, NKJV). The kind of obedience God is looking for is shown by Moses' careful and detailed compliance with the instructions he was given for setting up the tabernacle (see Exodus 40:1-33).

270 So named because later Greek visitors thought they portrayed the legendary Memnon, supposedly king of Ethiopia and son of Eos, goddess of the dawn. Memnon was said to have been killed by Achilles during the Trojan War. Weighing almost 1,300 tons, the statues are the height of a modern six-storey building.

271 A stela describes the temple as being built from "white sandstone, with gold throughout, a floor covered with silver and doors covered with electrum." Electrum is an alloy of gold and silver. It was especially prized since silver was less plentiful than gold in ancient Egypt, most Egyptian silver having to be imported from mines in Anatolia in modern Turkey. Greek historian and geographer Strabo says that most of the temple fell in an earthquake in 27 BC.

272 Medinet Habu is the name commonly given nowadays to the mortuary temple of Ramses III on the west bank of the Nile at Luxor.

273 Work on the third pylon was continued by Seti I and completed under Ramses II.

274 Under Amenhotep III the Egyptian empire reached its apogee, with a corresponding increase in the nation's belief in her ability to stand against the one true God.

275 Egyptian slaves were not always badly treated, In addition to food and lodging, they received a yearly allowance of oils, clothing and linen, whilst hours of work were reduced

in extreme heat. Since the standard of living was so high in the Two Lands compared to that in surrounding nations, many may have been materially better off than they had been when free. The shortcomings of the Israelites' spiritual perspective are evident in the weight they attached to such benefits.

276 The Law of Moses recognised the possibility that someone might desire to stay indentured even though having the right to claim his liberty: "But if the man shall plainly declare, 'I prefer my master, my wife, and my children, and I would rather not go free,' then his master shall bring him before the judges and shall publicly bore his ear with an awl, and after that he will be a slave forever." (Exodus 21:5-6, TLB).

277 We may infer that it was Moses' increasing experience of the love of God that resulted in one who first "hid his face, because he was afraid to look at God" (Exodus 3:6) within a relatively short time afterwards asking, "Now show me your glory" (Exodus 33:18).

278 Alfred, Lord Tennyson, *The Lotus-eaters*.

279 Each of these alternatives is seen in the differing destinies of the protagonists of Exodus. Israel was (1) set apart to be "a holy nation" (Exodus 19:6); (2) dedicated to the service of God as "a kingdom of priests" (Exodus 19:6); (3) to be kept free of all "the diseases [God] brought on the Egyptians" (Exodus 15:26); (4) made "fruitful" (Exodus 1:7); (5) given abundant "silver and gold and ... clothing ... plundered [from] the Egyptians" (Exodus 12:36); and (6) promised that God would "come to you and bless you" (Exodus 20:24); whereas Egypt was (7) not separated, for "the LORD [made] a distinction between Egypt and Israel" (Exodus 11:7); (8) (for the most part) determined to continue serving false gods, the exception being those who "went up with [Israel out of Egypt]" (Exodus 12:38); (9) beset by diseases of both man and beast (Exodus 9:1-12); (10) left barren with the death of her first-born (Exodus 12:29-30); (11) brought to the edge of starvation as livestock died and the land was progressively "ruined" (Exodus 8:24 and 10:7); and (12) cursed through the judgment that the Lord brought "On all the gods of Egypt" (Exodus 12:12).

280 One consequence of this is that understanding and giving effect to the gospel does not require intelligence or expertise in the way that humans habitually understand these terms. It is so simple that a child can grasp its essentials, yet at the same time so profound that eternity will be insufficient to plumb its depths.

281 Presumably when the people "withdrew from Moses' presence" (Exodus 35:20) this was so that they could discuss matters amongst themselves and decide what to do.

282 There is an element of seasonality to some aspects of service, in that there will be times when one set of attributes is more to the fore than another. This is worth bearing in mind if our own skills are not in demand in quite the way we might wish. Regardless of the season, however, there will always be ways in which we can serve.

283 Pharaoh had an extensive retinue and many servants, but these did not enable him to resist the power of the few ragged men who came before him in the name of the Almighty. In addition to the vizier the other main officers of state were the two Overseers of the Treasury (concerned with reception and allocation of commodities, raw

materials and finished goods, tribute and plunder), Overseer of the Granaries of Upper and Lower Egypt (in charge of harvesting, storage and recording of the wheat and barley crops), Viceroy of Kush (the pharaoh's deputy in Nubia and Lower Sudan as far south as the Fourth Cataract of the Nile) and the First Prophet or High Priest of Amun at Thebes (principal adviser on spiritual matters). Under these came a host of lesser officials including the Chief Steward, Superintendent of Works, Master of the Horse, Scribe of the Recruits, First and Second Heralds, King's Secretary and Butler, together with chamberlains, pages and fan-bearers.

[284] The fact that "The LORD was pleased with Abel and his offering, but he rejected Cain and his offering" (Genesis 4:4-5, GNT) was a consequence of Cain's bringing only "some of his harvest ... [whilst] Abel brought the first lamb born to one of his sheep, killed it, and gave the best parts of it as an offering" (Genesis 4:3-4, GNT). In other words, Abel set apart the very best for God, but Cain was grudging and half-hearted, assuming that he could keep back the best for himself. Thus it was "By faith [that] Abel offered God a better sacrifice than Cain did" (Hebrews 11:3) since faith leads us to be unstinting in our dealings with the Almighty and service of him. Those the Bible commends for such wholeheartedness include Caleb (Numbers 14:24), all who gave towards building of the Temple in Jerusalem (1 Chronicles 29:9) or swore to seek God under King Asa (2 Chronicles 15:15), King Hezekiah (2 Chronicles 31:21) and the early Christian community in Rome (Romans 6:17) – each worthy examples for later generations to emulate and follow.

[285] This is not to have us grovel and cower before him but so that he might bless us, for those who are humble he will "save" (2 Samuel 22:28, Psalm 18:27); them he "guides" (Psalm 25:9), sustains" (Psalm 147:6), "crowns ... with salvation" (Psalm 149:4), and to them he "gives grace" (Proverbs 3:34 and James 4:6, GNT), causing them to "rejoice in the LORD" (Isaiah 29:19). Unless we yield to God's direction and control, we will necessarily experience less blessing than we would otherwise.

[286] The word discipline is related to disciple, which means "follower".

[287] Ananias and Sapphira provide a New Testament parallel (see Acts 5:1-11).

[288] Israel's service of God was (and remains) so important that to prevent it is a capital offence. God told Pharaoh through Moses that "you refused to let [my son] go; so I will kill your firstborn son." (Exodus 4:23).

[289] Perhaps mould on the wood neutralised whatever caused the water to become bitter, though that is pure speculation.

[290] God's abundant provision is also seen in the quail which God "drove ... in from the sea ... [and] ... brought ... down all around the camp to about three feet above the ground, as far as a day's walk in any direction" (Numbers 11:31) and which "came and covered the camp" (Exodus 16:13). This is by no means as far-fetched as it might at first sound. There are many instances both recent and ancient of extraordinary things falling from the sky in large numbers. Random examples include spiders (Santo Antonio da Platina, Brazil, 2012), frogs (Brignoles, France, 1977), cubes of meat (Olympia Springs,

Kentucky, 1876), golf balls (Punta Gorda, Florida, 1969) and worms (Jennings, Louisiana, 2007).

291 The abundance of God's provision is such that the Israelites were even "restrained from bringing more [donations for building of the tabernacle], because what they already had was more than enough to do all the work." (Exodus 36:6-7). See also the restraint on taking more than we need which is recounted in Exodus 16:19-20 and 25-30.

292 This phrase appears in "the song of Moses the servant of God and the song of the Lamb" (Revelation 15:3).

293 Aaron's authority was symbolised by his anointing with oil (see Exodus 40:12-16). To keep control over vassals and allies in Asia the sons of local rulers would be taken to Egypt as young men as hostages for their fathers' good behaviour. They would be brought up with the Egyptian royal children to "serve their lord and stand at the portal of the king". In due course they would be sent back to their homelands having been anointed by the pharaoh himself.

294 The artificial lake symbolised achieving *Ma'at* through creating a harmonious environment and exercising control over nature, whilst cementing diplomatic relations with the Mitanni signified success in foreign policy. The overarching theme was the personal excellence of the king, exemplified by the stability and reach of royal power and its continuous renewal, emphasising the reliability of royal patronage and the benefits that would flow from the recipient's continued loyalty.

295 Isis means "throne" and as a personification of the throne she was an important representation of the king's power. By the New Kingdom she had assimilated many of the roles of Hathor and came to be depicted with the headdress typical of that goddess, comprising cow horns with a sun-disc between them. It is not impossible for the topography of Akhet-aten to have been read in terms of this symbol, thereby bringing royal associations together with those relating to Aten and linking the site with the seat of kingship as well as with worship of Akhenaten's chosen deity. If so, this would doubtless have strengthened the pharaoh's conviction that the site of his new city was divinely ordained.

296 The temple to Horus at Edfu was built on the site where he and his wicked uncle supposedly met in mortal combat.

297 As already observed, these were not the only elements of the old beliefs to survive under the new regime, at least in the opening years of Akhenaten's reign. The name of Aten was initially rendered by reference to other gods, whilst at first the king was content to identify himself and Nefertiti with Shu and Tefnut (see note 101).

298 The public role of a princess seems largely to have ended once her father ceased to occupy the throne. Akhenaten's sisters Satamun, Isis, Henuttaunebu and Nebetah vanished from official monuments after their brother became pharaoh.

299 This desire, evident throughout the Old Testament, is even more clear in the New: Christ's coming was characterised not only by "new teaching"(Mark 1:27) but ushered in

"new tongues" (Mark 16:17), a "new covenant" (Luke 22:20), a "new command" (John 13:34), "new life" (Acts 5:20), service in a "new way" (Romans 7:6, TLB), the opening of "a new and living way" (Hebrews 10:20, NKJV) and "new birth" (1 Peter 1:3, NRSV), all of these presaging "new heavens and a new earth" (2 Peter 3:13, NRSV), "the new Jerusalem" (Revelation 3:12) and "a new song" (Revelation 5:9 and 14:3). Each believer is to be a "new creation" (2 Corinthians 5:17), a "new man" (Ephesians 2:15), to put on a "new self" (Ephesians 4:24 and Colossians 3:10) and will be given "a new name" (Revelation 2:17). This crescendo of renewal culminates in the Lord's triumphal declaration, "I am making everything new!" (Revelation 21:5).

[300] It was against this backdrop that the Lord told Israel, "If you follow my decrees and are careful to obey my commands ... You will still be eating last year's harvest when you *have to move it out to make room for the new.*"(Leviticus 26:3 and 10, emphasis added).

[301] It is important to keep these things in proper perspective, for they are pure grace on our Maker's part. Not only is he sovereign and may do as he pleases but also there is neither right nor basis for any human being to require him to explain himself, as shown by his reply to Job's questioning: "Who is this that darkens my counsel with words without knowledge? Brace yourself like a man; I will question you, and you shall answer me." (Job 38:1).

[302] The Lord does not disrespect or disregard the past. Neither does he go back on his word. Jesus said, "Do not think that I have come to abolish the Law [of Moses] or the Prophets; I have not come to abolish them but to fulfil them. I tell you the truth, until heaven and earth disappear, not the smallest letter, not the least stroke of a pen, will by any means disappear from the Law until everything is accomplished." (Matthew 5:18). By stating that "every teacher of the law who has been instructed about the kingdom of heaven is like the owner of a house who brings out of his storeroom new treasures as well as old" (Matthew 13:52), Christ emphasised that the new does not override the old. Rather, the former complements the latter and vice versa.

[303] We need to tread carefully in approaching one particular characteristic of the Almighty which nowadays carries an overwhelmingly negative connotation. When he commands, "Do not worship any other god, for the LORD, whose name is Jealous, is a jealous god" (Exodus 34:14) this has to be seen in context. Jealousy is part of the language of love, closely linked to God's characterisation of his relationship with Israel as being akin to that between husband and wife. God has the same exclusive right to the devotion and lifelong faithfulness of his people as a spouse has of their partner. This is hardly an unreasonable demand, for in return he gives of himself in greater measure than any human being can fully conceive. The result is that God will neither put up with the rivalry of other claims on his people's affections, nor with unfaithfulness on the part of his beloved. Thus, "Whoever sacrifices to any god other than the LORD must be destroyed." (Exodus 22:20).

[304] An omer "is one tenth of an ephah" (Exodus 16:36), making it a measure roughly equivalent to four pints.

305 In this context, keeping of the Sabbath stands in some degree as a marker for obeying all divine laws.

306 It therefore applies no matter what work may need to be done: "Six days you shall labour, but on the seventh day you shall rest; even during the ploughing season and harvest you must rest." (Exodus 34:21).

307 Love so much encapsulates the divine nature that it is possible to say, "God is love" (1 John 4:8). Though justice requires that sin must be punished, love is still uppermost, hence: "Do I take any pleasure in the death of the wicked? declares the Sovereign LORD. Rather, am I not pleased when they turn from their ways and live?" (Ezekiel 18:23).

308 The Lord is therefore at pains to emphasise how important it is that we should remember these things, hence: "Never forget these commands that I am giving you today. Teach them to your children. Repeat them when you are at home and when you are away, when you are resting and when you are working. Tie them on your arms and wear them on your foreheads as a reminder. Write them on the doorposts of your houses and on your gates." (Deuteronomy 6:6-9, GNT, substantially repeated in Deuteronomy 11:18).

309 Monotheism brings unity, and therefore order, to what is diverse and disparate in a polytheistic schema, with Creation unified in its dependence on a transcendent but immanent God. The Almighty similarly works to integrate the heart, mind and soul of man, such being part of the process by which we are increasingly "conformed to the likeness of [Christ]" (Romans 8:29).

310 With the fundamental distinction that until the death and resurrection of Jesus sin was merely covered over by the Old Testament system of animal sacrifice. Only the once-and-for-all atonement of Christ's shed blood dealt with sin for all time and led to victory over death.

311 Israel was told not to forget "the things your eyes have seen" (Deuteronomy 4:9, NKJV), "the covenant of the LORD your God which He made with you" (Deuteronomy 4:23, NKJV), "the covenant of your fathers" (Deuteronomy 4:31, NKJV), "the LORD who brought you out of the land of Egypt, from the house of bondage" (Deuteronomy 6:12, NKJV) and "the LORD your God" (Deuteronomy 8:11, NKJV). There are in addition three warnings: of prosperity causing pride and leading people to forget God (Deuteronomy 8:14), of destruction in the event of forgetting the Almighty and following false gods (Deuteronomy 8:19) and of the need "not [to] forget how [Israel] provoked the LORD your God to wrath in the wilderness." (Deuteronomy 9:7, NKJV).

312 Joshua was in due course to lead Israel across the Jordan into the Promised Land, directing the campaigns that delivered the greater portion of Canaan to the Twelve Tribes by the time of his death. He was divinely chosen to succeed Moses, for God told Moses, "Take Joshua son of Nun, a man in whom is the spirit, and lay your hand on him." (Numbers 27:18). Acting first as the prophet's "assistant" (Exodus 24:13 and 33:11), he proved his outstanding military and leadership ability against the Amalekites (Exodus 17:8-13), becoming Moses' right-hand man and trusted companion. So much so that

"Moses set out with Joshua his assistant, and ... went up on the mountain of God" (Exodus 24:13), even though the people "trembled with fear ... [and] stayed at a distance" (Exodus 20:18). Joshua evidently stayed on the mountain throughout the forty days of Moses' sojourn there, since "when [he] heard the noise of the people shouting, he said to Moses, 'There is the sound of war in the camp'" (Exodus 32:17) and Moses had to correct his misapprehension. Joshua's bravery and godliness were in further evidence when he became one of the twelve spies sent to scout out Canaan (Numbers 13:1-13). Above all, he was eager for the things of God, lingering in the divine presence for as long as possible; when "Moses would return to the camp [from the Tent of Meeting] ... his young assistant Joshua son of Nun did not leave the tent." (Exodus 33:11).

[313] A memorial was also set up after the battle against the Amalekites: "Moses built an altar and called it The LORD is my Banner. He said, 'For hands were lifted up to the throne of the LORD.'" (Exodus 17:15-16). In Jewish thought, raising two hands with outstretched fingers symbolises acceptance of Torah and the furtherance of its role in uniting heaven and earth through the intermediary of human consciousness. It is a symbol both of submission to God and a plea for his intervention.

[314] The pharaoh and his chief queen deputised for Amun and Mut in consummating afresh the latter pair's Sacred Marriage. For this purpose they spent some days in seclusion in the Harem of the South before returning to Karnak with their divine companions, whilst all the while the people feasted.

[315] From the time of Amenhotep III, the journey was often made by boat. The statue of Amun-Ra would stop at the temples of Mut and Khons to collect images of those deities, all three idols then being taken to the quayside for embarking aboard splendidly bedecked barges. Gangs of men hauling on papyrus ropes dragged these vessels upstream, accompanied by an honour guard of chariots and infantry with guidons and pennants aflutter.

[316] Together with the Feasts of Trumpets (Leviticus 23:23-25) and tabernacles (Leviticus 23:33-38), these make seven major festivals mandated by Scripture. In addition, there were New Moon festivals (Numbers 10:10) plus feasts once every seven years to mark Sabbath years (Exodus 23:10-11) and once every fifty years to mark Jubilees (Leviticus 25:8-55). On top of these, there were various celebrations of human devising, including Purim (marking the frustration of Haman's plan to kill all Jews during the reign of Xerxes; Esther 9:18-32) and Hanukkah (on the anniversary of the Maccabees' rededication of the Jerusalem Temple after its desecration under Antiochus IV). The Feast of Trumpets was a one-day celebration, whereas the Feast of tabernacles took place over eight days.

[317] Also called the Feast of Weeks (Exodus 34:22) since it took place seven weeks after Passover, this was the feast which in the Christian calendar is called Pentecost. Stipulations relating to the pilgrim feasts were sufficiently important for them to be repeated in substantially similar wording in Exodus 34:18-23.

[318] The month of *Abib* (later also called *Nisan*) is equivalent to modern mid-March to mid-April. It therefore fell in the Egyptian harvest season of *Shemu*.

319 The joyfulness which God wishes to see at his feasts is of a different order from the indulgence, excess and "revelry" (Exodus 32:6 and 1 Corinthians 10:7; see also Colossian 2:23) that habitually mark pagan celebrations.

320 Obedience to divine command invariably blesses the giver every bit as much as the receiver, though often in ways that we are not able to see or appreciate fully at the time. The Israelites may quite conceivably have known that leaving land fallow allows soil to regain moisture and thus increases its productivity in succeeding years. It is, however, most unlikely that they knew it also helps break the lifecycle of insects such as locusts (which have a seven-year cycle). Letting land lie fallow does not of itself add nutrients back to the soil. Before the advent of modern fertilisers, this required crop rotation of the kind pioneered in England by 'Turnip' Townshend (1674-1738).

321 Just outside the temple entrance was the last of these six lay-bys, which was subsequently entirely rebuilt by Ramses II and enclosed within his new courtyard.

322 God authorised Moses if need be to go even further: "If in spite of these two miracles they still will not believe you, and if they refuse to listen to what you say, take some water from the Nile and pour it on the ground. The water will turn into blood." (Exodus 4:9, GNT). This was a foretaste of the first plague (the plague of blood), when "The LORD said to Moses, 'Tell Aaron, 'Take your staff and stretch out your hand over the waters of Egypt – over the streams and canals, over the ponds and all the reservoirs' – and they will turn to blood. Blood will be everywhere in Egypt, even in the wooden buckets and stone jars.'" (Exodus 7:19). The authenticity of the biblical account is frequently evidenced by its incidental details, such as the comment that during the first plague "all the Egyptians dug along the Nile to get drinking water, because they could not drink the water of the river." (Exodus 7:24). The sand along the river bank would have acted as a filtration system, allowing potable water to be extracted. Exodus 12:34 similarly bears the mark of eyewitness description.

323 God also told Moses that "Pharaoh will refuse to listen to you – *so that* my wonders may be multiplied in Egypt." (Exodus 11:9, emphasis added). It was the Egyptian king's very disobedience that set the stage for the Almighty to display his power in greater and greater measure.

324 It is noteworthy that in this verse the blood of the Passover lamb is said to have been a sign for Israel, not for God or for the "destroyer" (Exodus 12:23) sent by him to smite Egypt. Nevertheless, the Lord went on to say that, "he [God] will see the blood on the top and sides of the door-frame and will pass over that doorway, and he will not permit the destroyer to enter your houses and strike you down." (Exodus 12:23).

325 Simultaneous references to the six days of Creation and the Sabbath day (to be found in Exodus 20:12 and many times subsequently) have a bearing on whether the former were, like the latter, days of twenty-four hours. In *Genesis and the Big Bang*, Dr Gerald L. Schroeder suggests there is no discrepancy between the six days of Creation spoken of by the Bible and the age of the universe currently indicated by cosmology (fifteen billion years or more). He reaches this conclusion by comparing the estimated age of the universe based on the space-time coordinates that presently exist on earth with those that

would have applied when looking forward from a point in time and space near to the first moments after the Big Bang. According to the Theory of Relativity, time varies from place to place depending on conditions such as gravity and velocity, so that a day experienced at this point as lasting for twenty-four hours would from our standpoint seem longer. Since expansion of the universe had the effect of stretching time, a doubling in size corresponding to a halving of time, he calculates that to us the first day would appear to last eight billion years, the second four billion, the third two billion, the fourth one billion, the fifth half a billion and the sixth a quarter billion, totalling 15.75 billion years.

[326] Earlier, Moses had been told, "And when you come into the land that the Lord will give you, just as he promised, and when you are celebrating the Passover, and your children ask, 'What does all this mean? What is this ceremony about?' you will reply, 'It is the celebration of Jehovah's passing over us, for he passed over the homes of the people of Israel, though he killed the Egyptians; he passed over our houses and did not come in to destroy us.'" (Exodus 12:25-27, TLB).

[327] Likewise God performed "miraculous signs … that you may tell your children and grandchildren how I dealt harshly with the Egyptians and how I performed my signs among them, and that you may know that I am the LORD." (Exodus 10:1-2).

[328] In Christian usage the Festival of Weeks became Pentecost. The former (representing in physical terms the fruitfulness of the Old Covenant) falls seven weeks after Passover since the Law was given seven weeks after leaving Egypt. The latter falls seven weeks after the death and resurrection of Christ, and represents the spiritual fruitfulness of the New Covenant.

[329] The world to which Egyptians believed they would return was called the Field of Reeds. It was conceived as an idealised form of Egypt, with tranquil waterways, verdant fields and abundant crops, plentiful food and reunion with loved ones. The ancient Egyptian word for reeds (*iaru* or *ialu*) has been suggested as the inspiration for the Elysian fields of the Greeks.

[330] Though this was the scheme that Amenhotep III inherited, under him the solar court at the royal temple in Thebes was built quite differently, being made open to the sun instead of enclosed. In this it harked back to earlier solar temples that had been raised in honour of Ra and was a foretaste of what was to come under Akhenaten, whose novel style and method of temple building is described in chapter 5.

[331] When Jacob died, "Joseph directed the physicians in his service to embalm his father Israel. So the physicians embalmed him, taking a full forty days, for that was the time required for embalming. And the Egyptians mourned him seventy days." (Genesis 50:3). It is not clear whether Joseph was also embalmed, though when the Israelites left Egypt "Moses took the bones of Joseph with him because Joseph had made the sons of Israel swear an oath [to that effect]." (Exodus 13:19).

[332] There was in fact no single Book of the Dead. Instead, a number of different versions of the tomb prayers have survived, with evidence that these were tailored to the means

and status of individuals. What we nowadays collectively call the Book of the Dead contains no synthesis of traditions and hence no single, consistent theology is expressed in its various versions. The major aim of the dead was to meet Osiris, become one with him and enter his following. The dead also wished to go aboard the barque of the sun god Ra and take part in his eternal journeys, by which the life force of humanity was renewed.

333 Indeed, sin means that "all of creation groans with pain, like the pain of childbirth" (Romans 8:22, GNT). Yet "the Spirit helps us in our weakness [and] … intercedes with sighs too deep for words." (Romans 8:26, NRSV).

334 Moses had "watched [the Israelites] at their hard labour" (Exodus 2:11). Though not personally enslaved in the sense of being "worked ruthlessly" (Exodus 1:13) and put to "hard labour in brick and mortar and with all kinds of work in the fields" (Exodus 1:14), he was appallingly treated nevertheless – wrenched from his family at a young age and forcibly adopted into an alien culture. It would have been astounding had these and other early experiences not left deep psychological scars. The fact that "Moses named [his son] Gershom, saying, 'I have become an alien in a foreign land'" (Exodus 2:22) shows the extent to which he came to share many of his people's trials and emotions. Certainly, he would readily have been able to identify with those who, like him, were "strangers in a land that is not theirs" (Genesis 15:13, NRSV).

335 Jewish thought sees circumcision as opening a rich channel of communication between earth and heaven. That puts an interesting slant on Moses being described as having "faltering [literally, uncircumcised] lips" (Exodus 6:12 and 30), since it opens the possibility that he might have been so deeply in touch with higher things that it was difficult for him to relate easily to those who remained earthbound, hence his need for Aaron as spokesman. These two together acted as a bridge between man and God, with Moses' gaze directed heavenward and Aaron's to more mundane or practical concerns.

336 To be blameless requires moral integrity, not sinless perfection. The reliability of God's promises is seen in how seriously he takes them. He repeatedly referred back to his covenant undertakings by way of showing that he kept these in mind and was determined to fulfil them (see for example Exodus 6:4 and 8).

337 It was so in the beginning when Adam and Eve were tempted to become "like God, knowing good and evil" (Genesis 3:5) and it will be so at the end when "the number of the beast is … [seen to be] man's number" (Revelation 13:18) – threefold repetition of the number six referring back to the day on which Adam was created and picturing man's recurring attempts to put himself in the position rightfully occupied by a Trinitarian God, whose number is seven (standing for perfection).

338 Several times God declared a "lasting ordinance": these relate to Passover (Exodus 12:14, 12:17 and 12:24), sinfulness and holiness (Exodus 12:19 and 28:43), priesthood in the line of Aaron (Exodus 29:9), ritual cleansing (Exodus 30:21) and observance of the Sabbath (Exodus 31:16). Each is of such a fundamental nature in terms of God's redemption purposes and the part they have to play in the New Covenant as well as in

the Old that any who transgress them are to be "cut off from Israel" or "cut off from the community of Israel" or "cut off from his people" (Exodus 12:15 and 19, 30:33 and 38).

339 God says that he "will turn against them and no longer consider them his people. The life of every living thing is in the blood, and that is why the LORD has commanded that all blood be poured out on the altar to take away the people's sins. Blood, which is life, takes away sins." (Leviticus 17:10-11, GNT). This emphasises the sanctity of all life; as a symbol of life, blood was to be treated with proper respect. After Cain murdered Abel, the Lord told him that "Your brother's blood is crying out to me from the ground" (Genesis 4:10, GNT).

340 This system was formalised with the building of the altar for the tabernacle (Exodus 30:1-5, 37:25-29 and 40:26-29) and in the regulations which governed its use, as set out in Exodus 30:6-10 and elsewhere.

341 The unleavened bread (*matzah*) which is the primary symbol of Passover (*Pesach*) not only carries a reminder of the speed of the departure from Egypt (Exodus 12:39) but also hints at the danger of pride. Leaven (food that has risen) is a symbol of the way in which pride puffs up, holding people back from experiencing the true freedom to which the Passover festival is directed. The regulations which appear in Exodus 12:43-47 confirm the universality of what God put in place through Passover, for from the very start aliens were allowed to share in it as long as they were circumcised.

342 The dire consequences of failing to abide by the requirements relating to a census are described in 1 Chronicles 21.

343 Holiness is the central theme of Leviticus, in which the word "holy" appears more often than in any other book of the Bible. The injunction to holiness is found time and again (see Leviticus 19:2, 20:7 and 26, 21:8 and 15, 22:9, 16 and 32), springing from the exhortation to "be holy, because I am holy." (Leviticus 11:45). The cleansing water of baptism pictures the washing away of sin, bringing purity and holiness and readying us for the new life of faith. The consecration of priests is described in Exodus 28:1 and 29:1-42.

344 King David prayed, "May my prayer be set before you like incense; may the lifting up of my hands be like the evening sacrifice." (Psalm 141:2). The last book of the Bible describes a vision of "four living creatures ... each holding ... golden bowls of incense, which are the prayers of the saints." (Revelation 5:8, NRSV).

345 As with the incense, careful instructions are given for making and using the oil (see Exodus 30:23-33).

346 A warning to be careful is first given with regard to "[going] up the mountain or [touching] the foot of it" (Exodus 19:12) but Israel was also to be careful "to do everything I [the LORD] have told you" (Exodus 23:13) and "not to make a treaty with those who live in [Canaan]" (Exodus 34:12 and 15), signifying circumspection in her dealings with both God and men.

347 Circumcision was a requirement for being allowed to partake in Passover. God told Moses, "No foreigner shall eat the Passover meal, but any slave that you have bought may eat it if you circumcise him first." (Exodus 12:43-44, GNT). Similarly, "A foreigner residing among you who wants to celebrate the LORD's Passover must have all the males in his household circumcised; then he may take part like one born in the land. No uncircumcised male may eat it. The same law applies both to the native-born and to the foreigner residing among you." (Exodus 12:48-49). At the same time, the injunction was to "Circumcise ... your heart" (Deuteronomy 10:16, NRSV).

348 In Judaism the spiritual value of circumcision is considered intricately bound up with its physical embodiment, for God told Abraham, "My covenant in your flesh is to be an everlasting covenant. Any uncircumcised male, who has not been circumcised in the flesh, will be cut off from his people; he has broken my covenant." (Genesis 17:13-14). Nevertheless, "'The days are coming,' declares the LORD, 'when I will punish all who are circumcised only in the flesh ... For all these nations are really uncircumcised, and even the whole house of Israel is uncircumcised in heart.'" (Jeremiah 9:25-26).

349 Further warnings and injunctions with regard to the inhabitants of Canaan are contained in Exodus 34:11-16. The Bible repeatedly stresses that all people without exception share a fundamental dignity and worth by virtue of being made in the image of God (Exodus 21:16 and 25-27) and thus murder is abhorrent to our Creator (Exodus 21:12-14), but equally, so is all sin for the Lord's "eyes are too pure to look on evil" (Habakkuk 1:13). Though he is merciful and gives ample opportunity for repentance, a just and holy God cannot and will not forever overlook wrongdoing. This context is vital in understanding God's sending "my terror ahead of [Israel] and [throwing] into confusion every nation you encounter." (Exodus 23:27).

350 Anger seems to have been at least part of the explanation for his acting contrary to God's instructions by striking the rock to bring forth water (Numbers 20:10-12). Though initially Moses was deprived of entry to the Promised Land for this, in his mercy God eventually allowed him to tread one of its mountains alongside Jesus, for when Christ was transfigured, the prophet stood nearby (see Mark 9:2-4). In this we glimpse how the failings, frustration and hardships of this life will be made good in the next.

351 The temptations of Moses in some degree mirror the temptations of Christ (see Matthew 4:3-4, 5-7 and 8-10).

352 Further examples of prompt answers to Moses' prayers can be found in Exodus 8:9-14, 9:29-30 and 10:18-19, amongst others.

353 The word "new" in the phrase "a new heaven and a new earth" (Revelation 21:1, NRSV) might more accurately be translated "renewed". The Lord offers similar renewal in the lives of individuals, repaying "the years the locust has eaten" (Joel 2:25).

354 Israelite religion and customs were anathema to Egyptians. When "Pharaoh summoned Moses and Aaron and said, 'Go, sacrifice to your God here in the land'" (Exodus 8:25), the prophet retorted that "The sacrifices we offer the LORD our God would be detestable to the Egyptians. And if we offer sacrifices that are detestable in

their eyes, will they not stone us?" (Exodus 8:26). Though this may to some extent have been a convenient excuse, the essential truth of it is shown by the fact that in an earlier generation "[The Egyptians] served [Joseph] by himself, [his] brothers by themselves, and the Egyptians who ate with him by themselves, because Egyptians could not eat with Hebrews, for that is detestable to Egyptians." (Genesis 43:32).

[355] God also says that he will give Israel "the land of Canaan ... as a possession" (Exodus 6:4 and 8), "a full life span" (Exodus 23:26) and "rest" (Exodus 33:14). In response to God's gifts, we are to "Give generously to [the needy] and do so without a grudging heart; then because of this the LORD your God will bless you" (Deuteronomy 15:10).

[356] This would seem to be the only way to account for the fact that Joshua did not know what was going on in the camp. He spoke of "the sound of war in the camp" (Exodus 32:17) and Moses had to correct him, saying, "...it is the sound of singing I hear" (Exodus 32:18). It is also consistent with Moses telling the elders to "Wait here for us until we come back to you" (Exodus 24:14), which suggests that he expected Joshua to stay on the mountain with him.

[357] There was no exaggeration in Jesus' saying that "the [Old Testament] Scriptures... testify about me, yet you refuse to come to me to have life." (John 5:39).

[358] For example, the so-called workmen's village which lay in the desert to the east of the city had no independent water supply or cultivable land. Food and drink thus had to be supplied from outside. In itself this was not unprecedented, for the same applied to the village that supplied workmen for the Valley of the Kings outside Thebes. Nevertheless, the environs of Akhet-aten were less salubrious than those of Thebes and hence the amount of locally grown produce that was available to the city as a whole would have been correspondingly less.

[359] One of the most distinctive aspects of the temples which Akhenaten built to his god was that they contained no cult images of the deity. Open to the sky, constructions such as the Gem-pa-Aten (the main temple of Akhet-aten) and Ḥwt Aten (the Mansion of Aten, a smaller temple about half a mile away) instead directed the gaze upwards towards the sun disc which was the outward symbol of Aten.

[360] Inertia in the face of threats to the empire from abroad also needs to be explained.

[361] The prospect of their finding re-employment as priests of Aten was slight. Though services in honour of this god were celebrated daily, they were simple in form and required fewer priests than other cults; there was no cult statue, so no need for someone to wash and care for it, and the pharaoh acted as High Priest, accompanied by his daughters and chief wife Nefertiti, so that the role of minor priests was limited. Worship consisted solely of singing hymns and making offerings of food, drink, flowers and perfume – often accompanied by burning incense and pouring libations – which were consecrated by touching the proffered goods with a special baton called a *hrp* so as to mark them as belonging to Aten. The etymology of *hrp* is uncertain. It might conceivably be linked with hyssop, an unidentified plant whose twigs were used for sprinkling in Jewish purification rites. The first biblical mention of hyssop is in connection with the

original Passover: the Israelites were told to "Take a bunch of hyssop, dip it into the blood in the basin and put some of the blood on the top and on both sides of the door frame." (Exodus 12:22).

362 The reaction of workers in Ephesus when it seemed that the preaching of St Paul would cause a drop in demand for their products and services shows the extent to which artisans might depend on custom generated by religious cults and the intense anger their loss of livelihood might arouse (see Acts 19:23-41).

363 The Lord "makes winds his messengers, flames of fire his servants" (Psalm 104:4) and correspondingly "makes his angels winds, his servants flames of fire." (Hebrews 1:7). There were "tongues of fire" (Acts 2:3) at the first Pentecost.

364 Though Moses took the lead in dealing with God, the Almighty did not intend that the prophet should be the only one to experience the divine presence. Moses was told, "There [in the Tent of Meeting] I will meet you and speak to you; *there also I will meet with the Israelites*, and the place will be consecrated by my glory." (Exodus 29:43, emphasis added).

365 The first biblical use of the phrase "*kavod YHWH*" ("Glory of the LORD") is when Moses told Israel, "In the evening you will know that it was the LORD who brought you out of Egypt, and in the morning you will see the glory of the LORD, because he has heard your grumbling against him." (Exodus 16:6-7). Similarly, God's telling Moses that he stood on "holy ground" (Exodus 3:5) on Horeb is the first mention of the word 'holy'. The conjunction of glory and holiness emphasises the new era inaugurated by the Exodus events. As well as the shining brilliance of the Lord's presence, glory is also used to describe the superlative honour that should be given to the Creator by everything in the universe.

366 God's presence in Israel's midst was likewise symbolised by "the bread of the Presence ... [which was] to be before me at all times." (Exodus 25:30). This was an extraordinary departure from all traditions of Egyptian religion. The worship of Amun was literally a matter of obfuscation, his hidden nature reflected in the way that temples built in his honour became steadily darker and more mysterious the further inside one penetrated, whereas the God of Abraham, Isaac and Jacob brought "light in the places where [his people] lived." (Exodus 10:23). The darkening or obscuring associated with Amun meant that at best he could only be tangentially present in the lives of his devotees, whilst the Lord was notable through his constant and obvious presence "in the sight of all the house of Israel during all their travels." (Exodus 40:38). Amun stood for that which was secret and unknowable. By contrast, the Lord granted "ability and knowledge" (Exodus 31:3 and 35:31).

367 The phrase has the sense of "Stop coming closer, as you are presently doing". There is an echo of something similar in Jesus' words to Mary Magdalene on the morning of his resurrection, when he said, "Do not hold onto me" (John 20:17). There are also hints of the circumstances surrounding Christ's rising from the dead when Moses was told to "Go to the people and consecrate them today and tomorrow. Make them wash their

clothes and be ready for *the third day*, because on that day the LORD will come down on Mount Sinai in the sight of all the people." (Exodus 19:10-11, emphasis added).

368 The timing of events, too, is within the sovereign control and gift of God, for "The wind [of his Spirit] blows wherever it pleases" (John 3:8): Nevertheless, the operation of free will means that some degree of leeway is delegated to humankind. It was in accordance with the counsels of heaven that "Seven days passed after the LORD struck the Nile" (Exodus 7:25) and "The LORD set a time ... and the next day ... did it" (Exodus 9:5-6) but, acting with divine authority, on another occasion "Moses said to Pharaoh, 'I leave to you the honour of setting the time for me to pray for you and your officials and your people that your houses may be rid of the frogs, except for those that remain in the Nile.'" (Exodus 8:9). When Pharaoh answered, "Do it tomorrow" (Exodus 8:10, TLB), "Moses replied, 'it shall be as you have said; then you will know that there is no one like the Lord our God. All the frogs will be destroyed, except those in the river.'" (Exodus 8:10-11, TLB). There are many happenings that we may be able to anticipate using natural abilities, but only God can know the precise moment when they will come to fruition. The prophet's divinely inspired ability to say exactly when the frogs would disappear removed the last vestiges of intellectual support for Pharaoh's continued defiance, since he could no longer pretend that the plagues were natural phenomena coming about by chance.

369 The conditionality that underlies God's promise to be continuously present with his people is shown in that the text of Exodus 29:45-46 begins with the word 'then' – a reference to fulfilment of the events described in the immediately preceding verses.

370 Probably the narrative singles out Moses' brother by name in order to emphasise that even a blood relative who had been the prophet's "mouth" (Exodus 4:16) and stood alongside him whilst miracles were performed was gripped by the same fright as everyone else.

371 From earliest times it seems to have been thought that no man could see God and live. Hence Jacob remarked after the encounter at Peniel, "I saw God face to face, and yet my life was spared." (Genesis 32:30). That the belief was well founded was confirmed when the Lord told Moses, "…you cannot see my face, for no-one may see me and live." (Exodus 33:20).

372 The phrase "fear of Isaac" (Genesis 31:42, KJV; and 31:53, KJV) seems to be used either as an alternative for "God of Isaac" or as a way of suggesting intimate relationship between the patriarch and his Maker. It is of paramount importance that we set the fear of God in its proper context, for the Lord does not wish fear to have a hold over his people. This is reflected in the fact that Moses twice issued the exhortation, "Do not be afraid" (Exodus 14:13 and 20:20) – on the first occasion advising the Israelites not to be fearful in the face of the things of this world (Pharaoh and his advancing army) and on the second telling them to bear up in the face of spiritual challenge. Scripture is full of examples of God telling people not to be afraid, these words being said to each of Abraham, Isaac and Jacob (Genesis 15:1, 21:17 and 46:3) and to many others thereafter. The advice from one of the disciples who was closest to Jesus is that "There is no fear in

love. But perfect love drives out fear, because fear has to do with punishment. The one who fears is not made perfect in love" (1 John 4:18).

[373] When God descended in this way, it was in a manner distinct from how he "came down to see the city and the tower [of Babel] mankind was making" (Genesis 11:5, TLB). On that occasion, he investigated what was going on but did not dwell, since the temple that was made was unsuitable for his presence. Its architects sought to use religion to project power and bolster their prestige, in the process demeaning worship and service of the Almighty and treating it as if it were restricted to one nation or group – in much the same fashion as Akhenaten apparently sought to do – rather than as a means by which the Lord might bless all people. The result was that they brought judgment on themselves.

[374] John Gillespie Magee Jnr, *High Flight*.

[375] There are mountain settings for many pivotal events in Scripture, including Elijah's stand against the four hundred and fifty prophets of Baal on Mount Carmel (1 Kings 18) and subsequent encounter with God in a "still, small voice" (1 Kings 19:12, KJV) on Mount Horeb; the Sermon on the Mount (Matthew 5:1-7:29); the time of solitary prayer which preceded Jesus' walking on the water and Peter's recognition that he was the Son of God (Matthew 14:23-33 and Mark 6:46-52); the feeding of the four thousand (Matthew 15:29-38); and the Transfiguration of Christ (Matthew 17:1-13 and Mark 9:1-13). The locations of the Sermon on the Mount and Transfiguration are unspecified, though traditionally they are identified with Mount Eremos and Mount Tabor respectively.

[376] Christ also demands that we take a step towards him, for we need to respond to his invitation to "Come and follow me" (Matthew 19:21, GNT; Mark 10:21, GNT; and Luke 18:22, GNT), "Come with me" (Mark 1:17, GNT), "Come to me" (Matthew 11:28, GNT), "Come with me" (Matthew 4:19, GNT; and Mark 6:31) or simply, "Come" (Matthew 14:29, GNT). His words are echoed by both the Holy Spirit and the Church, for "The Spirit and the bride say, 'Come.'" (Revelation 22:17, GNT).

[377] Exodus frequently emphasises the importance of obedience and the need for it if we are to honour God as we ought. Its material is arranged so that blessing is seen to follow from obedience. Hence the statement that "all the Israelites did just what the LORD had commanded Moses and Aaron" (Exodus 12:50) is linked in the very next verse to the fact that "on that very day the LORD brought the Israelites out of Egypt by their divisions." (Exodus 12:51). Indeed, the same connection is explicitly made by God himself, for he promises that "Whenever I cause my name to be honoured, I will come to you and bless you." (Exodus 20:24).

[378] The song which Moses and the Israelites sang on emerging from the Red Sea (Exodus 15:1-18), with its talk of God's having "become my salvation" (Exodus 15:2) and his people being "[brought] in and [planted] ... on the mountain of [his] inheritance – the place, O LORD, you made for your dwelling, the sanctuary, O LORD, your hands established. The LORD will reign for ever and ever" (Exodus 15:17-19) confirmed the spiritual elevation which took place as Israel was freed once and for all from her former

slavery. It does so in terms which emphasise that these things were sovereign works of God, not the result of human activity.

³⁷⁹ The intention that Israel should be a means by which God blesses all mankind is also apparent from the first: "By the power of your arm they will be still as a stone – until your people pass by, O LORD, until the people you bought pass by." (Exodus 15:16). God's mercy towards all men is the more striking given that the people who are spoken of in this verse are the sinful nations which will "hear and tremble" (Exodus 15:14), be gripped with "anguish" (Exodus 15:14), "be terrified ... [and] seized with trembling" (Exodus 15:15) and upon whom "terror and dread will fall" (Exodus 15:16) at the approach of Israel's army.

³⁸⁰ Some of what is involved in heaven's breaking into earth is evident in the language used to describe the tent of meeting (in Hebrew, *'ohel mo'ed*). The word *mo'ed*, often rendered "appointed season" or "appointed time", is linguistically related to *ed*, meaning both "eternity" and "witness". So the tent of meeting was almost a *kairos* moment made flesh – a point in space and time where eternity and the uncreated met the finite and the creature, where sacred and profane collided and where the heavenly bore witness to the earthly about itself. Moreover, the two letters which make up the word *ed* (*ayin* meaning, eye and *dalit* meaning, door) show eternity to be that higher realm which lies beyond and can sometimes be glimpsed through the door of the physical world; not an infinite duration of everyday experience, but something supremely more intense and satisfying experienced in a higher, spiritual realm, the ultimate "life ... to the full" (John 10:10) of which Jesus spoke.

³⁸¹ The need to ready ourselves for the coming of the heavenly King is a refrain of both Old and New Testaments: "The voice of one crying in the wilderness: "Prepare the way of the Lord; Make straight in the desert; A highway for our God." (Isaiah 40:3, NKJV, the gist of which is quoted in Matthew 3:3, Mark 1:3, Luke 3:4 and John 1:23).

³⁸² In Egypt placing a statue of a god in its temple was believed to bring about the literal presence of the deity in that place. Each year these statues would be paraded publicly so that the god could appear to the people. By contrast, unlike its pagan equivalents, the sanctuary envisaged in Exodus was not meant to be understood literally as God's abode, at least not to the extent this might suggest that the Almighty can in any way be constrained in time, space or action. Its function was instead to make tangible the concept of God as immanent (present in the world). The divine Presence in the camp was something to keep the people focussed on their goal of entering into Canaan, but it was also a foretaste of what is to come at the end of time when the Lord will be permanently with his people in the ultimate Promised Land, for "the throne of God and of the Lamb will be in the city, and his servants will serve him ... [and] they will not need the light of a lamp or the light of the sun, for the Lord God will give them light." (Revelation 22:3 and 5).

³⁸³ In terms of the Old Testament dispensation, this was a moment to mirror its New Testament equivalent, when at the death of Jesus "The curtain of the temple was torn in two" (Matthew 27:51, Mark 15:38 and Luke 23:45), symbolising the decisive action that

had been taken to deal with human sin and thereby remove the root cause of separation between God and man.

384 Solomon's dedication of the Temple in Jerusalem saw similar happenings: "When Solomon had finished praying, fire came down from heaven and consumed the burnt offering and the sacrifices; and the glory of the LORD filled the temple. And the priests could not enter the house of the LORD, because the glory of the LORD had filled the LORD's house." (2 Chronicles 7:1-2, NKJV).

385 His doing so is a measure of how the set purposes and unchanging nature of the Almighty sit alongside the fact that he responds according to changes in circumstance and the differing characters of human beings. He singled out Moses with an eye to his potential, for whatever failings he may have had in youth the prophet showed almost from the first the essential humility that made him so powerful an instrument in the hands of God. An example of this quality is seen in the fact that "Moses agreed to stay with the man [Jethro]" (Exodus 2:21, which could equally be rendered as "Moses was content to dwell with the man"), though this was an astonishing come-down for one who only shortly beforehand had been a prince of Egypt. Egyptians would most probably have regarded Midianites as uncivilised savages, and even their chiefs and priests would have been beneath the notice of a pharaoh and his kin.

386 There is huge disparity between the weight of God's judgment and the depth of his love. Sin is punished to the third and fourth generation, but he "[shows] love to a thousand generations of those who love [him] and keep [his] commandments." (Exodus 20:6).

387 The word balance appears only four times in the Bible, and in all of these instances it is used either in the sense of a set of scales or in the accounting sense of a residue to be paid. Nevertheless, balance is a concept integral to understanding of God, his Word and its application to our lives. It is present in the now and not yet of the Kingdom of God, in the potential which may be realised through the exercise of Free Will and in the Almighty's willingness to respond to prayer. In the sense of harmony it is also part of what is meant by *shalom* and it underlies the need for a proper weighing in terms of spiritual discernment.

388 Later descriptions of "a throne, in appearance like a sapphire stone" (Ezekiel 1:26, NKJV, and a similar wording in Ezekiel 10:1, NKJV) suggest a link with the throne room of God. The jewel is also mentioned as part of the foundations of the heavenly city (see Revelation 21:19).

389 The Malqata palace lies at the southern end of the Theban necropolis. Newly built at Amenhotep III's command as Per-Hai (House of Rejoicing), it was his residence during the latter part of his reign, becoming known as the Splendour of Aten.

390 So it would seem according to the letter which Yapahu of Gezer sent to his Egyptian overlord (Amarna letter EA 298).

391 Further references to fire and cloud as harbingers of the presence of God can be found in Exodus 13:22, 14:19, 14:20, 14:24, 19:16, 24:15, 24:16, 24:18, 33:9, 33:10, 34:5,

40:35, 40:36, 40:37 and 40:38 (cloud) and Exodus 13:21, 14:24, 19:18, 24:17 and 40:38 (fire).

³⁹² Dalits (*Broken Ones*) were formerly known as Untouchables.

³⁹³ A further intriguing aside concerns the information that Pharaoh "took six hundred of the best chariots, along with all the other chariots of Egypt, with officers over all of them." (Exodus 14:7). In the Eighteenth Dynasty chariot wheels with four spokes were in the process of being superseded by a design with six spokes, the latter being both lighter and stronger, producing an altogether more reliable machine. Reference to the best chariots could therefore be to the six-spoke variety which would presumably have been issued to frontline forces, and the other chariots would most probably have been the four-spoke version, which was doubtless used by reservists or second rank units. This is the kind of detail unlikely to have been captured by someone making up the story later, long after chariots with four spokes had fallen out of use. A similar point applies to the word rendered into English as "officers", which literally means "third man". Though Egyptian chariots had a crew of two, during initial battlefield deployments these were often accompanied by a "chaser" armed with bow and spears, whose job was to dismount at an appointed spot and then be ready to kill or capture enemy crewmen, rescue any of their own crews who were beleaguered, and soak up opposition chariot attacks whilst the more manoeuvrable Egyptian vehicles wheeled about to charge the enemy from behind. In a sense these chasers were thus forerunners of the German *Panzergrenadier* or Soviet *Tankdesantniki* who rode into battle on tanks during the Second World War.

³⁹⁴ Amongst cultures familiar to Israel in later times, Shamash and Utu were respectively the Akkadian and Sumerian solar gods. The bewildering array of deities from which Egyptians could choose is described in Appendix 4.

³⁹⁵ Yet the religion of Akhet-aten led down a blind alley and the king's reforms failed to take root. It is uncertain to what extent worship of Aten was ever genuinely adopted and taken to heart outside the immediate circle of the royal family and a few courtiers. Within a few years of the king's death there was little to show for the massive investments in this cult. It is a poignant illustration of the fact that, "If the LORD does not build the house, the work of the builders is useless." (Psalm 127:1, GNT).

³⁹⁶ This supposition would probably make Akhenaten's grandfather and predecessor-but-one Thutmose IV the Pharaoh described in Exodus 2. The oppression described in Exodus 1 doubtless took place under earlier rulers.

³⁹⁷ The Lord specifically stated that "Against all the gods of Egypt will I execute judgment" (Exodus 12:12). The plagues and disasters that befell this nation were thus expressly designed to show that the Egyptian deities were false gods and reveal their powerlessness in the face of the Almighty. Ancient Egypt was one of the most polytheistic of all societies, having well over one hundred gods and goddesses (see Appendix 4).

398 It seems that Jewish folk memory preserved recollection of a link, albeit tenuous, between Moses and Akhenaten; the first century AD historian T. Flavius Josephus, himself a Jew, placed them as contemporaries, and Sigmund Freud seems to have picked up on this in his last published work, *Moses and Monotheism*, in which he argued that the religion of Amarna influenced Judaism. Since the incontrovertibly established facts of Akhenaten's reign and legacy are few, speculation abounds, but this work contends that it is more credible to put it the other way round. If Akhenaten's father (Amenhotep III) were the Pharoah of the Exodus, one can readily imagine that what Akhenaten saw or heard about as a youngster must have profoundly influenced his subsequent actions.

399 Amenhotep III's eldest son, Crown Prince Thutmose, died whilst still a child. The killing of Egyptian firstborn is recounted in Exodus 11:4-7 and 12:29-30. The precise mechanisms by which these deaths were brought about are impossible for now to say, though Exodus' description of contaminated water supplies, rotting animal carcasses and swarms of gnats and flies offers a wide range of possibilities, of which dysentery, typhus, cholera, malaria and sand-fly fever are some of the more obvious. Bubonic plague is also a possibility, traces of this having been found at Akhet-aten (see Appendix 1).

400 Nevertheless, when we have eliminated the impossible, then whatever remains, however improbable, must be the truth. (*Pace* Sir Arthur Conan Doyle, as put in the mouth of Sherlock Holmes in *The Sign of Four*).

401 After his death the people returned to their old gods and habitual forms of worship, and the dignity of monarchy was again proclaimed in time-honoured manner. Despite some continuing occupation Akhet-aten was abandoned by officialdom, and attempts (albeit faltering and only partly successful) were made to sweep away artistic aberrations sponsored by the former king. Generations to come made strenuous efforts to recover the imperial greatness of years gone by, most notably under Seti I and his son Ramses II, although in the event the high watermark of Egyptian power and influence proved to have irretrievably passed.

402 As to the future, God has declared that "there will be a highway between Egypt and Assyria. The people of these two countries will travel back and forth between them, and the two nations will worship together. When that time comes, Israel will rank with Egypt and Assyria, and these three nations will be a blessing to all the world. The LORD Almighty will bless them and say, 'I will bless you, Egypt, my people; you, Assyria, whom I created; and you, Israel, my chosen people.'" (Isaiah 19:23-25, GNT).

403 The import of the biblical narrative is that the oppression of Exodus 1:11-14 took place at a much earlier date than the events of Exodus 2:1-20, since otherwise there would be an insufficient lapse of time to account for the Israelites being in bondage for over four hundred years, as Genesis 15:3 and Exodus 12:40-41 require.

404 The traditional reckoning (the High Chronology) was determined by the accession of Thutmose III, which was dated to 1504 BC. Modern usage recalculates this date as 1479 BC (the Low Chronology). There has been thought to be a fair degree of assurance about the date when Thutmose III came to the throne, since this can be correlated to two lunar

observances recorded during his reign, though the New Chronology proposed by David Rohl casts doubt on this.

405 Heliacal rising describes the moment when a heavenly body appears above the horizon just before sunrise, an event which is seasonal because of the movements of the earth and brightness of the sun at different times of year. In Egypt the dog-star Sirius (regarded as the goddess Sopdet) disappeared from view for seventy days in midsummer, appearing again before dawn on the eastern horizon at the end of this period. Its return normally forecast the start of the annual Nile flood a few days later. It was thus considered an event of central importance, marking the beginning of the Egyptians' New Year, providing the means of fixing the first month of their old calendar and being considered a propitious time for crowning a new monarch. In the process, it emphasised the harmony between divine kingship and the natural world as a new king and a new Egypt rose from the floodwaters of the Nile, in which the old king as the murdered god Osiris was believed to float.

406 The limits on our ability to date ancient happenings accurately are amply demonstrated by the volcanic explosion that partially destroyed the Aegean island of Thera (present-day Santorini) in the second millennium BC. This is credited with unleashing a tsunami which brought down the Minoan civilisation of Crete. Radiocarbon dating currently puts the eruption at about 1623 BC plus or minus 20 years, though archaeological evidence points to a date of 1550 to 1500 BC. The scope for argument is illustrated by the fact that radiocarbon dating can often produce date ranges spanning 200 years or more, whilst interpretation of archaeological evidence for such an event is seldom straightforward. The explosion that devastated Thera is thought to have been violent enough to throw up a cloud of volcanic ash and debris that would have been visible from the peninsula of Sinai. Flashes of lightning within this cloud would have produced a phenomenon akin to that seen by the Israelites: a "pillar of cloud by day [and a] pillar of fire by night" (Exodus 13:22; see Plates VI to IX for modern-day examples). It is not beyond the bounds of possibility that a huge tsunami could have played havoc with sea levels sufficient to affect the waters of the Red Sea. When the Indonesian island of Krakatoa exploded on 27 August 1883, it created a tsunami over one hundred feet high in places. The pressure wave generated by the colossal final explosion radiated from the epicentre at 675 mph, rocking ships as far away as England and South Africa.

407 The fact that schematic or aggregate figures might be used does not mean that statements based on them are false or inherently unreliable, merely that they need to be interpreted in a different way from modern expressions of time. If we say that something will take 'just a second' that statement is not rendered untrue merely because the task takes twenty seconds, for all we meant to convey was the idea of a short time span.

408 The nearest thing so far found occurs in a partly erased autobiographical text in the tomb of Amenhotep son of Hapu, overall supervisor of works during the reign of Amenhotep III. This seems to indicate the taking of a census and infilling of the ranks of workmen after the occurrence of some unnamed event – presumably traumatic since otherwise it would have been proclaimed elsewhere. A slight degree of corroboration for this supposition comes from a carving on the back of the temple at Luxor, part of which

has been deliberately cut away, referring to difficulties encountered during its construction.

409 Whilst there was at least some form of continued occupation at Akhet-aten for a considerable time after the death of Akhenaten, this appears to have been by private individuals. All indications are that the city ceased to be a functioning capital shortly after its creator's death. Certainly, by the time Tutankhamun came to the throne in 1339 BC or thereabouts Memphis either was already or shortly thereafter again became the centre of government and administration.

410 Those who came after Akhenaten swiftly reversed the naming policies of the Amarna years; Tutankhamun, for example, was originally called Tutankhaten (Living image of Aten) and his wife Ankhesenamun was once named Ankhesenaten. It is uncertain whether new names were forced on this couple, though the fact that Aten's sun-disc was used on shrines which formed part of the boy king's funerary equipment would be consistent with a last statement of personal allegiance to the abandoned sun-god on the part of the one who was buried alongside them.

411 The River Arnon rises in the mountains of Gilead in modern Jordan and flows westwards into the Dead Sea. Heshbon, Aroer and the towns along the Arnon were amongst the first to fall to the invading Israelites, being overrun before Joshua led the tribes across the River Jordan to begin the conquest of Canaan proper. It is thus reasonable to treat three hundred years prior to the anointing of Saul as marking the start of Israel's conquest of Canaan.

412 The book of Judges gives figures for alternate oppressions and deliverances which appear to total four hundred and ten years. Adding this to an unspecified number of years of Joshua's leadership and the judgeships of Eli and Samuel gives a figure more like four hundred and eighty years than the three hundred referred to in Judges 11:26. In practice, it is likely that periods of oppression and deliverance overlapped. For example, some Israelite tribes may have been under the heel of one nation or group of nations at the same time as other tribes were subject to quite distinct groups. Use of schematic or aggregate figures has already been noted.

413 The River Eleutheros lies far inside Lebanon, beyond Israelite territory. In the remains of Byblos (which sits on the coast about thirty miles south of the western mouth of the Eleutheros) Maurice Dunand found parts of a large doorway or portal bearing the cartouches of Ramses II, and there are rock carvings of Ramses II dating from the second, fourth and fifth years of his reign at the mouth of the Dog River between Beirut and Byblos. Keeping to the coast as far as the Eleutheros would have enabled Egyptian forces travelling overland to link with troops or supplies sent by ship to Byblos, then under Egyptian control or influence. It should, however, be noted that there is an emerging view amongst Egyptologists (based on study of Egyptian war reliefs) that Ramses II did conduct a campaign in Palestine during the eighth year of his reign. The extent to which this involved striking at Israelite power centres (rather than merely crossing lands controlled by Israel) is presently a matter of conjecture – the main Egyptian objectives seem to have lain in Ammon, Moab and the Negev.

⁴¹⁴ The Bible says that "Jabin king of Canaan, who reigned in Hazor" (Judges 4:2, NKJV) and his general Sisera "for twenty years ... harshly oppressed the children of Israel" (Judges 4:3, NKJV). For much of the periods of oppression described in Judges the Israelites were confined to the hill country where lack of chariots placed them at less of a disadvantage against better armed adversaries.

⁴¹⁵ The Egyptian word for Israel in this inscription is written with the determinative for people rather than land, implying that she did not have a king or kingdom at this point. The context nevertheless implies that Israel was just as strong as the other Canaanite city-states that are mentioned on the stele, and was not merely a nondescript tribe. The "well of waters of Nephtoah" mentioned in Joshua 15:9 and 18:15 may conceivably use a Hebrew variant of Merneptah.

⁴¹⁶ If the oppression took place under Ramses II and the exodus under Merneptah, the wording of this stele would be even more difficult to credit. Far from Israel's then being "destroyed", on that hypothesis Merneptah's pursuing chariots would have recently come to grief (Exodus 14) and the Israelite forces been victorious against the Amalekites (Exodus 17:8-13). If this had been the case it is doubtful that Egypt would have had the appetite for sending any kind of expedition beyond her northern borders for some time to come.

⁴¹⁷ 1 Chronicles 7:20-27 gives a genealogy for Joshua, but the Bible nowhere specifically says how old he was at the time of the exodus or when he first led his people into Canaan. Scripture nevertheless speaks of Caleb in terms that suggest he was a near contemporary of Joshua, and Caleb is said to have been forty when Moses sent him to explore the Promised Land (see Joshua 14:7). If Joshua were the same age, then important turning points in his life (his entry into Canaan first as a spy and then as leader of Israel) would have come at the ages of forty and eighty, just as equivalent moments did for Moses (his flight to Midian followed by his subsequent return to Egypt). For Joshua to have been forty when he was commissioned to scout out the Promised Land is consistent with his being described at one point as Moses' "young assistant" (Exodus 33:11) and yet at the same time being of sufficient age and experience to serve as Israel's commander in battle against the Amalekites (Exodus 17:9-10). In *Antiquities of the Jews* 1:29 Josephus estimates Joshua to have been forty-five at the time of the exodus and eighty-five on leading the Israelites into Canaan.

⁴¹⁸ Thutmose IV was most probably the grandfather of Akhenaten. The Bible might be thought to require a "long period" (Exodus 2:23) for his reign, though in fact the time period to which this verse refers is the length of Moses' stay in Midian, marriage to Zipporah and birth of his first son. Most modern scholars tend to estimate the duration of Thutmose IV's rule at ten years or so, although others hazard that it could have been as much as thirty-five years. Very little is known with any degree of certainty about what happened during this pharaoh's time on the throne, though the first known references to Aten are found then.

⁴¹⁹ Amenhotep III is thought to have acceded to the throne around 1391 BC and to have reigned for thirty-eight years.

⁴²⁰ Amongst the rulers whose cities were taken by the invading Israelites, the Bible names "Horam of Gezer" (Joshua 10:33) and "Jabin of Hazor" (Joshua 11:1). These appear to be titles rather than personal names, Jabin meaning "the discerner" or "the wise" and Horam perhaps equating to "highness" or "exalted one". The Amarna Letters also feature correspondence from rulers of the same cities, though seemingly using family or given names – Abdi-Irsi and Abdi-Tirsi in the case of Hazor and Adda-danu in the case of Gezer – making it impossible to say for sure if these are identical to their biblical equivalents.

⁴²¹ As reflected in Hosea 5:8. The warlike character and martial skills of the tribe of Benjamin are referred to in Genesis 49:27, Judges 20:16 and 1 Chronicles 8:40 and 12:2.

⁴²² Pella fell within the territory allocated to the tribe of Gad. 'T' and 'G' sounds are easily transposed, as with 'T' and 'D' in the German 'Tochter' and its English equivalent, 'Daughter'.

⁴²³ Gebel (modern Dschebel) lay on the coast about twenty-five miles north of Beirut.

⁴²⁴ Though the identification is not without its critics, many equate these with Hebrews. Strictly speaking *Habiru* or *Apiru* are not completely synonymous with *Sa-Gaz*, though use of the terms overlaps. In the Amarna Letters they seem to be interchangeable, with Sa-gaz being used in letters originating from the more northerly cities, and Habiru in those coming from regions further south. The etymology of *Sa-Gaz* is uncertain, apparently being connected both with the Sumerian *habbatu* (brigand, highway robber) and Akkadian *saggasu* (aggressor). In each case, the sense is of fierce, lawless people who threaten existing settled communities and operate outside the normal confines of civilised society. *Habiru* or *Apiru* is also sometimes rendered as *The Dusty Ones*, a fitting epithet for a race of slaves, though a reminder too of our origins and common humanity, for God "knoweth our frame, he remembereth that we are dust" (Psalm 103:14, KJV).

⁴²⁵ Not all those to whom the terms Sa-Gaz or Habiru were applied need necessarily have been part of Joshua's army – the Amarna Letters show that confusion and panic was the order of the day, so the appellation may not always have been used consistently or with precision. Since conflicts of the sort described in the book of Joshua have tended throughout the ages to lead to an upsurge in brigandage, it is conceivable that armed groups displaced from areas taken by the Israelites might have formed roving bands which then preyed on weaker adversaries. Something of this kind may lie behind the activities of the man the Amarna Letters call Labayu, whom a number of the pharaoh's correspondents accused of assorted outrages. Such activity could only have weakened the opposition which its victims were able to mount to an Israelite attack, giving an interesting perspective on God's telling Moses that "I will send the hornet ahead of you to drive the Hivites, Canaanites and Hittites out of the way" (Exodus 23:28). Amarna Letter EA 289 says, "Are we to act like Labayu when he was giving the land of Shechem to the Habiru?"

⁴²⁶ This is consistent with what God had told Abraham: "Then the LORD said to [Abraham], 'Know for certain that your descendants will be strangers in a country not their own, and they will be enslaved and ill-treated four hundred years.'" (Genesis 15:13).

Since "Jacob lived in the land of Egypt seventeen years" (Genesis 47:28, KJV), it may be that an Egyptian change of heart towards Israel began a mere thirteen years after the death of the patriarch. Certainly, on his deathbed Joseph spoke in terms that are suggestive of this, whilst also pre-figuring the exodus: "God will surely come to your aid and take you up out of this land to the land he promised on oath to Abraham Isaac and Jacob." (Genesis 50:24). The period of 430 years during which Israel was in Egypt mirrors an equivalent period of God's apparent silence between the Old and New Testaments, for from the days of Nehemiah (approximately 432 BC) to the birth of Christ Israel received no further divine revelation.

[427] The *Story of Two Brothers*, an Egyptian text thought to date from about 1225 BC, has similarities to the story of Joseph. It tells how a young man was falsely accused of adultery by the wife of his older brother after he rejected her advances.

[428] Egyptian records contain references to famines at various points in the nation's history, though widespread starvation was fairly rare. When it did occur, it usually resulted from a poor Nile flood. The so-called "famine stele" on the south-east side of Sehel Island tells of a seven-year famine that is said to have struck during the reign of the third dynasty king Djoser (thought to have come to the throne around 2691 BC to 2625 BC). The causeways which lead both to the pyramid of Sahure (said to have reigned from 2487 BC to 2475 BC) and the pyramid of Unas (Wenis) show emaciated famine victims. Unas was the last king of the fifth dynasty, believed to have ruled at some point between 2375 BC and 2345 BC. The difficulties inherent in dating are shown by the fact that Unas' pyramid is ascribed to him on the basis of a small inscription incised on its south face by Prince Khaemwese, son of Ramses II, without which there would be nothing to identify the building's owner. Since Khaemwese lived fourteen dynasties and over a thousand years after Unas, this attribution must be open to question. Dating of the famine stele is likewise problematic: its language and layout suggest that it was carved in the Ptolomeic period, some two thousand years after the events it purports to relate.

[429] The so-called Semna Despatches, which are commonly dated to the reign of Amenemhet III, deal with surveillance of the habitually troublesome southern border with Nubia. They report routine patrols and checks on population movements rather than large-scale campaigns.

[430] The pattern described in Genesis 47:20-22 was not unique and is consistent with the experience of other cultures in the region. Famine and its economic consequences lie at the root of debt jubilees in several religions of the ancient Near East. Harvest cycles led to widespread periodic default on debt, causing forfeiture of collateral and concentration of wealth in the hands of leaders. Steps which the Athenian leader Solon took in 599 BC to relieve the consequent hardship (including cancellation of debts, restitution of land seized by creditors, the setting of minimum prices for commodities and flooding the money supply with state-issued coinage) were copied by the Romans in their Lex Aternia of 454 BC. God's solution is to be found in the requirement for a jubilee every fifty years, when debts were to be forgiven, land left untilled, certain alienated property restored and slaves freed (see Leviticus 25:11).

431 Some forty miles wide, the Faiyum is the second broadest stretch of arable land in Egypt after the Nile delta.

432 The wisdom and efficacy of Joseph's preparations is shown by comparison with the dire famine and disease which struck Egypt in 1085 AD when the Nile flood failed for seven years in succession. On that occasion, divine warning had presumably either been absent or gone unheeded.

433 If the Execration Texts do belong earlier than the Thirteenth Dynasty this might on its face seem to make a connection with the enslavement and oppression of Israel less compelling. Yet there were two Twelfth Dynasty kings who came after Amenemhat III, and on his deathbed Joseph spoke to his brothers in terms that could be taken to mean that circumstances were already becoming difficult for them, saying, "I am about to die. But God will surely come to your aid and take you up out of this land to the land he promised on oath to Abraham, Isaac and Jacob." (Genesis 50:24).

434 Pithom is usually identified with the modern Tell al-Maskhuta, though not all agree on this. Heliopolis (On) was also referred to as Pi-Atum (the estate of the god Atum), which biblical writers might conceivably have rendered as Pithom.

435 Chemicals released by decomposing straw make clay more pliable and homogeneous. Hence bricks made with straw are stronger than those made without. For centuries the farmers of Egypt ploughed these mud bricks into their fields since the straw made them rich in nutrients. In doing so, they unwittingly destroyed much evidence of ancient Egyptian civilisation.

436 There was a dearth of wood in Egypt. Supplies were sought from Canaan, Lebanon and further afield.

437 Avaris, which eventually became a district of Pi-Rameses As-naktu (meaning *The house of Ramses Great in Victory*) is of earlier foundation than the Ramesside capital. There is evidence of prolonged Semitic occupation at Avaris, though dating this reliably and determining to what extent it might mark the presence of Israelite slaves is still the subject of debate. Pi-Rameses is thought to have been founded first by Ramses I whilst he served in the army under Pharaoh Horemheb. Largely abandoned when the Twenty-first Dynasty moved its capital to Tanis, Pi-Rameses then effectively became a quarry and a source of ready-made monuments. Nevertheless, its name appears in a list of Twenty-first Dynasty cities, and it had a revival in the tenth century BC during the Twenty-second Dynasty under Sheshonq I, who sought to emulate Ramses II.

438 Some Jewish traditions have it that Moses' parents named him Chaver (meaning, friend) whilst his grandfather called him Avigdor (meaning, father protector) and Pharaoh's daughter named him Minios. This would make Moses (Moshe) a Hebrew translation or transliteration of Minios. Moses sounds like the Hebrew for "draw out", reflecting the fact that the infant was drawn out from the waters of the Nile.

439 These were the Horus name, the Two Ladies name, the Gold Horus name, the throne name and a personal name given at birth. The latter was the Son of Ra name, being preceded by Sa Re. Some pharaohs had multiple names within each of these categories.

Ramses II, for example, used six Horus names at various times. Not all the different names for each ruler have been uncovered. In *Pharaohs and Kings: a biblical quest*, David Rohl argues persuasively that "Shishak king of Egypt" (1 Kings 11:40 and 14:25 and 2 Chronicles 12:2 and 12:9) could be a Semitic rendering of a form of the name Ramses. For the reasons given above, this does not necessarily mean that Ramses II was the pharaoh to whom the Bible was referring on this occasion. As far as identification is concerned, in and of itself a reference to Shishak in 1 Kings and 2 Chronicles may take us no further forward than does the title Pharaoh in Exodus.

440 It is generally thought that Ramses I reigned from 1292-1290 BC and Ramses II from 1279-1213 BC.

441 The names of Tiaa and Pyikhia appear in the mortuary chapel of Tiaa's grandfather, an official named Sobekhotep. This chapel contains the only known reference to the House of the Royal Children. The mummies of Tiaa, Pyikhia and Amenemotep were reburied in the so-called Sheikh Abd el-Qurna cache along with several others. Tentamun, who died in the same year as her father, was buried in the Valley of the Kings in tomb KV43 together with her father and a brother called Amenemhat.

442 It is probably safe to conclude that none of the princesses ever left Egypt because Amenhotep III is unlikely to have lied when he told a foreign petitioner for his daughter's hand in marriage that "From olden times, no king's daughter has been given in marriage outside of Egypt". In a later age a diminished Egypt evidently relaxed this rule, however, for "Solomon made an alliance with Pharaoh king of Egypt and married his daughter." (1 Kings 3:1).

443 The life of such a princess may have been comparatively luxurious, but was almost certainly heavily constrained. The harems of ancient Egypt were called *kheneret*, which is related to words meaning restrain, confine and prison.

444 In one single temple alone at Thebes (dedicated to Mut, consort of Amun) some 600 statues of Sekhmet were placed on the orders of Amenhotep III. A total of 745 of these statues have been found thus far, with more coming to light all the time. These are not small figurines but enormous objects of homage and supplication, twice human size, weighing over a ton apiece. Many refer to towns and villages whose existence is otherwise unknown, suggesting depopulation, perhaps by reason of the departure of large numbers of Israelites or death of the native firstborn.

445 The Hebrew for the word "firstborn" (*bekhore*) is linguistically related to that for "chosen" or "choice youth" (*bakhur*). It is therefore possible that Exodus' speaking of the killing of Egyptian firstborn is a literary device – a formula somewhat akin to the English "flower of the land", though also a self-conscious reference to God's having said, "You [Pharaoh] refused to let [my firstborn son, Israel] go; so I will kill your firstborn son." (Exodus 4:23).

446 Of itself this is not conclusive. The same was true of other heirs to the throne, including the elder brother of Ramses II, and mortality rates were high even amongst royalty. Crown Prince Thutmose held the titles Governor of Memphis, Director of the

Prophets of North and South and High Priest of Ptah. Unlike most Egyptian princes, he does not seem to have been kept in the background, for a number of monuments relating to him have been found (see the introduction to chapters 8 and 10 for a brief summary of the religious beliefs that made this unusual).

[447] Amongst other things that suggest disruption at this time, it seems that the course and flow of the Nile was changing. At Thebes the river was evidently narrowing, since gates on the east bank were moved westwards to keep them alongside the water's edge, with a mirror image of this process being carried out on the opposite bank. If the gap in documentation is a result of the events recounted in Exodus, it would be reasonable to assume that the Ten Plagues took place in whole or in part during the twelfth year of Amenhotep III's reign. Further work is needed if this supposition is to be substantiated since at present the dates do not dovetail completely, though it fits neatly with Amenhotep III's issuing a third (and final) set of Commemorative Scarabs in the eleventh year of his reign.

[448] If this epidemic had struck Egypt during the reign of Akhenaten's father it is within the bounds of possibility that it could still have been raging in neighbouring lands, whether or not it had burned itself out in the place of origin.

[449] In the ancient Near East divine names were habitually accompanied by the name of the place where the relevant god was worshipped.

[450] Amenhotep II's successor Thutmose IV is omitted from this table.

[451] The losses suffered by Egypt's army when it pursued the fleeing Israelites slaves were severe: "The best of Pharaoh's officers are drowned in the Red Sea." (Exodus 15:4). The word 'officer' in this context may designate chariot commanders, though see also note 393.

[452] Egyptian chariots had a crew of two, whilst their Hittite equivalents had a crew of three: *seneny* (charioteer), *qer'iu* (shield-bearer) and *kedjen* (chariot-driver) – though see also note 394. The Amarna Letters do not mention chariots, as is to be expected if Egypt's chariot force were then being rebuilt from scratch.

[453] The Bible does not say that Pharaoh was killed. Since it would doubtless have been considered demeaning for him to engage in combat against slaves, it is logical to infer that he and his staff officers would have watched the pursuit from a safe distance.

[454] Some degree of economic and political recovery is likely to have come swifter than replacement of the lost charioteers. As might be expected if he were the Pharaoh of the exodus, the reign of Amenhotep III saw international diplomacy largely replacing the relentless military campaigning of his predecessors, though despite any hardship and deprivation Egypt may have suffered earlier his rule culminated in a series of magnificent jubilee pageants celebrated in Thebes.

[455] Ramses II is usually said to have been born in 1303 BC and to have ruled from 1279 BC to 1213 BC. The tenor of the biblical narrative is that the Pharaoh of the exodus was come relatively new to the throne at the time Moses returned from Midian; the

implication of God's "[concern] about [the Israelites'] suffering" (Exodus 3:7) is that he would have moved swiftly to commission Moses once "all the men who wanted to kill [him were] dead" (Exodus 4:19).

⁴⁵⁶ Further evidence of the extent to which foreigners were recruited into the armed forces is provided by the Wilbour Papyrus. This lists farmers in the middle of the country during the twelfth century BC, a number of whom have foreign names. It is widely assumed that these were veterans from overseas who had been settled on the land at the end of their period of army service. Lists of slaves and servants in the same papyrus suggest that a high proportion of these were of Asiatic (Semitic) origin.

⁴⁵⁷ The economic effect of the Black Death (commonly thought to have killed something in the region of one third of the population of Europe during the outbreak of 1346 to 1353) provides a yardstick for comparison. Widespread death from plague loosened the bonds of feudalism, and the survivors of a decimated peasantry found their bargaining position much improved. Pressure on the land was reduced, workers were in short supply and wages began to creep upwards. Existing ideas and hierarchies were repeatedly challenged, leading to political upheaval, revolt and repression.

⁴⁵⁸ During the New Kingdom the priesthood became a highly specialised profession. In addition to their cult functions the chief priests were increasingly required to be secular administrators. In this they were assisted by a bevy of officials and functionaries both religious and secular. The temples of Amun in particular received such enormous endowments and gifts both from commoners and from grateful pharaohs that the First Prophet or High Priest of this god eventually needed four senior prophets to serve alongside him. Together they supervised not only a host of minor clergy such as bearers of floral offerings, but also a chief steward and overseers for the various temple granaries, storehouses, cattle, huntsmen, peasants, weavers, craftsmen, goldsmiths, sculptors, shipwrights, draughtsmen, record-keepers and police.

⁴⁵⁹ Dissolution of the monasteries in England under Henry VIII provides an imperfect glimpse of the dislocations which may have accompanied closure of temples under Akhenaten. Abrupt loss of employment opportunities and welfare provision formerly provided by monasteries caused real hardship for many, though redistribution of monastic land also led to some becoming wealthy and probably resulted in overall economic stimulus. By contrast, wealth sequestered from temples seems to have been directed either to consumption in the form of offerings to Aten or to largely unproductive investment through wasteful, unnecessary and ultimately abandoned construction projects at a time when Egypt could ill afford either.

⁴⁶⁰ Akhenaten may have been born at any time between about 1385 and 1375 BC, that is, between six and sixteen years into his father's reign. The first documentary record of him so far found appears to date to year thirty of Amenhotep III's kingship, say 1361 BC or thereabouts.

⁴⁶¹ Since he would have been relying only on those events that were within direct or indirect Egyptian knowledge, it is hardly surprising that his concept of God, how he works and what he requires of man was incomplete. The Egyptians are most unlikely to

have known in any detail of things that happened to their former slaves after the loss of their pursuing chariots in the Red Sea, as recounted in Exodus 14. Though they had a string of border look-out posts like the "Migdol [meaning watchtower]" (Exodus 14:2) which lay near the Israelites' camp "by the sea, directly opposite Baal Zephon" (Exodus 14:2), the Hebrew tribes would most probably have passed beyond the last of these when they crossed the Red Sea and headed further into the Sinai Peninsula.

[462] If this final confirmation of the Almighty's judgment on the gods of Egypt were caused by an earthquake it would most probably have happened after the Israelites left Egypt. As they gathered at Mount Sinai immediately before the giving of the Ten Commandments "the whole mountain trembled violently" (Exodus 19:18). Exodus makes no specific mention of earth tremors in connection with the Ten Plagues.

[463] Although he was an Egyptian, Manetho seems to have written exclusively in Greek. The complete text of the *Aegyptiaca* has not been preserved. Fragments are known through quotations and references in other works.

[464] Amenophis is the Greek form of Amenhotep. Intriguingly, Amenhotep III's master of works (who masterminded and supervised the pharaoh's great building projects) was Amenhotep-son-of-Hapu, a name which bears more than a passing resemblance to Amenophis son of Paapis. The similarity lends credence to the identification of the Pharaoh Amenophis of Manetho's account with Amenhotep III. So highly regarded was Amenhotep-son-of-Hapu during his lifetime that he was granted the unprecedented honour of his own funerary temple and was deified in the Ptolomaic period.

[465] The population of Akhet-aten has been variously estimated, from 20,000 to as many as 50,000 inhabitants. Since not all its ruins have been excavated, even the higher figure may be an underestimate. By way of comparison, it is reckoned that during the Eighteenth Dynasty Thebes covered something like 1,500 acres and had a population in the order of 90,000.

[466] This does not require Akhenaten to have been the Pharaoh of the exodus, given that Moses remained leader of the Israelites during their forty years in the wilderness.

[467] About the Jewish rising against the Romans from AD 66 to AD 70, in which Josephus was an active participant.

[468] Countless examples show that, whilst a culture which belongs to a subservient or minority group will generally absorb influences from the dominant culture more readily than vice versa, nevertheless there will often be a flow of ideas and influences in the opposite direction. A culture as resilient as that of Jewish monotheism was well equipped to stand its ground in the face of Egyptian beliefs, as attested by Moses' readiness to identify himself with the former rather than the latter.

[469] Further work on the Psalms was carried out after the Babylonian exile so as to bring them into the form in which they exist today.

[470] Further detail on population is given in Appendix 2.

⁴⁷¹ The extraordinary fruitfulness of the Israelites is shown by the fact there were only seventy who first came to settle in Goshen (see Exodus 1:1-5). For these few over the course of the next four hundred years to have produced the number of descendants described in Numbers 1:21-46 is remarkable, but not mathematically impossible.

⁴⁷² By the Thirteenth Dynasty even in Upper Egypt the number of what the Egyptians called Asiatics (usually meaning by this Semites from beyond their north-eastern borders) was considerable. One official of the time had no fewer than forty-five in his household. They acted as cooks, brewers, seamstresses, vine-dressers, dancers and in a variety of other menial tasks, but some also attained positions of trust and responsibility. At least one held the relatively prestigious position of doorkeeper at a temple of Sesostris II.

⁴⁷³ These figures rely heavily on conjecture and extrapolation, though it seems that by this time slaves were at least as numerous in Rome as freedmen (non-citizens). Some estimate that at the height of Roman power in the mid second century AD the aggregate slave population of the Empire as a whole may have approached ten million, nearly one sixth of the total. Since it is supported by accurate census returns, a less speculative comparison is provided by the United States. In 1860 slaves accounted for just over a third of the inhabitants of the Upper and Lower South (the eleven States which together formed the Confederacy), the total population of those regions being 9,003,372, of which 5,482,222 were free and 3,521,150 slaves.

⁴⁷⁴ Where the figure is rounded to "about six hundred thousand men on foot, besides women and children" (Exodus 12:37) that is presumably for ease of narrative in a context that does not call for the precise detail required when listing results of a census. Attempts have been made to explain away the large numbers as (1) relating to a later time, perhaps that of King David or (2) being symbolic, though it is not clear of exactly what, or (3) not reflecting the fact that the word now rendered as thousands (*eleph*) might originally have meant clan, leader or family group, in which case the total would more likely be between 5,000 and 72,000 (depending on exactly how figures are recalculated). In truth, none of these interpretations of the text is wholly satisfactory.

⁴⁷⁵ More precise analyses of demographic change have tended to lower the estimates of total population rather than to increase them. The most recent attempt raises the total to four million but is not based on rigorous demographic analysis (and its methodology results in lowering the area of agricultural land to 20,000 square kilometres). It is generally thought that population in the Nile Valley outweighed that in the Delta by a factor of fifteen to thirteen. As far as known, no population estimates have yet sought to take account of the lost towns and villages recorded on statues of Sekhmet (see note 444).

⁴⁷⁶ Akhenaten, his father Amenhotep III and his grandfather Thutmose IV ruled in the second half of the Eighteenth Dynasty (see Appendix 1).

⁴⁷⁷ The demographic make-up of Roman Egypt is reasonably well documented, with about 300 papyri recording census returns from this period. These detail not only members of families living in the Nile Valley but also their slaves and lodgers. Nevertheless, deriving overall population figures is problematic since the two principal sources are contradictory. First century BC Greek historian Diodorus Siculus put the

population of his day at 3 million, whilst Josephus (writing a century later) gave a total of 7.5 million excluding Alexandria, to which Diodorus ascribed a population of 300,000. The modern tendency is to prefer the figures given by Diodorus Siculus, but the truth could lie anywhere between his total and that given by Josephus.

478 As well as the episodes recorded in the Bible when Egypt supported peoples from abroad during times of famine during the days of Abraham (Genesis 12:10) and Joseph (Genesis 41:53-42:2), surplus grain from The Two Lands is known to have succoured the Hittites during a famine in the reign of Merneptah in about 1211 BC.

479 In addition to domestic production, tribute or imports from overseas could have helped sustain a population beyond what Egypt was able to feed from her own resources, though there is nothing to suggest this was necessary.

480 That they formed an even greater proportion cannot be ruled out, for the slaves "multiplied and spread; so [much that] the Egyptians came to dread the Israelites" (Exodus 1:12).

481 This is an estimated twenty times the inhabitants of Jerusalem under the Jebusites, who (despite an initial Israelite sacking under Joshua) controlled that city until its conquest by King David (see 2 Samuel 5:6-7). Archaeological research has so far revealed twenty-two layers of occupation at Hazor, spanning 2,700 years from the early Bronze Age in the twenty-ninth century BC to the Hellenistic period of the second century BC. The city was strategically located so as to control the point where trade routes from north, east and west converged in northern Canaan. Amongst other things, Hazor was important in the trading of tin (one of the components of bronze). Cuneiform tablets from the reign of King Zimri-Lin of Mari in the eighteenth century BC record that his contemporary King Hammurabi of Babylon thought Hazor important enough to warrant keeping two ambassadors there. Its site covers 225 acres, twice the size of Canaanite Megiddo.

482 For example, the Bible records that "Caesar Augustus issued a decree that a census should be taken of the entire Roman world [which was] the first census that took place whilst Quirinius was governor of Syria." (Luke 2:1-2). It is reasonable to suppose that an educated man like Josephus would have known at least the broad outline of the census results for Roman Palestine, just as his equivalent nowadays might be expected to know the rough population of his own and indeed various other countries. Quite apart from matters of general knowledge, as a member of the Jewish elite and a leading figure in the revolt of AD 70, it could well have been Josephus' business to know the manpower resources that were at the disposal of the rebels and the disposition of forces which were employed in the defence of Jerusalem. Tax revenues would likewise have been a major pre-occupation of those responsible for administration of the incipient Jewish state, and these would largely have been a function of population. Moreover, Josephus says that he acted as negotiator between the Romans and the Jewish rebels during the siege of Jerusalem, in which his parents and his first wife died. In the light of all this, he is unlikely to have produced casualty figures that were completely invented.

483 No attempt is made to place a figure on the numbers involved, presumably since the Israelites were unable to make an accurate count. Hence a standard expression for a large multitude is adopted. This suggests that where precise numbers appear elsewhere in the book of Joshua they were used carefully, lending credence to their reliability.

484 Until the middle of the nineteenth century some contended that Nineveh never existed, or at any rate that there could not at that time have been such a large conurbation as the Bible describes, for Scripture says that "Nineveh was a very large city with many villages around it – so large that it would take three days to walk through it" (Jonah 3:3, TLB). The sceptics' assertions were disproved when the city's remains were excavated by Austen Henry Layard from 1845-47. It turned out that Nineveh was indeed massive but had been so completely obliterated by the Babylonians under Nabipolassar in 612 BC that all which remained of it were two mounds (tells).

485 These being the dimensions posited in the model used by the National Centre for Atmospheric Research in Boulder, Colorado, as described in note 178.

486 For the reasons given above, this would seem to be at the high end of the range suggested by Scripture.

487 NATO armies typically work on the basis of two to five metres between dismounted soldiers moving in open column. Though this formation is normally used in daylight, it can be employed at night with the use of night-vision equipment. The crossing of the Red Sea did not take place in pitch blackness, for the pillar of cloud "brought darkness to the one side [the Egyptians] and light to the other [Israel]" (Exodus 14:20). Allowing three square yards per person may nevertheless be too conservative, since fear is likely to have caused the Israelites to pack in more tightly than they might otherwise. They may consequently have adopted something like close column, with between one and three metres between individuals. This formation is normally used in blackout conditions or for marches in restricted terrain since it takes maximum advantage of the traffic capacity of a route and provides less dispersion, albeit at the expense of a slower rate of movement.

488 Though Scripture records that "the Israelites went through the sea on dry ground" (Exodus 14:22), this might be meant by way of contrast with the "wall of water on their right and on their left" (Exodus 14:22) rather than indicating that there was no moisture at all in the land over which they passed. Presumably conditions underfoot would have been akin to a beach after the tide has gone out.

489 Daybreak in Egypt at the start of June occurs at around 5.00 am, the exact time depending on precise date and location. (The likelihood is that the Ten Plagues proceeded at the rate of one per month, beginning in August and carrying through to the succeeding May, placing the Israelites' likely departure date from Egypt as late May or early June; see chapter 6 and Appendix 4 for the circumstances surrounding each plague and their probable timings.)

490 The supposition is that a group whom the Egyptians called the Peleset were the people known to us as Philistines.

⁴⁹¹ There was a well-trodden route along the coast from Egypt to Canaan that was called the Way of the Philistines.

⁴⁹² The suggested timings of the plagues follow the schema set out in chapter 6.

⁴⁹³ It might also involve a swipe at Baal. Later generations of Israelites called him Baal-Zebub (Lord of the Flies), a pun on his title of Baal-Zebul (Lord of Lords or Baal the Prince) (see 2 Kings 1:2, 1:3, 1:6 and 1:16).

⁴⁹⁴ Though Amun, Ra and Aten were the major sun-gods, the other deities in this list also had powerful solar connections. The cat goddess Bastet was linked to the rising sun, whilst as "finisher of the world" Atum represented the sun as it set. The right eye of the sky-god Horus was considered to be the sun and his left the moon. Khepri was god of rebirth and sunrise, Khnum god of sunset. Nefertum, god of healing and beauty, stood for the first sunlight whereas Ptah, god of fertility, the arts and craftsmanship, was also sometimes said to represent the sun at night. Sekhmet was goddess of war, plagues and the sun, Sopdu god of war and the scorching heat of the summer sun.

⁴⁹⁵ Perhaps alternatively capable of being rendered, "the great mountain". The Hebrew word *midbar* (usually translated into English as desert or wilderness) is a generic term for a wild or unsafe place.

⁴⁹⁶ Given the paucity of grazing land and watering holes, and bearing in mind that there was friction between different tribes over their use – as when "shepherds came along and drove [Jethro's daughters] away] from the well where they came to draw water]" (Exodus 3:17) – Moses might have been better advised to keep to uncontested areas, but he was clearly not someone to be deterred by the prospect of encountering opposition or challenge.

⁴⁹⁷ Throughout Exodus the names Horeb and Sinai seem to be used interchangeably, the former appearing thrice (Exodus 3:1, 17:6 and 33:6), the latter ten times (Exodus 19:11, 19:18, 19:20, 19:23, 24:16, 31:18, 34:2, 34:4, 34:29 and 34:32). Some take from this that Horeb might have been one of the peaks of Sinai; Christian tradition identifies Horeb with Jebel Catherina in the south of the Sinai Peninsula, which has two peaks, today called Mount Horeb and Jebel Musa (in Arabic, the Mountain of Moses). Another tradition identifies Mount Horeb with Ras es-Safsaf (Willow Peak, 6,500 feet high) and Mount Sinai with Jebel Musa (the Mountain of Moses, 7,400 feet high). Alternatively, Horeb might be the Semitic term for what was known to non-Semites as Sinai. The etymology of Sinai is doubtful, though probably connected to the nearby Desert of Sin.

⁴⁹⁸ At one point the Israelites "travelled along the desert road of Moab." (Deuteronomy 2:8).

⁴⁹⁹ Numbers 33:1-49 lists "the stages in the journey of the Israelites when they came out of Egypt by divisions under the leadership of Moses and Aaron." (Numbers 33:1). There is no reason to view this as anything other than a more or less contemporaneous account, since it is specifically said that "At the LORD's command Moses recorded the stages in their journey." (Numbers 33:2). Eleven camps are noted between leaving Egypt and camping "in the desert of Sinai" (Numbers 33:15; see also Exodus 19:1-2), though it was

not until "the third month after the Israelites left Egypt – on the very day – [that] they came to the Desert of Sinai ... and Israel camped there in the desert in front of the mountain." (Exodus 19:1-2). This is consistent with the seven weeks which tradition has it elapsed between leaving Egypt and the granting of the Law, if three months is intended to mean a period that straddled the end of one month and the beginning of another with a full month in between.

[500] Passover lambs had been slaughtered on "the fourteenth day [of the previous month]" (Exodus 12:6) and Israel had left Egypt the next day.

[501] This began with an Amalekite attack on the Israelite camp and continued for the whole of the following day, with Moses interceding with God on behalf of Israel "until the sun set" (Exodus 17:12, NRSV), so presumably those who had been in combat would have needed a period of rest to recuperate and tend their wounds afterwards.

[502] Biblical writers clearly considered the Desert of Sin and the Desert of Sinai to be distinct. The latter was probably even more desolate than the former; the "ai" component means ruin or desolation, as in the Canaanite town of that name which Joshua's army "burned ... and made ... a permanent heap of ruins, a desolate place to this day" (Joshua 8:28).

[503] The distance between Rephidim and Horeb as the crow flies need not have been great. A mountainous landscape cut by deep ravines combined with the encumbrance of a baggage train, the elderly and infirm and substantial flocks would have made it sensible for the main body of the Israelites to take a roundabout route, keeping to the valleys, whilst Moses and those who accompanied him to witness the miraculous provision of water could have taken a short cut across country.

[504] The same northern Italian city is called Milan in English, Mailand in German and Milano by the natives. One group in Northern Ireland speaks of Londonderry, another of Derry.

[505] Since the exception is a quotation from "the blessing that Moses the man of God pronounced on the Israelites before his death" (Deuteronomy 33:1), this was presumably added after the prophet's passing by someone who was unaware of why Moses had exclusively used Horeb hitherto. By contrast, Moses did not employ Horeb at all in Leviticus or Numbers, which refer only to Sinai.

[506] The Romans generally thought of Arabia as being the region lying beyond their control in the Arabian Peninsula, which Ptolemy had divided into three parts: Arabia Deserta, Arabia Petraea and Arabia Felix. Rome did not annex the erstwhile Nabatean Kingdom to form its province of *Arabia Petraea* (also known as *Provincia Arabia* or simply *Arabia*) until decades after St Paul's death. The conquest took place in AD 106 under Emperor Trajan.

[507] The jury is out on whether the traditional identification of Mount Sinai is correct. Simcha Jacobovici, Adjunct Professor in the Religious Studies Department of Huntington University, Canada argues persuasively that Horeb was another mountain in

the Sinai Peninsula, Hashem el-Tarif: see his article in the Jerusalem Post on 25 September 2013.

508 There is agreement on the translation of only a single phrase from amongst the various graffiti at Serabit el-Khadim: לבעלת (*l b'lt,* meaning 'to the Lady'). This would seem to be a reference to Hathor, who was patron goddess of the miners and was known as the Lady of the Turquoise. As well as being part of one of the titles of Hathor, *ba'lat* (the lady) is the feminine equivalent of Baal (Lord), the major Canaanite god. Hence the presence of this word is said by some to support the view that the language of the graffiti is Semitic. Also tentatively identified is the word *m'hb,* meaning 'loved'.

509 Huge quantities of turquoise were mined over this period. They were carried down Wadi Matalla to a garrisoned port at el-Markha, then shipped to Egypt where they were used both for jewellery and to provide pigment for paint.

510 These most probably would have spoken a Semitic language such as Canaanite, to which both Phoenician and Hebrew are related.

511 They may have been involved in repair or extension work on the temple (which was enlarged during the New Kingdom, latterly by Akhenaten's father Amenhotep III) or have toiled in the mines. Even if such work was not amongst the routine employments of Israelite slaves, Hebrews may have been used in exceptional circumstances or where manpower was short. The notoriously grim environment of the mines might also conceivably have been a punishment for runaways.

512 Examples include (1) a letter to Senedjemib Inti from Fifth Dynasty monarch Isesi (who reigned from about 2414 BC to 2375 BC), which says that "His Person [the pharaoh] wrote with his fingers"; (2) the Prophecy of Neferti, which states that King Sneferu "stretched out his hand to his box of writing materials and took a papyrus roll and a palette (*gstj*). Then he wrote down what the chief lector priest of Neferti said"; (3) a stela of Amenhotep II which contains the text of a letter to Usersatet, viceroy of Nubia, which is said to be a copy of "a royal letter which his Person [the pharaoh] made with his own hand to (the viceroy)". As regards (2) it should be noted that the Prophecy of Neferti was in fact composed during the early Twelfth Dynasty (about 650 years after the time of Sneferu), but presumably it purported to record something a king might actually have done.

513 Papyrus is known to have been invented by the start of the First Dynasty since two blank rolls of it were found in a storeroom of the tomb Den at Saqqara, which dates from that time. By the first millennium BC at the latest, Egypt was exporting rolls of papyrus to other states in the Near East – a trade which indicates that pen and ink were displacing the more cumbersome method of using a stylus to impress cuneiform symbols on clay tablets.

514 The words "writing", "book" and "ink" are common to all branches of the Semitic tongue, suggesting that these things were known to the earliest Semites before they separated into different races. Abraham hailed from "Ur of the Chaldeans" (Genesis, NKJV), cradle-land of the oldest forms of writing. Since he came from a literate culture

and had the free time that comes to someone who "became very wealthy" (Genesis 26:13) it is not difficult to envisage that he would have passed the ability to read and write to his descendants. At least some of those who lived in close proximity to Abraham and his family in their new homeland also appear to have been literate: near the Canaanite city of Hebron "where Abraham and Isaac had stayed" (Genesis 35:27) and the patriarchs were buried (see Genesis 23:19, 25:9, 35:27 and 49:29-31) lay Kiriath-Sepher, which means "scribe-town". That this name was extremely ancient is attested by the fact that by the time of Joshua it was styled differently and it was necessary to remind people that "Debir [was] ... formerly called Kiriath Sepher" (Joshua 15:15). Jews remained highly literate throughout the ages, their literacy rates far exceeding those of Gentiles in Mediaeval Europe, for example.

[515] The divine element should not, of course, be overlooked. The "two tablets of the Testimony" (Exodus 32:15) were so saturated with the Word of God that they were "inscribed on both sides, front and back. The tablets were the work of God; the writing was the writing of God, engraved on the tablets." (Exodus 32:15-16).

[516] It is of course likely that in the early stages after coming out from Egypt few Israelites apart from Moses were literate, slave-owners seldom being keen to see their charges too highly educated. The fact that Moses was told to "write this [the account of Israel's defeat of the Amalekites] on a scroll as something to be remembered and make sure that Joshua hears it" (Exodus 17·14) suggests that the latter could not read but had to have the words recited to him.

[517] Papyrus was first manufactured in Egypt as early as the second millennium BC.

Index of Scripture References

Roman numerals in bold refer to illustrations.

Genesis.
1:1 (p. 284).
1:2 (p. 283, 292).
1:3 (p. 39, 109, 175, 282, 292, 293).
1:4 (p. 38)
1:6 (p. 39, 109, 175, 282, 292, 293).
1:9 (p. 39, 109, 175, 282, 292, 293).
1:10 (p. 38, 282).
1:11 (p. 39, 109, 175, 292, 293).
1:11-12 (p. 282).
1:12 (p. 38, 282).
1:14 (p. 39, 54, 109, 175, 292, 293).
1:14-18 (p. 282).
1:18 (p. 38, 282).
1:20 (p. 39, 109, 175, 292, 293).
1:20-22 (p. 282),
1:21 (p. 38, 282).
1:22 (p. 282).
1:24 (p. 39, 109, 175, 292, 293).
1:25 (p. 38, 282).
1:26 (p. 109, 175, 292).
1:27 (p. 80, 89, 108, 110).
1:28 (p. 38, 128, 282).
1:31 (p. 38, 80, 282).
2:2 (p. 56).
2:4 (p. 111, 293).
2:6 (p. 111).
2:7 (p. 109, 111, 283).
2:10-14 (p. 282).
2:15 (p. 32).
2:19 (p. 268).
2:22 (p. 291).
2:24 (p.110).

3, passim (p. 269).
3:1 (p. 39).
3:5 (p. 309).
3:8 (p. 48).
3:23 (p. 187).
4:1 (p. 270).
4:3-4 (p. 302).
4:4-5 (p. 302).
4:6-7 (p. 268).
4:7 (p. 268).
4:10 (p. 310).
4:14 (p. 187).
6:14 (p. 39).
7:12 (p. 292).
9:1 (p. 38).
11:4 (p. 195).
11:5 (p. 315).
11:31 (p. 334).
12:3 (p. 271).
12:10 (p. 200, 331).
14:19-20 (p. 108).
14:20 (p. 289).
15, passim (p. 133).
15:1 (p. 314).
15:3 (p. 319).
15:13 (p. 271, 309, 323).
15:16 (p. 226, 297).
15:19-21 (p. 237).
16:13-14 (p. 108).
17:1 (p. 108, 172).
17:5 (p. 293).
17:13-14 (p. 311).
18, passim (p. 292).
18:3 (p. 113).
18:18 (p. 22).
18:25 (p. 125).
19:26 (p. 24).
21:17 (p. 314).
21:34 (p. 237).
22, passim (p. 291).

22:8 (p. 108, 267).
22:18 (p. 298).
23:19 (p. 336).
24, passim (p. 265)
25:1-2 (p. 266).
25:9 (p. 336).
26:1 (p. 237).
26:4-5 (p. 298).
26:8 (p. 237).
26:13 (p. 336).
26:14-15 (p. 237).
26:15 (p. 287).
26:18 (p. 237).
29, passim (p. 265).
29:32 (p. 73).
30:13 (p. 217).
31:42 (p. 314).
31:53 (p. 314).
32:22-32 (p. 292).
32:24 (p. 279).
32:30 (p. 279, 314).
33:20 (p. 108).
34, passim (p. 266).
34:25-29 (p. 300).
35:27 (p. 336).
37:3 (p. 255).
39:20 (p. 299).
40:1-2 (p. 299).
40:21 (p. 299).
40:22 (p. 299).
41:29-30 (p. 211).
41:48-49 (p. 211).
41:53-42:2 (p. 331).
41:57 (p. 200).
43:32 (p. 312).
46:3 (p. 314).
46:6 (p. 211).
46:8-14 (p. 38).
46:17 (p. 209).
46:27 (p. 164).

47:1-12 (p. 210).
47:11 (p. 214).
47:20-22 (p. 211, 324).
47:26 (p. 211).
47:27 (p. 229, 298).
47:28 (p. 324).
48:14 (p. 197).
49:3 (p. 59, 69, 73).
49:5-6 (p. 27).
49:7 (p. 43).
49:10 (p. 105, 118).
49:13 (p. 75).
49:15 (p. 183).
49:16 (p. 121, 134).
49:19 (p. 11).
49:20 (p. 151, 165).
49:21 (p. 167).
49:22 (p. 135).
49:24 (p. 68).
49:27 (p. 91, 323).
49:29-31 (p. 336).
50:3 (p. 308).
50:24 (p. 324, 325).

Exodus.
1:1-5 (p. 38, 330).
1:6 (p. 118).
1:6-7 (p. 128).
1:7 (p. 118, 229, 301).
1:8 (p. 154, 212, 218, **I**).
1:9 (p. 170).
1:9-10 (p. 229).
1:10 (p. 285).
1:11 (p. 24, 99, 138, 212, 214).
1:11-14 (p. 102, 319, **II**).
1:12 (p. 38, 118, 128, 145, 331).
1:13 (p. 145, 309).
1:13-14 (p. 24).

337

1:14 (p. 138, 181, 309).
1:15-21 (p. 16).
1:15-22 (p. 271).
1:16 (p. 41, 102).
1:17 (p. 265).
1:18 (p. 265).
1:19 (p. 265).
1:20 (p. 38).
1:20-21 (p. 17).
1:22 (p. 102, 114, 138, 286).
2:1-2 (p. 267).
2:1-3 (p. 16).
2:1-20 (p. 203, 215, 319).
2:2 (p. 38, 114).
2:3 (p. 39, 70, 114, **III**).
2:4 (p. 16, 115).
2:5 (p. 198, 286).
2:5-6 (p. 16, 265).
2:7 (p. 115).
2:7-8 (p. 16).
2:8 (p. 115).
2:8-9 (p. 16).
2:8-10 (p. 215).
2:9 (p. 114).
2:10 (p. 16, 70, 265, 267).
2:11 (p. 171, 265, 309).
2:11-12 (p. 14, 177).
2:13 (p. 171).
2:13-14 (p. 15).
2:14 (p. 15, 108, 265, 267).
2:15 (p. 17, 163).
2:15-21 (p. 265).
2:16 (p. 17, 116).
2:17 (p. 34, 265).
2:18 (p. 294).
2:19 (p. 163, 265).
2:20 (p. 294).
2:21 (p. 18, 265, 317).
2:22 (p. 18, 70, 309).
2:23 (p. 19, 169, 322).
2:23-25 (p. 127).
2:24 (p. 153).
2:25 (p. 143).

3:1 (p. 18, 19, 48, 67, 191, 196, 217, 243, 245, 265, 333).
3:2 (p. 19, 186, 189, 196, 245).
3:2-3 (p. 19).
3:3 (p. 20, 200).
3:4 (p. 20, 62, 109).
3:5 (p. 47, 49, 67, 147, 187, 245, 274, 313).
3:6 (p. 20, 48, 64, 189, 274, 291, 301).
3:7 (p. 20, 99, 143, 328).
3:7-8 (p. 109).
3:7-9 (p. 48).
3:8 (p. 21, 102, 157, 163, 165, 190).
3:9 (p. 20).
3:10 (p. 21, 23, 48, 113, 139).
3:11 (p. 143, 268).
3:12 (p. 21, 48, 180, 268).
3:13 (p. 267).
3:14 (p. 21, 108, 109, 280, 2956).
3:15 (p. 12, 21, 154).
3:16 (p. 100).
3:16-17 (p. 154).
3:17 (p. 72, 333).
3:18 (p. 117, 199, 243, 272).
3 19 (p. 128).
3:20 (p. 21, 281).
3:21 (p. 21, 271).
3:21-22 (p. 289).
3:22 (p. 85).
4:1 (p. 22).
4:2 (p. 148).
4:3 (p. 149).
4:3-4 (p. 22).
4:4 (p. 149).
4:5 (p. 22).
4:6-7 (p. 22).
4:8 (p. 161).
4:8-9 (p.22).
4:9 (p. 161, 307).

4:10 (p. 22, 171).
4:11 (p. 32).
4:12 (p. 22-3).
4:13 (p. 23).
4:14 (p. 23, 71).
4:14-16 (p. 268).
4:16 (p. 314).
4:17 (p. 67, 287).
4:18 (p. 62, 266).
4:18-26 (p. 95, 102).
4:19 (p. 208, 278, 328).
4:20 (p. 103, 117,149).
4:21 (p. 37, 78, 178, 281).
4:22 (p. 40).
4:22-23 (p. 37, 270).
4:23 (p. 145, 302, 326).
4:24 (p. 294).
4:24-26 (p. 117).
4:26 (p. 294-5).
4:27 (p. 114, 243).
4:27-28 (p. 71, 265).
4:29 (p. 114).
4:29-30 (p. 103).
4:29-31 (p. 48-9).
4:30 (p. 114-5, 117, 171).
4:30-31 (p. 161).
4:31 (p. 117, 143, 161, 171).
5:1 (p. 23, 49, 133, 169, 198, 199, 272).
5:2 (p. 33, 34, 79, 143, 147, 198, **IV**).
5:3 (p. 199, 243, 272).
5:4 (p. 169-70, 181).
5:4-5 (**V**).
5:5 (p. 170).
5:6 (p. 99, 143).
5:6-8 (p. 212-3).
5:6-9 (p. 33-4).
5:9 (p. 144, 170, 181).
5:10 (p. 99).
5:10-12 (p. 170).
5:11 (p. 181).
5:12 (p. 170, 213).
5:13 (p. 99, 181).
5:14 (p. 99).

5:15 (p. 99).
5:15-16 (p. 170).
5:17-18 (p. 170).
5:18 (p. 178, 181).
5:19 (p. 99).
5:20-21 (p. 103).
5:22 (p. 104).
5:22-23 (p. 104).
6:1 (p. 282).
6:1-8 (p. 264).
6:2-3 (p. 21, 218).
6:3 (p. 108).
6:4 (p. 193, 309, 312).
6:5 (p. 153).
6:6 (p. 145, 198).
6:6-7 (p. 40, 108, 179).
6:7 (p. 28).
6:8 (p. 193, 309, 312).
6:9 (p. 118, 133, 140, 145).
6:10-11 (p. 264).
6:12 (p. 171, 309).
6:13 (p. 294).
6:14-19 (p. 267).
6:14-27 (p. 271).
6:16-25 (p. 273).
6:20 (p. 267).
6:26 (p. 40, 287).
6:27 (p. 294).
6:28 (p. 264).
6:29 (p. 128, 298).
6:30 (p. 171-2, 309).
7:1-2 (p. 114, 148).
7:1-5 (p. 264).
7:2 (p. 128).
7:3 (p. 37, 161).
7:4 (p. 287).
7:5 (p. 171).
7:6 (p. 295, 297).
7:7 (p. 194).
7:8 (p. 264).
7:8-10 (p. 113).
7:10 (p. 30, 242, 294).
7:11 (p. 30, 32, 113, 180, 194).
7:12 (p. 31, 242).

Index of Scripture References

7:13 (p. 271).
7:14-20 (p. 270).
7:14-25 (p. 241).
7:16 (p. 23, 49, 198, 199, 272).
7:19 (p. 172, 307).
7:20 (p. 30, 149, 172, 194, 295).
7:21 (p. 172).
7:22 (p. 30, 32, 180, 271).
7:23 (p. 34).
7:24 (p. 307).
7:25 (p. 314).
8:1 (p. 23, 49, 198, 272).
8:1-15 (p. 241).
8:2 (p. 271).
8:2-4 (p. 288).
8:5 (p. 149).
8:6 (p. 30, 194).
8:7 (p. 30, 32, 180).
8:8 (p. 34).
8:9 (p. 314).
8:9-14 (p. 311).
8:10 (p. 314).
8:10-11 (p. 314).
8:12-13 (p. 31).
8:14 (p. 288).
8:15 (p. 34, 37).
8:16-17 (p. 288).
8:16-19 (p. 241).
8:17 (p. 194).
8:18 (p. 31).
8:19 (p. 14, 271).
8:20 (p. 23, 49, 198, 272).
8:20-21 (p. 270).
8:20-32 (p. 241).
8:21 (p. 194, 271).
8:21-22 (p. 288).
8:23 (p. 128, 161).
8:24 (p. 301).
8:25 (p. 311).
8:26 (312, **VI**).
8:27 (p. 243, 272).
8:27-28 (p. 199).
8:28 (p. 34).
8:29 (p. 35).

8:30-31 (p. 178).
8:32 (p. 34, 37).
9:1 (p. 23, 49, 198, 272).
9:1-7 (p. 241).
9:1-12 (p. 301).
9:2 (p. 271).
9:3 (p. 194).
9:4 (p. 39, 128).
9:5-6 (p. 314).
9:6 (p. 39).
9:7 (p. 271).
9:8-12 (p. 241).
9:9 (p. 194).
9:11 (p. 32, 147).
9:12 (p. 37).
9:13 (p. 23, 49, 198, 272).
9:13-15 (p. 270).
9:13-35 (p. 241).
9:16 (p. 9).
9:17 (p. 172).
9:18 (p. 101, 288).
9:19 (p. 31, 35, 37).
9:20 (p. 14, 35, 37).
9:21 (p. 149).
9:22 (p. 264).
9:23-26 (p. 288).
9:25 (p. 195).
9:27 (p. 35).
9:27-28 (p. 34).
9:29 (p. 36).
9:29-30 (p. 311).
9:30 (p. 36, 189).
9:31-32 (p. 36).
9:33 (p. 149).
9:34 (p. 34, 37).
9:35 (p. 271).
10:1 (p. 37, 161).
10:1-2 (p. 307).
10:1-20 (p. 241).
10:2 (p. 191).
10:3 (p. 23, 49, 143, 198, 272).
10:4 (p. 271).
10:4-6 (p. 288).
10:7 (p. 36, 37, 301).
10:8 (p. 49).

10:9 (p. 112).
10:10-11 (p. 48, 49).
10:11 (p. 171, 196).
10:12 (p. 36).
10:13-14 (p. 241).
10:13-15 (p. 287, **VII**).
10:15 (p. 195).
10:16-17 (p. 36, **VIII**).
10:18-19 (p. 36, 311).
10:20 (p. 37).
10:21 (p. 288).
10:21-29 (p. 241).
10:22 (p. 195).
10:22-23 (p. 287).
10:23 (p. 313).
10:24-27 (p. 49).
10:25-26 (p. 233).
10:26 (p. 52).
10:27 (p. 37).
10:28 (p. 36-7, 278).
10:29 (p. 278).
11:1 (p. 264).
11:2 (p. 112).
11:2-3 (p. 289).
11:3 (p. 270).
11:4-6 (p. 290).
11:4-7 (p. 319).
11:7 (p. 39, 128, 301).
11:8 (p. 142, 177).
11:9 (p. 307).
11:10 (p. 37).
12:1-14 (p. 158).
12:6 (p. 334).
12:12 (p. 95, 156, 241, 301, 318).
12:13 (p. 161, 172-3).
12:14 (p. 163, 173, 309).
12:15 (p. 173, 310).
12:15-16 (p. 158).
12:16 (p. 181).
12:17 (p. 173, 287, 309).
12:18-20 (p. 173).
12:19 (p. 173, 309, 310).
12:21 (p. 117).
12:22 (p. 172, 313).

12:23 (p. 173, 179, 289, 307, **IX**).
12:24 (p. 173, 309).
12:25-27 (p. 308).
12:27-28 (p. 274).
12:29 (p. 186, 195, 199).
12:29-30 (p. 37, 216, 241, 301, 319).
12:31-32 (p. 49).
12:33 (p. 103, 271).
12:34 (p. 198, 307).
12:35-36 (p. 103).
12:36 (p. 233, 298, 301).
12:37 (p. 214, 229, 330).
12:37-38 (p. 229).
12:38 (p.14, 38, 229, 301).
12:39 (p. 310).
12:40-41 (p. 40, 210, 319).
12:41 (p. 287).
12:42 (p. 186).
12:43-44 (p. 311).
12:43-47 (p. 310).
12:48-49 (p. 295, 311).
12:50 (p. 315).
12:51 (p. 287, 315).
13:1-2 (p. 272).
13:3-16 (p. 290).
13:9 (p. 161).
13:11 (p. 297).
13:13 (p. 40).
13:14-16 (p. 162).
13:17 (p. 96-7, 237).
13:18 (p. 99, 199).
13:19 (p. 218, 308).
13:20 (p. 235).
13:21 (p. 52, 196, 318, **X, XI**).
13:22 (p. 186, 317, 320).
14:1-4 (p. 98).
14:2 (p. 235, 329).
14:2-3 (p. 244).
14:4 (p. 37).
14:5-6 (p. 37-8).
14:6-7 (p. 219, 220).

339

14:7 (p. 318).
14:8 (p. 97, 104).
14:9 (p. 274).
14:10 (p. 104, 118, 190).
14:11 (p. 175).
14:12 (p. 136, 139).
14:13 (p. 57, 104, 201, 314).
14:13-31 (p. 95).
14:14 (p. 92, 97, 104).
14:15 (p. 149).
14:16 (p. 149).
14:17 (p. 97).
14:18 (p. 97).
14:19 (p. 51, 287, 317).
14:19-20 (p. 98, 194, **XII**).
14:20 (p. 98, 194, 234, 317, 332).
14:21 (p. 98, 234, 272).
14:21-22 (p. 39, 98, 242).
14:22 (p. 98, 332).
14:23 (p. 98, 287).
14:23-28 (p. 242).
14:24 (p. 317).
14:24-25 (p. 98, 234).
14:25 (p. 234).
14:26-28 (p. 98).
14:27 (p. 234).
14:27-28 (p. 219, 220, 234).
14:29-30 (p. 98-9).
14:30 (p. 99, 195).
14:31 (p. 97, 99, 118, 188).
15:1 (p. 79, 274).
15:1-18 (p. 315).
15:1-2 (p. 34).
15:2 (p. 315).
15:3 (p. 96, 127).
15:4 (p. 79, 327).
15:5 (p. 200).
15:6 (p. 80, 128).
15:7 (p. 96).
15:7-8 (p. 80).
15:8 (p. 188).

15:9 (p. 96).
15:9-10 (p. 80).
15:11 (p. 69, 155, 161, **XIII**).
15:12 (p. 200).
15:13 (p. 140, 155, 274).
15:13-16 (p. 102).
15:14 (p. 316).
15:15 (p. 316).
15:16 (p. 181, 190, 316, **XIV**).
15:17-19 (p. 315).
15:20 (p. 115, 283).
15:21 (p. 116).
15:22 (p. 243, 263, 273).
15:22-25 (**XV**).
15:23-24 (p. 164).
15:24 (p. 63, 71, 118, 180).
15:25 (p. 274).
15:25-26 (p. 297).
15:26 (p. 164, 179, 299, 301).
15:27 (p. 147, 164).
16:1 (p. 243, 243-4).
16:1-35 (p. 50, 230, 293).
16:2 (p. 71, 118, 180, 278).
16:3 (p. 23).
16:4 (p. 133, 154).
16:6-7 (p. 313)
16:6-8 (p. 290),
16:8 (p. 133, 176, 282).
16:9-10 (p. 193).
16:10 (p. 186, 196).
16:13 (p. 50, 230, 302).
16:15 (p. 178).
16:18 (p. 147).
16:19 (p. 147).
16:19-20 (p. 303).
16:20 (p. 177).
16:25-30 (p. 303).
16:28 (p. 147).
16:29 (p. 178).
16:32 (p. 55, 154).
16:36 (p. 304).

17:1 (p. 100, 243, 244).
17:1-2 (p. 278).
17:1-7 (p. 50, 230).
17:2 (p. 133).
17:3 (p. 71, 118, 180).
17:4 (p. 63).
17:5 (p. 117, 245).
17:5-6 (p. 244).
17:6 (p. 117, 245, 278, 333).
17:7 (p. 118).
17:8 (p. 99, 100).
17:8-13 (p. 244, 305, 322).
17:8-16 (p. 95, 274, 287).
17:9 (p. 100, 149).
17:9-10 (p. 322).
17:9-13 (p. 180).
17:10 (p. 144).
17:11 (p. 100).
17:12 (p. 99, 334).
17:13 (p. 99, 100).
17:14 (p. 152, 154, 157, 249, 279, 336, **XVI**).
17:15-16 (p. 306).
18:1 (p. 148, 294).
18:2 (p. 117).
18:2-3 (p. 117).
18:3-4 (p. 18).
18:4 (p. 71, 289).
18:5-6 (p. 294).
18:7 (p. 294).
18:8 (p. 181).
18:9 (p. 116).
18:9-11 (p. 181).
18:10 (p. 116, 294).
18:11 (p. 148).
18:12 (p. 116, 117-8, 163, 181, 196).
18:13 (p. 130, 299).
18:13-27 (p. 17).
18:14 (p. 130).
18:15 (p. 131).
18:15-16 (p. 277).
18:16 (p. 131).
18:18 (p. 130, 299).

18:19 (p. 132).
18:20 (p. 130, 168).
18:21 (p. 189-90, 288).
18:21-22 (p. 131-2).
18:23 (p. 193).
18:24 (p. 130).
18:25-26 (p. 130).
18:27 (p. 116).
19:1 (p. 124, 243).
19:1-2 (243, 244, 333, 334, **XVII**).
19:2 (p. 235, 244).
19:3-6 (p. 53).
19:5 (p. 122).
19:5-6 (p. 39, 299).
19:6 (p. 38, 161, 174, 301).
19:7-8 (p. 117).
19:9 (p. 186, 196).
19:10-11 (p. 52, 314).
19:11 (p. 175, 190, 333).
19:12 (p. 52, 175, 310).
19:12-13 (p. 180-1).
19:13 (p. 164).
19:14-15 (p. 290).
19:15 (p. 175).
19:16 (p. 102, 188, 317).
19:16-19 (p. 78).
19:18 (p. 190, 318, 329, 333).
19:20 (p. 180, 186, 190, 191, 331).
19:21 (p. 189, 274).
19:22 (p. 52).
19:23 (p. 52, 175, 333).
19:24 (p. 52).
19:25 (p. 290).
20:1 (p. 296, 299).
20:1-19 (p. 291).
20:2 (p. 125, 132, 154).
20:3 (p. 125).
20:3-17 (p. 129).
20:4 (p. 125).
20:4-6 (p. 88).
20:5 (p. 140).
20:6 (p. 127, 155, 317).

Index of Scripture References

20:7 (p. 88, 112, 126, 154).
20:8 (p. 126, 155).
20:9-10 (p. 181).
20:11 (p. 155).
20:12 (p. 126, 307).
20:13-17 (p. 127).
20:15 (p. 298).
20:16 (p. 127).
20:17 (p. 106).
20:18 (p. 188, 306).
20:18-19 (p. 189).
20:18-21 (p. 181).
20:19 (p. 118, 139).
20:20 (p. 63, 144, 189, 314).
20:21 (p. 63, 67, 189).
20:22 (p. 191).
20:22-23 (**XVIII**).
20:24 (p. 88, 193, 301, 315).
20:25 (p. 272).
20:26 (p. 272).
21:1 (p. 125).
21:2-11 (p. 298).
21:5-6 (p. 301).
21:12-14 (p. 311).
21:15 (p. 297).
21:16 (p. 311).
21:17 (p. 297).
21:18-22 (p. 266).
21:23-25 (p. 132).
21:24 (p. 266).
21:25-27 (p. 311).
21:28 (p. 112).
21:29-32 (p. 112).
21:33-36 (p. 266).
22:1-15 (p. 128).
22:3 (p. 298).
22:4 (p. 298).
22:5 (p. 298).
22:6 (p. 298).
22:7 (p. 298).
22:9 (p. 298).
22:11 (p. 127, 298).
22:12 (p. 298).

22:14 (p. 298).
22:16-17 (p. 143).
22:18 (p. 131).
22:19 (p. 297).
22:20 (p. 304, **XIX**).
22:21 (p. 117, 128, 143, 157).
22:22 (p. 128, XX).
22:22-24 (p. 143).
22:24 (p. 143).
22:25-27 (p. 143).
22:27 (p. 9, 143, 155).
22:28 (p. 176).
22:29 (p. 179).
22:29-30 (p. 176).
22:31 (p. 174-5).
23:1 (p. 127).
23:1-2 (p. 124).
23:2 (p. 124, 127, 155).
23:3 (p. 124).
23:4 (p. 144).
23:4-5 (p. 132).
23:6 (p. 143, 155).
23:6-8 (p. 124).
23:9 (p. 294).
23:10-11 (p. 159, 306).
23:12 (p. 155, 181, 294).
23:13 (p. 128, 134, 175, 310, **XXI**).
23:14 (p. 158).
23:15 (p. 158, 159).
23:16 (p. 159).
23:17 (p. 158).
23:18 (p. 173).
23:19 (p. 142).
23:20-32 (p. 102).
23:22 (p. 289).
23:26 (p. 312).
23:27 (p. 190, 311).
23:28 (p. 323).
23:33 (p. 176).
24:1 (p. 67, 118, 191, 279).
24:2 (p. 279).
24:3 (p. 133).
24:3-4 (**XXII**).

24:4 (p. 279).
24:4-5 (p. 173).
24:6 (p. 130).
24:6-7 (p. 195).
24:7 (p. 133, 146).
24:8 (p. 133, 164).
24:9-10 (p. 25, 279).
24:9-11 (p. 118, 195, 196).
24:11 (p. 186, 279).
24:12 (p. 125, 129, 191).
24:13 (p. 180, 305, 306).
24:14 (p. 118, 312).
24:15 (p. 317).
24:15-18 (p. 187).
24:16 (p. 317, 333).
24:17 (p. 186, 318).
24:18 (p. 180, 317).
25:1 (p. 39, 192).
25:2 (p. 264).
25:3-7 (p. 82).
25:8 (p. 192).
25:9 (p. 81).
25:10 (p. 81).
25:10-16 (**XXIII**).
25:10-20 (p. 297).
25:12-16 (p. 81).
25:15 (p. 55).
25:17 (p. 81, 181, 187).
25:18-21 (p. 81).
25:19 (p. 283).
25:21-22 (p. 193).
25:22 (p. 187, 190).
25:23 (p. 283).
25:23-29 (p. 297).
25:29 (p. 54).
25:30 (p. 196, 313).
25:31 (p. 81, 283).
25:31-39 (p. 297).
25:31-40 (p. 54).
25:34 (p. 81).
25:36 (p. 54, 81, 283).
25:38 (p. 54).
26:1-37 (p. 297).
26:2 (p. 283).
26:6 (p. 81).

26:8 (p. 283).
26:11 (p. 81).
26:16 (p. 283).
26:30 (p. 82).
26:31 (p. 54).
27:1 (p. 283).
27:1-8 (p. 297).
27:2 (p. 283).
27:8 (p. 82).
27:9 (p. 283).
27:9-19 (p. 297).
27:11 (p. 283).
27:12 (p. 283).
27:13 (p. 178).
27:13-16 (p. 283).
27:18 (p. 283).
27:20-21 (p. 186).
28:1 (p. 310).
28:2-42 (p. 297).
28:3 (p. 178-9).
28:4 (p. 47).
28:6 (p. 81).
28:8 (p. 81).
28:9-12 (p. 81).
28:29 (p. 81-2).
28:35 (p. 274).
28:42-43 (p. 272).
28:43 (p. 309).
29:1-42 (p. 310).
29:9 (p. 309).
29:11 (p. 196).
29:43 (p. 54, 313).
29:44-46 (p. 192).
29:45-46 (p. 187, 314).
30:1-5 (p. 310).
30:2 (p. 283).
30:6-10 (p. 310).
30:10 (p. 163).
30:11 (p. 39).
30:11-12 (p. 174).
30:12 (p. 40, 161).
30:13-16 (p. 174).
30:17 (p. 39).
30:18-19 (p. 174).
30:20-21 (p. 274).
30:21 (p. 309).

341

30:22 (p. 39).
30:23-33 (p. 310).
30:29 (p. 174).
30:33 (p. 310).
30:34 (p. 39).
30:34-38 (p. 174).
30:35 (p. 174).
30:38 (p. 310).
31:1 (p. 39).
31:1-5 (p. 83).
31:2-3 (p. 110).
31:3 (p. 186, 313).
31:6 (p. 83, 179).
31:6-11 (p. 83-4).
31:11 (p. 82).
31:12 (p. 39).
31:13 (p. 56, 155, 162).
31:13-17 (p. 147).
31:14-15 (p. 181).
31:16 (p. 309).
31:17 (p. 162, 181).
31:18 (p. 54, 67, 264, 333).
32:1 (p. 57, 115, 181).
32:1-29 (p. 180).
32:2 (p. 156).
32:2-4 (p. 57).
32:3-4 (p. 85).
32:4 (p. 57, 79, 115, 156).
32:5 (p. 57, 115).
32:6 (p. 57, 307).
32:7 (p. 118).
32:8 (p. 118).
32:9-11 (p. 63).
32:11 (p. 127, 155, 284).
32:11-12 (p. 63, 89).
32:12 (p. 284).
32:13 (p. 63, 154, 284).
32:14 (p. 89, 127, 181).
32:15 (p. 336).
32:15-16 (p. 336).
32:17 (p. 306, 312).
32:18 (p. 57, 312).
32:19 (p. 279).
32:19-20 (p. 35, 177, 284).
32:21 (p. 115).
32:22-24 (p. 115, **XXIV**).
32:23 (p. 71).
32:25 (p. 57, 70, 115, 144, 156).
32:26 (p. 102).
32:26-35 (p. 95, 102).
32:27 (p. 144).
32:28 (p. 144).
32:29 (p. 102).
32:30 (p. 57).
32:30-31 (p. 63).
32:32 (p. 165).
32:33 (p. 165).
32:33-34 (p. 144).
32:35 (p. 144).
33:1 (p. 297).
33:2-3 (p. 187).
33:3 (p. 295).
33:4-6 (p. 187-8).
33:5 (p. 85).
33:6 (p. 245, 333).
33:7 (p. 181, 279)
33:7-11 (p. 196).
33:9 (p. 186, 190, 196, 317).
33:10 (p. 317).
33:11 (p. 14, 16, 62, 113, 180, 181, 279, 305, 306, 322).
33:12 (p. 65, 72, 143, 188).
33:12-13 (p. 34).
33:12-23 (p. 196).
33:13 (p. 60, 64, 66, 154).
33:14 (p. 184, 188, 312).
33:15-16 (p. 64, 188, 196).
33:17 (p. 65, 143, 188).
33:18 (p. 64, 67, 187, 301).
33:19 (p. 67, 68, 69, 89, 155).
33:20 (p. 65, 279, 314).
33:21 (p. 67, 68, 69).
33:21-22 (p. 67, 69).
33:22 (p. 68).
33:23 (p. 67, 69).
34:1 (p. 193, 279).
34:2 (p. 175, 191, 333).
34:2-5 (p. 191).
34:4 (p. 331).
34:4-9 (p. 196).
34:5 (p. 186, 317).
34:6 (p. 89, 143, 155).
34:6-7 (p. 126, 127, 148, 280).
34:7 (p. 126, 155, 195).
34:8 (p. 147, 274).
34:8-9 (p. 63).
34:9 (p. 63, 64).
34:10 (p. 71-72, 179, 193, 196).
34:11-16 (p. 311).
34:12 (p. 175, 310).
34:14 (p. 88, 304).
34:15 (p. 175, 310).
34:17 (p. 176).
34:18 (p. 158).
34:18-23 (p. 306).
34:19 (p. 142).
34:20 (p. 148, 179).
34:21 (p. 305).
34:22 (p. 159, 305).
34:24 (p. 72).
34:25 (p. 173).
34:26 (p. 143).
34:27 (p. 279).
34:28 (p. 72).
34:29 (p. 86, 112, 284, 333).
34:30 (p. 76, 86, 188-9).
34:31 (p. 86).
34:32 (p. 87, 179, 333).
34:33-35 (p. 87).
34:34 (p. 110).
34:35 (p. 280).
35:1-35 (p. 290).
35:2 (p. 147, 181).
35:3 (p. 147).
35:5 (p. 148).
35:10 (p. 141).
35:20 (p. 301).
35:20-22 (p. 140).
35:22 (p. 112).
35:25-26 (p. 141).
35:26 (p. 112).
35:27-29 (p. 141).
35:29 (p. 112).
35:30-31 (p. 141).
35:31 (p. 164, 186, 313).
35:31-33 (p. 83).
35:34 (p. 141, 179, 283).
35:35 (p. 84, 141).
36:1 (p. 138).
36:1-2 (p. 179).
36:2 (p. 137).
36:3 (p. 103, 138).
36:4-5 (p. 86).
36:6 (p. 144).
36:6-7 (p. 303).
36:8-38 (p. 297).
36:9 (p. 283)
36:13 (p. 81).
36:15 (p. 283).
36:18 (p. 81).
36 21 (p. 283).
37:1 (p. 283).
37:1-9 (p. 297).
37:6 (p. 283).
37:8 (p. 283).
37:10 (p. 283).
37:10-16 (p. 297).
37:17 (p. 283).
37:17-24 (p. 297).
37:22 (p. 283).
37:25 (p. 283).
37:25-29 (p. 310).
38:1 (p. 283).
38:1-7 (p. 297).
38:2 (p. 283).
38:8 (p. 112, 142).
38:9 (p. 283).
38:9-20 (p. 297).
38:11-15 (p. 283).
38:18 (p. 283).
38:21-31 (p. 284).
38:26 (p. 229).

Index of Scripture References

39:1-31 (p. 297).
39:5 (p. 81).
39:32 (p. 176-7).
39:33-41 (p. 177).
39:36 (p. 196).
39:42 (p. 177).
39:42-43 (p. 143, 177).
40:1-33 (p. 300).
40:2 (p. 177).
40:12-15 (p. 72).
40:12-16 (p. 303).
40:13 (p. 283).
40:19 (p. 297).
40:21 (p. 297).
40:23 (p. 297).
40:24 (p. 297).
40:26-29 (p. 310).
40:27 (p. 297).
40:29 (p. 297).
40:30-31 (p. 174).
40:32 (p. 297).
40:34 (p. 44, 186, 192, 297).
40:34-35 (p. 196).
40:35 (p. 82, 192, 318).
40:36 (p. 318).
40:36-38 (p. 146, 196).
40:37 (p. 318).
40:38 (p. 78, 186, 313).

Leviticus.
11:44-45 (p. 297).
11:45 (p. 191-2, 310).
16:1-34 (p. 158).
17:10-11 (p. 310).
19:2 (p. 310).
19:19 (p. 298).
19:30 (p. 56).
20:7 (p. 310).
20:25 (p. 128).
20:26 (p. 310).
21:8 (p. 310).
21:15 (p. 310).
22:9 (p. 310).
22:16 (p. 310).
22:32 (p. 310).

23:23-25 (p. 306).
23:33-38 (p. 306).
24:20 (p. 266).
25:11 (p. 324).
25:8-55 (p. 306).
26:2 (p. 56).
26:3 (p. 304).
26:10 (p. 304).

Numbers.
1:2 (p. 229).
1:21-46 (p. 229, 230, 330).
1:47 (p. 229).
2:4-31 (p. 229).
3:12 (p. 272).
6:24-26 (p. 283).
6:27 (p. 283).
10:10 (p. 306).
10:12 (p. 243).
10:25 (p. 99).
10:26 (p. 99).
10:27 (p. 99).
10:28 (p. 99).
10:31 (p. 266).
11:5 (p. 23, 138).
11:6 (p. 118).
11:29 (p. 62).
11:31 (p. 302).
12:1 (p. 71, 115, 117).
12:3 (p. 16, 34).
12:6-8 (p. 264).
12:10 (p. 115).
12:16 (p. 243).
13:1-13 (p. 306).
13:3 (p. 243).
13:21 (p. 243).
13:26 (p. 243).
14:2 (p. 71).
14:23 (p. 146).
14:24 (p. 302).
14:39-45 (p. 289).
14:40-43 (p. 146).
14:43-45 (p. 289).
17:5 (p. 282).
17:10 (p. 282).

20:1 (p. 243).
20:8 (p. 278).
20:10-12 (p. 311).
20:11 (p. 278).
20:12 (p. 71, 278).
24:9 (p. 271).
26:45 (p. 209).
27:14 (p. 243).
27:18 (p. 305).
32:13 (p. 146, 208).
33:1 (p. 144, 333).
33:1-49 (p. 235, 333).
33:2 (p. 279, 333).
33:3 (p. 214).
33:3-15 (p. 244).
33:5 (p. 214).
33:8 (p. 243).
33:12 (p. 244).
32:13 (p. 146).
33:14 (p. 244).
33:15 (p. 244, 333).
33:36 (p. 243).
34:3 (p. 243).
34:4 (p. 243).

Deuteronomy.
2:8 (p. 333).
2:26 (p. 243).
4:9 (p. 305).
4:15 (p. 245).
4:23 (p. 305).
4:24 (p. 186).
4:29-30 (p. 299).
4:31 (p. 305).
6:6-9 (p. 305).
6:12 (p. 305).
7:1 (p. 237).
8:2-3 (p. 55).
8:3 (p. 83).
8:11 (p. 305).
8:14 (p. 305).
8:19 (p. 305).
8:20 (p. 299).
9:7 (p. 305).
9:10 (p. 54, 264).
9:23 (p. 299).

10:16 (p. 311).
11:18 (p. 305).
12:31 (p. 33).
15:7-8 (p. 179).
15:10 (p. 312).
16:14 (p. 159).
18:10-12 (p. 299).
20:1 (p. 287).
20:2 (p. 287).
20:5 (p. 287).
20:9 (p. 287).
20:17 (p. 237).
25:19 (p. 157).
28:58 (p. 279).
29:20-21 (p. 278).
29:27 (p. 279).
30:10 (p. 279).
30:11-14 (p. 300).
31:9 (p. 279).
31:19 (p. 279).
31:22 (p. 279).
31:24 (p. 279).
32:4 (p. 68).
32:25 (p. 266).
33:1 (p. 334).
34:1 (p. 72).
34:4 (p. 72).

Joshua.
1:1-2 (p. 208).
3:15-16 (p. 51).
8:28 (p. 334).
9:14-15 (p. 224).
10:33 (p. 323).
11:1 (p. 209, 323).
11:4 (p. 232).
11:10 (p. 209).
11:10-11 (p. 210).
11:17 (p. 210).
13:1 (p. 224, 287).
13:2 (p. 287).
13:2-3 (p. 224, 237).
13:2-7 (p. 224).
14:7 (p. 293, 322).
15:9 (p. 322).
15:15 (p. 336).

343

18:15 (p. 322).
19:24-31 (p. 209, 218).
23:7 (p. 284).
24:29 (p. 208).

Judges.
1:34 (p. 207).
4:2 (p. 322).
4:3 (p. 322).
6:2 (p. 206).
6:6 (p. 206-7).
6:11 (p. 206).
7:1-22 (p. 288).
11:14 (p. 206).
11:26 (p. 206, 214, 321).
16:23 (p. 287).
20:16 (p. 323).

1 Samuel.
8:5 (p. 296).
8:7-9 (p. 296).
8:10-18 (p. 296).
13:1 (p. 206).
16:7 (p. 104).

2 Samuel.
5:4 (p. 206).
5:6-7 (p. 331).
7:8 (p. 266).
11:15 (p. 264).
22:2 (p. 68).
22:28 (p. 302).

1 Kings.
3:1 (p. 326).
4:30 (p. 147).
6:1 (p. 205, 206, 214).
8:9 (p. 244).
9:1-3 (p. 275).
11:40 (p. 326).
14:25 (p. 326).
18, passim (p. 315).
18:16-46 (p. 291).
19:8 (p. 244).
19:12 (p. 291, 292, 315).
19:12-18 (p. 267).

2 Kings.
1:2 (p. 333).
1:3 (p. 333).
1:6 (p. 333).
1:16 (p. 333).

1 Chronicles.
7:20-27 (p. 322).
8:40 (p. 323).
12:2 (p. 323).
16:29 (p. 51).
21, passim (p. 310).
29:9 (p. 302).

2 Chronicles.
5:10 (p. 244).
7:1-2 (p. 317).
12:2 (p. 326).
12:9 (p. 326).
15:15 (p. 302).
31:2 (p. 273).
31:21 (p. 302).

Nehemiah.
12:27 (p. 273).

Esther.
3:13-14 (p. 271).
4:11 (p. 275).
9:18-32 (p. 306).

Job.
38:1 (p. 304).

Psalms.
4:4 (p. 292).
18:2 (p. 68).
18:27 (p. 302).
19:14 (p. 69).
24:8 (p. 95).
25:1 (p. 191).
25:9 (p. 302).
28:2 (p. 191).
29:2 (p. 51).
40:2 (p. 69).
46:10 (p. 104).
61:3 (p. 95).
63:4 (p. 191).
74:16 (p. 80).
74:16-17 (p. 178).
78:49 (p. 289).
86:4 (p. 191).
91:12 (p. 191).
92:15 (p. 69).
96:8-9 (p. 51).
100:2 (p. 51).
103:8-10 (p. 68).
103:13 (p. 68).
103:14 (p. 22, 96, 323).
104:4 (p. 313).
104:16-23 (p. 224, 277).
106:19 (p. 244).
110:7 (p. 191).
116:13 (p. 191).
119:48 (p. 191).
121:1 (p. 191).
123:1 (p. 191).
127:1 (p. 15, 318).
133:1 (p. 102).
133:3 (p. 102).
134:2 (p. 191).
139:13 (p. 96, 265).
139:14 (p. 80).
141:2 (p. 310).
142:1 (p. 191).
143:8 (p. 191).
147:6 (p. 302).
149:4 (p. 302).

Proverbs.
3:34 (p. 302).
27:19 (p. 113).
29:18 (p. 83).

Isaiah.
2:6 (p. 287).
14:12 (p. 284).
19:23-25 (p. 319).
26:4 (p. 68).
29:19 (p. 302).
40:3 (p. 316).
43:19 (p. 274).
45:20 (p. 96).
49:15 (p. 291).
55:9 (p. 278).
55:11 (p. 55).
60:1 (p. 86).
61:1 (p. 24).
66:13 (p. 291).

Jeremiah.
1:5 (p. 264).
9:25-26 (p. 311).
29:11 (p. 140).
29:13 (p. 19, 277).

Ezekiel.
1:26 (p. 317).
10:1 (p. 317).
18:23 (p. 305).

Daniel.
2:29 (p. 290).
2:47 (p. 290).
3:27 (p. 19).

Hosea.
5:8 (p. 323).

Joel.
2:25 (p. 311).
2:28 (p. 186).
2:28-29 (p. 84).

Amos.
3:7 (p. 277).

Jonah.
3:3 (p. 332).

Habakkuk.
1:13 (p. 311).

Zephaniah.
3:17 (p. 66).

Index of Scripture References

Malachi.
2:11 (p. 295).
2:14-15 (p. 295).
3:18 (p. 128).
4:4 (p. 244).

Matthew.
2:15 (p. 200-1).
2:16 (p. 271).
3:3 (p. 316).
4:2 (p. 293).
4:3-4 (p. 311).
4:5-7 (p. 311).
4:8-10 (p. 311).
4:19 (p. 315).
5-7 (p. 290).
5:1-7:29 (p. 315).
5:6 (p. 193).
5:16 (p. 86).
5:17–7:6 (p. 297).
5:18 (p. 304).
5:24 (p. 96).
5:38-42 (p. 266, 300).
5:44 (p. 96).
5:48 (p. 297).
6:9 (p. 18).
6:19-20 (p. 137).
6:21 (p. 137).
7:7-8 (p. 277).
10:26 (p. 290).
11:7-9 (p. 265).
11:28 (p. 315).
11:29 (p. 68, 142).
11:29-30 (p. 192).
12:8 (p. 56).
12:26 (p. 270).
12:30 (p. 40).
12:39 (p. 294).
12:45 (p. 145).
13:43 (p. 86).
13:52 (p. 304).
14:20 (p. 193).
14:23-33 (p. 315).
14:29 (p. 315).
15:29-38 (p. 315).
15:37 (p. 193).
16:6 (p. 173).
17:1-8 (p. 55, 267).
17:1-13 (p. 291, 315).
17:2 (p. 280).
19:21 (p. 315).
20:20 (p. 280).
20:22 (p. 67).
22:37-40 (p. 70).
22:40 (p. 127).
23:37 (p. 291).
25:1 (p. 18).
25:5 (p. 18).
25:14-30 (p. 147, 283).
25:21 (p. 24).
26:28 (p. 164, 300).
27:50 (p. 25).
27:51 (p. 25, 275, 316).
28:19-20 (p. 23).

Mark.
1:3 (p. 316).
1:17 (p. 315).
1:27 (p. 303).
2:27 (p. 296).
3:35 (p. 289).
4:22 (p. 290).
6:31 (p. 315).
6:42 (p. 193).
6:46-52 (p. 315).
8:8 (p. 193).
8:18 (p. 80).
9:1-8 (p. 55, 267).
9:1-13 (p. 291, 315).
9:2 (p. 298).
9:2-4 (p. 311).
9:4 (p. 298).
10:5 (p. 297).
10:9 (p. 297).
10:21 (p. 315).
10:38 (p. 67).
12:30 (p. 70).
14:24 (p. 164, 300).
15:38 (p. 25, 275, 316).
16:15 (p. 160-1).
16:17 (p. 161, 304).

Luke.
2:1-2 (p. 331).
3:4 (p. 316).
4:18 (p. 24).
6:21 (p. 193).
6:38 (p. 138).
8:17 (p. 290).
9:17 (p. 193).
9:28-36 (p. 55).
10:25-37 (p. 132).
11:2 (p. 18).
11:9 (p. 277).
11:20 (p. 264).
11:23 (p. 289).
11:25 (p. 145).
12:2 (p. 290).
12:13-21 (p. 147).
12:24 (p. 266).
12:27 (p. 266).
13:34 (p. 291).
18:22 (p. 315).
19:11-27 (p. 283).
19:40 (p. 267).
22:19 (p. 163).
22:20 (p. 300, 304).
23:45 (p. 275, 316).
24:44 (p. 280).

John.
1:1 (p. 110, 298).
1:2 (p. 110).
1:3 (p. 110, 292).
1:14 (p. 56, 298).
1:23 (p. 316).
1:29 (p. 148).
1:50 (p. 175).
3:8 (p. 314).
4:14 (p. 163).
4:24 (p. 51).
5:39 (p. 312).
6:35 (p. 56, 155, 280).
6:41 (p. 56, 155).
6:48 (p. 56, 155).
6:51 (p. 56, 155).
7:38 (p. 50).
8:12 (p. 56, 280).
8:31-32 (p. 139).
8:44 (p. 31).
10:7 (p. 280).
10:10 (p. 41, 57, 129, 140, 316).
10:11 (p. 280).
10:14 (p. 18, 280).
11:25 (p. 280).
13:34 (p. 304).
14:6 (p. 89, 280).
14:12 (p. 175).
14:15 (p. 143).
15:1 (p. 280).
15:15 (p. 113).
18:6 (p. 69).
18:36 (p. 287).
20:17 (p. 313).
20:21 (p. 23).

Acts.
1:3 (p. 293).
1:9 (p. 293).
2:3 (p. 88, 313).
2:15-18 (p. 84).
2:17 (p. 186).
4:32 (p. 298).
5:1-11 (p. 274, 302).
5:20 (p. 304).
5:29 (p. 265).
7:20 (p. 15).
7:22 (p. 15, 22, 248, 267, 270).
7:23-24 (p. 266, 292).
7:25 (p. 15, 70).
7:30 (p. 245, 266, 292).
7:38 (p. 245).
7:58 (p. 264).
8:1 (p. 264).
13:18 (p. 208).
19:23-41 (p. 313).

Romans.
1:20 (p. 266-7, 277).
5:8 (p. 163).
5:14 (p. 282).
6:6 (p. 274).

345

6:17 (p. 302).
7:6 (p. 304).
7:7 (p. 134).
7:10 (p. 164).
8:1 (p. 164).
8:17 (p. 282).
8:21 (p. 24, 274).
8:22 (p. 309).
8:26 (p. 309).
8:28 (p. 66).
8:29 (p. 305).
8:32 (p. 113).
9:9 (p. 226).
12:1 (p. 51).
12:19 (p. 266).

1 Corinthians.
1:18-19 (p. 194).
3:9 (p. 132, 146, 175, 282).
3:16 (p. 49, 165, 181).
5:7 (p. 163, 173).
6:19 (p. 49).
7:7 (p. 292).
7:23 (p. 274).
9:7 (p. 96).
10:2 (p. 163).
10:4 (p. 69).
10:7 (p. 307).
10:11 (p. 162).
10:13 (p. 96).
12:21 (p. 111).
13:12 (p. 67).
14:33 (p. 145).

2 Corinthians.
3:13 (p. 112).
3:13-18 (p. 87).
3:18 (p. 278).
4:16 (p. 292).
4:17 (p. 24).
5:17 (p. 304).
5:21 (p. 163, 275).
6:16 (p. 49-50, 165).
7:1 (p. 293).

9:7 (p. 138).
10:4-5 (p. 287).
11:14 (p. 31, 284).
12:7 (p. 16).
12:9 (p. 16).

Galatians.
1:17 (p. 246).
3:7 (p. 40).
4:24 (p. 245).
4:25 (p. 246).
5:22 (p. 18, 68).
5:22-23 (p. 270).
6:7 (p. 189).

Ephesians.
2:10 (p. 23, 66).
2:15 (p. 304).
3:20 (p. 19, 79, 142).
4:11-12 (p. 283).
4:24 (p. 304).
5:21 (p. 293).
5:29-32 (p. 292).
6:10 (p. 97).
6:11 (p. 104).
6:12 (p. 30-1).

Philippians.
2:12 (p. 132, 192).
2:15 (p. 86).
2:25 (p. 96).
3:17 (p. 282).

Colossians.
2:15 (p. 95).
2:16-17 (p. 160).
2:23 (p. 307).
3:10 (p. 304).
3:22 (p. 293).

2 Thessalonians.
2:9 (p. 294).
2:9-10 (p. 31).

1 Timothy.
1:18 (p. 96).
6:12 (p. 96).
6:15 (p. 126).

2 Timothy.
1:13 (p. 282).
2:3-4 (p. 96).
2:15 (p. 24).
3:8-9 (p. 269).

Philemon.
1:2 (p. 96).

Hebrews.
1:3 (p. 298).
1:7 (p. 313).
3:2 (p. 87).
8:1 (p. 148).
9:4 (p. 55).
9:8-10 (p. 274).
10:20 (p. 304).
10:31 (p. 189).
11:3 (p. 302).
11:23 (p. 15, 114).
11:24 (p. 70).
11:26 (p. 69).
11:27 (p. 69, 104, 265).
12:18-22 (p. 190)
12:21 (p. 189).
12:22 (p. 190).
12:24 (p. 190).
12:25 (p. 190).
12:28-29 (p. 51).
12:29 (p. 186).
13:8 (p. 50, 181, 196).
13:20 (p. 148).

James.
1:5 (p. 178).
2:10 (p. 134).
4:6 (p. 302).

1 Peter.
1:3 (p. 304).

4:10 (p. 284).

2 Peter.
1:5-7 (p. 280).
3:9 (p. 226).
3:13 (p. 304).

1 John.
4:8 (p. 126, 305).
4:10 (p. 32).
4:18 (p. 104, 139, 315).

Revelation.
1:4 (p. 156).
1:8 (p. 21).
1:12 (p. 275).
2:1 (p. 275).
2:5 (p. 275).
2:17 (p. 304).
2:24 (p. 290).
3:5 (p. 165).
3:12 (p. 304).
5:5 (p. 68, 96).
5:6 (p. 68, 96).
5:8 (p. 310).
5:9 (p. 304).
5:13 (p. 274).
11:18 (p. 293).
12:7-9 (p. 271).
13:18 (p. 309).
14:3 (p. 304).
15:3 (p. 69, 148, 303).
17:14 (p. 188).
20:2 (p. 271).
20:10 (p. 271).
21:1 (p. 311).
21:3 (p. 290).
21:5 (p. 304).
21:6 (p. 21).
21:19 (p. 317).
21:22-23 (p. 53),
22:3 (p. 316).
22:5 (p. 316).
22:13 (p. 21).
22:17 (p. 315).

Subject Index

Actium, battle of — 263 (n 6)
Ahmose, pharaoh — 285 (n 160)
Akhenaten, pharaoh
  army, use of by — 95, 219-20, 221, 286 (n 169)
  Aten, relationship to — 28-9, 46-7, 61, 77, 106-7
  birth of — 60, 328 (n 460)
  bodyguard of — 286 (n 169)
  co-regency with his father and — 204
  dates of the reign of — 251
  daughters of — 76, 295 (n 231, 232), 312 (n 361)
  diseases of — 281 (n 127)
  economic dislocation under — 220-21
  Eighteenth Dynasty and — 251, 330 (n 476)
  family relationships of — 60, 76, 122-3
  foreign policy under — 12, 60, 218, 228, 286 (n 170)
  harem of — 123
  increasing corruption under — 221
  influences on — 60, 72-3, 198-9, 224, 328 (n 461)
  Israelite conquest of Canaan and — 209-10
  language of inscriptions and — 77
  military capability in the reign of — 95, 218-19
  monotheism of — 60, 107, 199, 290 (n 200)
  mother of — 295 (n 236)
  motivation of — 12, 184, 198-9, 222, 227
  name, meaning of — 77, 106, 264 (n 11)
  name, new, choice of — 28, 106
  name of, original — 28
  official portrayal of — 76-7, 122-3
  physical deformity of — 60, 76, 281 (n 127)
  policies, economic effect of — 220-21, 228
  reaction to the reforms of — 13, 184-6
  religious beliefs of — 19, 28-9, 60-61, 106, 152-3, 290 (n 200)
  sequestration of temple funds by — 221
  sisters of — 276 (n 95), 303 (n 298)
  sons of — 77, 152, 295 (n 232)
  temple closures under — 95, 328 (n 459)
  treatment after death of — 13, 185-6, 205, 319 (n 401)
  unfinished tomb of — 221
  upbringing and education of — 60
  viziers of — 299 (n 260)
  wives and concubines of — 123
Akhet-aten
  abandonment of — 44, 321 (n 409)
  boundary stelae of — 45, 222
  bubonic plague and — 216, 319 (n 399)
  deficiencies of — 44, 295 (n 234), 312 (n 358)
  extent of — 272 (n 66)
  hieroglyph for — 45, 303 (n 295)
  layout of — 45, 46, 272 (n 66)
  location of — 44, 264 (n 8), 272 (n 66)
  meaning of — 45, 264 (n 8), 329 (n 465)
  population of — 46
  temples of — 46
  tombs of — 203, 225, 251, 261
Aldred, Cyril

Amarna Letters, the — 209-10, 218, 227, 251, 323 (n 420), 323 (n 424), 323 (n 425), 327 (n 452)
Amarna period, the
  art forms of — 12, 76-7, 280 (n 125)
  building styles of — 45, 77
  meaning of — 251, 264 (n 8)
Amarna, Tell el (see Akhet-aten)
Amenemhet III, pharaoh
  agricultural affairs and — 211-12
  daughter of — 211
  harvest goddess, veneration of — 211
  Hyksos and — 210-11
  Joseph and — 211-12
  Nile floods and — 211
  Nile god, veneration of — 211
  reorganisation of administration — 211
  turquoise mines and — 248
Amenemhat IV, pharaoh — 248
Amenhotep I, pharaoh — 204
Amenhotep II, pharaoh — 93, 203, 217, 251, 285 (n 167)
Amenhotep III, pharaoh
  army and — 95
  Aten and — 137, 266 (n 26), 317 (n 389)
  Beautiful Feast of the Opet and — 306 (n 315)
  changing course of the Nile and — 327 (n 447)
  children of — 276 (n 95)
  Commemorative Scarabs of — 149, 327 (n 447)
  co-regency with Akhenaten and — 204
  dates of the reign of — 251
  death of firstborn son and — 215-6, 227, 276 (n 95), 319 (n 399)
  decline in luxury goods and — 220
  depopulation during the reign of — 227, 230, 326 (n 444)
  earthquakes and — 329 (n 462)
  Eighteenth Dynasty and — 330 (n 476)
  exodus and — 203, 209
  gap in official records for — 216
  labour shortage and — 220
  mass burials and — 215
  mercenaries, use of — 220
  mother of — 137
  names of — 225
  nickname of — 225
  palaces of — 136, 195, 216, 317 (n 389)
  paternity of — 137
  Sekhmet, veneration of — 215, 226
  temple design under — 308 (n 330)
  titles of — 225
  viziers of — 299 (n 260)
  wife of — 136, 149, 276 (n 95)
  Yahweh and — 217
Amenhotep son of Hapu — 320 (n 408), 327 (n 464)
Ammit, devourer, the — 168, 239, 242, 252, 276 (n 96)
Amun
  Beautiful Feast of the Opet and — 158, 160
  closure of temples to — 95, 328 (n 459)
  defacing of images of — 29, 107
  depiction of — 61
  festivals in honour of — 158, 160
  First Prophet (Chief Priest) of — 277 (n 102), 301 (n 283)
  influence of — 93

347

Moses and Pharaoh

meaning of the name of	276 (n 98)	etymology of	263 (n 1)
nature of	93, 276 (n 98), 313 (n 366)	famine and	211, 215, 270 (n 55), 324 (n 428)
priesthood of	92, 328 (n 458)	Festival of Drunkenness and	156
primacy of	28, 92-3, 252, 284 (n 157)	foundation of the state of	263 (n 1)
Second Prophet of	277 (n 102)	gods and goddesses of	239-42
snakes and	269 (n 42)	gods of, parading statues of	46, 316 (n 382)
Theban Triad and	136, 158	government of	299 (n 260), 301 (n 283)
titles of	92, 276 (n 98), 285 (n 162)	legal system of	123-4, 131
war and	92-3	Lower	44, 242, 257, 263 (n 5), 269 (n 45)
Antikythera Mechanism, the	270 (n 50)	mines of, copper	94, 263 (n 3)
Anubis	60, 168, 239, 242, 252, 276 (n 96)	mines of, turquoise	94, 263 (n 3)
		names for	263 (n 5)
Apiru (see Habiru)		papyrus and, invention and use of	335 (n 513), 336 (n 517)
Apis bull, the	252, 276 (n 94)	population of	230-31
Antiochus IV	306 (n 316)	priests, role and functions of the	328 (n 458)
Aten		religious festivals of	158, 273 (n 71)
artistic representation of	60-62, 77	scribes, teaching of	29
design of temples to	46, 77	trade routes of	263 (n 3)
first references to	322 (n 418)	unification of	263 (n 5)
hieroglyphics for	107, 277 (n 101), 303 (n 297)	Upper	44, 255, 257, 263 (n 5), 269 (n 45), 328 (n 472)
hymns to	61, 199, 224, 277 (n 100)	Egyptians, the ancient	
		afterlife beliefs of	77, 168-9, 308 (n 329)
name of, manner of writing the	77, 107	architectural achievements of	12
prevalence of the cult of	77	astronomy and	269 (n 43)
primacy of	106-7	Book of the Dead and	308 (n 332)
relationship to royalty of	28, 61-2, 273 (n 74)	calendar and	269 (n 43)
		engineering and	32, 270 (n 48)
style of worship of	312 (n 359)	Israelite customs and	311 (n 354)
temples to	44, 77, 312 (n 359)	mathematics and	32, 269 (n 43)
		medicine and	269 (n 43)
titles of	107	occult practices and	30, 31,32, 131
visible symbol of	19, 61, 77, 252	science and	30, 32
Augustus Caesar (Octavian)	263 (n 6), 331 (n 482)	treatment of slaves by	300 (n 275)
		Execration Texts, the	212, 227, 325 (n 433)
Ay, pharaoh	221		
Bastet	239, 285 (n 163)	Famine Stele	324 (n 428)
Big Bang, the	307 (n 325)	Fisher, Clarence Stanley	213, 254
Black Death, the	328 (n 457)	Freud, Sigmund	223, 254, 319 (n 398)
Bunyan, John	293 (n 218)		
Breasted, James Henry	123, 253	Great Pyramid of Giza, the	12, 263 (n 7)
Byzantium	263 (n 6)	Habiru	
Canaan		Amarna Letters and	210
boundaries of	253	Egyptian references to	217-18
child sacrifice and	270 (n 51)	Israelites and	323 (n 425)
etymology of	253	meaning of	323 (n 424)
inhabitants of	237-8	Hammurabi, Code of	296 (n 240 and 241)
population of	231-3		
Cassius Dio (Lucius Cassius Dio Cocceianus)	232, 253	Hammurabi, ambassadors of	329 (n 481)
Cheops (Khufu), pharaoh	12	Hathor, goddess	239, 241, 242, 247, 248, 254, 276 (n 94), 296 (n 237), 303 (n 295), 335 (n 508)
Cleopatra, queen	263 (n 6)		
Confederacy, slave population of	330 (n 473)		
David, king	96, 205, 206, 264 (n 13), 266 (n 22), 330 (n 474), 331 (n 481)		
		Hatshepsut, queen	158, 160, 254, 264 (n 10), 295 (n 236)
Diggers, the	298 (n 254)		
Djoser, pharaoh	324 (n 428)	Hittites, the	207, 219, 237, 255, 285 (n 166), 286 (n 170), 331 (n 478)
Doyle, Sir Arthur Conan	319 (n 400)		
Dunand, Maurice	254, 321 (n 413)		
Egypt			
administrative divisions (nomes) of	257	Homer	286 (n 168)
agricultural year and	288 (n 186), 306 (n 318)	Horeb, Mount	
		location of	243-6
army of	93-5	meaning of	266 (n 25)
artistic conventions of	76, 280 (n 125-6)	Mount Sinai and	243-6, 333 (n 497)
border posts of	327 (n 461)		
bull cults of	56, 276 (n 94)	Horemheb, pharaoh	221, 258, 325 (n 437)
chariots and	94, 219, 285 (n 167), 318 (n 393), 327 (n 452)	Horus	61, 152, 255, 303 (n 296), 333 (n 494)
crops of	270 (n 55)		
empire of	12, 94		

348

Subject Index

Hume, David — 78, 281 (n 133), 288 (n 185)

Hyksos, the
  chariots and — 285 (n 167)
  etymology of — 255, 285 (n 161)
  expulsion from Egypt of — 92, 285 (n 161)
  Fifteenth Dynasty and — 259
  foundation of Avaris and — 252
  introduction of the wheel and — 255, 285 (n 161)
  Israelites and — 210-11
  Second Intermediate Period and — 259
  settlement in Egypt of the — 210, 255

Isesi, pharaoh — 335 (n 512)
Isis — 152, 240, 241, 242, 255, 296 (n 237)
Islam — 52, 122, 293 (n 219)

Josephus, Titus Flavius
  Jewish Revolt and — 329 (n 467)
  Joshua and — 322 (n 417)
  Moses and — 223, 264 (n 14), 319 (n 398)
  name, original — 255
  population figures and — 330 (n 477), 330 (n 482)
  reliability of — 223
  writings of — 223, 255, 263 (n 4)

Kamose, pharaoh — 285 (n 160)
Karnak — 136, 158, 256, 260, 268 (n 40), 270 (n 48), 273 (n 70), 306 (n 314)
Kearney, Denis — 269 (n 44)
Kings, Valley of the — 12, 46, 260, 312 (n 358), 326 (n 441)
Kiya, queen — 256, 281 (n 129), 296 (n 237)
Kochba, Simon bar — 232, 256
Krakatoa — 320 (n 406)
Kyle, Melvin Grove — 212, 256
Layard, Austen Henry — 332 (n 484)
Lepsius, Karl Richard — 211, 256
L'Ouverture, Toussaint — 288 (n 182)
Ma'at — 93, 107, 123, 124, 152, 158, 168, 240, 241, 242, 256, 276 (n 96), 296 (n 238), 303 (n 294)

Macalister, Robert Alexander Stewart — 256, 270 (n 51)
Magee, John Gillespie Jnr — 315 (n 374)
Manetho — 223, 226, 227, 256, 285 (n 161), 329 (n 463 and 464)
Memnon, colossi of — 136, 300 (n 270)
Merneptah, pharaoh — 207, 208, 322 (n 415 and 416), 331 (n 478)
Middle Kingdom, the — 29, 204, 210, 248, 257, 285 (n 162)
Monasteries, Dissolution of the — 328 (n 459)
Montu — 93, 136, 240, 242, 257

Nabipolassar, king — 332 (n 484)
Narmer, king — 263 (n 5)
National Center for Atmospheric Research, the — 287 (n 178), 332 (n 485)
Naville, Edouard — 212, 257
Neferti, the Prophecy of — 335 (n 512)
Nefertiti, queen
  artistic representation of — 61, 76, 122, 123
  Aten, relationship to — 62
  chief wife of Akhenaten as — 46, 61, 76, 122, 123, 257

  children of — 122, 295 (n 231)
  meaning of — 273 (n 73)
  prominence given to — 123, 277 (n 101)
  religious role of — 312 (n 361)
New Kingdom, the — 28, 92, 93, 131, 198, 230, 231, 252, 257-60, 263 (n 2), 268 (n 37), 286 (n 168), 303 (n 305), 328 (n 458)

Old Kingdom, the — 203, 225, 254
Osiris — 152-3, 240, 241, 242, 258, 295 (n 232), 296 (n 237), 308 (n 332), 320 (n 405)

Peleset, the (see Philistines)
Penrose, Roger — 282 (n 137)
Pharaoh
  crowns of — 263 (n 5)
  divinity of — 196, 225
  foreign vassals and — 93, 285 (n 164)
  legal system and — 123-4
  meaning of — 258, 263 (n 2)
  names of — 325 (n 439)
  officials of — 299 (n 260), 301 (n 283)
  prostration before — 196, 317 (n 390)
  representative of the gods as — 196, 225
  son of Amun as — 92
  symbols of kingship of — 92, 269 (n 45)
  titles of — 225
  usage of as a name for the king — 258, 263 (n 2)
Philistines — 237-8, 287 (n 175), 332(n 490), 333 (n 491)
Philo (Herennius Philon) — 258, 263 (n 4)
Pilate, Pontius — 9, 263 (n 4)
Psalms, the — 224, 329 (n 469)
Ptolemy — 334 (n 506)
Ra — 240, 241, 242, 258, 273 (n 72), 276 (n 94 and 99), 290 (n 198), 296 (n 237), 308 (n 330 and 332)
Ramses I, pharaoh — 258, 325 (n 437), 326 (n 440)
Ramses II, pharaoh
  battle of Kadesh and — 255, 256, 285 (n 165 and 166)
  Beautiful Feast of the Opet and — 158
  building projects and — 300 (n 273), 307 (n 321)
  campaigns of — 207, 219, 321 (n 413)
  chariots and — 219-20, 285 (n 166)
  dates of the reign of — 258, 326 (n 440), 327 (n 455)
  death of elder brother of — 227, 326 (n 446)
  exodus and — 203, 206-8, 213-14, 226
  names of — 284 (n 154), 325 (n 439)
  oppression of Israel under — 322 (n 416)
  population of Egypt under — 230
  revival of Egypt under — 319 (n 401)
  store cities and — 212-13
  terminology during the reign of — 217-18
  Yahweh and — 217-18
Ramses III, pharaoh — 286 (n 168), 300 (n 272)

Red Sea
  computer modelling for parting of — 287 (n 178)
  time needed for crossing of — 233-5, 332 (n 487)

349

Yam Suf and	50-51		
Rhind, Alexander Henry	215, 258	scientific explanation for	101, 288 (n 186), 289 (n 187-9)
Roman Empire, slave population of	229, 231, 330 (n 473)		
Rome	229, 330 (n 473)	timing of	101
Sa-Gaz (see Habiru)		Tennyson, Alfred Lord	301 (n 278)
Saul, king	96, 206, 224, 226	Thera (see Santorini)	
Sekhmet	215, 226, 227, 240, 241, 242, 258, 285 (n 163), 326 (n 444), 333 (n 494)	Thermodynamics, Second Law of	293 (n 220)
		Thutmose III, pharaoh	217-8, 254, 264 (n 10), 285 (n 164), 319 (n 404)
Semna Despatches, the	259, 324 (n 429)	Thutmose IV, pharaoh	
Senusret I, pharaoh	284 (n 157)	dates of the reign of	260, 322 (n 418)
Seqenenre II Tao, pharaoh	285 (n 160)	daughters of	215
Serabit el-Khadim	247-9, 263 (n 3), 335 (n 508)	Dream Stele and	260
		Eighteenth Dynasty and	330 (n 476)
Seth	93, 152, 240, 241, 242, 259	Moses and	208
		oppression of Israel and	203, 215
Seti I, pharaoh	217, 230, 300 (n 273), 319 (n 401)	relationship to Akhenaten of	322 (n 418)
		Townshend, 'Turnip'	307 (n 320)
		Trajan, emperor	334 (n 506)
Shelley, Percy Bysshe	284 (n 154)	Tutankhamen, pharaoh	
Sheshonq I, pharaoh	325 (n 437)	Aten, allegiance to	321 (n 410)
Schroeder, Dr Gerald L.	262, 307 (n 325)	change of capital by	321 (n 409)
Siculus, Diodorus	259, 330 (n 477)	change of name of	321 (n 410)
Sinai, mines of	263 (n 3)	paternity of	77, 281 (n 129)
Sneferu, pharaoh	335 (n 512)	Restoration Stele and	268 (n 40)
Solomon, king	206, 214, 226, 326 (n 442)	wife of	321 (n 410)
		Unas (Wenis), pharaoh	324 (n 428)
Solon	259, 324 (n 430)	Uraeus	39, 77, 107, 260, 285 (n 163)
Strabo	259, 300 (n 271)		
Sullivan, Louis	281 (n 132)	Wadjmose, pharaoh	285 (n 160)
Tacitus, Cornelius	259, 263 (n 4)	West, Rebecca	296 (n 239)
Taharqo (aka Taharka), pharaoh	204	Wilbour Papyrus	328 (n 456)
Ten Plagues, the		Wright, Frank Lloyd	281 (n 132)
duration of	209	Wooley, Charles Leonard	260
gods of Egypt and	239-42		